Handbook of Culture and Memory

FRONTIERS IN CULTURE AND PSYCHOLOGY

Series Editors
Chi-yue Chiu
Ying-yi Hong
Michele J. Gelfand

Books in the Series

Culture and Group Processes
Edited by Masaki Yuki and Marilynn Brewer

Handbook of Culture and Consumer Behavior
Edited by Sharon Ng and Angela Y. Lee

Handbook of Imagination and Culture
Edited by Tania Zittoun and Vlad Glăveanu

Handbook of Culture and Memory
Edited by Brady Wagoner

Handbook of Culture and Memory

EDITED BY BRADY WAGONER

OXFORD
UNIVERSITY PRESS

OXFORD
UNIVERSITY PRESS

Oxford University Press is a department of the University of Oxford. It furthers
the University's objective of excellence in research, scholarship, and education
by publishing worldwide. Oxford is a registered trade mark of Oxford University
Press in the UK and certain other countries.

Published in the United States of America by Oxford University Press
198 Madison Avenue, New York, NY 10016, United States of America.

© Oxford University Press 2018

Library of Congress Cataloging-in-Publication Data
Names: Wagoner, Brady, 1980– editor.
Title: Handbook of culture and memory / edited by Brady Wagoner.
Other titles: Culture and memory
Description: New York : Oxford University Press, [2018] | Series: Frontiers
in culture and psychology | Includes bibliographical references and index.
Identifiers: LCCN 2017007444 | ISBN 9780190230814 (hardcover : alk. paper) |
ISBN 9780190230821 (pbk. : alk. paper)
Subjects: LCSH: Culture—Psychological aspects. | Memory—Social aspects. |
Collective memory.
Classification: LCC HM621 .H3446 2017 | DDC 306.01/9—dc23
LC record available at https://lccn.loc.gov/2017007444

9 8 7 6 5 4 3 2 1

Paperback printed by Webcom, Inc., Canada
Hardback printed by Bridgeport National Bindery, Inc., United States of America

CONTENTS

CONTRIBUTORS

Jens Brockmeier
Department of Psychology
The American University of Paris
Paris, France

Steven D. Brown
School of Management
University of Leicester
Leicester, England, UK

Mario Carretero
Facultad Latinoamericana de Ciencias
    Sociales
Buenos Aires, Argentina

Constance de Saint Laurent
Department of Humanities and Social
    Sciences
Université de Neuchâtel
Neuchâtel, Switzerland

Merlin Donald
Department of Psychology
Queen's University
Kingston, Ontario, Canada

Astrid Erll
Institute for English & American
    Studies
Goethe Universitat
Frankfurt, Germany

Dieter Ferring
Department of Psychology
University of Luxembourg
Esch-sur-Alzette, Luxembourg

Mark Freeman
Department of Psychology
College of the Holy Cross
Worcester, MA

Sara Kauko
Department of Anthropology
Emory University
Atlanta, GA

Naohisa Mori
Sapporo Gakuin University
Hokkaido, Japan

Kyoko Murakami
Department of Psychology
University of Copenhagen
Copenhagen, Denmark

Katherine Nelson
Department of Psychology
The Graduate Center—City University
    of New York
New York, NY

Paula Reavey
Department of Psychology
London South Bank University
London, England, UK

Bradd Shore
Department of Anthropology
Emory University
Atlanta, GA

Kotaro Takagi
Aoyama Gakuin University
Tokyo, Japan

Floor van Alphen
Facultad Latinoamericana de Ciencias
    Sociales
Buenos Aires, Argentina

Brady Wagoner
Department of Communication and
    Psychology
Aalborg University
Aalborg, Denmark

James V. Wertsch
Department of Anthropology
Washington University
St. Louis, MO

Tania Zittoun
Department of Humanities and Social
    Sciences
Université de Neuchâtel
Neuchâtel, Switzerland

Introduction

*Remembering as a Psychological
and Social–Cultural Process*

BRADY WAGONER ∎

Long approached as mental faculty for retaining the past, memory has in recent decades been increasingly reconceptualized as an activity intimately entwined with and constituted by social and cultural life. This growing convergence of perspectives has happened within many theoretical and disciplinary fields, which in the past have often either ignored one another or been openly hostile. This book seizes the opportunity to develop a genuine interdisciplinary dialogue on the ways in which memory and culture mutually constitute one another. The reconnection brings us back to the ancient Greek myth of Mnemosyne, the goddess of memory, who gave birth to the nine muses on which all human culture rests. In this understanding, memory takes on a dynamic and constructive form that works at the intersection of a community's continuity with the past and innovation for the future. This book similarly builds on key ideas from the past in order to arrive at new approaches for integrating culture and memory into unified theoretical frameworks. This introduction sets the groundwork for these developments by exploring the different meanings assigned to the terms "culture" and "memory," outlining key principles of memory built upon in this volume (namely constructiveness, intersubjectivity, contextualism, and the use of diverse media), and providing a preview of the book's contents.

CULTURE AND MEMORY: TOWARD INTEGRATION

The terms culture and memory are both generic within contemporary discourse, and each has a long, complex history. In *Keywords*, Williams (1983) claims that "Culture is one of the two or three most complicated words in the English language" (p. 87), being used to describe civilization, a nation, fine arts (high culture), symbol systems, social practices, material artifacts, among others. Valsiner

(2012) comments, "Culture is in some sense a magic word—positive in connotations but hard to pinpoint in any science that attempts to use it as its core term" (p. 6). Memory has, on the other hand, been used in relation to phenomena as diverse as modifications of neuronal networks in sea snails all the way up to how human societies relate to their traditions. From a historical perspective, Danziger (2008) has shown how the concept and use of memory has changed in accordance with social practices, values, and technologies of a given society through its multifarious history. External memory technologies (books, calendars, stained-glass windows in cathedrals, etc.) have changed not only the means of remembering but also the so-called internal organization of memory. The most dramatic conceptual shift occurred with the spread of literacy: Memory changed from being seen as a performance in public space to an internal, individual event. Similarly, the Reformation and its iconoclasm led to replacement of imagery by verbal association in the practice of mnemonics (Yates, 1966).

Culture and memory have intersected in discourse mainly to describe how a social group relates to its traditions, often a national group. This social/cultural form of memory tends to be put into contrast with individual/biological memory (see Brockmeier, Chapter 2, this volume). Thus, there is, on the one hand, a group's memory that relies on a social and spatial framework of roles and relations together with material structures and objects and, on the other hand, an individual's memory stored in the brain. Early forerunners in memory studies already problematized this division: Frederic Bartlett (1932) showed how people remember stories and images through their group conventions. In contrast to Ebbinghaus' nonsense syllable approach, Bartlett highlighted how remembering involves "an effort after meaning," whereby we connect something present to previous experiences. Through this and the dynamics of interactions, social life conditioned both what is remembered and how it is remembered (Wagoner, 2017b). Maurice Halbwachs (1950/1980, 1925/1992) was even more radical in arguing that even the most private forms of memory, such as those found in dreams, are still inherently social because they rely on the social product of language. We must thus look to the relations of social life to understand how individuals' memory is prompted and rescripted through others. Finally, Lev Vygotsky (1987) thought the impressive advances in memory ability seen through human history and ontogeny could not be easily accounted for simply by the "natural" process of evolution and biological maturation. Instead, he shifted the analytic focus to how human beings make use of diverse cultural technologies to organize and aid memory—such as knots on a rope, monuments, the method of loci, or simply "chunking" information into manageable units.

Many contemporary developments in psychology, sociology, and anthropology pick up on these leads to explore memory at the intersection between individual and social–cultural processes, viewing neither as sufficient unto themselves. Although we can make distinctions between the memory of individuals and groups, this will always remain somewhat arbitrary: Individuals are not atoms of memory, any more than groups have a mental unity of their own. Thus, rather than a fast and hard distinction, it is more a difference of emphasis on either how groups organize the means by which individuals remember or how individuals are entangled with and make use of these socially organized means. Following Vygotsky, the unit of analysis becomes an active agent or agents using cultural tools to remember (Wertsch, 2002; see also Wertsch, Chapter 11, this volume). Cultural tools range from physical tools and bodily practices to language and theoretical systems (Donald, Chapter 1, this volume; Nelson, Chapter 8, this volume). They are taken over from a social group and function to *mediate* memory, as culture in action. Mediation implies a transformation of a relation through the intervention of a new factor, such as remembering *through* a picture card or knot on a rope. Contributors to this volume consider narratives taught in school (Carretero & van Alphen, Chapter 12), told within the family (Shore & Kauko, Chapter 4), or found in film and literature (Erll, Chapter 13), memorials and rituals to the dead (Murakami, Chapter 5), and conversations with others (Brockmeier, Chapter 2) as mediators that transform our relation to the past and, as a consequence, the present. This book analyzes the conceptualization, production, distribution, consumption, and use of these cultural mediators in remembering. Culture in this approach operates through us as a medium of experience and a resource for action as well as a constraint. This is rather different from the way culture has typically been understood in psychology, especially cross-cultural psychology.

When culture has been approached in psychology, it tends to be treated as a kind of homogeneous container that people belong in as a function of language, traditions, and geopolitical borders. Culture is studied as an independent variable for comparing the scores of people living in different countries or regions on some standardized questionnaire or task. The aim of this approach is to arrive at generalizations about the typical mentality of people living in different areas of the world and test whether they are the same as people living in the "West." Nisbett (2003), for example, argues that those living in the *individualistic* cultures of Europe and North America tend to analytically focus on objects and their attributes in their perception and memory, whereas *collectivistic* cultures of Asia tend to focus holistically on relations. Cross-cultural studies of this kind have been helpful in showing that studies done in the "Western" world often do not generalize well elsewhere (Henrich, Heine, & Norenzayan, 2010), but they also have conceptual difficulties. Approaching culture through broad characterizations (e.g., individualist and collectivist) ignores the diversity of mentalities found in a given society, contextual variability, and changes over time. For example, does it make sense to talk of "*the* India culture" given its 1,612 different languages, 675 precolonial kingdoms, and caste and religious segregations (Valsiner, 2007, p. 21)? Although India is considered a collectivist culture, we can still point to important cultural practices such as meditation that are highly individualistic. Moreover, group and national boundaries in the contemporary globalized world are themselves porous and dynamic: Ideas, people, and practices are spread easily throughout the world and adapted to local environments (Bartlett, 1923; Robertson, 1992). Should these people and practices be considered part of the receiving group's culture or as foreign bodies within it? Finally, the nation (or even more "the Western world") is itself an "imagined community" that relies on a myriad of cultural devices for its construction and maintenance rather than a self-evident category that can be used as a transparent variable (Anderson, 1983; Billig, 1995; Carretero & van Alphen, Chapter 12, this volume; Wertsch, Chapter 11, this volume). This is not to say we cannot compare people living within different social and cultural environments but, rather, that the comparison needs to be done at the level of single cases, which are sensitive to local knowledge and relationships at a granular level (Cole & Gray, 1972). In short, culture is not an explanation of differences in cognition but, rather, what needs to be explained.

We live through culture that exists *in* us, *with* us, and *around* us (Cole, 1996). Humans relate to their environment based on the fact that they live in a world of objects full of preexisting meanings and that these meanings, as they are experienced, become personalized (Valsiner, 2007). As such, the social–cultural environment and mind cannot be analyzed as independent and dependent variables but, rather, need to be seen as being mutually constitutive of one another. Shweder (1991) explains this principle as the defining feature of cultural psychology:

> No sociocultural environment exists or has identity independent of the way human beings seize meanings and resources from it, while every human being has her or his subjectivity and mental life altered through the process of seizing meanings and resources from some sociocultural environment and using them. (p. 74)

Methodologically, this means working with meaningful material, embedded in particular social contexts with other people and objects. Laboratory experiments are still possible within this approach but cannot be considered neutral contexts for revealing causal relationships between variables. The analytic focus shifts to explore the process by which people are both continually shaped by and actively create culture through their lives. In relation to memory, we both use cultural tools of remembering taken over from our social group (e.g., narratives, images, and mnemotechnics) and make them available to others in public acts of remembering. Recognizing the dialectic between personal and collective aspects of culture leads us to be careful in not reading off the use from the content or intended use of cultural artifacts: A statue, flag, or narrative will mean different things to different people on different occasions as a function of their relationships, goals, and personal history. This approach thus circumscribes the notion of culture to the meaningful resources and constraints that are inseparably interwoven into people's lives and used to mediate higher mental functions, such as memory. These resources are social in origin but become personalized by individuals in accordance with their particular life circumstances. As such, human remembering is both a personal and a social–culturally situated process: It is personal in that it expresses a unique life history and concerns, and it is social–cultural in that it is deeply enmeshed in social relationships and meanings provided by different groups. Mediators of memory (i.e., culture in action) thus provide a crucial link connecting individuals and collectives.

In summary, although the concepts of culture and memory remain open to allow for the diversity of approaches found in this volume (see recommendations from Jahoda (2012) on not attempting to define culture too strictly), they imply here dynamic and closely intertwined processes for human beings rather than independent and dependent variables. Moreover, this volume moves beyond viewing them both through fixed, spatial metaphors (namely containers) and instead considers them as temporal processes involving continuous construction and reconstruction, which puts into focus issues of change, history, conflict, future goals, and so on. In the next section, I outline a number of assumptions that come out of this broad approach. These are by no means new ideas, but outlining them will be helpful to prepare the ground for the chapters that follow.

SOME PRINCIPLES OF MEMORY

Remembering Is Constructive

Memory is not a thing, substance, or faculty for storing the representations of past but, rather, a process or activity of using the past to meet current needs for action. In a dynamic world filled with change, the person's flexible use of the past takes precedent over its literal reproduction. There are, of course, social contexts in which the literal accuracy of details in memory is deemed highly important—such as traditional school exams or courts of law—but this is the exception rather than the rule (see "Remembering Is Contextual"). This approach to remembering, as an active and flexible construction or reconstruction, was first forcefully put forward in psychology by Frederic Bartlett (1932) in his classic work *Remembering: A Study in Experimental and Social Psychology*. However, the idea can be traced back much earlier to the German philosopher Hermann Lotze's notion of "the activity of memory" (Northway, 1940). Bartlett famously described the concept thus:

> Remembering is not the re-excitation of innumerable fixed, lifeless and fragmentary traces. It is an imaginative reconstruction or construction, built out of the relation of our attitude towards a whole active mass of organised past reactions or experience, and to a little outstanding detail which commonly appears in image or in language form. (p. 213)

In contemporary discussions, the concept of "construction" has taken on two subtly different meanings (Wagoner, 2017a; see also Brockmeier, Chapter 2, this volume). One account has made construction a synonym for "distortion" and "inaccuracy" in memory. This has typically been assessed against the fixed and literal standard of what a computer does with information. Here, memory is often treated more as a distinct faculty than an activity involving processes that would often be treated in separation (e.g., feeling, imagination, and meaning-making). In contrast, the other account of construction understands variability in remembering as being part of a person's situated adaptation to the environment. Thus, it highlights memory's functional and creative characteristics, which can lead to both memory accuracy and inaccuracy. In the place of accuracy, memory is assessed in this account primarily according to how it changes a person–environment relation, either opening or closing avenues for action and agency (Brown & Reavey, 2015; see also Brown & Reavey, Chapter 7, this volume). Whether a memory enhances or restricts our agency will depend on the context and thus needs to be accessed in relation to it (discussed later).

The latter meaning of construction was advocated by Bartlett (1932) and is further developed by contributors to this volume. Bartlett's approach is particularly helpful for our purposes of connecting culture and memory in that he first theorized constructiveness in relation to how social groups retain and change their cultural patterns (Wagoner, 2017b). This approach was later used as an analogy to theorize remembering on an individual level. In both cases, Bartlett was interested in the negotiation of the need for continuity through time and the need to innovate for the future. The greatest stimulus to innovation and the development of new cultural forms and experiences on both individual and group levels was for Bartlett contact between people with different backgrounds. Construction here is not done out of nothing but, rather, involves the weaving together of diverse already existing cultural streams; it is an active and often reflective improvisation with the various resources and constraints of the moment. The past then serves as a source for innovation in the present, as the medieval art of memory had also understood it (Carruthers, 1990). Thus, construction is not simply the fitting of something to an already existing plan but, rather, a living response oriented to the future from which something new can emerge. As such, the development of our memories retains some degree of unpredictability. In this volume, we see how new modes of memory emerge through evolution and child development (Donald, Chapter 1; Nelson, Chapter 8), how people continuously update autobiographic memories as a function of the situation and changing conceptions of self (Brown & Reavey, Chapter 7; de Saint Laurent & Zittoun, Chapter 9; Freeman, Chapter 3; Takagi & Mori, Chapter 6), and how groups mobilize and reshape memory through material and symbolic resources (Carretero & van Alphen, Chapter 12; Murakami, Chapter 5; Shore & Kauko, Chapter 4; Wertsch, Chapter 11). Given the multiple social and cultural inputs into constructive remembering, it might even be preferable to refer to it as "co-constructive," rather than simply "constructive," in order to highlight its intersubjective and dialogical dimensions. This is the focus of the next section.

Remembering Is Intersubjective

Following Durkheim's insight that the categories of thought and memory emerge from group interactions, Halbwachs (1950/1980, 1925/1992) influentially argued that all human memory is essentially social. This is so because memory necessarily relies on "social frameworks"—that is, the people who make up a group and the systems of meaning that unite them. When we remember, we effectively place ourselves within a group's perspective and elaborate along its lines. We are constantly prompted by others to recall and rescript our memories according to what we have heard from them. Thus, the "social" here should be taken in its strong sense as being irreducible to a collection of individual contributions (Olick, 1999). We have the illusion that our memories originate in ourselves, says Halbwachs, only because individuals belong to multiple groups and may move between their social frameworks in remembering. Halbwachs (1950/1980) vividly describes how our experience comes into being infused with various social relationships even when we are alone:

> Our memories remain collective . . . and are recalled to us through others even though only we were participants in the events or saw the things concerned. In reality, we are never alone. Other men need not be physically present, since we always carry with us and in us a number of distinct persons. I arrive in London and take walks with different companions. An architect directs my attention to the character and arrangement of city buildings. A historian tells me why a certain street, house, or other spot is historically noteworthy. A painter alerts me to the colors in the parks, the lines of the palaces and churches, and the play of light and shadow on the walls and facades of Westminster and on the Thames. A businessman takes me into the public thoroughfares, to the shops, bookstores, and department stores. . . . Many impressions during my first visit to London—St. Paul's, Mansion House, the Strand, or the Inns of Court—reminded me of Dickens' novels read in childhood, so I took my walk with Dickens. In each of these moments I cannot say that I was alone, that I reflected alone, because I had put myself in thought into this or that group . . . I can still feel the group's influence and recognize in myself many ideas and ways of thinking that could not have originated with me. (pp. 23–24)

Halbwachs was right to highlight the social dimensions of our memory and experience, but he often overemphasized the role of group processes at the expense of attending to what the individual brings to memory. The fact that people move between frameworks suggests that the individual is not simply the automaton of the group but, rather, is active in weaving together different social experiences, as Bartlett (1932) had emphasized (discussed previously). In the previous quotation by Halbwachs, we see the inherent *tension* of an interdependent self and other, relating to some object (e.g., a city). Contrary to epistemologies that view the knower as rooted in either an individual or a collective, Marková (2003) has argued that the triad of self–other–object should be the basic unit of analysis in psychology and other social sciences (see also Moscovici, 1984). This focus avoids both the upward reduction of memory to collective processes and the treatment of individuals as independent atoms of memory. Bartlett's (1932) famous studies of repeated reproduction of folk tales brilliantly illustrated that memories are both increasingly conventionalized toward group patterns and transformed according to personal factors, such as interests, emotions, and an individual's particular life history (see Wagoner, 2017b). The individual cannot be dissolved in the group any more than he or she can be exclusively separated from it. Individuals construct memories with and in relation to commonly shared symbols, rituals, and events, but they also create their own particular variations of them in the process. Nonetheless, communities may externalize parts of this collective reservoir—for example, in monuments—such that it can appear to have at least a semi-independent status from its users.

Somewhat counterintuitively, it is precisely in the process of becoming part of a cultural community that a sense of individuality develops. The infant begins life in "a primordial sharing situation," in which there is little differentiated in his or her experience between self, other (typically the mother), and an object of reference (Werner & Kaplan, 1963, p. 42ff). The self emerges out of social interaction in repeated action contexts with structured social positions, such as giving and receiving; gradually the child is able to take the perspective of the other toward oneself because he or she has previously occupied the opposing position in a social act (Gillespie, 2005; Mead, 1934; see also Nelson, Chapter 8, this volume). This provides the mechanism behind self-reflection in general and what is today often called "meta-memory" or "meta-cognition," referring to our ability to monitor and control our remembering and thinking (Nelson, 1996). Remembering becomes a kind of dialogue (either internal or external) through which we take different perspectives of others on our own experience, as in the previous quotation from Halbwachs (1950/1980). This is also the more radical meaning of "construction" in Bartlett's (1932) work, in which we "turn around upon [our] own schema and construct them afresh" (p. 206). However, we can be more explicit than him here in arguing that this process is itself inherently social, even if internally so. The incorporation of others' perspectives into one's self can sometimes lead to "source monitoring" problems, especially among children. But the fact that we frequently confuse perspectives does not mean they are always fused—the triad of self–other–object remains primary for human beings. The next section considers how the contextual constraints help to ground and stabilize memory and social relations.

Remembering Is Contextual

Human memory relies on social relationships and perspectives, but there are also a constellation of other factors through which memories are constructed, such as spaces, objects, and social practices. These also function to ground social relationships and interactions. No person, or organism for that matter, exists apart from its environment or *umwelt*. Thus, to fully understand an act of remembering, we need to consider how it is enmeshed in a network of relations, extending from the immediate setting to the broader social–cultural milieu to which the person belongs (Brown & Reavey, 2015). This network of relationships has been discussed by applying the notion of context, but this is a polysemic term that itself needs explanation (Stone & Bietti, 2015). Typically, context has been evoked in psychology as a "cue" to an already formed internal memory or an external constraint on what can be publically shared (e.g., obedience or conformity). Thus, the mind is here viewed as an entity already abstracted from the world and its relations and then placed in it as an independent thing in an empty container. In contrast, a social–cultural approach views context as being both "that which surrounds" and "that which weaves together" (Cole, 1996, p. 132ff). The first helps us to understand that at any moment we belong to a hierarchy of contexts:

> A teacher gives a lesson, which is shaped by the classroom it is a part of, which in turn is shaped by the kind of school it is in, which in turn is shaped by the community, and so on. (p. 134)

Human action can only be understood against this background of a meaningful prestructured environment, much like a figure only appears against a ground. The second understanding of context highlights how persons, actions, objects, and so on are threaded together in action as parts of a meaningful whole that gives them coherence. The boundaries between the parts here are mutable and dynamic rather than clear-cut or static. This is because cognition is *distributed* between complementary and shifting internal and external resources (Sutton, Harris, Keil, & Barnier, 2010).

Thus, rather than adopt a language of how one element (e.g., emotion) affects another (e.g., memory), contributors to this volume focus on the holistic context and its dynamic relations as the starting point for their inquiry. At the outermost level of context, contributors illustrate how cultural traditions extending long before one's birth continue to shape one's relating to the past in the form of traces in the environment, narrative, images, and rituals (see especially Freeman, Chapter 3; Wertsch, Chapter 11; Carretero & van Alphen, Chapter 12; Erll, Chapter 13). At a narrower level of context, the specific setting (or sometimes called "situation") in which remembering occurs establishes definite constraints and possibilities. The chapters of Part II, in particular, show the specificities of remembering in different cultural contexts or settings. Rather than assume the divergences in memory between settings are a sign of distortion or false memory, we should expect to see differences if the whole setting is involved. For example, remembering episodes of sexual abuse in the context of a trial will show marked differences from doing so within the context of therapy. Every constructed memory is a "setting level achievement" that cannot be reduced to any single factor within the whole (Brown & Reavey, Chapter 7). This does not mean we need to entirely abandon the distinction between real and confabulated memories, although we should perhaps consider them as being on more of a continuum. Takagi and Mori (Chapter 6) have developed an ecological approach to testimony that can reveal whether a person actually came in contact with a past environment through an analysis of the narrative he or she tells under interrogation. In relation to laboratory experiments, contextualism does not lead us into throwing out research done there; instead, it forces us to include the broader social–cultural milieu of participants and to recognize the specific norms of the laboratory setting—for example, how people are more guarded and focused on the accurate recall of details (Bartlett, 1932; Middleton & Edwards, 1990). The next section considers the cultural tools that are given life through action in context and also how people are active in constructing context with them.

Remembering Occurs with and Through Diverse Media

Human beings actively construct settings of recall for others and themselves, as can be seen in the organization of a family home and objects that populate it (Shore & Kauko, Chapter 4), assistance technologies that supplement for memory decline (Ferring, Chapter 10), monuments and rituals to war dead (Murakami, Chapter 5), and even whole cities (Boyer, 1996). It is in this feature of changing the environment in order to remember that Vygotsky (as quoted in Bakhurst, 1990) saw as what was distinctive to the way human beings remember:

> The very essence of human memory is that human beings actively remember with the help of signs. It is a general truth that the special character of human behaviour is that human beings actively manipulate their relation to the environment, and through the environment they change their own behaviour, subjugating it to their control. As one psychologist has said [Dewey], the very essence of civilization consists in the fact that we deliberately build monuments so as not to forget. In the knotted handkerchief and the monument we see the most profound, most characteristic and most important feature, which distinguishes human from animal memory. (p. 210)

The importance of the concept of mediation to a social–cultural approach to memory has already been noted (see also Wertsch, Chapter 11, this volume). Memory and experience come into being and take form through various material and symbolic media. In Vygotsky's theory, human beings construct external signs, which they use to regulate and control their own behavior; this is possible because the sign has "reverse action"—in giving it meaning, it later acts back on its creator and on others. Following Vygotsky's approach, this has typically been investigated with a focus on verbal language, but even he attended to other kinds of mediators, such as picture cards used to aid memory (Vygotsky, 1987) or knots on a rope used as an accounting practice in many preliterate societies (Vygotsky & Luria, 1930). The material basis of many mediating artifacts is the focus of Murakami (Chapter 5; see also Radley, 1990) and figures prominently in a number of other chapters in this volume as well. The role of place in setting up conditions for memory (see "Place Memory" in Casey, 2000) is also present to some degree in Murakmi (Chapter 5) and Shore and Kauko (Chapter 4).

Although language and narrative are powerful and central media of memory, we need to be careful not to reduce all mediated memory to this form. Donald (Chapter 1) argues that the first evolutionary level of human culture involved interaction based in body language, imitation, and routine actions with objects. This is where tool use and skilled action emerged. It is also on this level of "event knowledge" that children first enter into culture through routines such as feeding, bathing, and going to bed (Nelson, Chapter 8). Connerton (1989) has argued that social scientists have typically neglected memory *incorporated* into one's body because of the bias toward *inscription* or written texts (see also Murakami, Chapter 5, this volume). Following Durkheim and Bourdieu, he describes how transmission of memory through body practice does not allow for the variations nor critical distance characteristic of language. It is thus little surprise that ritual actions continue to be a stable means of cementing and transmitting traditions in groups of all sizes, from repeated family vacations (Shore & Kauko, Chapter 4) to national commemorations (Carretero & van Alphen, Chapter 12; Murakami, Chapter 5). Of course, a group's stories also interrelate with its body practices, which bring us to the next level in Donald's scheme (Chapter 1): the narrative mode. Cultural psychologist Jerome Bruner (1990, 1991, 2002) has argued that narrative is the medium through which our common sense, sharing of experience, and sense of self are derived. All societies create myth stories and institutions to transmit them between generations, whether in the family, religious ceremonies, national celebrations, or formal schooling. The character of the narrative and memory will also be shaped by the technology that carries it (Erll, Chapter 13). For example, spoken language depends much more on the situation in which it occurs, whereas written language is relatively decontextualized in order to communicate with more distant and generalized interlocutors. Furthermore, the spread of literacy and written texts fed into memory's conceptualization as a kind of inscription stored in the individual (Danziger, 2008). It also set the conditions for Donald's (Chapter 1) third level of culture: theoretical knowledge. New technologies such as film, television, and the Internet continue to transform memory today (Erll, Chapter 13).

PREVIEW OF THE BOOK

This book is divided into four thematic sections to provide the reader with various entry points into the text. Part I, "Concept and History of Memory," explores different conceptualizations of memory at its intersection with culture and how it has changed through time. It covers the prehistoric emergence of memory in collectives (Chapter 1), recent shifts away from the notion of memory as an individual archive in the brain (Chapter 2), and how human memory itself is deeply shaped by one's group history (Chapter 3). In Chapter 1, Merlin Donald analyzes how a group's shared experience, skill, and knowledge (i.e., "cultural memory") is transmitted and adapted through time and provides the basis for the development of individual human memory. He traces how cultural memory has evolved in relation to embodied, narrative, and institutional modes of representation (or "mimetic," "mythic," and "theoretical," respectively), arguing that the prime driver of early evolution of mind and memory was tool mastery rather than language. In Chapter 2, Jens Brockmeier describes recent changes in our understanding of memory from the traditional archive metaphor of memory to new alternatives.

He criticizes the archive metaphor for the assumption that memory is individual, biological, and works according to the logic of storage. This model, he argues, should be replaced with one that focuses on remembering as an inherently social practice, thus foregrounding its societal and cultural dimensions. The chapter concludes with the development of a model of remembering as conversation. In Chapter 3, Mark Freeman asks how second-hand information is metabolized into memory, focusing on those culturally rooted aspects of our history (including events before our birth) that have yet to become explicit parts of our life story. He invents the concept of "narrative unconscious" to describe this process and in so doing grapples with questions surrounding the "owning" of a history as "our past" that we were not directly involved in (whether as a victim or a benefactor). All three chapters in Part I thus problematize the clean separation of individual and collective memory by illustrating the many mutual lines of intersection between them. Remembering necessarily extends beyond the individual cranium into distributed networks of people, artifacts, ideas, and social practices that reach back into history.

Part II, "Cultural Contexts of Remembering," zooms in on the dynamics of remembering in four different contexts or settings: the family (Chapter 4), commemoration (Chapter 5), giving testimony in a court of law or police interrogation (Chapter 6), and contexts in which we deal with difficult autobiographical memories such as how child sexual abuse is discussed in therapy (Chapter 7). Each chapter in this section also offers a new interdisciplinary theoretical approach to the issues that arise from the specificities of the context under consideration. In Chapter 4, Bradd Shore and Sara Kauko explore the family as a distributed memory system that incorporates spaces, objects, narratives, sensory experiences, power relations, and a range of other phenomena. The family is a fundamental human institution and has been an exemplary place to search for "collective memory" since Halbwachs (1925/1992) introduced the concept. Shore and Kauko take the analysis a step further by analyzing the different degrees of collectivity in individuals' autobiographic memories of family life and the "landscape" of different factors that support them. In Chapter 5, Kyoko Murakami examines the context of commemoration with a case study of the "remembrance poppy," a material artifact for remembering World War I. She highlights how discourse, materials, bodily movements, inarticulate feelings, and the environment come together in commemorative practices. Using theories of materiality, ritual, and ornaments, she paints a multidimensional picture of the place cultural artifacts play in memory. In Chapter 6, Kotaro Takagi and Naohisa Mori aim to develop an ecological approach to giving testimony as a social practice. After reviewing the early history of testimony research, they critically examine recent cognitive and discursive approaches. The starting point for a new alternative theory is found in Neisser's (1982) notion of "repisode," which refers to the invariant features of a recurrent situation rather than a single episode as covered by the term "episodic." Combining this concept with those of Gibson (1979) and Bartlett (1932), they arrive at a new ecological approach to remembering that is illustrated with the case of a murder testimony. In Chapter 7, Steven D. Brown and Paula Reavey focus on the dynamics of difficult autobiographical memories (what they call "vital memories") and what they mean for the self. In contrast to the typical approach obsessed with accuracy and the pathological nature of these memories, they attend to the creative and nuanced ways in which people productively manage their pasts. Their account is based on the "expanded model of memory," which considers the place of discursive practices, artifacts, and other "setting level" conditions that make it possible.

Part III, "Memory Through the Life Course," then takes a developmental perspective, focusing on characteristics of remembering during different life phases—namely infancy through early childhood (Chapter 8), adolescence (Chapter 9), and old age (Chapter 10). Examples of adult memory processes can be found in the other parts of this volume. Key to Part III is how memory develops in and out of interactions with others. For example, children in early life come to master the conversational tools that enable them to organize and prompt their own memory. But there are other important developments before this stage. In Chapter 8, Katherine Nelson explores how in the early years of life, memory emerges as a multiple-level system through exposure to the different layers of culture in social interaction (cf. Donald, Chapter 1). Children first appropriate culture through event knowledge derived from repeated action sequences coordinated between self and other. Only later do they come into the cultural world of narrative and its explicit temporal relations, causes and results, and the motivations of actors. It is on this foundation that autobiographical memory and a conscious sense of self develop. In Chapter 9, Constance de Saint Laurent and Tania Zittoun focus on the functions of autobiographical memory in the transitional years of adolescence. They highlight its role in the construction of the self, relating with others, and directing our actions toward the future. The last of these—the directive function—connects memory with imagination, in that the past is mobilized for the purpose of projecting a future. A model of memory in life transitions is put forward that integrates self, other, cultural tools, past recalls, and future prospects. This is illustrated with a longitudinal case study of a Swiss teenager that shows how changes in the social–cultural context can trigger development and the reorganization of autobiographical memories. In Chapter 10, Dieter Ferring describes memory decline in old age (especially in relation to degenerative diseases such as dementia and Alzheimer's disease). In this context, culture tools supplement for loss in the form of *assistive technologies* (e.g., smart homes and other semiotically organized environments that provide external support to memory) and *symbolic resources*, which are mobilized to fill the meaning gap created by a disease such as Alzheimer's disease. Throughout the life course, we see how memory is dynamic and evolving in relation to new constraints and possibilities provided by our social–cultural environment as well as our biology.

Part IV, "Memory, History, and Identity," shifts the focus to more large-scale collective phenomenon, exploring how nations construct memory (Chapters 11 and 12) and the ways in which memory circulates beyond national borders through literature, film, and digital media (Chapter 13). These chapters highlight the relationship between history and collective memory, on the one hand, and collective memory and identity, on the other hand (see also Murakami, Chapter 5). In Chapter 11, James Wertsch analyzes national memory in two metaphoric "locations": (1) in the confrontation of different "mnemonic communities" over how to remember the past and (2) in the deep-lying codes and habits carried forward in a group's cultural traditions. In relation to the latter, he points to the "narrative templates" from which specific narratives of historical events are constructed. Like all cultural tools that mediate our relationship to the world, these both empower us and simultaneously obscure what we aim to understand. Wertsch illustrates these dynamics with an example of how the 2008 war between Russia and Georgia is remembered by Russians through an analogy with World War II, where the former Soviet Union was forced to enter the war as a result of foreign aggression. In Chapter 12, Mario Carretero and Floor van Alphen analyze differences between history and collective memory that emerge from different understandings of history education—namely as a means of creating national identification (the "romantic" account) or critical citizens (the "enlightened" account). This is not to say that people simply remember according to the official account propagated in schools and other sites—counterversions of the past do arise. Thus, we need to be careful to distinguish between production and appropriation of historical narratives. The authors go on to outline and illustrate six dimensions that constitute students' master narrative of national history, such as a "we" versus "them" structure, heroic accounts of key figures, and an essentialist concept of the nation. Finally, they show how master narratives are (re)-enacted through patriotic rituals in national celebrations. In Chapter 13, Astrid Erll discusses the fundamental "mediatedness" of memory by examining how cultural memory is continuously transformed as it travels from one medium to another (e.g., in literature, archives, film, photographs, and digital media), across time, space, and culture—a process she calls "remediation." The dynamics of remediation leads to "premediation," which preforms the understanding of new events according to a familiar media schema. Whereas earlier memory theories tended to neglect the formative role of media technology in the transmission of memory, she argues it becomes particularly central in our globalized, digitalized, and media-saturated world. These transcultural dynamics of memory are illustrated with examples of how World War I, World War II, 9/11, and other historic events have been reconstructed in diffusion through various media. Thus, in this volume, we journey from the prehistoric development of human memory to its modern form in the globalized, multicultural world of today.

ACKNOWLEDGMENT

I am grateful to Ignacio Brescó for his comments on an earlier draft of this chapter.

REFERENCES

Anderson, B. (1983). *Imagined communities*. London, UK: Verso.

Bakhurst, D. (1990). Social memory in Soviet thought. In D. Middleton & D. Edwards (Eds.), *Collective remembering* (pp. 203–226). London, UK: Sage.

Bartlett, F. C. (1923). *Psychology and primitive culture*. Cambridge, UK: Cambridge University Press.

Bartlett, F. C. (1932). *Remembering: A study in experimental and social psychology*. Cambridge, UK: Cambridge University Press.

Billig, M. (1995). *Banal nationalism*. London, UK: Sage.

Boyer, M. C. (1996). *The city of collective memory: Its historical imagery and architectural entertainments*. Cambridge, MA: MIT Press.

Brown, S. D., & Reavey, P. (2015). *Vital memory and affect: Living with a difficult past*. London, UK: Routledge.

Bruner, J. (1990). *Acts of meaning*. Cambridge, MA: Harvard University Press.

Bruner, J. (1991). The narrative construction of reality. *Critical Inquiry, 18*, 1–21.

Bruner, J. (2002). *Making stories: Law, life, literature*. Cambridge, MA: Harvard University Press.

Carruthers, M. (1990). *The book of memory*. Cambridge, UK: Cambridge University Press.

Casey, E. (2000). *Remembering: A phenomenological study*. Bloomington, IN: Indiana University Press.

Cole, M. (1996). *Cultural psychology: A once and future discipline*. Cambridge, MA: Harvard University Press.

Cole, M., & Gray, G. (1972). Culture and memory. *American Anthropologist, 74*(5), 1066–1084.

Connerton, P. (1989). *How societies remember*. Cambridge, UK: Cambridge University Press.

Danziger, K. (2008). *Marking the mind: A history of memory*. Cambridge, UK: Cambridge University Press.

Gibson, J. J. (1979). *The ecological approach to visual perception*. Boston, MA: Houghton Mifflin.

Gillespie, A. (2005). G. H. Mead: Theorist of the social act. *Journal for the Theory of Social Behaviour, 35*(1), 19–39.

Halbwachs, M. (1980). *The collective memory*. New York: Harper & Row. (Original work published 1950)

Halbwachs, M. (1992). *On collective memory*. Chicago, IL: University of Chicago Press. (Original work published 1925)

Henrich, J., Heine, S. J., & Norenzayan, A. (2010). The weirdest people in the world? *Behavioral and Brain Sciences, 33*, 61–135.

Jahoda, G. (2012). Critical reflections on some recent definitions of "culture." *Culture & Psychology, 18*(3), 289–303.

Marková, I. (2003). *Dialogicality and social representations: The dynamics of mind*. Cambridge, UK: Cambridge University Press.

Mead, G. H. (1934). *Mind, self and society: From the standpoint of a social behaviorist*. Chicago, IL: University of Chicago Press.

Middleton, D., & Edwards, D. (1990). Conversational remembering: A social psychological approach. In D. Middleton & D. Edwards (Eds.), *Collective remembering* (pp. 23–46). London, UK: Sage.

Moscovici, S. (1984). The phenomenon of social representations. In R. Farr & S. Moscovici (Eds.), *Social representations* (pp. 3–68). Cambridge, UK: Cambridge University Press.

Neisser, U. (1982). John Dean's memory: A case study. In U. Neisser (Ed.), *Memory observed: Remembering in natural contexts* (pp. 139–159). New York, NY: Freeman.

Nelson, T. O. (1996). Consciousness and metacognition. *American Psychologist, 51*, 102–116.

Nisbett, R. E. (2003). *The geography of thought.* New York, NY: Free Press.

Northway, M. L. (1940). The concept of "schema": Part I. *British Journal of Psychology, 30*, 316–325.

Olick, J. (1999). Collective memory: The two cultures. *Sociological Theory, 17*, 333–348.

Radley, A. (1990). Artefacts, memory and a sense of the past. In D. Middleton & D. Edwards (Eds.), *Collective remembering* (pp. 46–59). London, UK: Sage.

Robertson, R. (1992). *Globalization: Social theory and global culture.* London, UK: Sage.

Shweder, R. (1991). *Thinking through Culture: Explorations in cultural psychology.* Cambridge, MA: Harvard.

Stone, C. B., & Bietti, L. M. (2015). *Contextualizing human memory: An interdisciplinary approach to understanding how individuals and groups remember the past.* London, UK: Routledge.

Sutton, J., Harris, C. B., Keil, P. G., & Barnier, A. J. (2010). The psychology of memory, extended cognition, and socially distributed remembering. *Phenomenology and the Cognitive Sciences, 9*(4), 521–560.

Valsiner, J. (2007). *Culture in minds and societies.* New Delhi, India: Sage.

Valsiner, J. (2012). Introduction: Culture in psychology—Renewed encounters of inquisitive minds. In J. Valsiner (Ed.), *The Oxford handbook of culture and psychology* (pp. 3–24). Oxford, UK: Oxford University Press.

Vygotsky, L. (1987). *The collected works of L. S. Vygotsky. Volume 4: The history of the development of higher mental functions.* New York, NY: Plenum.

Vygotsky, L., & Luria, A. (1930). *Ape, primitive man and child: Essays in the history of behaviour.* New York, NY: Harvester Wheatsheaf.

Wagoner, B. (2017a). What makes memory constructive? A study in the serial reproduction of Bartlett's experiments. *Culture & Psychology, 22*(2).

Wagoner, B. (2017b). *The constructive mind: Bartlett's psychology in reconstruction.* Cambridge, UK: Cambridge University Press.

Werner, H., & Kaplan, B. (1963). *Symbol formation: An organismic–developmental approach to the psychology of language and the expression of thought.* Hillsdale, NJ: Erlbaum.

Wertsch, J. (2002). *Voices of collective remembering.* Cambridge, UK: Cambridge University Press.

Williams, R. (1983). *Keywords.* Oxford, UK: Oxford University Press.

Yates, F. (1966). *The art of memory.* Chicago, IL: University of Chicago Press.

PART I

Concept and History of Memory

The Evolutionary Origins
of Human Cultural Memory

MERLIN DONALD ■

Cultural memory can be broadly defined as a shared storehouse of collective experience, skill, and knowledge. It is distinct from biological memory inasmuch as it is registered, edited, and transmitted in a population of organisms rather than in a single organism. Cultural memory cannot typically be contained entirely within a single brain. Its traces are distributed across many brains, in widely varying versions, and cannot be retrieved in whole from any single individual. Moreover, its contents are under constant revision. Cultural memory is thus a dynamic cognitive system that differs significantly from biological memory systems both in the nature of its storage and retrieval systems and in that of its function and content.

Cultural memory is also parasitic on biological memory; in fact, cultural memory is one of the major cognitive products of human social networks built on a cognitive platform provided by the biological memory systems of the brain. It is a distributed storage system that can generate and accumulate a massive amount of memory material very quickly, recoding the memory contents of a population by reprocessing that material in a variety of interactive public representational systems. These systems generate even more variability and imaginative activation in individuals so that memories stored in cultural systems greatly exceed the capacity of any individual to track or comprehend them.

Cultural memory systems can transmit memories from the deep past, transform them into a format compatible with the present mindset of a population, and shape the future formation of developing minds (Assman, 2006; Halbwachs, 1980; see also Nelson, Chapter 8, this volume). Elaborate interactive memory systems of this kind are uniquely human; in fact, they might be singled out as the signature cognitive feature that distinguishes the human mind from those of its close primate relatives.

The key difference between cultural memory and the biological memory systems of the brain lies in its social roots, especially interactive skills and social interdependency (Tomasello, 1999). Human beings perform their major memory work in groups. They construct memory in culture, relying heavily on one another's memories for building and verifying personal versions of events. Bartlett (1932) developed the idea of reconstructive remembering in some detail, showing how social forces can greatly influence the personal process of remembering events (see also Wagoner, this volume). People collaborate extensively in interpreting, borrowing, correcting, and editing their memories. They constantly interact in the creation and refinement of their shared memory records, and these records are held in social networks that are correspondingly complex, overlapping, and often contain many contradictory versions of events. Even highly personal memories are greatly influenced through the filter of shared culture. Because cultural memories accumulate rapidly and are transmitted across generations in subtle ways, the deepest cultural memories are usually buried so far beneath the surface of culture that very few, if any, of the adult members of a culture are even aware of their existence. Yet these deep memories dominate the representational style of every culture, and as the history of empires can testify, they have proven very difficult to eradicate.

Cultural memory systems carry forward a society's world view, customs, and wisdom, allowing new generations to add new items to the storehouse while providing a means whereby developing individuals can assimilate their cultural past. They inevitably carry a strong set of biases and predispositions, and this biasing process tends to stabilize cultural norms and align the beliefs, customs, and values of the members of a given culture. However, the specific content of cultural memory can change radically over time, even in a small cultural group, and is thus inherently unpredictable.

For that reason alone, extreme developmental plasticity is a necessity in the human child, whose dependency on cultural memory is unique in the biosphere. Flexibility and adaptability are paramount factors in sustaining the individual developing in the context of a complex, constantly changing culture. Cultural memory systems constitute an inherently unpredictable (but not chaotic) cognitive ecology within which the human mind develops and functions throughout the lifespan.

In the course of its evolution, cultural memory has been, of necessity, finetuned to the social–cognitive skills available in human ancestors to support various degrees of social interactivity. In this regard, the relation of brain to cultural memory has necessarily been a two-way one, with brain evolution sensitive to emerging developmental conditions and cultural evolution constrained by the brain's innate interactive capacities. In a true Darwinian manner, this two-way interdependency has changed over time as cultural memory has developed new tools; it has gradually drifted from a brain-dominated process in the Lower Paleolithic to a culturally dominated process in recent centuries, as the momentum of cultural memory has grown in its formative influence.

Time parameters have played a crucial role in this shift; the rate of current cultural (including technological) change is such that biological evolution is simply too slow to cope with the stresses now threatening human survival. Nevertheless, it remains true in principle that cultural memory systems should not exceed the human brain's capacity to deal with the imposed memory load, without the risk of increasing the threat of species extinction.

The memory system of a culture is thus much more than a repository of past experience and knowledge. It is also an active cognitive force that influences thought and the representation of reality. It structures the collective intellectual activity of a population by linking together, in a set of complex social networks, the cognitive resources of an entire population. Within its embrace, networks of people exchange perceptions of reality, make decisions, share memories, form consensus on what will be remembered (and forgotten), and stimulate one another to generate thoughts and representations that are otherwise extremely unlikely to appear in socially isolated individuals.

The next section discusses cultural memory as a distributed cognitive system, and the section that follows outlines the important role of material artifacts in the evolution of human cultural memory. The following four sections introduce a proposed hierarchical model that might prove useful as a platform for further study. The model proposes that human cultures tend to construct interactive cognitive hierarchies that govern thought and memory in individuals and make possible a coordinated community of mind. The seeds of these cognitive hierarchies are preserved in mass distributed memory systems that include material artifacts that form part of the "cognitive ecology" that influences cognitive activity in any given cultural moment.

A DYNAMIC, DISTRIBUTED COGNITIVE PROCESS

The memory system of a culture amounts to more—usually much more—than the sum total of what the members of the community have stored in their brains at a given time. It contains algorithms that govern cognitive activity in social networks, and it can thus be viewed as a dynamic *process*. A cultural memory system includes habits of mind, systems of cooperation and organization, and creative skills that drive the social–cognitive interactions that make human culture possible. The process aspect of a cultural memory system, even in a small population, contains far more information than anyone could know or remember, and much of that information, especially procedural and strategic information, is largely invisible to the user (just as operating systems are invisible to the average computer user).

This feature of cultural memory is crucial because it determines the range of options available to a society for solving the various cognitive challenges it may face. For example, thought processes can differ enormously in tracking causality. In a culture dominated by animistic beliefs, there is a strong tendency to interpret and explain disasters in terms of external agents, such as demons or gods, and to actively search for effective ways to placate those agents. Those tendencies are transmitted in infancy and childhood, and they can influence people for life, fixing their minds into a specific thought strategy.

Another population of people from the same gene pool, raised in a different social–cognitive ecology—for example, modern society—will tend to interpret and represent the same events in memory very differently, not only because they frame them so differently in terms of causality but also because they attend to completely different aspects of their experiences (Bruner, 1986; Cole, 1996). These differences in the way things and events are remembered are not trivial; they reflect a different cognitive strategy and imply a significant shift in the way the brain's resources are employed in adapting to the environment. Thus, the influence of cultural memory goes deeper than the remembering process; it actively shapes the thought processes that dominate in a given society. This topic is expanded further in the next section.

The combined memory resources of a social network may be labeled as a "distributed" system, to use a term borrowed from computing science. The term is appropriate in this application because, like its computational counterparts, cultural memory systems distribute memory resources across many locations in a larger computational system (society) that includes many processors (minds). Computational distributed systems carry out their operations by sending messages between many networked processors, and human cultures carry out their cognitive operations in networks of minds (processors) linked by a system of communication, whether oral, written, or electronic. The parallels with computational networks are clear.

There are also significant differences to take into account. The differences between human cultures and machines are significant not only in their unique storage and retrieval properties but also in the kinds of memories they can encode. The most important differences between humans and machines concern the nature of the cognitive activity that can be supported by the larger distributed memory system. As advocates of artificial intelligence have discovered in their efforts to simulate basic processes such as social event perception in machines, brains and computers are very different in what they can and cannot achieve, as well as in how they achieve it; this is a thoroughly studied and complex topic (Weizenbaum, 1976) that needs no further elaboration here.

However, despite the differences between human and machine intelligence, there are parallels that make this term—distributed systems—a useful metaphor (developmental evidence also supports this use of the term; Cole & Engestrom, 1993). Most social networks are cognitive systems that distribute their operations across the minds and resources of a number of individuals, and each person embedded in such a network becomes a component in the system, just as processors are in a computing network. This has consequences: To become an effective part of a social network, a person must be able to conform to a certain standard of thought and behavior, and perform certain operations, while meeting the performance parameters demanded by the system. Any mind functioning as part of a social network must therefore sacrifice a significant degree of autonomy and obey the strictures imposed by the network.

The validity of this statement is easily seen in the computer-mediated social networks of modern organizations, in which control of an operator's attention can often be calibrated down to the fraction of a second (Auletta, 2009; Postman, 1993; Taylor, 1911). However, it is also true of more "natural" or informal social networks such as those traditionally formed by governments, corporate cultures, and religious systems. Such networks have always placed enormous constraints on the skills people need to function in, and be accepted by, the social network. In training and educating their potential members, priority is given to the special skills and attitudes required for access to and understanding of the contents of the shared memory system. Once validated, individuals become cognitive elements inside the larger system, carrying out their assigned tasks in the context of an administrative hierarchy driven by a common purpose.

In theory, cognitive work can be distributed anywhere in a network where technical competence can be found; but other cognitive factors, such as trust, special interests, and intentionality, inevitably come into play. The management of a cultural memory process is always a highly political matter. This applies in many specific contexts, from the simplest reconstruction of family history (see Shore & Kauko, Chapter 4, this volume) to the coordinated cognitive work entailed in operating large engineering projects and the management of a modern banking system or major film production. Even in the New Stone Age, members of a tribal culture had to master a massive number of special skills that were dictated by the need to survive within their social circle and physical ecology (Trigger, 2003). Those skills were rigidly encoded in a cultural memory system. Failure to acquire those skills and thought strategies is usually fatal. Human beings have always been beholden to their cultural memory systems, and they remain so.

Although cultural memory systems lack the organic unity and internal drive for coherence of a mind, they are nevertheless true cognitive systems in that they perform operations such as remembering, perceiving, assessing, deciding, and acting, usually in a cooperative manner. Organizations and corporations are, first and foremost, cognitive systems of this kind. They exist mostly to perform cognitive functions for society by sharing resources. For example, corporations such as IBM and Siemens link together the resources of tens of thousands of highly trained people, together with tools such as electronic communications networks, for the ultimate purpose of inventing and producing better tools—in this case, better cognitive tools. Each corporation has a massive memory system and a corporate culture for its proper use, which must tap directly into the personal memory systems of employees for skills, knowledge, and planning. Meantime, it must maintain a larger corporate memory system independently of those of its human element, using hard media. By merging people with machines, such a system can acquire cognitive capabilities that single individuals cannot match, just as individual brains have unique capabilities that cannot be matched (yet) by any existing nonbiological network.

Full-blown cultures are much broader distributed cognitive systems than corporations, and they are more complex than most other formal organizations, such as governments and military establishments. This is due to their comprehensiveness—governments and corporations always exist within the larger context of culture—but also especially to the fact that cultures are less tied down to explicitly symbolic operations. Much of their functional role plays out in modes of representation that may be regarded as "irrational" by enthusiasts of a more explicitly rational bent.

In fact, the so-called irrational tendencies of the human mind are by far the deepest and most primal—in the sense of being basic and coming first—of human intellectual proclivities. These "mimetic" modes of thought and representation are the foundation on which explicitly symbolic systems must be constructed (Donald, 1998a). In that sense, cultural memory systems are by far the most complex distributed systems on Earth; they encompass not only the basic social cognitive systems that tie human societies together but also all the corporate and governmental organizations under their aegis.

Mostly informal in their origins, cultures can not only learn and remember but also serve as generators for the shared mental representations essential for the smooth functioning of human society. Cultures that share mind can only achieve a unified cognitive community by producing ideas and values that have been thoroughly vetted in the minds of the entire population, providing a common ground for cooperation. Formal organizations serve specialized roles within this kind of larger cognitive–cultural environment. They also contribute very substantially to cultural memory, but the greater weight of cultural memory still falls outside their generative reach.

These are crucial points: An adequate evolutionary scenario of human cultural memory must account for much more than the explicitly symbolic features of the human mind—that is, more than language and symbolic thought. It must also account for the overwhelming importance of nonverbal, or so-called nonrational or irrational, modes of representation in cultural memory.

THE EARLY ROLE OF MATERIAL ARTIFACTS IN EVOLVING CULTURAL MEMORY

Cultural memory has taken several million years to evolve. The earliest clear manifestation of the existence of a special kind of human cultural memory in human ancestors are stone tools, which can be dated back at least to 3.3 million years before present (McPherron, Alemseged, & Marean, 2010). Stone tools are not particularly unique—humans can make tools from many materials—but they are very important because they are more likely to be preserved, whereas tools made from more perishable materials usually do not survive for long. Stone tools are thus an index of tool use in general, and their degree of refinement can be taken as a more general measure of human progress in evolving the cognitive prerequisites of refined skill.

The ability to invent and refine stone tools was a revolutionary change because it opened up a new set of possibilities for the ways in which the human species could radically modify its adaptive options. Tools can be regarded as weapons in the fight for survival. They are really surrogates for the kinds of adaptations that, in other species, might have taken millions of years to evolve. Weapons such as antlers, talons, fangs, stingers, and tusks are the kind of tools most animals need to survive, and they evolved over very long periods of time. In contrast, tools that could serve some of the same purposes as tusks and stingers were invented by early humans and disseminated widely within a fraction of a single lifetime. The weapons available to humans in their fight for survival could thus, at least in theory, change radically and fast; those of other species could not.

Because the weapons available to a species are often used, quite literally, as criteria that define the species and to specify their nature, it is fair to say that species *Homo* was the first to become able to change its nature on relatively short notice. By that criterion, human nature has been a moving target for a long time, periodically under revision. One could not imagine a more radical departure from previous evolutionary change than a species with the capacity to deliberately shape and redefine its own basic survival-related toolset.

Comparing societies at different stages of development, it is clear that cultural memory has evolved over time from a constant and creative interaction of biological and technological forces. This is a classic case of a positive feedback loop whereby A (brain) produces B (tool), and the presence of B leads to modifications of A (in this case by influencing selection pressure), which, as a result, enables A to produce more of B and to modify B, and so on. There is a strong argument in favor of such positive feedback from material culture to genetics very early in human evolution, when species ancestral to humans first became able to invent tools and altered their environment, thus changing the evolutionary pressures affecting their survival and reproduction (Baldwin, 1896). The human mastery of tools and tool manufacture changed both the evolutionary environment and the selection pressures that shaped the direction of evolution. This phenomenon resembles what biologists call "niche construction," whereby organisms alter the environment in which they live (e.g., beavers), creating a changed set of circumstances that affects the direction of their evolution. The interaction changes the environment, creating a two-way feedback loop between organism and environment (Odling-Smee, Laland, & Feldman, 2003; Sterelny, 2012).

Of course, the open-ended potential of this development in hominins was not evident in the earliest Oldowan stone tool culture, which was very limited in scope, and did not change significantly for hundreds of millennia. However, a more radical shift became evident in the Lower Paleolithic, between 1.8 and 1.0 million years ago, when early humans started to fashion a more complex toolset from the hardest, sharpest materials available: flint and obsidian. This innovation, which defined the so-called Acheulian tool culture, eventually culminated in the master toolkit used by early sapient humans. This toolkit could be used to create tools from other tools, usually by using the hard, sharp stone tool to shape softer materials, such as wood, hide, soft stone, and bone. For example, it became possible to make wooden spears with flint cutting tools. This ability, to make tools with other tools, altered the normally closed nature of niche construction. It also opened the door to an accelerated extension of human toolmaking powers, exploding in the late Upper Paleolithic approximately 60,000 years ago, signaling the unique and rapid adaptability of anatomically modern humans.

Tools and the complex cooperative skills needed to maintain a tradition of toolmaking and tool use over generations depended on special cognitive capacities that started to emerge more than 3 million years ago. Certain crucial brain adaptations were necessary for the development of complex skills evident in early stone toolmaking cultures. Those adaptations were probably rooted in changes to the frontocerebellar system, which is a key component in the neural support of efficient procedural learning. In particular, these changes had to permit the kind of active, self-critical, rehearsal skills necessary for the mastery of even the simplest Oldowan toolmaking (Donald, 1998b). Moreover, the skills involved in making good stone tools usually require some pedagogical guidance from others. A useful description of the complexities of sustaining simple toolmaking skills is provided by Toth and Schick (2009).

Moreover, some further evolution of archaic human social skills was necessary for sustaining the more complex Acheulian tool culture that existed for more than 1 million years. Such cultures are complex enough to demand efficient social networks for their continuance. Hutchins (1995) suggested the term "networks of practice" for the rituals and patterns of group behavior that sustain tool use in such domains as navigation and migration. Such networks can be held together in a variety of ways that are best described as nonverbal. They can be sustained by behavior patterns that are embedded in, and transmitted through, cultural memory systems.

Stone toolmaking is solid evidence for the successful transmission of cultural memory across generations. Although it is true that the transmission of local traditions has been demonstrated in other species (Whiten, 2011), it constitutes the earliest permanent memory record of a uniquely human kind of tool culture that demands a capacity for *self-guided rehearsal*. Tools are not typically designed to preserve memory, but tools themselves store information in their form and use patterns, and they may prove informative to the user in many other ways. Moreover, the ideas driving their invention and use had to be preserved.

In this context, stone tools can be viewed as affording an important selection advantage for those hominins able to sustain a cultural memory system linked to material culture. As stone tools became more sophisticated in design, they also provided their users with information that showed what to aim at in manufacturing them. Later in human evolution, this was also true of other products of material culture, such as markers, monuments, hearths, and built structures. Those also left traces of their possible functions, indicating something about the lifestyles of past inhabitants. They also contained within themselves implicit guidelines for their manufacture. Design alone can tell future generations how tools might be used. Their mere existence points to possibilities that might otherwise not have been realized.

The importance of the material cultural record is thus not merely its historical value to researchers. The material record itself is informative. It has been useful as an instructive device throughout human evolution. Tools are packed with useful information for future generations, and they are an important component of cultural memory. Their rediscovery can even serve to restore knowledge that might otherwise have remained forgotten (the rediscovery of classical civilization during the early Renaissance is one of the clearest examples of this, albeit on a more abstract level). The existence of a physical record points its future discoverers to the reimagining of ideas that might have been lost for centuries. Finding a tool from a foreign civilization is a potentially rich and suggestive discovery, capable of carrying an idea forward across time and space and possibly leading to important and perhaps crucial changes in a cultural skill set. Material devices often impose a pattern of discipline and cooperation in their use, and they also stimulate the creative imagination.

This may seem obvious in a modern context. However, in a fundamental sense, the material components of cultural memory have been a pedagogical reality in human society for a very long time. They entered into the evolutionary process very early, and played a crucial role from the start, as the human mind started to diverge from its primate pattern.

A POSSIBLE SCENARIO

It is an important challenge for cognitive neuroscience to establish in detail the path humanity took in evolving the brain capacities needed to create a cultural memory system. In the abstract, viewed in terms of potential cognitive architectures, there are many ways in which this outcome might have been achieved. In fact, however, humans are primates, very closely related to modern chimpanzees; humans are genetically as close to chimpanzees as chimpanzees are to gorillas. This closeness imposes some serious constraints on theoretical speculation. Given the conservative evolutionary history of the brain, it suggests that some of the signature capabilities evident in human higher cognition might be, at least partly, attributable to nonbiological factors, such as culture and technology.

Regardless of its origins, the cognitive gap between humans and our two closest relatives, and even more remotely related primate species, is enormous. The common ancestor we share with chimpanzees obviously underwent a series of modifications that widened the cognitive gap between the mentalities of both ancient and modern primates and formed the characteristic mental capabilities of modern humanity. However, the cognitive distance traveled during human evolution is too large for a conventional gradualistic explanation; this points to a special role for a novel factor, such as culture, in human cognitive evolution.

In fact, the cognitive distances in this case are so great that it is fair to claim that human beings constitute a whole new order in biology (Deacon, 1997; Donald, 1991). Radical changes have occurred in at least a dozen basic parameters of primate cognition (Donald, 2001). Changes on this scale imply that a critical threshold has been crossed in human evolution, introducing a novel set of evolutionary factors that pushed humanity over that threshold.

One candidate for such a factor was culture, in its new role as a collective memory system that could accumulate knowledge in social networks and carry that knowledge across generations, influencing neural epigenesis. There might also have been a revolutionary shift in the effect of culture as an evolving cognitive ecology so that algorithms stored in cultural memory gradually became increasingly capable of releasing latent, or unrealized, brain potential, much as the availability of a symbol set has revealed a hitherto unrealized potential for comprehending symbols in the enculturated apes such as Kanzi (Savage-Rumbaugh et al., 1993).

This introduces the possibility of a novel factor in human cognitive evolution that might help explain its uniqueness: a co-evolutionary relationship between brain and culture, an emergent brain–culture symbiosis. As culture becomes more complex and assumes the role of defining the human cognitive ecology, the very complexity and unpredictability of that ecology provides a selection factor favoring a major increase in the plasticity of the human brain and also in its social competency.

In most species, including primates, culture can be regarded almost as an epiphenomenon of social cognition, to be accounted for as a byproduct of innate behavioral tendencies; culture is thus secondary to the innately programmed mental abilities of the species. As a result, it shows relatively little variation between groups, and those variations are typically due to environmental differences. In contrast, human cultures are highly variable, differing along many dimensions, so that the prevalence of any social trait under study in a given culture—for example, violence, egalitarianism, altruistic behavior, deference to authority, promiscuity, and cooperation—can be shown to be nullified or reversed in another. Material culture can also be so fundamentally different between cultures—for example, the presence of writing and literacy—that it imposes very different epigenetic regimes, affecting the modes of thought and memory, and the cerebral architectures that support them.

Material culture evolved into a major player fairly early in hominid evolution. As humanity continued to evolve, material cultural innovations such as writing influenced the pattern of neural epigenesis and cognitive development in a more profound sense, eventually to such a degree that symbolic technologies now dominate the formation of the higher cognitive systems of the brain on the level of functional architecture. For example, the set of skills commonly defined in neuropsychology as higher cognition in modern human beings depends on access to and skills that were assimilated from a massive shared cognitive system whose operations can be defined by the properties of both the individual brain and the network or networks into which it has been embedded. The most obvious examples are writing and musical skills, both related to literacy. The network in these cases changes the course of individual development so that the mature adult's mind and brain have been defined largely by the degree to which cultural algorithms, such as literacy, have been assimilated.

The outcome of this arrangement is complex; modes of cognition that dominate in one culture do not necessarily dominate in another. Nor does every cognitive possibility characteristic of the human species develop spontaneously in every healthy adult as such things tend to do in other species. The possibilities that are realized are very much a function of the particular cultural memory systems in play during development.

This kind of heavy developmental influence depends utterly on immersion in certain kinds of cultural environments. Those environments are now so influential that they have actually become what might more appropriately be called human cognitive ecosystems. This scenario demands considerable neural plasticity, and there is good evidence that humans have a higher degree of plasticity than other primates or mammals, especially in the most recently evolved regions of the brain.

Radical shifts in the role of culture in cognitive evolution have occurred gradually during a period of at least 2 million years, possibly more. From the paleontological and archaeological record, there is evidence of at least three major transition periods in human prehistory that meet good evidential standards for a major cognitive–cultural shift. In each of these, human culture has evolved further in the direction of becoming an indispensable memory bank for crucial adaptive information related to releasing potential that was latent in the human brain to create the powerful distributed cognitive system that we can identify as cultural memory (Table 1.1).

A three-stage scenario for human cognitive and cultural evolution follows from a broad survey of evidence from several academic disciplines (Donald, 1991, 1993, 1999, 2010). The details of the evolutionary and neuropsychological argument have been reviewed and updated extensively elsewhere (Donald, 2008, 2012a, 2013) and are not reconsidered here. Table 1.1 outlines the main stages relevant to the emergence of modern forms of cultural memory. The essence of the proposal is that cultural memory was wired into the human cognitive apparatus of thought quite early in hominid evolution and was one of the driving forces that pushed it in a unique direction, toward a brain–culture symbiosis.

Taken together, the modes of representation in Table 1.1 were intended to account, in evolutionary terms, for the complex modes of mental representation available to the modern mind. These modes were labeled mimetic, mythic, and theoretic because the governing mode of representation was different during the three postulated stages. In brief recapitulation, the *mimetic mode* is action-oriented, embodied, and employs an analog logic; the *mythic mode* is rooted in storytelling, archetypes, and autobiographical memory, employing an event-representational logic closely allied to mimesis, from which it sprang; and the *theoretic mode* is institutional and dependent on information technology—its internal logic resembles Bruner's (1986) notion of "paradigmatic" or analytic thought. It grew as a consequence of long experience with the technologies of literate expression and the gradual institutionalization of habits of thought.

Table 1.1 PROPOSED SUCCESSIVE STAGES OR "LAYERS" IN THE EVOLUTION OF PRIMATE/HOMINID CULTURE, USING A COGNITIVE CRITERION FOR CLASSIFICATION[a]

Stage	Species/Period	Novel Forms of Representation	Manifest Change	Cognitive Governance
Episodic	Primate	Complex episodic event perceptions	Improved self-awareness and event sensitivity	Episodic and reactive; limited voluntary expressive morphology
Mimetic (first transition)	Early hominids, peaking in H. erectus; 4 M–0.4 Mya	Nonverbal action modeling	Revolution in skill, gesture (including vocal), nonverbal communication, shared attention	Mimetic; increased variability of custom, cultural "archetypes"
Mythic (second transition)	Sapient humans, peaking in H. sapiens sapiens; 0.5 Mya–present	Linguistic modeling	High-speed phonology, oral language, oral social record	Lexical invention, narrative thought, mythic framework of governance
Theoretic (third transition)	Recent sapient cultures	Extensive external symbolization, both verbal and nonverbal	Formalisms, large-scale theoretic artifacts and massive external memory storage	Institutionalized paradigmatic thought and invention

[a] Note that each stage persists into the next and continues to occupy its cultural niche; thus, fully modern human societies incorporate aspects of all four stages of hominid culture. The Upper Paleolithic seems to be situated pretty clearly in the oral–mythic cultural tradition, but set the stage for later expansions.

SOURCE: Reprinted with permission from Harvard University Press.

Some aspects of the model directly address the nature of cultural memory. The main points are evident from an overview of Table 1.1. The following points should be kept in mind when reviewing the stages:

1. Each stage of the cultural–cognitive system was built on a preexisting platform.
2. Each stage introduced a major new mode of representation into cultural memory.
3. Previous modes of representation were retained within the emerging cultural–cognitive structure as each new mode of representation emerged.
4. These stages were not static; they emerged only very gradually, in a nonlinear manner, over long periods of transition.
5. The first, or mimetic, stage was the product of a reorganization of the hominid executive brain as co-evolved with the increasing importance of tools in hominid social life.
6. Because languages are socially constructed entities, the universal presence of languages implies that some form of culture and cultural memory (mimesis) had already emerged before languages existed, satisfying the cognitive preconditions necessary for the emergence of protolanguage.
7. Languages were the negotiated product of essentially mimetic minds trying to establish a common means of sharing mental representations.
8. The mythic stage was a product of spoken language having evolved to the point where storytelling—the symbolic encapsulation of large and complex event representations—became widespread in human society, eventually producing a symbiosis between autobiographical memory and cultural memory (Donald, 2012a; Nelson, 1996; see also Nelson, Chapter 8, this volume).
9. The theoretic stage emerged as a dominant form fairly recently, and it was largely a product of socially entrained habits of thought and the institutionalization of pedagogy; its current dominance in science and economic management reflects the successful application of material culture and technology to cognitive ends.

It can be said with some confidence that a reciprocal relationship between brain and culture appeared quite early in human prehistory, and the result was an early redirection of the course of cognitive evolution away from modularity and specialization toward learning, plasticity, cross-modal integration, executive skills, and social interdependency. There is substantial empirical and theoretical support for this idea (Deacon, 1997; Donald, 1991, 2001; Tomasello, 1999, 2008, 2014).

Thus, in the human case, cognitive evolution is so closely tied to cultural memory that it must be tracked in terms of cultural evolutionary steps. Cultural memory in this model consists of layers of publicly accessible mental representations superimposed on a base episodic layer of personal memory. The base layer was inherited from our common ancestor with Miocene apes. This is a cascade model of cognitive evolution in the sense that the three postulated cognitive–cultural stages were not independent of one another; each successive development was built upon, and closely interwoven with, its predecessors. Thus, the complex interweaving of cultural memory with the mature forms of adult cognition tended toward increasingly greater complexity. These succeeding layers each operated according to a distinctive internal logic.

The logic of mimesis is embodied action metaphor. The logic of mythic culture is the elaborated representation of social events. The logic of theoretic culture is really derivative of written symbols and machine logic, as reflected in symbolic logic and mathematics. In modern humanity, these modes of representation have different degrees of depth in terms of their hold on the human psyche, roughly reflecting the order in which the features of the modern human mind emerged. Thus, mimetic cultural memories should be the most difficult to eradicate or conquer. Narrative memory, constituting the deepest mythological ideas of a society, is less resilient but nonetheless very difficult to conquer or replace. As might be expected, the later-evolved forms of mental representation, those linked to a theoretic stance, are less deep, less mandatory in personal cognitive development, and more vulnerable to conquest or disruption.

These stages reflect more accurately the real-world complexity of human memory structure than traditional solipsistic accounts based solely on evidence from the laboratories of experimental psychology (for a discussion of the "isolated mind" model, see Donald, 2000). When social networks are taken into account as an active player in constructing memory, it is probably wise to combine the traditional categories of human memory—implicit versus explicit, episodic versus semantic, procedural versus declarative, and so on—with the layers of cognitive–cultural evolution described previously. In doing so, it becomes evident that every aspect of biological memory played a role at each of the three stages. The voluntary, collective elaboration of procedural memory may have dominated the first transition; the interpretation of episodic event memory in social networks dominated the second; and the extreme refinement of semantic memory, and its formal embedding into a system of material symbols, dominated the third. However, all the innate memory systems of the brain have contributed to each stage in some manner. The resultant layering of public representational systems created a superordinate memory system that is generated, and largely resides, in the social networks of culture, which remain based in the irrational but immensely powerful cerebral circuitry driving the mimetic mode.

COGNITIVE GOVERNANCE

Cognition in social networks requires governance. The layers of superordinate cultural memory representation listed in Table 1.1 are both created by and imposed upon individuals. The three modes of representation play somewhat independent roles in the governance of modern society, reflecting their place in the evolutionary succession, where each succeeding layer of representation has played a distinct role in the cognitive governance of the social networks of culture.

Early in human evolution, before language or symbolic thought were a possibility, a culture of action and skill necessarily predominated in human life. The evolutionary evidence suggests that ancient hominins became *skilled* before they became *articulate*. Nonverbal networks of practice were the only way a culture could remember skills and effective patterns of tool use. This was a limited means of preserving tradition and left little room for innovation, but it evidently worked for a very long time—in fact, for most of human prehistory. It is worth reiterating that the internal logic of mimesis does not rule out some small degree of lexical invention. The home signs created by deaf non-signers are perhaps the best evidence that mimetic communication can work, to a limited degree, to sustain a network of practice without needing the complexities of grammars and large vocabularies. Moreover, those skills can be transmitted across generations through emulation and ritual practice, without a fully developed language.

This mimetic governing tendency rules the apprenticeship learning networks of society, which are still dominant in the modern transmission of many nonverbal skills and customs. This is played out in the way athletic skill, craft, dance, performance art, and theater are sustained. It is also evident in both formal and informal rules of social ritual—and this mode still governs those aspects of human life.

Cultural memory in early hominin prehistory seems to have consisted largely of coordinated skills—procedural memories embedded in social networks—that were largely ordered around the learning and transmission of ritualized action patterns. These resemble the networks of practice observed by Hutchins (1995), within which social relationships and cooperative work can thrive, while language plays a very minor role.

Much later in human evolution, after spoken language began to dominate human social life, the oral tradition came into its heyday. Mythologies and the narrative mode of thinking (Bruner, 1986) ruled human thinking and remembering, while mimetic rituals and apprenticeship cultures continued to thrive within a new framework.

Finally, many millennia after agriculture and literacy were established, the institutions required to sustain a complex culture based on empirical science and analytic thought were gradually established. With this, "theoretic" culture ascended to a position of governance in human affairs. Theoretic culture is still in a minority position globally, and it continues to rely on the two previous modes of representation for its cognitive platform. However, it rules the human world. It dominates in science, technology, the financial markets, and even many of the arts.

TOWARD A HIERARCHICAL MODEL OF CULTURAL MEMORY

Cultural memory systems are a valid object of study in their own right, and the social sciences need a more adequate model of this important and uniquely human phenomenon. It is clear from examining Table 1.1 that the properties of the human brain, taken alone, cannot account for the features of the distributed cognitive–cultural system of the human species. The brain's innate memory systems provide the basic creative circuitry that drives the system, and they impose a series of constraints on cultural memory insofar as humans must be able to gain access to its contents relatively easily and must also be able to generate, understand, and use those contents for various purposes. These constraints were absolute in the early evolution of human culture, when the brain was the dominant partner. The relationship between the mind and its cultural storehouse—the interface between mind and cultural memory—was not really problematic until the invention of writing and mathematics.

However, the relatively recent proliferation of complex machine-dominated environments, novel computational logic, and sophisticated robots has changed the picture. The human–machine interface has become a crucial design question not only for individuals but also for large corporate entities, such as governments. The artifacts of earlier cultures were much simpler, and they necessarily reflected the way the human mind naturally functioned. This is no longer the case. The relationship between human and machine has now become a critical consideration because the category of cultural memory can legitimately be extended to include even the most esoteric kinds of computation, mathematics, and bioengineering, which are, after all, part of the contents of our distributed cultural memory system, but operate on quite different principles, and have increasingly distinct properties that are incompatible with the design of the human brain.

These developments are in danger of leaving the brain's innate memory strategies in the dust, so to speak. Access is now a very major issue: We cannot google our biological memory banks; we cannot even catalog them. However, we can engineer massively improved access to the virtually infinite cultural memory banks of modern society. We can even choose whether or not to make such knowledge universally accessible. As mentioned previously, the modes of operation of computational memory systems are very different from those of biological memory systems. Representational forms that were central to traditional human cultural life, such as mythologies, performance-based expressive behavior, art, music and dance, ritual, and even systems of moral/ethical representation, are not, strictly speaking, necessary components of the new technological environment.

The fundamental design features of cultural memory are now an open question. We have choices to make that were, quite literally, unthinkable a mere generation ago. Our present situation can be taken as an excellent example of emergent evolution, whereby a new order of complexity emerges—in this case, in a distributed cognitive system with new properties—that is still completely dependent on the needs of its foundational platform for its perpetuation and use but is nevertheless in a position to dominate the hierarchy, much as organic cognitive systems came to dominate the underlying processes supporting multicellular life forms.

In summary, as hominid cognitive resources have become increasingly entangled with cultural memory systems, the evolutionary course followed by the human brain has departed dramatically from the traditional primate pattern of cognitive evolution. This has led humanity in a unique evolutionary direction in which the species has become increasingly more reliant on a cultural memory system whose properties are radically mutable on short notice.

INDIVIDUALS VIEWED AS CARRIERS OF CULTURAL MEMORY

Cultural memories are enduring and can transcend many lifetimes. Individual humans have become, in a very real sense, the temporary carriers of cultural memory. Individual brains fix and instantiate—in idiosyncratic ways special to each individual—the customs, skills, and knowledge assimilated from a cultural past. Every aspect of the human brain's innate memory apparatus, implicit and explicit, can be employed to this end. In effect, the human species has put cultural memory to use as a storehouse of epigenetic and developmental programs for building adaptive phenomes out of genetic raw material. Moreover, those programs can be changed relatively quickly if necessary.

The result is a biologically novel phenomenon: the person-as-cultural-specimen. The developing brain is culturally neutral; given the appropriate epigenetic environment, it can masquerade as an exemplar of virtually any culture, whether Bushman, Chinese, French, Russian Orthodox, and so on, without prejudice. It can even masquerade as a robotic component in a human–machine system, as any assembly-line employee can verify. Mature adult brains carry an enormous amount of cultural memory material, and they can often absorb more than one cultural tradition, including multiple versions of such basic things as languages, habits of thought, and even personality traits.

Episodic, mimetic, and mythic culture are unifying concepts that express the dominant cognitive quality of the individual mind in relation to society. They determine the very general properties of the kind of mental control processes that determine how an individual thinks or remembers. In traditional societies, it is the balance between mimetic and mythic components that sets the governing standard. Theoretic elements may be present in some degree, but they are typically in the background. When Bellah (2011) tried to apply these categories to the ancient civilizations of Greece, India, China, and Israel, he claimed to have found evidence that theoretic culture—a culture in which the process of thinking itself came under examination—had started to develop at that time in all four of these so-called Axial civilizations. My own reaction to his claim (Donald, 2012b) was that Greece was the only one that had met all the criteria for institutionalized theoretic culture, and this for only a short time at the high point of Periclean Athenian society. Otherwise, none of these societies, including Greece, contained even a subculture of a theoretic nature. Even today, theoretic culture is a minority elite culture that exists only as a subculture within a few highly developed nations. It is undoubtedly in a governing position, given that the global economy and the Internet are entirely under its command, but there is no guarantee this situation will sustain itself over the long term.

Regarding the position of the individual in modern society, the profusion of cultural memory material can both liberate and constrain the cognitive options available to a person. Some of the assimilated habits that the human brain can implement are primarily cognitive in nature (e.g., the inferential skills of a mathematician or a computer programmer); others may involve encoding complex sensorimotor sequences (e.g., the skills of a weaver or professional athlete) or social mannerisms (e.g., a particular way of expressing respect for authority, such as in the rules of the Japanese or British aristocracy, as opposed to those of a star punk rock guitarist). Amazingly, several of these modes can coexist in the same multicultural brain. There is no way to predict whether and when such complexity might free the individual to live a more enriching life or lead to confusion, disintegration, or even a major breakdown.

Cultural memory provides much of the raw material for assembling an adult person. The individual has a great deal of work to do during the course of self-assembly, but cultural memory plays the defining role in setting out a range of possibilities available during development (see Nelson, Chapter 8, this volume). On a personal level, individuals may believe that they can control, or at least influence, this process. However, in a single lifetime, most individuals will only manage to create very minor variations on what they have absorbed from the cultural memory banks they inherit.

In this sense, the contribution of the individual brain to an evolving collective memory system can easily be exaggerated, relative to the larger social–cognitive equilibrium that preserves the cultural memory record. The larger cognitive–cultural system dominates. Each individual brain carries the responsibility for maintaining internal coherence and integrity in the assimilated system as it self-assembles, altering its contents somewhat where possible or deemed necessary. However, even this modification is usually only achievable by close interaction with the distributed cognitive–cultural apparatus of society. Even the most radical individuals in human history, those who broke the existing mold, so to speak, of their societies—Socrates, Buddha, Jesus, and Genghis Khan—were very much of their historical time and place.

The tension between individual and cultural memory is a perpetual fact of human life. To be effective, the individual brain must develop a strategy to operate as an active functional component within the much larger distributed memory system of society. This interactive role defines adaptive success for each new generation and is a central creative factor influencing the shape of cultural memory systems over time. At the same time, individuals undergo individuation and form an identity, usually in contradistinction to their immediate social environment. The outcome of this arrangement reveals a unique symbiotic interdependency between the evolving brain and cultural memory; even the representational options available to the growing mind are ultimately set out by culture. Concepts of time and space, motivational and emotional priorities, behavioral norms, stories of origin, attitudes to hierarchy and social class, ideals of self-fulfillment, and even the balance of power between the mythic, mimetic, and theoretic elements come largely from the surrounding culture.

CONCLUSION

Personal growth is a dynamic process that seldom remains stable for long, and cultural memory reflects that dynamism on a social level. A cultural memory system is best regarded as a work in progress, undergoing constant revision and redesign by groups of people working in social networks. It is vulnerable to decreases, as well as increases, in its overall cognitive power and effectiveness. Cultural memory can sustain a culture but can also destroy it, depending on the needs of the moment, and those needs are determined by a combination of cognitive, social, and political factors too complex to discuss in this short chapter. This dynamism applies equally to local memories shared by small kinship groups and to widely disseminated memories shared by very large populations. The needs of a cognitive community change continuously and require continuous updating to remain current and effective. This constant need to update the system is normally manageable, but in times of social crisis it can place a strain on individual members of society, sometimes passing the point of no return, where a society quite literally disintegrates from within.

No limit to human inventiveness has been clearly established. It is a changing capacity, rooted in the networked brains of our species and greatly amplified by technological innovation. As memory technology develops, it changes the possibility space for both mind and society, and for this reason, the future development of memory technology cannot be predicted with any certainty. A consequence of this is that the future forms of cultural memory are also uncertain.

Despite their dependency on the creative contributions of individual human beings, cultural memory systems are not subject to many of the constraints that act on personal memory. Cultural memory systems routinely outlive individuals, and depending on available memory technologies, they have no inherent capacity limits. They are able to sustain many contradictory ideas at the same time, and they can register many competing viewpoints, with no theoretical limit on either the content or the number of such conflicts to be sustained at any given time. However, because the larger process must ultimately be filtered through the individual minds that make up a culture, the governance of every cultural memory system, and especially access to it, remains a highly political matter (Halbwachs, 1980).

Elaborate cultural memory systems can be extraordinarily robust, such as those that can preserve an informal system of laws for centuries after conquest by another group or rebuild a city destroyed by war. This is because memories reside in many people and objects simultaneously; in other words, it is due to the distributed nature of storage in the system. Different components of cultural memory systems are lodged in distinctive ways in the memory systems of individuals and institutions, but no single individual can store or comprehend the entire system. In addition, because the larger cultural memory system does not constitute a mind and lacks conscious unity, it can never be fully aware of the resources it holds, whether in its population or in material culture. However, a group, using its scattered memory resources and the codes and artifacts preserved in the remnants of a damaged material culture, can some-times reconstitute an entire cultural memory system even after it has sustained serious injury—for example, the reconstruction of Hebrew centuries after it was declared a dead language.

This complex cognitive–cultural arrangement, which enables human beings to construct and remember an almost unlimited amount of information and knowl-edge, is the signature cognitive feature that distinguishes the unique mentality of human beings. Such an extraordinary adaptation seems to have no precedent in the history of life on Earth. Its domination by technology is the major engineer-ing challenge of our time. Material culture in general, which includes the elec-tronic communications systems surrounding the planet, has played a critical role in releasing cultural memory from the constraints inherent in the brain's limited innate memory systems. The technologies of cultural memory are now moving so fast that the most pressing questions about cultural memory are now concerned at least as much with its future as with its past.

REFERENCES

Assman, J. (2006). *Religion and cultural memory*. Stanford, CA: Stanford University Press.

Auletta, K. (2009). *Googled: The end of the world as we know it*. New York, NY: Penguin.

Baldwin, J. M. (1896). A new factor in evolution. *American Naturalist, 30*, 441–451, 536–553.

Bartlett, F. (1932). *Remembering: A study in experimental and social psychology*. Cambridge, UK: Cambridge University Press.

Bellah, R. (2011). *Religion in human evolution: From the Paleolithic to the Axial Age*. Cambridge, MA: Harvard University Press.

Bruner, J. (1986). *Actual minds, possible worlds*. Cambridge, MA: Harvard University Press.

Cole, M. (1996). *Cultural psychology: A once and future discipline*. Cambridge, MA: Harvard University Press.

Cole, M., & Engestrom, Y. (1993). A cultural–historical approach to distributed cogni-tion. In G. Salomon (Ed.), *Distributed cognitions: Psychological and educational con-siderations*. New York, NY: Cambridge University Press.

Deacon, T. (1997). *The symbolic species: The co-evolution of language and the brain*. New York, NY: Norton.

Donald, M. (1991). *Origins of the modern mind: Three stages in the evolution of culture and cognition*. Cambridge, MA: Harvard University Press.

Donald, M. (1993). Précis of *Origins of the Modern Mind* with multiple review and author's response. *Behavioral and Brain Sciences, 16*, 737–791.

Donald, M. (1998a). Mimesis and the executive suite: Missing links in language evolu-tion. In J. R. Hurford, M. Studdert-Kennedy, & C. Knight (Eds.), *Approaches to the evo-lution of language: Social and cognitive bases* (pp. 44–67). Cambridge, UK: Cambridge University Press.

Donald, M. (1998b). Hominid enculturation and cognitive evolution. In C. Renfrew & C. Scarre (Eds.), *Cognition and material culture: The archaeology of symbolic storage*. Cambridge, UK: McDonald Institute for Archaeological Research.

Donald, M. (1999). Preconditions for the evolution of protolanguages. In M. C. Corballis & I. Lea (Eds.), *The descent of mind* (pp. 120–136). Oxford: Oxford University Press.

Donald, M. (2000). The central role of culture in cognitive evolution: A reflection on the myth of the isolated mind. In L. Nucci, G. Saxe, & E. Turiel (Eds.), *Culture, thought and development* (pp. 19–38). New York, NY: Erlbaum

Donald, M. (2001). *A mind so rare: The evolution of human consciousness.* New York, NY: Norton.

Donald, M. (2008). How culture and brain mechanisms interact in decision making. In C. Engel & W. Singer (Eds.), *Better than conscious? Decision-making, the human mind, and implications for institutions* (pp. 191–225). Cambridge, MA: MIT Press.

Donald, M. (2010). The exographic revolution: Neuropsychological sequelae. In L. Malafouris & C. Renfrew (Eds.), *The cognitive life of things: Recasting the boundaries of the mind* (pp. 71–79). Cambridge, UK: McDonald Institute Institute for Archaeological Research.

Donald, M. (2012a). Evolutionary origins of autobiographical memory. In D. Berntsen & D. C. Rubin (Eds.), *Understanding autobiographical memory: Themes and approaches* (pp. 269–289). New York, NY: Cambridge University Press.

Donald, M. (2012b). An evolutionary approach to culture: Implications for the study of the Axial Age. In R. Bellah & H. Joas (Eds.), *The Axial Age and its consequences* (pp. 47–76). Cambridge, MA: Harvard University Press.

Donald, M. (2013). Mimesis theory re-examined, twenty years after the fact. In G. Hatfield & H. Pittman (Eds.), *The evolution of mind, brain and culture* (pp. 169–192). Philadelphia, PA: University of Pennsylvania Press.

Halbwachs, M. (1980). *The collective memory.* New York, NY: Harper & Row Colophon Books.

Hutchins, E. (1995). *Cognition in the wild.* Cambridge, MA: MIT Press.

McPherron, S. P., Alemseged, C. W., & Marean, C. W. (2010). Evidence for stone-tool-assisted consumption of animal tissue before 3.39 million years ago at Dikika, Ethiopia. *Nature, 466,* 857–860.

Nelson, K. (1996). *Language in cognitive development: The emergence of the mediated mind.* New York, NY: Cambridge University Press.

Odling-Smee, F. J., Laland, K. N., & Feldman, M. W. (2003). *Niche construction: The neglected process in evolution.* Princeton, NJ: Princeton University Press.

Postman, N. (1993). *Technopoly: The surrender of culture to technology.* New York, NY: Knopf Doubleday.

Savage-Rumbaugh, E. S., Murphy, J., Sevcik, R. A., Brakke, K. E., Williams, S. L., & Rumbaugh, D. M. (1993). Language comprehension in ape and child. *Monographs of the Society for Research in Child Development, 58*(3–4), 1–222.

Sterelny, K. (2012). *The evolved apprentice: How evolution made humans unique.* Cambridge, MA: MIT Press.

Taylor, F. W. (1911). *The principles of scientific management.* New York, NY: Harper.

Tomasello, M. (1999). *The cultural origins of human cognition.* Cambridge, MA: Harvard University Press.

Tomasello, M. (2008). *Origins of human communication.* Cambridge, MA: MIT Press.

Tomasello, M. (2014). *A natural history of human thinking.* Cambridge, MA: Harvard University Press.

Toth, N., & Schick, N. (2009). *The cutting edge: New approaches to the archaeology of human origins.* Bloomington, IN: Stone Age Institute Press.

Trigger, B. (2003). *Understanding early civilizations*. New York, NY: Cambridge University Press.

Weizenbaum, J. (1976). *Computer power and human reason: From judgement to calculation*. San Francisco, CA: Freeman.

Whiten, A. (2011). The scope of culture in chimpanzees, humans and ancestral apes. *Philosophical Transactions of the Royal Society. Series B, Biological Sciences, 366*(1567), 997–1007.

From Memory as Archive to Remembering as Conversation

JENS BROCKMEIER ■

In memoriam Oliver Sacks (1933—2015)

Over long periods in the cultural history of the West, people's thoughts and ideas about their memory and the nature of their memories were amazingly stable and uncontested. During these periods, human memory seemed like something given and taken for granted. This, to be sure, cannot be said for the present. Some might dispute that there is *a* notion of memory and, indeed, such a thing as memory at all. Yet even those who are confident about memory's conceptual state and ontological status today agree that our idea of memory is in the midst of reconstruction—that there is a remodeling taking place at a variety of sites.

In this chapter, I take a closer look at this remodeling. My aim is to get a sense of possible future outlines of our understanding of remembering and forgetting. There is no understanding without concepts. Sometimes, if things get complicated, such understanding is described in terms of not only concepts but also models. Memory models typically have a conceptual and a metaphorical aspect, often without a clear borderline between them. My first question is, What are the established memory models? If we wanted to stress the metaphorical aspect of these models, we could also speak of fossilized metaphors—of metaphors that have become so common and taken for granted that they are not perceived any more as metaphors but as direct representations of assumed realities. My second question is, What are conceivable conceptual and metaphorical perspectives that might guide a new, possibly alternative, understanding of remembering and forgetting—if we insinuate, for once, that the present reconstruction and remodeling will go on?

I begin by inspecting the busiest present construction sites. In particular, I am interested in a number of developments in the memory sciences as well as in other fields of social and technological memory studies. These developments have challenged three assumptions that have long been fundamental for our idea of remembering; in fact, they have been fundamental for our cultural notion of memory. By cultural notion, I refer to today's dominant ideas of the nature and significance of what happens when we remember—ideas that are explicitly and implicitly articulated in various discourses, be they theoretical or common sense, academic or literary, scientific or artistic; they are also enacted in many of our individual and collective practices of remembrance and reminiscing.

What are these three assumptions? The first one is that memory is an individual affair; it is the human individual who is the site, carrier, and performer of remembering and forgetting. The second assumption, already broached, is that memory is a biological function and integral part of the individual organism or one of its organs, the brain; it is a "natural kind." There are several levels of biological and neuroscientific memory research—for example, one is concerned with systems of neuronal networks. The third assumption is that memory works according to the model of a storage; it is an archive of the past. This model appears in a number of variants. Even more time-honored than the two other ones, its first and most influential articulation was given by Plato. Ever since, it has been used to describe what most of today's neuroscientists conceive of as the basic mechanisms of memory—the encoding, storing, reconsolidating, and recalling of information.

Although I characterized these as the culturally dominant assumptions both in the memory sciences and in everyday discourse, we should be aware that they are challenged in various fields of memory studies. They are especially questioned in those fields in which the social, collective, and cultural dimensions of remembering are given center stage, which is a focus quite different from neurocognitive and neurophysiological research. It is exactly these dimensions, as the critique goes, that the individuo-centered, naturalistic, and archivalist frameworks elude; more than this, they are systematically excluded. The field of social and cultural research overlaps in part with other areas of memory studies: autobiographical and biographical studies (based in the social sciences and the humanities); studies of life writing, trauma, and testimony (in the humanities); and narrative and discursive studies of remembering and forgetting (based in the humanities, the social sciences, and medicine and health sciences). Finally, there is the emerging field of digital memory studies, which is concerned with new mnemonic and interactional technologies and their social, psychological, and cultural implications—with special attention given to Internet-based communication and the human–computer interface.

However, it is not just a fundamental critique of traditional psychological and neuroscientific models of memory that has been put forward in these areas. What have also emerged are new visions of remembering and forgetting—new concepts, metaphors, and perspectives of how to understand the complexities of memory beyond what many view as traditional reductionism.

There is, however, the danger of viewing this picture as one of a clear-cut contrast between traditional psychological (i.e., cognitive) and neuroscientific research, on the one hand—research that typically conceives of itself as culture-independent and committed to universal standards of scientificity—and a field of culturally oriented memory studies mainly localized in the social sciences and the humanities, on the other hand. It is a danger because the assumption of this contrast comes with the idea of a unified field of scientific memory research. Although the neurosciences have been characterized as unified by a common "neuromolecular mode of thought" (Rose & Abi-Rached, 2013), there is little agreement on how to map memory and the many neurocognitive systems or brain centers in which it has been divided, let alone nailing down the putatively naturalist ontology, the neurophysiological substrate, of these systems and centers. In particular, this concerns the neurocognitive idea of multiple memory systems that postulates distinct (semantic, episodic, autobiographical, and many other) memory units. Even if not necessarily related to these distinctions, a number of mnemonic phenomena are also directly attributed to specific locations in the brain, or perhaps more precisely, neurological findings are associated with mnemonic phenomena (Medved & Brockmeier, 2016). For example, the hippocampus and other parts of the limbic system are thought to be essential for what is called the consolidation of information assumed to take place in the transition from short-term memory to long-term memory, as in the formation of episodic and autobiographical memories.

Relations of neurological and psychological phenomena are investigated in a plurality of disciplinary contexts: within experimental and naturalistic settings, on several epistemological levels and within different categorical orders (neurological, psychiatric, psychotherapeutic, psychoanalytic, rehabilitative, and philosophical). Accordingly wide is the spectrum of research protocols and practices, ranging from neurophysiological research on the cellular and subcellular molecular level to functional neuroanatomy, neurocognitive (mostly digital imaging-based) study of neuronal networks and brain areas and traditional memory experimentation in cognitive and social psychology. Finally, this spectrum also includes research with clinical populations, such as in neurotraumatology, gerontology, and dementia studies.

Although this entire research landscape is concerned with mnemonic phenomena, much of what occurs here is not coordinated or interrelated. Often, researchers in one field are unaware of developments in other fields and, indeed, of their very existence. The notorious insularity of various academic and professional cultures does not make things easier. Academic protocols typically exclude that scientists within, for example, experimental biomedical research (which by far consumes the most research funds in this area), social psychology, or clinical psychiatry would consider research studies from a field that is not their own. In addition, their conceptual and epistemological frameworks of research are hardly compatible. How are you to cohere the biochemical study of sea slug neurons, the dynamics of "false memories" in an ethnically mixed group of New Yorkers remembering the terrorist attacks of September 11, 2001, and clinical trials testing vaccines against amyloid beta to comprehend and treat Alzheimer's disease?

This picture becomes even more telling if we included memory studies in the social sciences, cultural studies, and humanities. Without addressing the question of whether there is such a thing as memory, we certainly can assert, vis-à-vis these highly diverse areas of investigation, that there is no such thing as memory research that could be captured in only one singular noun.

All these fields are expanding, but—and this makes this scenario even more puzzling—they are expanding in various directions; the chapters in this volume are a case in point. Against this backdrop, I next discuss models of remembering and forgetting that can be said to be hegemonic in many memory sciences and, due to their scientific background, are typically also taken for granted in other fields of memory studies and everyday understanding, at least in what is seen as the domain of individual remembering. I then turn to what I call novel and alternative perspectives. Unavoidably connected to this is the question of whether there will be, and can be at all, one overarching concept and model of memory.

CONSTRUCTION, RECONSTRUCTION, AND OTHER WAYS TO SAVE THE ARCHIVE

Obviously, it is misleading to draw a clear disciplinary borderline between areas of memory research that challenge traditional models and others that do not, between conceptual changes that allow for new visions and changes that strive to consolidate old views. As just outlined, this is even the case within the neurosciences. Consider the archivalist understanding of memory and the central role it has played for the Western idea of remembering and forgetting. This notion has been so basic—indeed, it is generally not even conceived of as a notion but, rather, a mere reflection of a given biological fact, a natural kind—that it has never been problematized, let alone questioned, by any leading memory scientists or in any textbook on the subject. One standard work, although perhaps the most authoritative, is *Principles of Neural Science*, with Eric Kandel as the lead editor. In all five editions of this work published during the past few decades, there are chapters on "learning and memory" that summarize the state of the art of neuroscientific research on explicit memory at the time. All reach the same conclusions: Memory, to quote from the last edition (Kandel, Schwartz, Jessell, Siegelbaum, & Hudspeth, 2013), is defined as "the process by which . . . knowledge is encoded, stored, and later retrieved" (Schacter & Wagner, 2013, p. 1441). In contrast with earlier versions, the 2013 edition adds a further qualification to the concept of memory as storage, namely that "the brain does not have a single long-term store of explicit memories. Instead the storage is widely distributed among many brain regions" (pp. 1446–1447). The third edition of *Principles of Neural Science* simply stated, "Learning is the process of acquiring knowledge about the world, memory is the retention or storage of that knowledge" (Kupfermann, 1991, p. 997).

Given that the basic account of memory as a storehouse in which knowledge or information is encoded, deposited, and retrieved has not changed, the qualification of the "distributed" nature of the storage in the latest edition of *Principles of Neural Science* is particularly interesting. It reflects the attempt to accommodate a new aspect to the standard view of remembering, but it does so without questioning the traditional storage model. Several developments have been instrumental for this new view. Some occurred within the neurosciences, such as the discovery of neuroplasticity and the advancement of neurobiological knowledge at the cellular and molecular levels; some occurred outside the neurosciences, including technological innovations such as neuroimaging, the Internet, and powerful computer simulation. Furthermore, what has changed, as already indicated, is the general cultural discourse on memory, with many of the new approaches in the social and human sciences addressing memory in a way quite different from traditional psychology and neuroscience (Olick, Vinitzky-Seroussi, & Levy, 2011; Radstone & Schwarz, 2010; Smith & Watson, 2010; Tota & Hagen, 2016).

The new view is closely connected to two trends that have emerged during the past several decades. One is that neuroscientists have increasingly come to localize the activities and operations of memory in a decentralized way—as distributed over many different areas of the brain and intertwined with diverse brain functions. Before that, memory was commonly viewed as a single and unitary faculty of the human mind and, in fact, as a function of information processing that in principle was operative throughout most of the animal kingdom. Keep in mind that the overwhelming majority of all neurobiological experiments on living brains have been performed on animals.

The second trend is that memory itself is viewed in a more dynamic way, as a process rather than a static entity or capacity—that is, more precisely, as an interplay of multiple processes. Whereas the 1991 edition of *Principles of Neural Science* focused on memory as the storage of knowledge, in 2013, the same warehouse account was associated with the idea of memory as a process (Kandel et al., 2013). Although the basic model according to which memories are stored in a mental or neuronal archive has not changed, memories now appear as undergoing changes and transformations even after being encoded, as the textbook chapter points out in detail. These transformations can take place at any stage of the archivalization, equally during "encoding," "storage," or "retrieval," unless the memories are lost—that is, forgotten or distorted ("false memories") beyond recognition.

Even this last idea is relatively new. Until the 1980s, almost all scientific and clinical psychologists assumed that our experiences are forever stored in a mental or neuronal archive, whether we are aware of it or not. In a study by Elizabeth and Geoffrey Loftus (1980), 84% of psychologists were convinced that all of our experiences are permanently encoded and that even if some seemed to be forgotten, they could eventually be recovered with the right experimental or therapeutic technique. On this account, as I described it in an earlier work, the villain Forgetting ultimately has no chance in his eternal struggle against the hero Remembering (Brockmeier, 2002). He must fail because his opponent,

Remembering, can rely on a most efficient mnemonic archive. The only difficulty for Remembering is to apply the right technique or cue needed to reconquer the past.

This view, however, was increasingly questioned by evidence primarily from outside the memory laboratories, yet also from within (Schacter, 1995). Schacter, one of the foremost neurocognitive memory psychologists of the past few decades, described the "elegant techniques used by cognitive psychologists to dissect memory" (Schacter, 1996, p. 6), only to concede that even these techniques often do not reach their objective because memories are anything but passive or literal recordings of reality. Drawing on relatively recent neuroscientific findings (i.e., from the 1990s), Schacter (1996) stated that "experiences are encoded by brain networks whose connections have already been shaped by previous encounters with the world" (p. 6). He went on to write that "this preexisting knowledge powerfully influences how we encode and store new memories, thus contributing to . . . what we will recall of the moment" (p. 6).

As a consequence, Schacter (2001) declared memory to be a "sinner" because it constantly violates the rules and regulations of proper archival behavior. These rules were posited by experimental memory psychologists since Ebbinghaus and the Göttingen School of memory psychology, establishing a tradition of conceptualizing and investigating memory that has dominated the discipline ever since (Danziger, 2008). Following the biblical notion of humans' mortal sins, Schacter distinguished seven sins of memory, including the sins of absent-mindedness, misattribution, suggestibility, and bias. As strange as this biblical analogy might appear in the context of neuroscientific theorizing, it has provided a framework for reconciling the traditional model of memory with new evidence. Schacter stated, "Even though they often seem like our enemies, the seven sins are an integral part of the mind's heritage because they are so closely connected to features of memory which make it work well" (p. 6).

In fleshing out the sins of memory theoretically and empirically, Schacter has elaborated a full-bodied metaphorical and conceptual complement to the dry formula presented in *Principles of Neural Science*. In both accounts, the traditional archival memory model is adapted to new evidence—evidence, however, that could also be viewed as contradicting this very model. Indeed, an alternative interpretation could draw on a massive body of recent neurobiological research demonstrating that nowhere in the neuronal and molecular organization of the brain is there anything remotely similar to a storehouse or to any other location where knowledge or information could be retained, as proponents of memory "traces" or "engrams" have postulated. Rather than questioning the, admittedly, venerable storage assumption, contradicting evidence has been integrated into the established model by adjusting it to the new findings. Hence, instead of a single long-term store, we now have a "widely distributed store," and instead of a memory working properly according to the commandment of archival correctness and reliability, we have a memory that is a sinner. Sins are regrettable but human. A sinner breaks the rules but acknowledges them.

The metaphor or analogy of sin and sinner even suggests an answer to the question why there is a memory model that does *not* do what it is supposed to do: adequately reflect what we do when we remember. Human remembering may not work like an archive, nor like an archivalist, but when this "failure" is conceived of as a moral transgression that is, like sinning, part and parcel of human nature, then the dysfunctional model can be taken as representing precisely the, at least in part, dysfunctional reality of human memory. If one accepts this metaphorical framework, one might even recognize some virtues in memory's sins (Hirst, Cuc, & Wohl, 2012; Randall, 2010; Schacter, 2001, Chapter 8). More important, however, is that the traditional architecture of memory has not changed, nor does it appear as if it had to do so.

These two research trends are reflected in the increasing use of a vocabulary of *construction* and *reconstruction* that is used for what happens during both storage and retrieval. Again, a look at any recent textbook suffices to get a sense of this (see, for a change, Gazzaniga, Ivry, & Mangum, 2013). Of course, this vocabulary and its metaphorical core are not new either. In retrospect, Schacter (1995) even discerns a "constructivist tendency" in all of 20th-century memory research. Prominently, Frederic Bartlett (1932) was one of those who introduced it to academic psychology, which arguably has contributed to the recent rediscovery of Bartlett (Middleton & Brown, 2005; Wagoner, 2017) that we observe even in quarters of experimental memory research, where for a long period of time no attention was paid to his path-breaking work *Remembering* (Bartlett, 1932).

The concept of *reconstructive memory* is meant to outline a compromise similar to the metaphor of the sinner; it accommodates contrary empirical findings from neurosciences and other memory studies in order to save the archival model. Consider, again, an alternative perspective: that our memories are not just *re*-constructions but, rather, constructions resulting from processes of interpretation that involve acts of fictional creation. This feature of remembering, a central concern for countless autobiographers, has often been described and examined and is by now well recognized—although clearly at odds with the hegemonic view. How, then, could it be reconciled with the idea of memory as a storage in which information is encoded and stored in order to be recalled in the future? "Reconstructive memory" gives an answer, write Roediger and DeSoto (2015): It refers to the idea that the retrieval of memories from one's inner storage "does not occur in some completely accurate form, as a video might replay a scene, but rather that recollection of memories involves a process of trying to reconstruct (rather than replay) past events" (p. 50). During this reconstruction, as already emphasized, memory can be distracted and disoriented, committing all kinds of mistakes. The same idea is configured by "reconstructive memory" but along less moralistic lines than suggested by the fall of the sinner. Roediger and DeSoto even take this argument one step further, maintaining that "systematic errors in memory are the primary evidence for its reconstructive nature" (p. 50).

Roediger is another established cognitive psychologist of memory (Roediger, Dudai, & Fitzpatrick, 2007). His authoritative explanation of reconstructive memory as an updated version of the archival model confirms Schacter and Wagner's (2013) account by adapting present conceptualization of memory to findings from the two research trends noted previously. Without this accommodation, these findings could potentially question the traditional archival model and give support to the more fundamental critique of the reductionism of (neuro) cognitive memory experimentation.

Having noted these "updates," I should however emphasize that there are a number of respects in which the archival model has not changed. What has remained unaltered is its fundamental presuppositions: First, memory is a biological entity or capacity (or network of systems), a natural kind, whose basic unit is the individual brain and whose basic "mechanisms," operative in all memory systems, are encoding, storing, and retrieval of information. Unaltered, too, is a consequence of this memory model: It ignores a number of essential aspects of human remembering and narrows down its complexity. I already broached various criticisms of the exclusion of people's social and cultural lifeworlds as a vital dimension of remembering. Ulric Neisser (1976, 1982), for one, extensively excoriated what he called laboratory-based "high-road" cognitive psychology. Building on Bartlett's (1932) idea of remembering as "effort after meaning," he proposed as an alternative to investigate naturalistic, ecological, and situated mnemonic practices. Neisser called this orientation "low-road" memory studies.

Since Bartlett and Neisser, many of the excluded aspects have become the subject of further research. In some quarters of psychology, a wider and more culture-sensitive view of memory and memory research has emerged. Brown and Reavey (2015; see also Chapter 7, this volume) have called it an "expanded view" of memory, which can be related to a tendency in recent philosophy to comprehend the human mind in a more de-individualized and "distributed" manner, as in conceptions of the "expanded mind" (Clark, 2011; Menary, 2010; Noë, 2009). Still, all of these new approaches to memory have taken on shape outside of the disciplinary domain of experimental psychology and neuroscience. As a consequence, the scope of memory studies outside of scientific psychology and neuroscience—in sociology, anthropology, history, literary, and cultural studies—has grown, and so has its impact on the formation of a more cultural understanding of remembering and forgetting(Brockmeier, 2015, Chapters 1–3). The awareness that there have already been, for approximately a century, various traditions of social and cultural memory research has likewise increased. Of these traditions, the by now well-known Durkheim–Halbwachs–Nora line is only one (Assmann, 2011; Olick et al., 2011; Radstone & Schwarz, 2010; Tota & Hagen, 2016).

To be sure, many of these efforts strive to overcome the fixation on the isolated and, at the same time, universal human mind or brain as the exclusive site of remembering and forgetting, widening the focus to everyday landscapes of social practices and material as well as digital artifacts. Also, because these practices and artifacts are themselves subject to historical change, a further trajectory has entered the picture: history. The role of historical change is twofold: It affects both how human beings remember and the concepts and models that they apply to explain what they do when they remember.

HOW PURE IS REMEMBERING?

As noted previously, I am particularly interested in contemporary changes in our understanding of remembering, especially if they are associated with the emergence of alternative visions that challenge the traditional archival notion and offer new ways to conceive of our mnemonic practices as cultural practices. What characterizes many of these postarchival approaches is that they use categories such as agency, meaning-making, and social interaction instead of categories that aim at identifying mechanisms of encoding, storing, and retrieval of information. In this way, acts of remembering turn into components of overarching actions and concerns of the remembering subject—a subject acting in a complex social world.

Viewed from this perspective, remembering is a form of life in Wittgenstein's (1953/2009) sense, a practice that does not exist as such, independent from the cultural world in which it takes place. Embedded in contexts of action, and mediated by as well as entangled with material objects, it also is intertwined with other psychological processes. This marks a further difference from the established psychological notion of memory. The traditional conceptualization of memory is closely colluded with strategies of experimentation meant to identify and quantitatively measure pure memory. Hence, "pure" memory has to be isolated from what are considered to be non-mnemonic forms. These forms comprise language and related activities, such as narrative and conversation; they also include other material and sign-mediated practices, including common memory aids such as writing, computing, or the use of "digital memory machines," as computers are sometimes called in the literature on digital memory (van Dijck, 2013). In cognitive and neurocognitive memory research, such practices are generally regarded as added a posteriori to a primordially pure (neuro-)cognitive memory process. Typically, such addition or imposition is viewed as distorting and falsifying or at any rate modifying the supposedly pre-semiotic nature of memory. And this nature is taken to be exclusively pre-semiotic even when the primordial memory is understood as imagistic, as in various cognitive theories of autobiographical memory. An example of the experimental creation of pure memories is the construct of variables—autonomous, accurate, and voluminous recollections—that underlie the Wechsler Memory Scale. This standardized test battery is one of the most commonly used clinical instruments for the measurement and assessment of memory.

I just outlined one alternative to this view—one that captures memories as inextricably intertwined with their interpretation and understands these interpretative acts as practices of a remembering subject rather than neuronal operations of the brain. At stake, then, are forms of agency that are part and parcel of the subject's lifeworld (even if it is true that an experimental memory lab can sometimes become a central part of an individual's lifeworld). In the case of autobiographical memories—the type of memories primarily considered in this chapter—all of this implies language, mostly in the form of narrative. Because language and narrative are complex cultural practices that are entangled with other practical and symbolic practices, the picture widens even more.

Elsewhere, I have examined the explanatory capacity and investigative potential of this "narrative alternative" to traditional memory models (Brockmeier, 2002, 2015). Yet to envision the autobiographical process as essentially organized through its narrative fabric is just one possible alternative. Another option, although partly overlapping and intertwined with the narrative alternative, takes center stage in the remainder of this chapter. This option unfolds the inherent social and intersubjective dimension of the autobiographical process. Specifically, I explore the notion of autobiographical remembering as a practice of conversation. Conversation has long been a proven model of interaction and communication in the human sciences; in hermeneutic philosophy, it is discussed as a model of consciousness and the mind. I am concerned here with how it is also establishing itself as a culturally sensitive model and metaphor of a new postarchival and postindividualist understanding of remembering and forgetting.

BEYOND THE SOCIAL–INDIVIDUAL DICHOTOMY

Of course, neither the idea nor the concept of conversational remembering is novel. Linguistic and communicative interaction, understood in a wide sense, has played an important role in many traditions investing social life, including social or collective remembering. These approaches include discursive psychology; conversation analysis; critical discourse analysis; sociocultural and Vygotskian approaches; and Bartlett-inspired studies of social remembering within cognitive, social, and organizational psychology. Moreover, there are sociological, historical, and anthropological approaches. If we can therefore state that the study of social or collective remembering is by now well established, we should, however, be aware that what is established is a particular concept of social remembering in tandem with a particular concept of individual remembering. What makes these concepts particular?

A widely shared conviction in these areas is that the social world affects the way individuals remember and forget, with conversation, discourse, and other forms of communicative interaction being pivotal in the process. This conviction is linked to the assumption that *what* is socially shaped are basic natural processes of remembering and their results—processes that are localized in the individual brain. Ultimately, then, it is *individual* processes—the neuronal processes underlying or even causing individual acts of cognition—through which we remember. These processes are the subject of external, social "influences" or "contexts" whose effects are typically described in traditional terms of shaping, ordering, organizing, and reconstructing. Also traditional is that these effects, as already noted, are viewed as a posteriori: They affect a memory after it has been retrieved and often result in memory distortion, falsification, repression, silencing, and other "sins."

This distinction between individual and social memory can be found in all the fields just outlined. Jan Assmann, historian of culture and theorist of social memory, defines it as the difference between two levels of memory, one he calls inner and the other social. Assmann (2008) writes,

> On the *inner level*, memory is a matter of our neuro-mental system. This is our personal memory, the only form of memory that had been recognized as such until the 1920s. On the *social level*, memory is a matter of communication and social interaction. (p. 109)

For social psychologist Harald Welzer (2010), there are two kinds of memory, one individual and one social. Whereas individual memory is located within a person, in whom it has a central organ, the brain, social memory "exclusively exists *between* subjects and not *within* them; its form of existence consists of communication" (p. 5). The difference between the two is a matter of their biological substrate:

> In contrast to those fields of memory research that are concerned with the memory of the individual person, research on social memory phenomena is confronted with the peculiar problem that social memory has neither a substrate in the sense of a remembering subject nor a central organ of an operating memory in the sense of a human brain. (p. 5)

Along these lines, the underlying operations of collective memory are conceived of as resulting from the interactional or sociocultural *context* that impacts on the "natural" mechanisms of memory.

Taking this approach one step further, social and cognitive psychologists William Hirst and Gerald Echterhoff study in their memory experiments the way individuals communicate about the past and how this contextual setting impacts on content, form, detail, frequency, emotional charge, veracity, and accuracy of their memories—for instance, by "social contagion." In examining the impact of communication both after and before the act of recollection, they are interested in acts of remembering "when they serve a communicative function" (Hirst & Echterhoff, 2012, p. 56). That is, what they do not inquire into is the question as to whether the very act of remembering itself is a collaborative or otherwise social activity because the point of departure of their research—as that of Tulving, Schacter, Assmann, Welzer, and many others—is that this very act is an individual process. In other words, Hirst and Echterhoff's experiments yield important insights into the *social behavior* of individual rememberers in conversational settings either after or before the act of recall, but they do not examine whether and in what sense remembering itself is a social process.

There is no doubt that the study of peoples' communicative and otherwise social behavior marks a significant advance over previous individual-centered paradigms in experimental memory research (see the survey in Hirst & Echterhoff, 2012). However, such research obviously does not help us scrutinize its own basic assumption according to which individual, "inner," "neuro-mental," or "neurobiological" processes of "pure recall" are organized in a fundamentally different manner from what is defined as social memory. Social memory, on this view, is operative in processes of face-to-face communication about the past—for example, in personal and familial encounters. It is also active in larger contexts of organizational, societal, and cultural practices and artifacts of remembering and remembrance. Surely, this is not only an academic agreement but also solid common sense: "What happens in the head," assert Hirst and Echterhoff, is different from "what occurs within and after a conversation" (p. 57), not to mention what occurs in larger societal and cultural contexts. Given the synchrony of everyday and academic discourse (that extends, within academic discourse, to both camps of individual and social memory research), who would doubt this picture of individual and social memory?

Vis-à-vis this solid consensus, it is astonishing that there are nevertheless some recent ideas that ignore or even defy the presupposition that the individual human brain is an autarkic system and that remembering therefore must be viewed as an individual act clearly separated from social processes of remembering and forgetting. These ideas, to which I turn now, are quite different in form and scope, even if they, too, mainly refer to processes of autobiographical remembering that, one might think, are particularly "individual." They have emerged in various places and contexts of thinking and scientific investigating, both within and outside of the academic domain, ranging from debates among social and human scientists to discussions about digital technologies, from the laboratory to autobiographical literature and fiction from the garden of science to the wilderness of literature, to use an expression by Daniel Albright (1994). Interestingly, at many of these construction sites of novel ideas of remembering we find particular attention paid to practices and concepts of conversation.

UNDERSTANDING THE REMEMBERING DYAD

Writers have always been at the forefront of the exploration of mind and memory. Since the onset of modernity, they have also been explorers of the autobiographical process, especially concerned with the narrative fabric of all things autobiographic. More than this, they have shown a strong interest in and, indeed, an affinity with unusual, complicated, and messy forms of remembering—of remembering in the wild. This distinguishes the approach to autobiographical memory of literature and the arts from that of academic psychology and neuroscience, which is predicated on the experimental study of "pure memory"—of remembering in the garden.

When in 2008 Pat Kavanagh, the wife of British writer Julian Barnes, died, it took him several years to write about his memories of her. Eventually, he published a short memoire, *The Loss of Depth* (Barnes, 2013), about their joint life and about what came afterwards. Although an experienced and prolific writer, Barnes explained that he had difficulty finding the right language and the adequate form or genre. In addition, he was not sure whether losing himself in his memories would mitigate or increase his pain. A vague, although deep-rooted, desire to give sorrow words was one of his reasons to carry on. Another reason was the same as that for countless others, writers or not, who have written about the death of a close and beloved person in order to come to terms with it. Evoking and writing down memories of one's partner can be a way to continue her presence even if she is absent; although she is forever physically absent, she is still present in one's memory and one's imagination. "The fact that someone is dead," Barnes writes, "may mean that they are not alive, but doesn't mean that they do not exist" (p. 90). There is nothing from keeping the conversation going.

To be sure, such conversation takes some effort, which has to do not only with the contradictory nature of grief and sorrow and with finding appropriate words and narrative forms; it also refers to the process of autobiographical remembering itself. Barnes and his wife lived together for more than 30 years. If two individuals have spent such a long period closely together, all the time living in the same present and remembering an increasingly common past together, it becomes difficult and sometimes even impossible to separate out their memories. Many memories do not just call back knowledge or experiences as if they were exclusively personal, private properties; rather, they only exist as intermingled, if not comingled, with the memories of the other. Barnes calls them memories in the first-person plural; we can also dub them interdependent memories or socially distributed or embodied memories. Not only do they exist in a shared present—in this case, the co-presence of a couple—but also they relate to experiences and events in the past that have often been jointly remembered, told and retold, and again jointly interpreted and commented on. Sometimes one individual of the remembering duo might bring up a version that is different from the version of the other. Perhaps together with the little dispute, this might trigger a difference of opinion that then might become a component of the memory of the jointly recalled previous memory—all of this depending on the specific situation in which it is told, the mood, and the intention of the rememberer at that moment.

So who is the rememberer? Whose memories are at stake? Meticulously, Barnes (2013) points out why it is impossible to individualize certain memories in hindsight. From the very beginning, they have existed only in dialogical form, bound to a shared vocabulary "of tropes, teases, short cuts, injokes, sillinesses, faux rebukes, amatory footnotes—all those obscure references rich in memory but valueless if explained to an outsider" (p. 88). Throughout the years, these highly personal forms of interaction have become conflated with the original memory, if an original memory can be identified at all. Such conflation is not surprising given what we know about the protean nature and the transformative character of remembering—all the more if it is a shared process and the recalled experience was already a shared experience in the first place. What makes up and carries out such autobiographical processes, and what keeps them open, creative, and contributes to their never exhausted intersubjective plasticity is not the individual but a remembering dyad—at least in this case it is a dyad; in principle, it can be any larger social unit. This dyad does not enter the scene of remembering *post festum*, socializing a primordial pure memory and transforming it into a collective one.

Rather, the dyad is from the outset the very subject, the carrier, and protagonist of the entire autobiographical process.[1]

This is not to say that the limits of the remembered and imagined presence of a dead person are not painfully manifest. "You ask yourself," as Barnes (2013) questions his own strategy of reminiscing and envisioning his wife, "what happiness is there in just the memory of happiness? And how in any case might that work, given that happiness has only ever consisted of something shared?" (pp. 79–80). He wonders whether solitary happiness can ever remind one of joined happiness. He replies, "It sounds like a contradiction in terms, an implausible contraption that will never get off the ground" (p. 80). In earlier days, the things he liked most were things he did together with Pat. Insofar as he liked doing things by himself, it was partly "for the pleasure of telling her about them afterwards" (p. 82), which meant to again frame them as shared experiences, in this way creating new, even if different, shared memories. In other words, the framing of the past in terms of joint experiences in the present—as conversation—appears to be equally possible within imagination. This is what Barnes, like many other people who have gone through similar experiences, reports in striking detail.

In describing his life of mourning and grief, Barnes (2013) gives an account of what it means to continue the conversations with his deceased wife and, in this way, keep their countless common memories alive. For Barnes, this is a normal and natural practice. It also entails that he takes on her part, including her part in the remembering dyad, which he had come to know as well as his own part. He even imagines her taking over his part, effortlessly moving back and forth between remembering and imagining—and there are many possible movements and combinations thereof. In this manner, he remains within the domain of their very personal language (which, as does every language, revolves around an I–you dyad) and their very personal remembering habits (which have always been first-person plural). Granted, Barnes notes, "outsiders might find this an eccentric, or 'morbid,' or self-deceiving, habit; but outsiders are by definition those who have not known grief. I externalize her easily and naturally because by now I have internalized her" (p. 103). He calls it the paradox of grief that allowed him to survive 4 years of Pat's absence because, in keeping the conversation alive, he had 4 years of her presence.

Barnes' remembered, imagined, and newly created conversations with a dead person do not appear that eccentric or morbid when we bring to mind that much of this kind of discourse can also be found among the living and the non-grievers, the outsiders, as Barnes has it. There are manifold forms of human thinking, imagining, and remembering that are intermingled with conversational activities. The most important instrument and practice of human cognition—language—is constitutively dialogical and conversational, whether it is viewed from a grammatical, semantic, or pragmatic standpoint, or whether at stake is its development. If the evolutionary and cultural uniqueness of human beings is essentially due to the cooperative way in which their cognition and their linguistic capacities are organized, as Michael Tomasello (2008, 2014) has argued, then it would be indeed incomprehensible if a crucial human cognitive ability such as remembering were left to the isolated individual. For Tomasello, social, cultural, and cognitive cooperation—especially what he calls shared or collective intentionality—is the key to human psychology. Shared or collective intentionality is the ability and motivation to engage with others in cooperative practices with joint goals and intentions. This also implies that the psychological processes in which collaborating individuals engage are jointly directed at something. They are intermingled within a common attentional frame—a frame that also comprises extended forms of mutual understanding ("mind reading") and conjoint acts of remembering and anticipating the future.

Tomasello's research brings additional support to the Vygotskian claim that our higher mental functions are not solitary activities but, rather, cooperative interactions that enmesh individual improvisation in a sociocultural matrix. Specifically, Tomasello (2014) makes the case for a notion of human *thinking* as inherently social and cooperative. He elaborates this notion in examining three fundamental aspects of thinking. One is representation: Humans can keep in mind the world that is not here-and-now using complicated symbolic systems such as language. The second is inference, which is the ability to draw conclusions from experiences and to learn. The third is self-monitoring, which is the capacity of self-control and self-reflection. Tomasello has elaborated his case with respect to thinking, yet, as I believe, it can be compellingly extended to remembering and its interactive and cooperative dynamic. Viewed this way, mnemonic activities are likewise fundamental intersubjective forms of representation, inference, and self-monitoring, with the latter becoming particularly evident in the autobiographical process.

From the perspective of Tomasello's sociocultural psychology and anthropology, we can inquire into a wide spectrum of intersubjective practices of shared remembering. Whereas we might localize Barnes' sophisticated and idiosyncratic forms of remembered and imagined memory talk at one end of the spectrum, we find widespread everyday practices of joint remembering at the other end. "I'm searching for my keys, did you see them somewhere?—You have misplaced them? Hmmm. Have you checked the green jacket you wore last night when we went to see Helen?—Of course I did . . ., but actually, I might have checked the brown one. . . . So let me take a look at the pockets of the green one. . . . Bingo, yes, there they are. . . ." Who, then, did the labor of memory in this primal scene of social remembering conversation?

Obviously, it was done by two people, two rememberers, two brains that complemented each other in a way that appears very simple but, according to Tomasello, is unique for the human species and humans' sophisticated sense of shared subjectivity. In fact, it is the basic of all cultural development. Humans are able to connect to others, Tomasello (2014) writes, "in a way that other primates seemingly are not, to form a 'we' that acts as a kind of plural agent to create everything from a collaborative hunting party to cultural institutions" (p. 3). Barnes (2013) shows that this "we" extends from hunting parties and the search for lost keys in the here and now to the past, to joint autobiographical memories, even to those memories that he called back in his conversations with his imagined partner Pat—"that they are not alive doesn't mean that they do not exist." Intuitively knowing and anticipating what Pat would have thought and said, he carries on their well-rehearsed dialogical practices of remembering—not so much to find some misplaced keys but to keep alive a sense of a life lived together, the life of a dyad full of normally rarely noticed moments of conversational remembering.

NEUROLOGY, CONVERSATION, AND CULTURAL COMMUNITIES OF MINDS

To conclude this discussion of alternative approaches to remembering as an inherently social practice—a practice that I suggest understanding after the model of conversation rather than the archival model of individual retrieval—I examine a phenomenon that in the research literature is known as "false memories" and to which I already referred at the beginning.

Drawing on extensive research by Daniel Schacter (Schacter, 1995, 2001; Schacter & Slotnick, 2004), Elizabeth Loftus (Loftus, 1984; Loftus, Doyle, & Dysert, 2008), and their collaborators, Oliver Sacks (2013) has dealt with how people confuse or are ignorant of what many psychologists call the sources of their memories. The underlying, although not explicated, assumption in this research is that every memory can be led back to an identifiable primordial event or experience, its "source"—which is an assumption that largely ignores the role of interpretation and creative fictionalization. Psychologists speak of source confusion when they believe that people erroneously misattribute memories or ideas to the wrong "source"—for example, presenting memories of others as their own. In one of his last essays on memory, Sacks has offered a novel view of this phenomenon. Combining empirical and theoretical, neurological and psychological, and clinical and literary considerations with his own autobiographical experience, he also has shed new light on the conversational nature of remembering.

A portion of "false memories" are traditionally viewed as resulting from "source confusion," with an important further distinction between those misattributions that are carried out consciously and intentionally and others that are carried out unconsciously and unintentionally. In the world of letters and public discourse, the first category is called plagiarism and has become the subject of many debates—academic, ethical, and legal. The second category captures unconscious and intentional memory confusions or substitutions, which Sacks (2013) calls cryptomnesia. This term, he thinks, needs to be better known because the very word plagiarism is so morally charged, so associated with deceit and theft, that it retains a sting even if it may be qualified as "unconscious plagiarism."

What exactly defines unconscious plagiarism or cryptomnesia, however, is difficult to determine. Ultimately, it is a cultural and historical question. Sacks reminds us of writers in various epochs who used or borrowed thoughts and memories of others both unknowingly and deliberately, mostly without any qualms—from Shakespeare to Wordsworth, Coleridge, and Mark Twain, to name a few. In clinical contexts, it is even more difficult to qualify forms of memory cryptomnesia in moral terms. For example, studying the experiences of individuals

with a neurotrauma who suffer from anterograde amnesia and thus have difficulty remembering new autobiographical experience, Maria Medved and I found
that many of these patients tried to give themselves the semblance of "normal
people" who *can* tell autobiographical stories about their recent past, a wish that is
more than understandable in a world in which personal identity is considered to
be closely compounded with autobiographical memory (Medved & Brockmeier,
2008). More precisely, in their stories about themselves, these individuals used
three narrative strategies. One we called "memory importation," which consisted
of transplanting an autobiographical memory of oneself from the time before to
after the neurotrauma. A second strategy we dubbed "memory appropriation"; it
used memories of others as one's own. The third one we named "memory compensation" because it was based on stories and conversational moves that aimed
to compensate for missing memories. From the viewpoint of neuropsychology
and neurological rehabilitation, all these strategies indicate important steps to
recovery after neurotrauma.

There are more arguments that plagiarism and cryptomnesia must be conceived of as larger social and cultural phenomena. Under closer scrutiny, most
of what we consider to be new and original ideas prove to be combinations of
elements from the collective imaginary—the encompassing symbolic space of a
culture (or the various cultural worlds) to which each person belongs and whose
potentials he or she uses, both consciously and, most of the time, unconsciously
(Brockmeier, 2017; see also Donald, Chapter 1, this volume). Consider language.
As we know from Wittgenstein (1953/2009), there is no way in which an individual can develop a private language or, for that matter, strictly private thoughts
and memories. Every thought and every word, even if it appears only within a
silent monologue, binds us into a larger cultural context of meanings and language games. Carrying with it the countless traces of earlier usage, every word
is part of a dialogue, an endless conversation, as Bakhtin (1981) noted. Speaking
a language connects us to a cultural intertext that extends into even the most
intimate thoughts, ideas, and memories of an individual (Brockmeier, 2005). The
claim to originality, it has been said, is based on the forgetting of what has been
voluntarily or involuntarily taken over from others.

In a memoir of his boyhood, Sacks (2001) showed that many of his interests
and impulses, although they seemed entirely his own, were the fruit of the suggestions of others that powerfully influenced him, with or without his awareness,
and then had been forgotten. Later, as a scientist, he encountered a comparable
forgetfulness. Often when he gave lectures on similar topics, he could not remember exactly what he said on previous occasions, one reason being that he could not
bear to look through his old notes. It was as if he were engaged in a conversation
extended over a long time in which one occasionally forgets what other conver-
sationalists and even oneself had already said on the subject at one point in the
past. At the same time, however, he perceives this as an advantage and strength
because losing conscious memory of what he explained before in another lecture,
and without a verbatim text, he discovers his themes afresh each time, considering previously unexamined sides or aspects of them. "This type of forgetting,"

Sacks (2013) notes, "may be necessary for a creative or healthy cryptomnesia, one that allows old thoughts to be reassembled, retranscribed, recategorized, given new and fresh implications" (p. 20).

From this kind of forgetting, there is only a small step to autoplagiarism, or autocryptomnesia. In effect, Sacks finds himself reproducing entire phrases or passages from his own previous works as if new, which may be the flip side of genuine forgetfulness. Is this forgetting, then, a condition of the possibility of creating something novel? Perhaps. Surely it facilitates and promotes it. Many artists have given positive answers to this question. The pianist Daniel Barenboim once said that he, as all pianists of course, knows well the important interpretations of a canonical piece of music but that it is essential for him to forget all of them and have an "empty mind" once he has started to play his own interpretation. Sacks (2013) reports about his own creative forgetting:

> Looking back through my old notebooks, I find that many of the thoughts sketched in them are forgotten for years, and then revived and reworked as new. I suspect that such forgettings occur for everyone, and they may be especially common in those who write or paint or compose, for creativity may require such forgettings, in order that one's memories and ideas can be born again and seen in new contexts and perspectives. (p. 20)

Not many memory psychologists have been interested in this creative and social dimension of remembering. Again, one of the few was Bartlett. For him, what he called the constructive nature of remembering shows in our ability to integrate various experiences and influences, present and past, in order to satisfy the "effort after meaning" in the here and now. Our facility to constantly reconstruct our memories within new present constellations was for Bartlett (1932) a unique strength—a form of agency that essentially contributes to the flexibility and adaptability humans need to live in an unstable world.

As Wagoner (2017)—points out, Bartlett originally used the term construction to describe the adaptive changes both individuals and social groups carry out in mentally reconfiguring their past. This ability allows us to apply past experience to new situations and to connect them with other influences—a capacity of integration that extends our possibilities for action in a constantly changing reality. Wagoner refers to Bartlett's (1958) last book, in which he argued that "perhaps all original ideas and developments come from the contact of subject-matter with different subject-matter, of people with different people" (p. 147).

Sacks' observations on this contact of memories and ideas with different memories and ideas, and of people with different people, can be viewed as reflecting a more recent surge or resurgence of ambiguous and messy memory and identity syndromes, which has yielded important experimental, forensic, and theoretical insights into the malleability and creativity of remembering and the autobiographical process in particular. These insights, too, belong to the larger cultural paradigm shift in our understanding of memory and remembering that is the background of this chapter. Importantly, they include that remembering occurs in a much less individual and self-referential manner than traditionally assumed. Remembering is anything but restricted to pure brain operations and archival "mechanisms"; it is distributed not only over several brain regions but also over a number of cognitive and emotive activities (e.g., the selection, evaluation, and interpretation of various mental states, some of which may be memories). It also extends over various social interactions and practices and involves material (including digital) objects and operations that take place in a number of locations. Memory, like all cognition, "might thus be multiply distributed, both within neural networks and across bodies, artifacts, and social groups" (Michaelian & Sutton, 2013, p. 6). The spatial distribution of social remembering can become quite convoluted, especially if it is understood not only as a cognitive system but also as a cultural and, that is, sign-mediated system (Brockmeier, 2002). In an attempt to overcome the individual focus and the "mind/brain container metaphor" altogether, Edwin Hutchins (2014) thus wants to shift the attention from the individual person and his or her surroundings to "cultural ecosystems" of cognition and memory operating at larger spatial and temporal scales.

The aspect of this new vision that I have foregrounded here is the dialogical nature of remembering. This aspect is little discussed in the cognitive sciences literature on the extended mind, distributed cognition, and cultural–cognitive ecosystems, a literature that is mainly concerned with the relationship between internal and external resources of the mind. It is also absent in mainstream memory research and neuroscience with its focus on monological scenarios of encoding, storing, and retrieval of information, all localized in the head of a single individual, as reviewed in the first part of this chapter. In contrast, I have suggested that these scenarios, rather than as monologues or relations between internal and external resources of the individual mind, are to be more appropriately understood as orchestrated like a conversation. There are many phenomena of "indifference" to sources of memories and ideas that demonstrate precisely this. For indifference is also openness. It allows us, as Sacks (2013) suggests, to easily "assimilate what we read, what we are told, and what others say and think and write and paint, as intensely and richly as if they were [our own] primary experiences" (p. 21).

My point, then, is that our minds are *inherently* social and cooperative, whether they build on primary experience; knowledge, thoughts, and images acquired from others; or ideas, imagination, and fantasy. Engaged in branching, never-ending conversations with others and ourselves, we are in touch with the entire collective imaginary of a culture and, in fact, of various cultural worlds. What dismissingly is called indifference is, from the viewpoint of a culturally informed psychology and philosophical anthropology, not primarily a malfunction or disorder that manifests itself in plagiarism and other cognitive sins. It is a human quality that allows us, to again borrow Sacks' (2013) terms,

> to see and hear with other eyes and ears, to enter into other minds, to assimilate the art and science and religion of the whole culture, to enter into and

contribute to the common mind, the general commonwealth of knowledge. (p. 21)

Whereas Tomasello emphasizes the evolutionary and phylogenetic origin of humans' distinctive sociocultural abilities of cooperation and shared intentionality, Sacks points to the neurological structures that make these abilities possible. From a developmental standpoint, Katherine Nelson (Nelson, 2007; see also Nelson, Chapter 8, this volume) has studied the same abilities demonstrating that each child has to develop them in order to enter a culture's "community of minds." And this inroad into cultural communities and their conversations about experiences, memories, and mental states starts early (Ornaghi, Brockmeier, & Grazzani, 2011).

Sacks (1990/2014) adds to this the perspective of a cultural neurology or cultural neuropsychology, if we see his neuropsychology in the wake of another neurologist, Alexander Luria. Cultural neuropsychology is an enterprise that investigates the cultural equivalents of neuropsychology and the neuropsychological equivalents of humans' cultural existence. Viewed from this vantage point, human remembering is both subjective and intersubjective: It is subjective because it continuously adapts memories to the subject's needs in the present, and it is intersubjective because it uses one's personal memories as well as those of others, ultimately, of the entire cultural community of minds. As a neurologist, Sacks reminds us that such subjectivity and intersubjectivity are not distortions, aberrations, or disorders but, rather, built into the very nature of human brains. They are not the exception but the rule according to which our minds/brains operate.

It is a unique feature of humans' cultural communities of minds that we are able to connect to re-presented experiences—including the experiences of others—in the same intense and emotional way as we do to our own actual lived experiences and realities. Autobiographical stories are a case in point because it is narrative that endows autobiographical memories with their actual existence, one that is inextricably intermingled with our interpretation of it. In drawing attention to the particular psycho-neurological quality of language and, specifically, of narrative, Sacks continues a research concern of Luria and another important neurologist, Kurt Goldstein (Medved & Brockmeier, 2015). Today, we have come to see that there is no neurophysiological mechanism in the brain for ensuring the truth or truthfulness of our memories and for distinguishing them from "memories" that someone else told us or that we "imported" from a written or filmed or otherwise enacted narrative. There is no neurobiological correlate that could indicate whether a particular mental state draws on my own experience or on that of someone else. Nor is there any functional brain imaging that could display a significant difference between activities of a brain that recalls a corroborated event in the past and one that imagines a purely fictional event in the present or one that anticipates this event in the future. In view of these findings, Sacks (2013) remarks that it is a wonder that "aberrations of a gross sort are relatively rare, and that, for the most part, our memories are relatively reliable" (p. 21).

I suspect that we can experience in all of these scenarios the same lived direct-ness and emotional intensity because they all are scenarios of meaning, which is to say they involve subjective and intersubjective acts of meaning-making (Brockmeier, 2014). However, the wonder of which Sacks speaks raises more questions. For example, does it happen despite the distributed and conversa-tional character of remembering or as a consequence of it? In other words, could it be that it is precisely the in-built subjectivity and intersubjectivity of human remembering, which is part of what Tomasello has described as the evolution-ary developed cognitive and emotional infrastructure of the human species, that allows and calls for our specific cooperative and conversational type of cultural intersubjectivity?

The ideas of memory that I discussed in the second part of this chapter sug-gest exactly this. They explore approaches to remembering and forgetting as an inherently cultural conversation, as a sort of reaching out to and interacting with others, and as a sharing and participating that would not be possible "if all our knowledge, our memories, were tagged and identified, seen as private, exclu-sively ours" (Sacks, 2013, p. 21). Like the "narrative alternative" mentioned previ-ously, they mark new and promising construction sites for a culturally sensitive psychology, neurology, and philosophical anthropology of remembering and forgetting.

NOTE

1. Elsewhere I have explained in further detail why it is more appropriate to use in this context the wider concept *autobiographical process*, which also comprises the dimen-sion of interpretation that is inseparably fused with all remembering, instead of the traditional terms *autobiographical memory* and *autobiographical remembering*. These terms tend to assume the existence of a memory per se that is independent from the process of its interpretation, although it is only in this process that it gains its mean-ing (Brockmeier, 2015, Chapters 4 and 5).

REFERENCES

Albright, D. (1994). Literary and psychological models of the self. In U. Neisser & R. Fivush (Eds.), *The remembering self: Construction and accuracy in the self-narrative* (pp. 19–40). Cambridge, UK: Cambridge University Press.

Assmann, J. (2008). Communicative and cultural memory. In A. Erll & A. Nünning (Eds.), *A companion to cultural memory studies* (pp. 109–118). Berlin & New York, NY: de Gruyter.

Assmann, J. (2011). *Cultural memory and early civilization: Writing, remembrance, and political imagination*. Cambridge, UK: Cambridge University Press.

Bakhtin, M. (1981). *The dialogic imagination*. Austin, TX: University of Texas Press.

Barnes, J. (2013). The loss of depth. In J. Barnes (Ed.), *Levels of life* (pp. 65–118). London, UK: Vintage.

Bartlett, F. C. (1932). *Remembering*. Cambridge, UK: Cambridge University Press.

Bartlett, F. C. (1958). *Thinking: An experimental and social study*. London, UK: Allen & Unwin.

Brockmeier, J. (2002). Remembering and forgetting: Narrative as cultural memory. *Culture and Psychology*, 8(1), 15–44.

Brockmeier, J. (2005). The text of the mind. In C. Erneling & D. M. Johnson (Eds.), *The mind as a scientific object: Between brain and culture* (pp. 432–452). New York, NY: Oxford University Press.

Brockmeier, J. (2014). Questions of meaning: Memory, dementia, and the post-autobiographical perspective. In L.-C. Hydén, H. Lindemann, & J. Brockmeier (Eds.), *Beyond loss: Dementia, identity, personhood* (pp. 69–90). New York, NY: Oxford University Press.

Brockmeier, J. (2015). *Beyond the archive: Memory, narrative, and the autobiographical process*. New York, NY: Oxford University Press.

Brockmeier, J. (2017). Picasso's masks: Tracing the flow of cultural memory. *Culture and Psychology*, 23(2), 156–170.

Brown, S. D., & Reavey, P. (2015). Turning around on experience: The "expanded view" of memory within psychology. *Memory Studies*, 8(2), 131–150.

Clark, A. (2011). *Supersizing the mind: Embodiment, action, and cognitive extension*. New York, NY: Oxford University Press.

Danziger, K. (2008). *Marking the mind: A history of memory*. New York, NY: Cambridge University Press.

Gazzaniga, M., Ivry, R. B., & Mangum, G. R. (Eds.). (2013). *Cognitive neuroscience: The biology of the mind* (4th ed.). New York, NY: Norton.

Hirst, W., Cuc, A., & Wohl, D. (2012). Of sins and virtues: Memory and collective identity. In D. Berntsen & D. C. Rubin (Eds.), *Understanding autobiographical memory: Theories and approaches* (pp. 141–159). Cambridge, UK: Cambridge University Press.

Hirst, W., & Echterhoff, G. (2012). Remembering in conversations: The social sharing and reshaping of memories. *Annual Review of Psychology*, 63, 55–79.

Hutchins, E. (2014). The cultural ecosystem of human cognition. *Philosophical Psychology*, 27(1), 34–49.

Kandel, E. R., Schwartz, J. H., Jessell, T. M., Siegelbaum, S. A., & Hudspeth, A. J. (Eds.). (2013). *Principles of neural science* (5th ed.). New York, NY: McGraw-Hill.

Kupfermann, I. (1991). Learning and memory. In T. M. Jessell, J. H. Schwartz, & E. R. Kandel (Eds.), *Principles of neural science* (3rd ed.). New York, NY: Elsevier.

Loftus, E. F., Doyle, J. M., & Dysert, J. (2008). *Eyewitness testimony: Civil & criminal* (4th ed.). Charlottesville, VA: Lexis Law Publishing.

Medved, M. I., & Brockmeier, J. (2008). Continuity amid chaos: Neurotrauma, loss of memory, and sense of self. *Qualitative Health Research*, 18(4), 469–479.

Medved, M. I., & Brockmeier, J. (2015). The narrative hinge between the neurology and the psychology of neurotraumatic responses. *Neurologie & Rehabilitation*, 21(6), 347–352.

Medved, M. I., & Brockmeier, J. (2016). When memory goes awry. In A. L. Tota & T. Hagen (Eds.), *The Routledge international handbook of memory studies* (pp. 445–457). London, UK: Routledge.

Menary, R. (Ed.). (2010). *The extended mind*. Cambridge, MA: MIT Press.

Michaelian, K., & Sutton, J. (2013). Distributed cognition and memory research: History and future directions. *Review of Philosophy and Psychology, 4*(1), 1–24.

Middleton, D., & Brown, S. D. (2005). *The social psychology of experience: Studies in remembering and forgetting.* London, UK: Sage.

Nelson, K. (2007). *Young minds in social worlds: Experience, meaning, and memory.* Cambridge, MA: Harvard University Press.

Noë, A. (2009). *Out of our heads: Why you are not your brain, and other lessons from the biology of consciousness.* New York, NY: Hill & Wang.

Olick, J. K., Vinitzky-Seroussi, V., & Levy, D. (Eds.) (2011). *The collective memory reader.* Oxford, UK: Oxford University Press.

Ornaghi, V., Brockmeier, J., & Grazzani, I. (2011). The role of language games in children's understanding of mental states. *Journal of Cognition and Development, 12*(2), 239–259.

Radstone, S., & Schwarz, B. (Eds.). (2010). *Memory: Histories, theories, debates.* New York, NY: Fordham University Press.

Randall, W. L. (2010). The narrative complexity of our past: In praise of memory's sins. *Theory & Psychology, 20*(2), 147–169.

Roediger, H. L., & DeSoto, K. A. (2015). The psychology of reconstructive memory. In J. Wright (Ed.), *International encyclopedia of the social and behavioral sciences* (2nd ed., pp. 50–55). Oxford, UK: Elsevier.

Roediger, H. L., Dudai, Y., & Fitzpatrick, S. M. (Eds.). (2007). *Science of memory: Concepts.* Oxford, UK: Oxford University Press.

Rose, N., & Abi-Rached, J. M. (2013). *Neuro: The new brain sciences and the management of the mind.* Princeton, NJ: Princeton University Press.

Sacks, O. (2001). *Uncle Tungsten: Memoires of a boyhood.* New York, NY: Vintage.

Sacks, O. (2013, February 21). Speak, memory. *The New York Review of Books, 60*(3), 19–21.

Sacks, O. (2014). Luria and "romantic science." In A. Yasnitsky, R. van der Veer, & M. Ferrari (Eds.), *The Cambridge handbook of cultural–historical psychology* (pp. 517–528). New York, NY: Cambridge University Press. (Original work published 1990)

Schacter, D. L. (1995). Memory distortion: History and present status. In D. L. Schacter, J. T. Coyle, G. D. Fischbach, M. M. Mesulam, & L.E. Sullivan (Eds.), *Memory distortion: How minds, brains and societies reconstruct the past* (pp. 1–43). Cambridge, MA: Harvard University Press.

Schacter, D. L. (1996). *Searching for memory: The brain, the mind, and the past.* New York, NY: Basic Books.

Schacter, D. L. (2001). *The seven sins of memory: How the mind forgets and remembers.* Boston, MA: Houghton Mifflin.

Schacter, D. L., & Slotnick, S. D. (2004). The cognitive neuroscience of memory distortion. *Neuron, 44*(1), 149–160.

Schacter, D. L., & Wagner, D. (2013). Learning and memory. In E. R. Kandel, J. H. Schwartz, T. M. Jessell, S. A. Siegelbaum, & A. J. Hudspeth (Eds.), *Principles of neural science* (5th ed., pp. 1441–1460). New York, NY: McGraw-Hill.

Smith, S., & Watson, J. (2010). *Reading autobiography: A guide for interpreting life narratives.* Minneapolis, MN: University of Minnesota Press.

Tomasello, M. (2008). *Origins of human communication.* Cambridge, MA: MIT Press.

Tomasello, M. (2014). *A natural history of human thinking*. Cambridge, MA: Harvard University Press.

Tota, A. L., & Hagen, T. (Eds.). (2016). *The Routledge international handbook of memory studies*. London, UK: Routledge.

van Dijck, J. (2013). *The culture of connectivity: A critical history of social media*. New York, NY: Oxford University Press.

Wagoner, B. (2017). *The constructive mind: Bartlett's psychology in reconstruction*. Cambridge, UK: Cambridge University Press.

Welzer, H. (2010). Re-narrations: How pasts change in conversational remembering. *Memory Studies, 3*(1), 5–17.

Wittgenstein, L. (2009). *Philosophical investigations* (4th rev. ed.). Chichester, UK: Wiley-Blackwell. (Original work published 1953)

Discerning the History
Inscribed Within

Significant Sites of the Narrative Unconscious

MARK FREEMAN ▪

At a most basic level, the central question to be explored in this chapter is the following: How does the world affect us? Specifically, how do the various phenomena that we encounter in the world—from concrete historical events to mediated representations, as may be found in books and films and other such "secondhand" sources—permeate us and become inscribed in memory? One might also ask: Where does all of this information "go" after we have encountered it, and how is it metabolized? Some dimensions of such experiences no doubt dissipate or even, perhaps, disappear. Other dimensions, however, seep into our psyches often in ways unbeknownst to us, thus becoming part of what is herein called the *narrative unconscious*. The narrative unconscious thus refers to those culturally rooted aspects of our histories that have yet to become an explicit part of our life stories, and it includes not only those events and encounters that occur in our lifetime but also those that precede us. By exploring some significant sites of the narrative unconscious, we may more readily discern the deep historical roots of our own psychological formation.

MEMORY, NARRATIVE, AND IDENTITY

Before addressing the idea of the narrative unconscious, it may be useful to provide some background about my own perspective on the relationship between memory, narrative, and personal identity. In a variety of works, distributed throughout approximately three decades of inquiry, I have been concerned to show the many and profound ways in which persons reconstruct and "rewrite" their pasts and, in turn, their selves. My first feature-length foray into these issues, *Rewriting the Self: History, Memory, Narrative* (Freeman, 1993), sought to explore the process at hand by close readings of a number of texts and by discerning, within these texts, the ways in which the history–memory–narrative triad played itself out. In addressing St. Augustine's classic *Confessions*, for instance, I was interested in exploring how his post-conversion vantage point in the present affected the way in which he viewed his past: Having ultimately "seen the light," he can now look backward and see the way in which God had steered his life this way and that, only to arrive at this very present moment. Although not the first text one might look toward to examine the relationship between culture and memory, it is in fact a profound instance of the hermeneutics of meaning-making, serving to inaugurate a radically new orientation to the task of self-understanding (Weintraub, 1978).

In addressing Helen Keller's *The Story of My Life* (1988), the focus shifted to language, specifically the way in which others' words and strategies of meaning-making had become folded into her mind and being. Keller, who had contracted a disease that had left her deaf and blind at 19 months of age, had been left in a highly primitive psychological state, unable to think, to act purposefully, or to relate meaningfully to the world. This changed with the arrival of her teacher, Annie Sullivan, who helped Keller understand the miracle of language. There was, however, an incident that served to cast into question some of Keller's incredible gains: Much of a story that she and others assumed was "her own" had in fact been written by someone else. Keller thus arrived at a startling and disturbing realization: "I cannot be quite sure of the boundary line between my ideas and those I find in books"—or in those ideas that derived from her teacher, Annie Sullivan, spelling things out on her hand—"because so many of my impressions come to me through the medium of others' eyes and ears" (p. 48). By her own account, she herself becomes a sort of postmodern pastiche self. "It is certain," she notes again at one point, "that I cannot always distinguish my own thoughts from those I read, because what I read becomes the very substance and texture of my mind" (p. 53). Keller's situation is of course unique in some ways. But it also raises the following questions: To what extent are our *own* memories "plagiarized," derived from others? To what extent are our life stories truly our own? What exactly does it mean—what exactly *can* it mean—to tell "one's own" story? Is autobiography even possible? In many respects, my immersion into the constellation of issues and questions posed by Keller's text was a foundational encounter with the relationship between culture and memory because it served to show just how linguistically and culturally saturated our ways of meaning-making—in this case, remembering and narrating—are.

Among the other texts I had explored at the time that served to highlight the relationship between culture and memory, one stands out as particularly significant. I am referring here to Jill Ker Conway's memoir, *The Road from Coorain* (1989), a story that recounts Conway growing up in the Australian bush, coming to terms with her own identity as a woman and an Australian, and, eventually, leaving her homeland to carry forward her own projects and plans. In large measure, Conway's narrative is a traditional one, in the sense of being about her own unique, personal circumstances. In addition, however, it is about her formation as a social being and about her own process of coming to consciousness about certain aspects of this formation that had remained occluded, hidden from view. Upon meeting a teacher who had been "impatient with Australian bourgeois culture," Conway eventually came to understand that she herself was being formed educationally in such a way as to minimize the influences of her own country. "We might have been in Sussex," she writes, "for all the attention we paid to Australian poetry and prose" (p. 99). She and her classmates would memorize Keats and Shelley, for instance, enthralled by their vivid descriptions of nature. But this had given them "the impression that great poetry and fiction were written by and about people and places far distant from Australia" (p. 99). What this had also done, Conway recognized, was give them the impression that their own natural world, which deviated greatly from these poetic descriptions, was somehow inferior, second-rate.

More important for present purposes were the discoveries Conway had made about the very earth beneath her feet. Her family had owned a large expanse of land, and she had always taken it to be theirs alone. But "Who," she would eventually ask, "were the rightful owners and users of the land I had always thought to belong to us?" (Conway, 1989, p. 170). She remembers having stumbled across aboriginal ovens and strange stones, which she herself had "heedlessly trodden upon" throughout much of her life. She had not really given these things a thought, her assumption being that they had merely been abandoned, by choice. Her lack of awareness, which came into view as she gazed backward upon her past, proved to be extremely disturbing.

From this point on, Conway (1989) writes, "I could never remember the image of my parents resting in the evening, sitting on the front veranda step at Coorain, quite the same again" (p. 191). For they would henceforth be suffused with her discoveries, permeated by the recognition that beneath her and her family's restful repose was a *history*, heretofore hidden, that would now become part of the story of her life.

To foreshadow a question to be taken up in greater detail later: To what extent did Conway need to "own" that hidden history? No one in her family had chased anyone off the land; whatever had happened had happened years ago and so could not possibly be any fault of her own. What exactly did she owe the "rightful owners" of that land? What might those of us living in the United States owe the Native Americans whose land we too may have "heedlessly trodden upon"? What might we owe to the multitudes of Africans who traveled across the ocean, only to be enslaved, both literally and figuratively, upon their arrival? One might answer these sorts of questions very simply by saying, "Nothing at all. We weren't there." And yet, this history, distant though it may be from our own first-hand experience, remains ours. It is part of our cultural memory, and even if none of it actually "registers" in our own personal lives—that is, even if we know virtually nothing of this distant era and have no sense of responsibility for it at all—it remains a chapter in our history. And once, like Conway, we begin to acquire some consciousness of it, it becomes part of our story as well.

ENCOUNTERING THE NARRATIVE UNCONSCIOUS

As relevant as Conway's story proved to be to my own "discovery" of the narrative unconscious, it was not until I traveled to Berlin, for the first time, that I began using the term (Freeman, 2002, 2006). The year was 1997; I had traveled to Berlin for a conference, and after several days exploring the city, I suddenly found myself undone, caught in an emotional vortex that was a mixture of horror, disbelief, and sorrow. Although I had certainly been prepared for some emotional challenges given my own Jewish background, my knowledge of some of the terrible events that had taken place there, and so on, the initial days of my visit passed unexceptionally. But then came a strange and utterly unanticipated experience, tied somehow to the ambience of the city itself. What I had said at the time was that death seemed literally to be in the air, invisible and yet tangible, as if the horrific events that had taken place there had somehow left behind ghosts of times past. The city had become truly menacing, and it had left me shaken.

The question I had to ask in the aftermath of the experience was, What exactly had happened? However much I felt that death was in the air, it was a stretch to think in these ghostly, almost paranormal, terms. I therefore had to conclude that whatever I felt was in the air I had presumably brought there, via my own hermeneutical "prejudices"—my expectations, my knowledge, my background, and, not least, my imagination. In other words, I must have carried with me enough of a storehouse of information, ideas, and images to "activate the undercurrents," as I had put it, of the spectacles observed. Memory, I wrote not long after this strange experience, thus emerges as "a curious amalgam of fact and fiction, experiences and texts, documentary footage, dramatizations, movies, plays, television shows, fantasies, and more" (Freeman, 2002, p. 199). It was exactly at this juncture that I began to entertain the notion of the narrative unconscious, which, I suggested, "refers not so much to that which has been dynamically repressed as to that which has been lived but which remains unthought and untold, i.e., to those culturally-rooted aspects of one's history that have not yet become part of one's story" (p. 193). In any case, and to make a long story short, I became interested in thinking about those dimensions of memory—and identity—that on some level may be said to go beyond the confines of an individual life.

The situation I am describing here is different in a number of ways from the one Conway had described. She had discovered a dimension of history that had never really been "unconscious," in the sense of unformulated experience. By her own account, she had been all but ignorant of it, such that whatever intimations she might have had as she trod upon those aboriginal ovens and stones were set aside. In my case, there is reason to believe that some of what I had encountered in the past, however mediated it may have been by sources outside the perimeter of my own first-hand experience, had somehow become sedimented in my mind, only to be released by that dreadful time in Berlin. With this release, I believe I learned something about the way in which second-hand sources—here, about the terrible plight of the Jews, among others—had become folded into my memory, dormant, awaiting an experience of the sort I had to come to light.

I also learned something about my Jewish identity—or at least I think I did. (There is no getting around the interpretative dimension, which, in a situation such as this, brings one into territory that cannot help but be downright speculative.) As I noted at the time, I am not an especially religious person. Nor did I know about specific family members who had been victims of the Nazis. My grandparents had arrived in the United States well before the Nazi era; both of my parents had been born in the United States; and although there had likely been some relatives who had perished at the hands of the Nazis, I did not have the kind of intimate connections that many others have. I therefore would not have expected to be as moved and disturbed as I in fact was. To state it crudely, I simply did not think I was *that* Jewish. But apparently I was, and am. I say this not only on the basis of the intensity of that emotional outburst but also on the basis of the fact that I had been left with an urgent desire to go to a synagogue somewhere in the city. I did not need to pray. Indeed, I did not need to enter the synagogue at all. It need not have been any particular one either—for instance, one that had been the site of some atrocity. It simply had to be a synagogue, a place where "my people" had been. How curious it was for this desire to have emerged given my own ambivalent relationship to Judaism. "My people": Had I *ever* thought in these terms?

Through it all, I cannot be sure whether all that I have described here was a function of my theretofore obscure Jewish identity. Since that time, in fact, I have wondered whether it might actually have had more to do with my identity as a *human*. I had jotted down some notes at the time that said as much: There had been a powerful feeling of *absence*; it was as if there was a great hole in the middle of history, and the sense of loss was massive. One way or the other, it had become clear that there were aspects of my history and of my own formation as a person about which I had been largely unaware. It had also become clear that the provoking "causes" of my experience in Berlin had been composed of realities, operating unconsciously, that were largely second-hand. Aspects of cultural memory, therefore, had apparently found their way into my history and had been living underground, as it were. Along these lines, perhaps we can speak of different "registers" or "orders" of autobiographical memory: those that have a first-order reference to the actualities of lived experience and those that have a second-order reference—that is, those that are "one step removed" from these actualities but that are still, in a distinct sense, part of "my past." "Memories," therefore, may consist of not only first-hand recollections drawn from lived experience but also those second-hand characteristics that are constitutive of "my past" and, in turn, "my story," and indeed "myself" (Freeman, 2010a, 2010b).

In this respect, there would seem to be no hard and fast dividing line between personal memory and "cultural memory" (see especially Brockmeier, 2002a, 2002b; Brockmeier, Chapter 2, this volume; Wang & Brockmeier, 2002). The ideas of "social memory" (Fentress & Wickham, 1992) and "collective memory" (Halbwachs, 1992) are relevant as well. But what exactly are these? Do any of these terms really have concrete referents? For Susan Sontag (2003), the answer is a firm

"No." On her account, "All memory is individual, unreproducible—it dies with each person" (p. 86). "Collective memory," therefore,

> is not a remembering but a stipulating; that this is important, and this is the story about how it happened, with the pictures that lock the stories in our minds. Ideologies create substantiating archives of images, representative images, which encapsulate common ideas of significance and trigger predictable thoughts, feelings. (p. 86)

Sontag is at least partially correct about this: Seen from one angle, memory is a purely individual matter. But as I have tried to show through the examples provided thus far, there is no separating what is wholly "mine" from what has been derived from without. And this is so not only in terms of the "what" of memory—that is, that which has issued from other sources—but also in terms of the "how"—that is, the way in which it emerges from within the fabric of extant storylines, genres, and modes of narration. Along these lines, "who we are can be understood only by taking into account the interpretive schemata provided by our society. We are individuals by thinking with culturally given concepts and actualizing culturally provided practices in a uniquely characteristic way" (Allan, 1993, p. 26).

As I have suggested via the idea of the narrative unconscious, we may be largely unaware of these processes. The situation is a curious one. Whatever it was that I had experienced in the past, both first-hand and second-hand, it had left me hermeneutically prepared to encounter the city of Berlin in the way I did; it had become inscribed in my being, my way of sensing, seeing, and feeling. Was all of this somehow "there," lying dormant, waiting to be released by just this encounter? Would I have known any of what I discovered had I not had that encounter? Possibly; but possibly not too. It is a humbling thought. Of course, what I have been describing here is but the proverbial tip of the iceberg. Think of all the texts and images and discourses that come one's way throughout the course of one's life. All of these leave deposits, imprints, residues. Some of these are concrete and vivid enough to become part of the explicit stories we tell ourselves about ourselves. Others, however, do not become part of these stories, maybe ever. They are part of the narrative unconscious; and whether they "rise to the surface," so to speak, will depend on what we encounter in our lives afterward.

THE POWER OF DEEP MEMORY

Here, I flesh out some of the ideas introduced in the previous section by turning to Eva Hoffman's (2004) *After Such Knowledge: Memory, History, and the Legacy of the Holocaust*. As Hoffman notes early in the book,

> I had grown up with a consciousness of the Shoah from the beginning. My parents had emerged from its crucible shortly before my birth. They had

survived, in what was then the Polish part of the Ukraine, with the help of Polish and Ukrainian neighbors; but their entire families perished. Those were the inescapable facts—the inescapable knowledge—I had come into. But the knowledge had not always been equally active, nor did I always want to make the inheritance defining.

Indeed, it was not until I started writing . . . that I began discerning, amidst other threads, the Holocaust strand of my history. I had carried this part of my psychic past within me all my life; but it was only now, as I began pondering it from a longer distance and through the clarifying process of writing, that what had been an inchoate, obscure knowledge appeared to me as a powerful theme and influence in my life. Until then, it had not occurred to me that I was in effect a receptacle of a historical legacy, or that its burden had a significance and weight that needed to be acknowledged. Now, personal memory appeared to me clearly linked to larger history, and the heavy dimensions of this inheritance started becoming fully apparent. (p. x)

As Hoffman (2004) goes on to note, she had listened to her parents' stories throughout her life. But they had died, as had most other survivors, the result being that she

felt more and more palpably that the legacy of the Shoah was being passed on to us, its symbolic descendants and next of kin. We were the closest to its memories; we had touched upon its horror and its human scars. If I did not want the "memory" of the Holocaust to be flattened out through distance or ignorance, if I wanted to preserve some of the pulsing complexity I had felt in survivors' own perceptions, then it was up to me. (pp. x–xi)

This meant that Hoffman "needed to reflect on [her] own and [her] peers' link to that legacy, to excavate our generational story from under its weight and shadow—to retrieve it from that 'secondariness' which many of us have felt in relation to a formidable and forbidding past. In a sense," she explains further, "I needed to address frontally what I had thought about obliquely: the profound effects of a traumatic history, . . . the kinds of knowledge which the Shoah has bequeathed to us, and the knowledge we might derive from it" (p. xi).

This meant exploring and interrogating what I have been calling the narrative unconscious, the "secondariness" at hand being explicitly linked to Hoffman's membership in the "second generation." On her account (Hoffman, 2004),

The second generation's story is a strong case study in the deep and longlasting impact of atrocity; and . . . children of survivors' very personal transactions with the past are a strong clue to the problems we must grapple with if we would grasp the meaning and consequences of historical horror. In their mediated but immediate relation to the Holocaust, children of survivors have had to live out and struggle with some of the defining issues that follow from atrocity: the internal impact of gratuitous violence and

the transmission of traumatic memories across generations; the emotional
intricacies of dealing with victims of persecution and the moral quandaries
implicit in dialogues with perpetrators; the difficulties of witnessing the pain
of others and of thinking about tragic pasts; and the relationship of private
memory to a broader understanding of history. (p. xii)

These words are loaded, indeed. How shall we understand the nature of "historical
horror"? What does it mean to speak of a "mediated but immediate relation to the
Holocaust"? How can this relation be both "mediated" and "immediate"? Should
we in fact speak of "the transmission of traumatic memories across generations"?
Can "memories" truly be transmitted in this way? And what about this ostensibly "private memory" about which Hoffman speaks? Insofar as it is linked to "a
broader understanding of history," *is* it private?

Hoffman acknowledges that, "while it has become routine to speak of the
'memory' of the Holocaust, . . . we who came after do not have memories of the
Holocaust. Even from my most intimate proximity," she writes, "I could not form
'memories' of the Shoah or take my parents' memories as my own" (p. 6). And
yet, she continues, there is a distinct sense in which her parents' memories *did*
become her own, albeit of a different order. She recalls her parents' first communications and how their "fragmentary phrases lodged themselves in my mind like
shards, like the deadly needles I remember from certain fairy tales, which pricked
your flesh and could never be extracted again" (p. 11). But there was more, much
more: "'You should have seen their faces,'" her mother had said. "'They were
not really human.'" Fantastic images would course through Hoffman's young
mind. "'We were hunted from all sides. There was nowhere to escape to.'" More
images: "Fields, trenches, pits of death, . . . barbed wire, skeletal figures, smoke,
intimations of mass death." If Hoffman is right, "Every child has such images
available right behind the eyelids." And eventually, "through literature and film,
through memoirs and oral testimony, these components of horror became part
of a whole generation's store of imagery and narration" (p. 12). According to
Hoffman, this awareness of pain and suffering "created an unconscious, or preconscious, ethics, and . . . in this system, just as war was the ground of being, so
pain was the ground of personhood" (p. 13). The result: She had "absorbed [her]
parents' unhappiness through channels that seemed nearly physical. The pain of
their psyches reverberated in my body almost as if they were mine" (p. 14).

There were larger events, such as the Warsaw uprising, that bore upon her life as
well. These too "would become my meaningful history, the history it is urgent to
know because it belongs to one's life, because it shapes ancestral fate and one's own
sensibility" (p. 18). Such are "the paradoxes of indirect knowledge," a knowledge
that continues to "haunt" Hoffman and others who "came after":

The formative events of the twentieth century have crucially informed our
biographies and psyches, threatening sometimes to overshadow and over-
whelm our lives. But we did not see them, suffer through them, experience
their impact directly. Our relationship to them has been defined by our very

"post-ness," and by the powerful but mediated forms of knowledge that have followed from it. (p. 25)

Hoffman is well aware of the dangers of framing things as she has. "It did not occur to me to think of myself as a 'child of Holocaust survivors' for many of my adult years," (p. 25) she admits. "Other threads of causality, influence, development seemed more important; or at least I gave them other names. . . . Identities are malleable and multidimensional," Hoffman continues, "and I am reluctant to fix my own through reifying labels. And yet, we do not only define ourselves; we are also defined by our circumstances, culture, the perceptions of others and— perhaps most of all—the force of an internalized past" (p. 27).

The challenge is how to think about this past. Referring back to some of the childhood images considered previously, Hoffman (2004) notes that "at first, it was not rational interpretation, or information, or anything like memories" (p. 33). Indeed, "The attic in my imagination . . . probably bore no relation to the actual attic in which my parents were hidden" (p. 34). What she did sense was "the huddled hiding; the despair, the fear, my father's alertness to danger, my mother's deep resignation. Those were among the molecular elements of my early world, as they were for so many of my background and generation" (p. 34). What she and others had received, therefore, were "the emotional *sequelae* of our elders' experience, the acid-etched traces of what they had endured" (p. 34). Questions abound: "How can the sequelae of catastrophe be passed on across generations? Or, more generally, what features of our parents' personalities enter us and make their deep impact? How do they become preserved or transformed within us, converted into liberating visions, or twisted into paralyzing knots?" (p. 61).

Reflecting further on the phenomenon at hand, Hoffmann (2004) too uses the very apt language of "haunting": "Something emerges from the past that we thought had been dead . . . but that has lain dormant in the turrets and caverns of the soul till it returns in the form of specters and shadows" (p. 65). These phenomena, she continues, "belong to the world of ghost stories and the gothic— psychologically speaking, a world of fantasy and inner distortion. For in the second generation, the anxieties, the symptoms, no matter how genuine in themselves, no longer correspond to actual experience or external realities." Indeed, she maintains, the second generation "has inherited not experience, but its shadows." This is not to diminish the power of the inheritance, for "wrestling with shadows," she notes, "can be more frightening, or confusing, than struggling with solid realities" (p. 66). The narrative unconscious looms especially large in this context, as does a broadly psychoanalytic account more generally. For Hoffman, such an account is in fact more consonant with the experience of survivors' children than with survivors themselves. "This is not only because the children are more psychologically-minded and understand their own experience in subjective terms; but because their experience belongs to the realm of the psychological, the internal theater of body and mind, rather than to the stage of external events" (p. 72). In this respect, she adds, "transferred loss, more than transferred memory, is what children of survivors inherit" (p. 73).

As Hoffman (2004) goes on to note, Halbwachs' idea of collective memory is surely relevant to present concerns because there is no question but that elements of the larger history into which she had been thrown had been operative in shaping her world (see Shils, 1981). Not unlike Sontag, however, she finds the idea problematic, "veering between a useful and a misleading fiction. For within such 'memory,' there is no subject who remembers, no process of remembering, no link between reflection and experience" (pp. 165–166). This is true, and the implication is clear enough: Insofar as we conceptualize memory in terms of first-hand experience alone, there is no justification for speaking of it in the present case. As previously discussed, however, it may be that there is no separating first-hand experience from the vast welter of second-hand sources that come our way. What this in turn suggests is that it may be useful to conceptualize memory differently. For Hoffman, the notion of "mediation" is central to her account: "Those who have not lived through the Shoah received its knowledge, at this late date, through mediations—sometimes several layers of them. We view it no longer directly, but through memorials, artistic representations, literature, film" (p. 178). But this is also true—and I say this cautiously—for those who *did* live through the Shoah and who returned to it throughout the course of their lives. For them, too, "memory" would bring in tow all kinds of extraneous, second-hand matter. It would also be conditioned by their ever-changing vantage point at the moment of remembering and narrating (Cohler, 2008; Schiff, Skillingstead, Archibald, Arasim, & Peterson, 2006). Do I need to put the word "memory" in scare quotes, as I just did? Or is it time to do away with them?

There are some dangers involved in moving in the direction I am suggesting here. As Hoffman (2004) argues,

> Impersonal memory, much more than embodied, personal remembering, is malleable in the extreme, and highly susceptible to deliberate shaping or exploitation—to propaganda and censorship, to tendentious selectivity and willful emphasis. It is, in other words, an instrument not so much of subjective reflection or understanding as of cultural agendas or ideological purposes. (p. 166)

Margalit (2002) concurs, underscoring "the urgent need and the ardent desire of authoritarian, traditional, and theocratic regimes to control collective memory, because by so doing they exercise monopoly on all sources of legitimacy" (p. 11). Such memory also risks being generic, stereotypical. My own experience in Berlin, removed as it was from first-hand memories, seems to have been the product of highly schematized and conventionalized images of people, places, and events. Bearing this in mind, we ought to be on our guard against too-pat renditions of the past, particularly in those circumstances in which "impersonal memory," as Hoffman puts it, is primary.

Should such "impersonal memory" be considered memory? Should "*false* memory" be considered memory? In this context, it might be helpful to briefly discuss another text that takes up some related issues. I am referring here to Binjamin

Wilkomirski's (1996) book *Fragments*, a "memoir" of a "wartime childhood" that had been hailed upon its publication as a masterpiece of autobiographical writing about the Holocaust, not least because Wilkomirski would "give up on the ordering logic of grown-ups" and "try to use words to draw as exactly as possible what happened, what I saw; exactly the way my child's memory has held on to it; with no benefit of perspective or vanishing point" (p. 4). Remarkable though the account was—and, as many readers have suggested, experientially accurate—it was too good to be true: The past he had written about turned out not to be his own. It is possible that Wilkomirski simply lied about his past. But the available evidence suggests something different and more pertinent to present concerns. What seems to have happened, in brief, was that Wilkomirski gave himself a history, a childhood, a past that he believed to have been his. On Stefan Maechler's (2001) account, "Wilkomirski did not one day decide to carefully construct a character and devise a story with which to deceive the world. His present-day identity arose, rather, over the course of four decades, unplanned and improvised, with new experiences and necessities constantly woven into it and contradictions smoothed over, though over time with less and less success" (p. 269). As Maechler goes on to suggest, Wilkomirski had created a kind of myth about this past. He was "one of those suffering children" whose story had to be told. This mythic story had been infused with "elements taken from humanity's remembrance of the Shoah" (p. 269), as Maechler states, with familiar images, events, and storylines. And this remembrance had gradually, but inexorably, become "his own."

Not unlike what occurred in the case of Helen Keller, remembering and imagining had become fused. There is, however, a significant difference between the two cases: Whereas Wilkomirski had supposedly been remembering but was in fact imagining, Keller had supposedly been imagining but had in fact been remembering. Most important for present purposes, in any case, is the commingling of what I called "first-order" autobiographical memory (i.e., that which could be tied to some concrete event or events in the past) and "second-order" memory (i.e., that which issued from without). The issue here, therefore, ultimately concerns the very idea of autobiographical memory. Memory, many would argue, is the internal, first-hand stuff; the rest is knowledge, which, the argument generally goes, gets imposed on memory. The problem, however, is that memory itself is always already infused with all sorts of extraneous matter—matter that can indeed be so phenomenologically compelling that one can (mis) take it wholly as one's own.

One may of course ask once again: Does it really make sense to speak of memory in a case such as Wilkomirski's? Acknowledging some of the obvious problems of doing so—not the least of which is the fact that the past he depicted was not factually his own—I believe it does. The main reason concerns the virtually inevitable commingling of first-order and second-order autobiographical memory. In addition, what we see in Wilkomirski's case is that this commingled memory, false though some of it was, was constitutive of his very identity. In a very real sense, he had become the person he had imagined himself to be, and at the root of it was his (presumed) past. Pragmatically speaking, the fact that this past turned out to have been crafted in error is immaterial. It was still *his*, and its impact on his identity is clear. Much the same may be said of Hoffman's situation: Factually speaking, her parents' memories were not her own. But pragmatically speaking, they were her own because they had come to reconstitute and reshape her past and, in turn, her identity. Along the lines being drawn, might it not be said that autobiographical memory refers to whatever constitutes the personal past, whether its sources are first-hand or second-hand, and personal identity that which is fashioned in its wake?

Brockmeier (2002b) speaks of memory being "distributed" in this context (see also Bruner, 2001; Donald, Chapter 1, this volume), this "larger layout of memory" being seen as "an array of texts, documents, and other artifacts that have become intermingled with the texture of one's own autobiographical memory" (p. 25). To be sure, the kinds of situations we have been addressing in this section of the chapter are to be distinguished from those tied to lived experiences. Hoffman is not her parents. She was not there. She was not a "victim"—at least not in the same way her parents had been. As for the Wilkomirski case, we certainly would not want to conflate his story with the stories of actual survivors. He too was not there, and he too was not a victim—at least not the particular victim he had imagined himself to be. The fact nevertheless remains: There is no fully disentangling the different registers of autobiographical memory that have been addressed herein. Autobiographical memory is a work of culture, and although it may at times be necessary to differentiate that which has been derived mainly from first-hand experience from that which has been derived from second-hand experience, the virtually inevitable commingling of the two, particularly as encountered in autobiographical narrative, leads us well beyond the more privatized conception of memory still dominant in much of the extant psychological literature.

MEANING, MEMORY, AND MORAL LIFE

In certain important respects, both Hoffman's and Wilkomirski's stories are about the "ownership" of the past; they are about what is, and is not, rightfully "theirs." What I want to explore now in more explicit fashion is the moral dimension of ownership, focusing especially on the question of what one *ought* to own— particularly when the past in question is not of one's own making.

Several years ago, my colleague and friend, Roger Frie, shared with me something about his own history that proved to be extremely disturbing—namely his discovery, through a family photograph, that his beloved grandfather had in fact been a member of the Nazi party. Frie (2014) asks,

> What does it mean to be caught in a web of history, to be part of a traumatic past over which we have no control? We are born into history and culture and it is through our family that we are connected to these larger dimensions of experience. Our families provide us with narratives, stories that enable us

to make sense of what we see and that implicitly shape what we know and remember at any moment in time. These narratives are an integral part of who we are, yet are not consciously organized. They remain largely unconscious, a compass by which our lives are pre-reflectively organized. At some stage, or at some point in life, we may be able to reflect on certain aspects of the narratives we inherit, and begin to question them, thus revealing new ways of seeing the world around us. I say "may," because a reflective, conscious understanding on our situation is never a given. . . . Initially at least, our place is made for us, unconsciously structured by the language we speak, the history we inherit, and the culture and traditions that constitute who we are. (p. 2)

Frie goes on in this piece to share a few tender words about his grandfather:

My experience of my grandfather was directly related to his work as an artisan. He created beautiful objects made of wrought iron, brass and copper. As a child I marveled at the way he could take a mass of metal and fashion it into a piece of art, much as a sculptor molds clay or chisels marble. His skills were recognized and in the years of hardship that followed the war he was able to find work to provide for the family. As I grew older, my grandfather showed me his craft and taught me some of the skills of metal work. He died quite suddenly when I was only fifteen and I mourned the loss of opportunity to do more with him. Later I used my grandfather's workshop to practice some of what I learned from him. To this day, working with my hands can evoke cherished memories of the time we spent together. (pp. 2–3)

"My grandfather was caring and kind, artistically gifted, and maintained a sense of humor in the face of the destruction and hardship wrought by war," Frie adds. "Although I knew early on that my grandfather belonged to the side of the perpetrators, I was always relieved that his history, and by extension my own, was not one of perpetration" (p. 3). With the discovery of the photograph that would eventually reveal the truth about his grandfather, he continues,

I found myself suddenly upended. My understanding of the narratives and memories by which I came to see the past had inalterably shifted. Knowledge of my grandfather's identity as a Nazi meant that I was the inheritor of an indelibly tainted history, connected however directly or indirectly with the perpetration of unimaginably heinous crimes. The fact that my grandfather appeared to be a "minor Nazi" was hardly consoling. It was the support lent by the rank and file that enabled the perpetration of mass murder to unfold. No matter how much I might want to disown this history, it is a part of my past, a part of who I am. (p. 8)

How, though, one might ask, was Frie *himself* culpable? In one very obvious way, he was not; like Hoffman, he was not there. In addition, there is really no indication that his grandfather himself perpetrated the kinds of dastardly deeds we all know about. Nevertheless, he writes,

> It seems clear to me now that I had been dissociating historical facts as a way of maintaining intact memories of my grandfather and avoiding uncomfortable, even forbidden family discussions. I may also have been protecting my mother and her siblings by not speaking more directly to the possibility of my grandfather's involvement. (p. 10)

This statement suggests that, on some level, Frie was aware of the possibility that his family might not have been quite as innocent as he had wished. This surely contributes to his sense of guilt and shame. But this possibility, real though it is, does not quite get to the heart of the problem at hand—or does not get us far enough. This is because *irrespective* of what he might have suspected or even known all along, the history in question was, in part, his. In fact, it is not really clear to me how much it *matters* that his grandfather happened to be implicated, for the history at hand would be much the same.

> "When I initially reflected on the questions I posed," Frie admits,
> I found myself wavering about whether to fully engage the past. After all, my grandfather's actions took place long ago, in an entirely differently time and place from my own. How was his political allegiance, his support of an immoral regime, possibly connected to me? In a purely chronological sense, I am one of those who "came after," and as such bear no direct responsibility for what happened before me. But any attempt to erase, or relativize the meaning of history in this way, is surely motivated by a singular wish for an unburdened past, for memory of a grandfather that is free of conflict. (pp. 12–13)

This is a wish, Frie recognizes, "that must ultimately fail." And so, "As much as I might want to step out of my historically defined position as a third-generation German, I am unable to" (p. 13).

I nevertheless ask, How much of his family's history does Frie need to own? How much of his *country's* history? But let us extend the questions here: How much do *we* need to own of *our* country's history? How much of a history of oppression, and violence, do I own as a white person, as a male, as a Jew, and so on? How far into the world do all these spheres of responsibility go? And where does it all end? *Does* it end, ever? These are difficult questions. I would not go so far as to say that we all deserve the designation of "perpetrator." That would be rather extreme. But on some level, we are responsible for everyone and for everything that goes on in the world—from the Black lives shot down in our midst all the way to the millions upon millions of more distant others who are starving or suffering in some other way. We are part of a history that has *led* to these things and allowed them to happen. None of what I am saying here should be taken to mean that we ought to take on every important cause or that we ourselves ought to suffer every possible site of suffering we can. What it does mean is that we need to reflect very carefully about our own historical position in the world and do what we can to own what is most urgent to own, at least for now, here, at this particular moment.

I was reminded of this during the course of my recent reading of Ta-Nehisi Coates's (2015) book *Between the World and Me*. As those of you who have read the book know, it is a quite remarkable account of being a "black body" in America, taking the form of a letter to his son. It is also very much about the narrative unconscious. The following is a particularly telling incident:

> Perhaps [he writes to his son] you remember that time we went to see *Howl's Moving Castle* on the Upper West Side. You were almost five years old. The theater was crowded, and when we came out we rode a set of escalators down to the ground floor. As we came off, you were moving at the dawdling speed of a young child. A white woman pushed you and said "Come on!" Many things now happened at once. There was the reaction of any parent when a stranger lays a hand on the body of his or her child. And there was my own insecurity in my ability to protect your black body. And more: There was my sense that this woman was pulling rank. I knew, for instance, that she would not have pushed a black child out on my part of Flatbush, because she would be afraid there and would sense, if not know, that there would be a penalty for such an action. . . . I turned and spoke to this woman [Coates continues], and my words were hot with all of the moment and all of my history. She shrunk back, shocked. A white man standing nearby spoke up in her defense. I experienced this as his attempt to rescue the damsel from the beast. He had made no such attempt on behalf of my son. And he was now supported by other white people in the assembling crowd. The man came closer. He grew louder. I pushed him away. He said, "I could have you arrested!" I did not care. I told him this, and the desire to do much more was hot in my throat. This desire was only controllable because I remembered someone standing off to the side there, bearing witness to more fury than he had ever seen from me—you. (pp. 93–94)

Where does the narrative unconscious enter the picture? Most explicitly, it enters in the form of Coates' fury, derived as it was from both the heat of the moment and the whole of his history, now surfacing. This was another shock of discovery, albeit one of a very different sort than Frie's. "I came home shook," Coates writes, partly due to the intensity of the event and partly due to the subterranean intensity of that history. The idea of the narrative unconscious can also be applied to his son, who, no doubt, would fold this frightening awful event, this trauma, into his own history, spread among countless others, also tied, in one way or another, to his black body; all of this would become part of his own "deep memory," as I called it previously, and deep identity. Finally, of course, the idea of the narrative unconscious can be applied to *us*, his readers, especially those of us who, as Coates puts it, "believe we are white" and who have inhabited a culture and world that is terribly fraught and that permeates our mind and our being root and branch, often in ways unbeknownst to us.

Many aspects of our historical inheritance are conscious or preconscious, able to be brought to mind given the right circumstances. But some are *unconscious*, which is to say they refer to those deep strata of history of which we may be largely, if not entirely, unaware. They are hidden, not so much in the sense of that which has been buried as that which remains unthought and thus not yet a part of the story we can tell. These dimensions of identity find their origins not in the personal particulars of a life but, rather, in the fabric of history.

The question I want to pose, In closing, is: How can this larger story be told? More to the point: How does one tell a story in which some of the most formative events were not actually a concrete part of one's life? To discern the workings of the narrative unconscious is difficult in itself. To tell its story brings the challenge at hand to another plane altogether. For it cannot be restricted to what is, or has been, present. In addition, it cannot be restricted to that stretch of time that exists between birth and death. And of course, it cannot be restricted to what goes on in the confines of "my" mind. What, then? The challenge, as always, is to find language that articulates and reveals rather than obfuscates and hides. In the present context especially, this language is less one of comprehension and prehension, grasping, than it is a kind of poetic being-before or being-with, one that somehow seeks to make present precisely that which eludes it. It is a tall order. In considering the narrative unconscious, that vast region of existence we call "the past" expands, moves beyond the particulars of "my life," into the world. The challenge of telling its story expands in turn. For this story is no longer bounded, no longer tied to that stretch of time between birth and death, no longer tied to discrete episodes and events, and indeed no longer tied to me alone but to the entire world through which my life acquires its distinctive meaning and form.

My own shock of discovery in Berlin was nothing like that of Roger Frie. There was no Nazi grandfather, no family silence, no shame per se—except the kind of shame that is bound up with being human, with being part of a species so capable of inflicting so much pain. Nor was it like that of Ta-Nehisi Coates. But it was a shock nonetheless, one that allowed me to discern some dimensions of my history that I had not encountered before. Narratives are with us in ways we do not quite know; they are part of our deep memory, which is itself composed, in part, of sedimented layers of history. By discerning the narrative unconscious—that is, by making the narrative unconscious conscious—we open ourselves to the possibility of exploring new forms of making sense and meaning of personal and social life.

REFERENCES

Allan, G. (1993). Traditions and transitions. In P. Cook (Ed.), *Philosophical imagination and cultural memory* (pp. 21–39). Durham, NC: Duke University Press.

Brockmeier, J. (2002a). Introduction: Searching for cultural memory. *Culture & Psychology, 8*, 5–14.

Brockmeier, J. (2002b). Remembering and forgetting: Narrative as cultural memory. *Culture & Psychology, 8*, 15–43.

Bruner, J. (2001). Self-making and world-making. *Journal of Aesthetic Education, 25*, 67–78.

Coates, T.-N. (2015). *Between the world and me.* New York, NY: Spiegel & Grau.

Cohler, B. J. (2008). Two lives, two times: Life-writing after Shoah. *Narrative Inquiry, 18*, 1–28.

Conway, J. K. (1989). *The road from Coorain.* New York, NY: Knopf.

Fentress, J., & Wickham, C. (1992). *Social memory.* Oxford, UK: Blackwell.

Freeman, M. (1993). *Rewriting the self: History, memory, narrative.* London, UK: Routledge.

Freeman, M. (2002). Charting the narrative unconscious: Cultural memory and the challenge of autobiography. *Narrative Inquiry, 12*, 193–211.

Freeman, M. (2006). Autobiographische Erinnerung und das narrative Unbeßuste [Autobiographical memory and the narrative unconscious]. In H. Welzer & H. J. Markowitsch (Eds.), *Warum Menschen sich erinnern können [Autobiographical memory in interdisciplinary perspective]* (pp. 129–143). Stuttgart, Germany: Klett-Cotta.

Freeman, M. (2010a). *Hindsight: The promise and peril of looking backward.* New York, NY: Oxford University Press.

Freeman, M. (2010b). The space of selfhood: Culture, narrative, identity. In S. R. Kirschner & J. Martin (Eds.), *The sociocultural turn: The contextual emergence of mind and self* (pp. 137–158). New York, NY: Columbia University Press.

Frie, R. (2014). Limits of understanding: Psychological experience, German memory and the Holocaust. *Psychoanalysis, Culture & Society, 19*, 255–271.

Halbwachs, M. (1992). *On collective memory.* Chicago, IL: University of Chicago Press.

Hoffman, E. (2004). *After such knowledge: Memory, history, and the legacy of the Holocaust.* New York, NY: Public Affairs.

Keller, H. (1988). *The story of my life.* New York, NY: New American Library.

Maechler, S. (2001). *The Wilkomirski affair: A study in biographical truth.* New York, NY: Schocken.

Margalit, A. (2002). *The ethics of memory.* Cambridge, MA: Harvard University Press.

Schiff, B., Skillingstead, H., Archibald, O., Arasim, A., & Peterson, J. (2006). Consistency and change in the repeated narratives of Holocaust survivors. *Narrative Inquiry, 16*, 349–377.

Shils, E. A. (1981). *Tradition.* Chicago, IL: University of Chicago Press.

Sontag, S. (2003). *Regarding the pain of others.* New York, NY: Farrar, Straus & Giroux.

Wang, Q., & Brockmeier, J. (2002). Autobiographical remembering as cultural practice: Understanding the interplay between memory, self, and culture. *Culture & Psychology, 8*, 44–64.

Weintraub, K. (1978). *The value of the individual: Self and circumstance in autobiography.* Chicago, IL: University of Chicago Press.

Wilkomirski, B. (1996). *Fragments: Memories of a wartime childhood.* New York, NY: Schocken.

PART II

Cultural Contexts of Remembering

The Landscape of Family Memory

BRADD SHORE AND SARA KAUKO ∎

The family has long been acknowledged as a key institution in both human evolution and human life (Browning, 1892; Davis & Daly, 1997; Fox, 1967). Because *Homo sapiens* evolved within the context of family organization, we would expect the family to have a privileged place in the evolution of human memory systems. Yet the multiplex relations between family and memory have not been fully explored. This chapter focuses on the importance of "family memory" as a significant human memory system and brings together insights from the literature on memory in cognitive psychology and the work on social memory by historians, sociologists, and anthropologists. Human groups exhibit a wide variability of family arrangements. Moreover, the family has been extended into much broader social categories that represent the expansion of de facto political institutions beyond the local household or village. Families proliferate into "kindreds," "lineages," and "descent groups" of many kinds, and so the analysis of family structure becomes the study of "kinship and social organization."

Although our research into family memory started with the question, "How is memory constituted through the family?" our journey through the literature has served to reverse the question. We learned to ask, "To what extend can we understand the family as a memory community?" The family is society's most important memory community. There are also many structural features that can define families: filiation, sharing a household, marriage, groups headed by siblings, eating together, sharing a hearth, having a common economy, and so on. A family is always understood as a unit that considers itself to be related through primary ties, usually, but not exclusively, filiation and marriage. Family memory is a primary aspect of personal and social identity and is supported by a large number of cultural institutions, such as kinship terminologies, genealogies, naming systems, kin reckoning techniques, photographs, stories/historical narratives, coats of arms, tartans, secret knowledge, heirlooms, and ancestor shrines. The goal shared by all of these mnemonics is to allow people to remember and identify each other as relatives or ancestors of one kind or another. The cultivation of family memory is a necessary and crucial aspect of family identity.

FINDING A PLACE FOR FAMILY MEMORY

In light of the scope of memory research, finding a conceptual home for family memory is challenging. Memory research has numerous disciplinary homes, including psychology, cognitive science, sociology, anthropology, history, literature, and cultural studies. Memory has been studied through the elaboration of a complex typology of different kinds of memory. The balkanization of memory into numerous subtypes has served both to illuminate and to complicate the field of memory research. To justify adding yet another subtype of memory, it is important to locate family memory within this analytical framework. We begin our exploration by finding a place for family memory among the many kinds of memory researchers have identified.

In the 19th century, researchers distinguished between short- and long-term memory. Short-term memory included the working memory system that holds objects of immediate attention for active access and manipulation, and it operates through an executive system that coordinates the different subsystems of working memory (visual, auditory, linguistic, etc.). John Anderson (1976) outlined a distinction within long-term memory between declarative (or explicit) memory ("knowing of"), subject to explicit recall and articulation, and procedural memory ("knowing how"), which is the implicit and not fully conscious recall of skills and routines, including the fully embodied muscle memory that allows the body to encode skilled movement. Endel Tulving (1972, 1983, 1985) proposed dividing declarative memory into episodic memory, which encodes the recall of events; procedural memory, which encodes information about sequences necessary to perform routines; and semantic memory, which deals with discrete information or facts.

In reference to the temporality of memory, Eugene Winograd (1988) has distinguished retrospective memory from prospective memory depending on whether the content of the memory is something from the past or an anticipated event in the future, which he calls "remembering to remember." Later in this chapter, we define a somewhat different conception of prospective memory that is of particular importance for family memory. Flashbulb memories are memory encodings that accompany shocking or emotionally salient events (Neisser, 1982). They are not necessarily memories of the triggering event itself but, rather, memories of where one was and what one was doing that are registered at the moment the event is experienced or reported and which become indelibly associated for the individual with the event.

Memory also underlies our understanding of space. Topographic memory is the encoding of mental maps and haptic information concerned with movement through space (Aguirre, Zarahn, & D'Esposito, 1998). Spatial memory in its allocentric and egocentric forms is neurologically specialized and an essential part of human spatial and social navigation (Shore, 2012, 2014). A related but distinct notion is the idea of consciously cultivated memory "spaces" made famous by Pierre Nora (1989) as "lieux de mémoire." Nora's concept of public places (e.g., museums, cemeteries, and monuments) or ritualized occasions (e.g., anniversaries and commemorations) links the evocative power of memory sites with the venerable notion of "locus of memory," the cognitive connection between memory and place. From a cognitive perspective, memory spaces are not forms of memory but, rather, act as memory affordances, occasions, and places deliberately constructed to evoke shared memory. *Lieux de mémoire* are a kind of spatial memory object. Like all memory objects, memory places serve to afford and cultivate memories. They constitute an objectified reservoir or catalyst of memory.

Family memory is a subset of autobiographical memory. Autobiographical memory is the network of salient events (episodic memory) and information (semantic memory) underlying an individual's sense of self. Conway and Pleydell-Pearce (2000) understand autobiographical memory as an aspect of what they term "the self-memory system" (SMS). Because it includes both episodic (event-based) and declarative (fact-based) memories, family memory is not a structurally distinct form of memory. Its coherence as a concept stems from the fact that it is organized around family experiences and also from its importance in the SMS. For both individuals and groups, family memory is an essential aspect of identity. Memorable experiences are presumed to be at least partially shared among or relevant to the identities of family members. Thus, from a content perspective, family memory is autobiographical memory dealing with family members and family experiences. Family memory has an important double life as an aspect of both personal and collective memory.

The phrase "family memory" is ambiguous in that it can refer to either memories *of* family held by anyone or memories of anything shared *by* family members. To avoid confusion, we use the term family memory to describe the intersection of these two concepts: memories held by family members that deal with family life—family events (both unique and repeated); ordinary family routines; family members remembered within the context of family life; and family-associated objects, rituals, and places. In terms of how far family extends, this will depend on the context and the society. The range of family memory can be as limited as specific events in the context of family life or as broad as the multigeneration history of an extended descent group, as long as the memories and the rememberers are understood to be related through kinship ties.

COLLECTIVE MEMORY

To the extent that family memory is shared to some degree by family members, it is a kind of collective memory. For this reason, family memory is of significance for historians, sociologists, and anthropologists as well as psychologists (Olick & Robbins, 1998). The idea of collective memory was proposed in 1925 by French sociologist Maurice Halbwachs (1992). A disciple of Emile Durkheim, Halbwachs was intent to demonstrate that all remembering is intrinsically social. Although it is individuals who carry out the act of remembering, the remembrances they access and the recollections they hold are inevitably socially constituted.

Families are likely to agree that they have a shared history that can be recalled or commemorated, despite the fact that the actual content of family memory is inevitably dynamic, changing over time and variable among family members. The truth value of the content of a presumably shared family memory is a common object of contestation among family members—a fact that does not generally undermine the felt importance of the concept of family memory in general.

The assumption that family memory is a form of collective memory rather than aggregated memories of individual family members is clearly problematical for psychologists. Halbwachs (1992) famously attempted to evade this problem by emphasizing the necessary social character of all personal memory:

> But individual memory is nevertheless a part or an aspect of group memory, since each impression and each fact, even if it apparently concerns a particular person exclusively, leaves a lasting memory only to the extent that one has thought it over—to the extent that it is connected with the thoughts that come to us from the social milieu. (p. 53)

Emphasizing the social origins of all memory allowed Halbwachs to treat collectivities, such as families, as sites of inherently collective remembering:

> I have limited myself hitherto to observing and pointing out all that is social in individual recollections—those recollections in which every person retrieves his own past, and often thinks that this is all that he can retrieve. Now that we have understood to what point the individual is in this respect—as in so many others—dependent on society, it is only natural that we consider the group in itself as having the capacity to remember, and that we can attribute memory to the family, for example, as much as to any other collective group. (p. 54)

However, even if our memories are always socially constituted, the fact of remembering being a fundamentally individual, cognitively orchestrated act still holds. The mechanisms of memory have been of interest to psychologists since the times of Ebbinghaus, Freud, and Bartlett. In the early 1930s, Bartlett argued that remembering was essentially a constructive process. Instead of paying meticulous attention to the fidelity and veracity of one's recollections, he argued, the focus ought to rest on the communicative processes that shape the form we give to our own memories and on which we ascribe meaning. Although he was critical of Halbwachs' postulation that all memory is social, he acknowledged the social dimension in individual remembering by contending that the mental schemata that orchestrate our remembering are products of our sociocultural surroundings. Moreover, the social context in which memories are retrieved influences the content of our remembrances. His focus on mental schemata and their dialectical relationship between the brain and the external world paved the way for subsequent research to approach memory as a process that is never static and more often than not characterized by its fallibility (Wagoner, 2013, 2017).

As anthropologists, we are sympathetic with Halbwachs' emphasis on the social character of human experience, yet we prefer a more nuanced approach to the collective nature of family memory that incorporates the psychologists' admonition that all actual remembering takes place in the individual. Collective memory does not simply happen as a consequence of joint experience. Furthermore, not all family memories are equally shared or equally remembered. What anthropologists and historians call "collective memory" is inherently subject to a variety of contextual contingencies and is produced through negotiated social processes, including the reification of some individuals' memories or versions of memories through the production of memory objects such as photographs, heirlooms, and stories. It also includes the marginalization and forgetting of some potential memories (Weltzer, 2005). Family memories are thus subject both to the vagaries of social negotiation and to individual differences in storytelling ability, organizing effort, and social power. In other words, all family members are not equally effective generators of family memories.

Although family memory is an aspect of both individual and collective memory, it can also be found seated at the intersection between what Jeffrey Olick (1999) deems "collective memory" and "collected memories." According to Olick, the "genuinely collective memory" is rooted in "public discourses about the past as wholes or narratives, and images of the past that speak in the name of collectivities" (p. 345). "Collected memories," in turn, refer to the accumulative individual memories that, when shared in a group, render the collective a "mnemonic community" (Zerubavel, 1996). This distinction serves as a useful tool to untangle the dichotomy between the social affordances of individual memory and the individual moorings of social memory.

We find the distinction between collective and collected memories particularly useful for our examination of family memory. For the present purposes, we recognize a necessary spectrum of sharedness in family memory and distinguish among three degrees of social memory. The first (SM1), following Halbwachs' (1992) argument, acknowledges all memory as having a degree of social influence. This is social memory in its most encompassing but weakest sense. The second type of social memory (SM2) consists of memories and practices of remembering that are socially distributed and transacted within groups. SM2 includes memories that are not necessarily fully empirically shared but that, through continuous negotiation, are woven into a collectively shared memory narrative. Finally, there is SM3, the most narrowly defined social memory concerning collective memories that are clearly reified into collective memory objects and unambiguously shared among a group.

The pyramid formed by these different strata of social memory is matched by a spectrum of three kinds of family memory. Like SM1, FM1 is the least collective form of family memory. FM1 refers to the inevitable social influence of family life on all its members' memories, even those that are not empirically shared. Most important, it functions as the ground on which the second type of family memory, FM2, is rooted. FM2 is family memory socially transacted and distributed through family talk and other concrete interactions. FM2 is made possible through continual negotiation, allowing the family to gradually create itself as a memory community. Although details and emphasis may vary among individual members of the family, FM2 includes memories that would be recognized in general terms by most family members. When shared in narratives and brought to the surface in communication, FM2 is momentarily reified, thereby creating an illusion of permanence. FM3 comprises strongly shared family memories objectively embodied in oft-repeated family stories, frequently viewed photographs, and other salient memory objects. FM3 represents a collective reservoir of collected and unchallenged family memories.

Many factors serve to enhance or prevent the full sharing of family memories. Psychologists caution that just as different storytellers or contexts of narration will affect the memories of their audience to different degrees, so too do public memorials have differential affordances for creating convergent memory effects on visitors. Coman, Brown, Koppel, and Hirst (2009) state that

> memorials can potentially change the memories of visitors one at a time, and thereby collectively all those who visit. If the change in individual memory is substantial and similar across visitors, a memorial can effectively shape the collective memory. On the other hand, if the change is minimal or different across individuals, the effect on collective memory will be minimal. The memory a person has of Jefferson is probably not changed dramatically by a visit to the Jefferson Memorial, but the image of Lincoln sitting Zeus-like in a building constructed in the style of a Greek temple is likely to remain with even the most casual tourist for years afterwards. This lasting image, replicated in the mind of each new tourist, may well serve as an anchor for the collective memory that these visitors have not only of the Lincoln Memorial, but of Lincoln himself. (pp. 128–129)

Not only do memory objects and places have different potentials for generating collective memory but also the interactional dynamics of the remembering group affect what gets remembered. Daniel Wegner (1986) considers social memory processes as "transactive memory," which he defines as "a set of individual memory systems in combination with the communication that takes place between individuals" (p. 186). For Wegner, collective memory such as that of families takes place within what he calls "transactive memory networks" (Wegner, 1986; Wegner, Erber, & Raymond, 1991; Wegner, Giuliano, & Hertel, 1985). Wegner and colleagues' theory of transactive memory involves understanding how the encoding, storing, and retrieval of information are facilitated by what previously was deemed "the group mind." In Wegner's (1986) view, collective memories are complex social transactions involving both numerous contextual contingencies and differential memory capacities and roles of individual members of the group:

If we ask a question of a person who is a well-integrated part of a transactive memory network, this person often is able to answer . . . with information well beyond his or her own internal storage. Asking any member of a family a question about the family's summer vacation, for example, can prompt the retrieval of several members' accounts of the experience. The success we have in retrieving certain items depends on the degree to which the person we begin with has location information about the items we label. Even if we ask the person to retrieve an item with an obscure label, however, the person may be able to help us enter the storage system. . . . There are a variety of potential paths to the information, and it may even be the case that no one knows, or everyone knows. Gaining entry to the group's stored knowledge is likely to be an efficient enterprise, however, even when we begin with a fairly inexpert member. This person may not have internal access to many items but is likely to have stored the main locations of information in the group.

The transactive quality of memory in a group is evident also in the transactions that take place during encoding and retrieval. In transactive encoding, people discuss incoming information, determining where and in what form it is to be stored in the group. . . . In this process, the very nature of incoming information can be changed, translated into a form that the group can store. (p. 190)

The transactive memory system is not necessarily sufficient to account for the exchanges of elaborated narratives of the past among group members. The framework of transactive memory tends to regard memories as analogous to information. This excludes the complex processes by which memories within a group are not just distributed but also can come to be shared, potentiating the collective consolidation of certain memory narratives while also sentencing others to be forgotten. Psychologists have paid increasing attention to the cognitive and social processes that enable social distribution and sharing of memory. Researchers have studied, for instance, the effects of conversational interactions and the differential influence of different narrators in affecting the "collective" memory of the group (Comen, Brown, Koppel, & Hirst, 2009; Hirst & Manier, 1996, 2008). In this vein, Hirst and Echterhoff (2008) examine the psychological groundings of collective memory through conversation practices. They contend that the existence and potential of any such thing as collective memory are rooted in the innate malleability of human memory (cf. Brockmeier, Chapter 2, this volume). This characteristic manifests itself particularly in conversations, in which the speaker–listener relationship can effectuate alterations in one's memories through social contagion, resistance, and induced forgetting. Apart from these mechanisms, the internal dynamics of the group, and the different conversational roles its members adopt can also influence what is later remembered and forgotten. Hirst, Manier, and Apetroaia (1997) have studied the "well-defined, mnemonically relevant roles" (p. 169) in family conversations. They present a model that shows how the mnemonic roles family members take as narrators, monitors, and mentors and also the dynamics between them can substantially impact the content of the narratives subsequently told and shared. Memory narratives are not fixed but, rather, actively shaped as much by the narrators as by the listeners and those who substantiate, corroborate, or dispute the contents of the story. This interactive feature anchored in intrafamilial communication is one of the most important factors giving shape to a cohesive notion of family memory.

FAMILY MEMORY AND HUMAN DEVELOPMENT

A possible objection to inclusion of family memory in the analytical toolkit of memory research is that it is an ad hoc category.[1,2] If memory can be said to organize itself around family, then why not include "cat memories" or "school memories" or any other context of remembering as basic forms of memory? Yet in relation to normal child development, secure attachment, and the formation of self-identity, family memory would seem to be far from arbitrary. Halbwachs (1992) noted that memories tend to associate with other memories and aggregate into distinct "memory systems": "It is correct that in reality memories occur in the form of systems. This is so because they become associated within the mind that calls them up, and because some memories allow the reconstruction of others" (p. 53). Because the family remains the primary context for early childhood development and a fundamental frame for identity formation for all humans, we propose that family memory represents a natural "memory system" of particular psychological and social significance. The inculcation and reinforcement of family memory through the transmission and retelling of family stories have been demonstrated to correlate significantly with other measures of psychological resilience in both children and the elderly (Bohanek, Marin, Fivush, & Duke, 2006; Caldwell, 2005; Duke, Fivush, Lazarus, & Bohanek, 2003; Fivush, Bohanek, Robertson, & Duke, 2004). From a developmental standpoint, family memory is a fundamental memory system.

Memories of family life unfold in differentiated developmental time. Family memories will inevitably be refracted not only through different family members' personal experiences and personalities but also in relation to their stage of development. In his chapter on family memory, Halbwachs (1992) emphasizes this dynamic character of family memory in relation to both the physical and social development of individuals and the developmental cycle of family life in any society:

> We might say inversely that, of the life of our parents, we know from direct experience only the part that begins several years after our birth. What precedes hardly interests us. In turn, when we ourselves become husbands and fathers, we pass through a series of states through which we have seen them also pass, and it seems that we can then identify ourselves with what they were at that time. But this still does not say enough. There is a whole period, which corresponds to the beginnings of the new household, when the new

family opposes the former family precisely because it is new and because it seems that it must create an original memory outside the traditional framework. (p. 80)

In other words, a grandparent's experience of family events will inevitably be very different from that of the grandchildren, as will that of children in different positions of birth order. These dramatic differences can be reduced somewhat by the existence of common family stories and other memory objects such as photographs, which provide a degree of shared perspective for family members on their family life.

Repeated family events such as vacations or ritual celebrations provide a shared framework for families within which individuals can update their identities in the context of family over developmental time. Shore (2008) has described the long-term memory effects of annual attendance at a camp meeting in north Georgia, where families return year after year to the same cabins on the same campground for spiritual and family renewal. The relatively stable setting and routine of camp meeting provide a fixed backdrop against which individuals assess the passage of their lives, and their families, and achieve a measure of identity updating. An elderly lady, a lifelong camper, described her experience as follows (as quoted in Shore, 2008):

> And it's funny because when you're young, you don't ever think about that. I mean these kids out here now, anybody below the age of like 20 is flat out playing, having fun and milking it for all it's worth. You know, but when you get older you begin to see that and you know it, especially if you're prone to notice that kind of thing, which I am. You can't help but notice it. That it's like you think: "Is that so and so or is that their son?" You know, that kind of thing. Especially when you're as old as I am because you know kids that I watched growing up have children now. I mean, you know. That's the way it works. And it has always been striking to me. Look at that picture. I've got all these little girls and my cousins, I've got pictures of all of them doing exactly the same thing that I was doing then. That is the thing about camp meeting. There is nothing like it. I can't think of anything like it. (pp. 113–114)

This is the effect of ritualized time and space. The simultaneous effects of stability and change, with new individuals occupying old slots, create a special context whereby the passage of time is at once blurred and acknowledged, and both collective and personal identities are updated.

As in the previous example, identity updating in modern Western societies often features older generations remembering themselves as young through contact with their grandchildren. As grandparents, they update their identities in multiple ways, coming to terms with their new status as generational elders but at the same time replaying to some extent their roles as parents and even recalling their own childhoods. Identity updating of the young through identification of the young with elders or ancestors is more common in traditional societies, in which there are more experiential continuities between old and young.

Early childhood memories are almost exclusively family memories. The earliest family memories for infants are preverbal, including early childhood memories encoded as sounds, images, and smells. A child's earliest memories are often subject to what has been called childhood amnesia, the inability of most children to recall memories of things that happened when they were younger than age 3½ years (Rubin, 2000). There appears to be both cultural and individual variation in the effects of childhood amnesia (Peterson, 2002; Peterson, Wang, & Hou, 2009). Memory researchers have suggested a variety of factors contributing to childhood amnesia, including neurological development; the emergence of a theory of mind (Welch-Ross, 1995); the emergence of a coherent sense of self (Conway & Pleydell-Pearce, 2000); and the acquisition of the ability to encode and understand experiences in language, especially in relation to maternal reminiscing (Nelson & Fivush, 2004; Peterson et al., 2009).

The phenomenon of childhood amnesia makes it difficult to ascertain exactly when family memory begins, depending on how far back childhood amnesia reaches for different individuals and whether one is willing to consider "forgotten" experiences that are not subject to verbal recall as memories. Early family memories will likely be those that have been encoded, preserved, and amplified by recording devices such as language (caretaker reminiscence) and photography.

A basic kind of routinized family memory is established through repeated routines that make up family life. For infants, the earliest routines are the simple "ritual" interactions that caregivers establish within the first months of an infant's life. In American culture, these ritualized interactions comprise peek-a-boo sequences and similar micro-rituals, which can scaffold the later development of more complex interactive routines (Garvey, 1977/1990; Piaget, 1962). These nonverbal or partially verbal micro-rituals are the elementary building blocks of episodic memory for children, and they provide the cognitive foundation for the earliest memory of family routine.

Once a child begins to use language, family memories inevitably become subject to conventional encoding and great elaboration. Events that repeat themselves are evoked through verbal labels, and toddlers learn to distinguish between expected events and unique or unexpected events. The latter produce fear or laughter or both. In this way, family life, and therefore family memory, becomes subject to being organized through typical event units that are the atoms of a young child's family routines. "Bath time," "nap time," and "time to eat" are some of the earliest event types in the life of the American toddler, and these become the basis of a generalized memory of family routine. Events can be organized into increasingly larger units, and as the child grows older, this kind of event chunking can be elaborated into a complex event structure that frames the episodic side of family memory.

THE ARCHITECTURE OF FAMILY MEMORY

As memory becomes "narrativized," family memory is subject to being organized through the chunking of events into coherent and repeatable "event clusters." Norman Brown (2005) characterizes event clusters as

> narrative-like memory structures that draw together information about events that are causally or thematically related. . . . Prior research indicates that these clusters play an important role in the organization of autobiographical memory and suggests that cluster formation is a by-product of normal processes required to plan, execute, evaluate, and discuss meaningful event sequences. (pp. 35–36)

Martin Conway and Helen Williams (2008) have extended the concept of event clusters into an elaborate schema of layered and embedded event structures of different timescales and themes to outline a basic architecture for autobiographical memory (see also Conway, 1997). Their schema organizes individuals' life stories into "life themes" (e.g., work and relationships) and "lifetime periods" (e.g., "high school years" and "my first marriage"). Both domains are associated with "general events" (e.g., "pay raise," "getting fired," and "dating"). Specific episodic memories are then associated with these general event types. It would be interesting to test this schema cross-culturally. Clearly, the specific categories framing autobiographical memory would be subject to considerable local and cultural variation, but the proposed general architecture might well be a cognitive universal.

Shore (2009) has studied the framing of episodic family memory in middle-class American family conversation and distinguishes between two kinds of family memory: specific events and generalized "routine" memories that take the form "we used to . . ." or "we always . . ." (p. 97), which are narrated in "ritual time" rather than "historical time." Shore divides the events of "lifetime periods" into epochal memories ("during my childhood"), "extended events" ("my senior year"), and "specific events" ("my junior prom night"). This chunking process is central to the organization of family memory, although the specific categories used will be historically and culturally variable.

In their study of autobiographical memory in adult men, Mihaly Csikszentmihalyi and Olga Beattie (1979) proposed that people organized their memories around general "life themes"—recurrent existential issues and problems that they sought to resolve. This raises the question of whether family narratives are also organized around such life themes. Although adult family narratives in the West do seem to manifest recurrent general themes, research on adolescents suggests that their autobiographical memory only becomes organized around coherent themes at approximately age 15 years (Habermas & Paha, 2001). This suggests a basic change in the organization of family memory as a function of the emergence of a stable conception of self. It also suggests the difference between family memory understood as a collective artifact of family life (as articulated by adults) and the heterogeneous collection of family memories of different individuals (and different generations) within a family.

COLLECTIVE ANCHORS FOR FAMILY MEMORY

Family memory is organized in relation to a wide variety of mnemonic artifacts. Family stories, photographs, rituals, landmark events, and places are well-known cognitive anchors for family identity. Often overlooked as a mnemonic for structuring family memory are taxonomic schemata such as genealogies and kinship terminologies. These taxonomies often encode aspects of family memory that are related to social class and status. Genealogies appear in cultural history with the rise of chiefdoms and elaborate social hierarchies in which social rank is justified in relation to noble or divine descent (Goldman, 1970, 1975; Sahlins, 1963). In many societies, descent group genealogies were part of oral history and were often kept by specialists, but with the advent of writing, genealogies were commonly written as part of recorded family histories.

Whereas extensive genealogies are found only in societies with marked status inequality, kin terminologies are ubiquitous. They provide mental maps for individuals to coordinate their family identities with others. Universally kin terminologies include both referential terminologies and terms of address. Referential terminologies (e.g., Mother, Father, Grandmother, Aunt, and Cousin) allow individuals to identify the family relationship of any two individuals whether to themselves or to others. They provide a perspective-neutral framework for classifying and thus remembering kin relations. On the other hand, terms of address (e.g., Mom, Granny, Sis, and Pop) allow for egocentric mappings of kin relationships, and thus these terms tend to be more contextually variable and subject to change compared to terms of reference (Shore, 2012). Commonly, people creatively extend the use of kin terms beyond the range of actual family members as a way of incorporating outsiders into the intimacy and moral obligations of family life.

Naming and kin terms not only afford remembering family relationships but also can afford social forgetting. A notable case of culturally mediated genealogical amnesia was documented for Bali by Hildred and Clifford Geertz (1964) in their study of Balinese teknonymy. Teknonymy is the practice of renaming parents ("father/mother of X") after the birth of children. These practices in Bali are normal for families of commoner status, shifting attention away from the historical depth and continuity of their lineages to an emphasis on their production of offspring rather than ancestors. Significantly, according to the authors, this teknonymy is not generally practiced by aristocratic families, who are known by enduring family titles that anchor them to the past rather than the future.

Through naming systems, kin terminologies, landmark events, and other commemorations, family memory is structured by an interesting combination of linear and cyclical time frames. Some memory artifacts, such as genealogies, family histories, photographs, and landmark places and events, contribute to a linear structure of family time as episodic. On the other hand, recurrent mnemonics such as repeated personal names and regular ritual events scaffold a more cyclical sense of family time. The best documented cultural model of cyclical family (kinship) time is the Australian aboriginal conception of "the dreamtime" or "the dreaming." Through complex combinations of ritual and myth in traditional Aboriginal groups, the unique developmental trajectories of individual lives are brought into relationship with recurrent cycles of social regeneration (Shore, 1996, Chapters 9 and 10; Stanner, 1966, 2011).

In modern Western contexts, landmark anniversary celebrations (e.g., sweet sixteen, the Latin American *quinceañera*, the silver wedding anniversary, and the centennial birthday) also provide an experience of family time that is simultaneously cyclical (in the form of familiar recurrent celebration) and linear (for the lives of the specific individuals celebrated). This mix of recurrent and unique time landmarks is a significant characteristic of family memory with important implications for the creation of stable identities incorporating change and continuity for family members.

An interesting variation of mnemonic family practices involves individuals who are conceived and treated as memory objects, embodied stand-ins for ancestors or deceased siblings. The most common way in which this identification is effected is through naming an infant after a dead relative, but there are many ways in which a child can be identified with an ancestor. Children can be conceived (consciously or unconsciously) as replacements for siblings or other family members who died before they were born. This sort of replacement identity can be experienced by the replacing individual as a form of identification with a family member he or she never knew and, depending on circumstances, grasped as either a positive aspect of the individual's identity or a troubling disruption of identity.

CLASS AND FAMILY MEMORY

Our treatment of genealogy and other forms of kin classification highlights the centrality of social stratification in the constitution of social memory. To our knowledge, there has been little comparative research done on different socioeconomic classes in terms of family memory. Moreover, we acknowledge that most of the work cited in this chapter focuses on Euro-American middle-class families. Although this does not imply that family memory practices are prevalent only in middle-class working families, we recognize that many of the memory practices discussed in this chapter are rooted in certain class privileges such as leisure time and purchasing power.

Annette Lareau (2003) maintains that middle-class families tend to spend less time together as a group than lower-middle-class and poorer families. The former organize their daily lives according to the family calendar, children's activities, and the parents' busy work schedules. Yet perhaps precisely because of this, they also focus more on concerted efforts to make time for the family (Daly, 2001). The middle-class family, as Gillis (2002) notes, is the family we live *by*, thus needing to be actively constructed in specific instances in order for it to match the ideal of the family we aspire to live *with*.

According to Lareau (2003), working-class family life revolves less around children's schedules because the family calendar is not dominated by the (over)scheduling of children's activities. Families of lower socioeconomic classes spend more time together as a family by virtue of usually occupying a smaller living space and having more unscheduled time. "Family time" thus unfolds as more spontaneous. What remains to be studied for working-class families are the kinds of memory work in which families engage and the kinds of memory narratives that emerge when the efforts to live by an idea of family are less concerted and more unselfconscious.

Although working-class and poor families may spend more time together as a family, they may also have fewer opportunities to engage in family conversations around the dinner table if both parents work different shifts. Similarly, chances to go on vacation may be scarce due to economic constraints. On the other end of the socioeconomic spectrum, we can also identify aristocratic and upper-class families with long traceable lineages. The emphasis on genealogy among wealthy, historically established families is usually less present among middle- and lower-class families. As Halbwachs (1992) argues, lineage and inheritance have, since the Middle Ages, served as the main definers of nobility and have found their way onto maps of collective memory. Thus, as porters of remembrances of who and what the family is, inherited titles, land, and knowledge of important past figures in the family shape the memories aristocratic families have of themselves and actively cultivate for the future.

In discussing family memory in terms of genealogies or heritage lines, we admittedly run the risk of equating family memory with recorded family history. Remembrances can, of course, be attached to ancestral portraits, possessed property, or inherited titles. However, family memory, as it is practiced by families, emerges in interactions between family members in which such material carriers of memory trigger and facilitate the interactive memory work. These practices can occur in any family with explicit or tacit interest in understanding and preserving its sense of self and projecting that self onto the future.

Where social classes come into play is in shaping the content of family memory, as well as in determining the kinds of environments that call for that memory to surface. Moreover, class can function as an important regulator of the narrative templates used to recount family stories. Whether modeled on positive upward mobility, economic success across generations, or resistance of the working class, the blueprints undergirding the shape of family narratives are an important factor in families' identity construction and in determining how family memories acquire their salience.

FAMILY NARRATIVE

Among the most common and best-studied anchors of family memory are narratives. Both family memory and practices of remembering often crystallize in specific narratives of the past. Family members reminisce about past times they have spent together, remind each other of specific past events, or discuss relatives who have already passed away. Some narratives are shaped by specific events, whereas others are framed in relation to recurrent events and celebrations that constitute the ritual life of families.

Family narratives are also anchored by landmark events. Landmarks events can be unique, such as births, deaths, or family tragedies, but family memories can also be grounded in recurrent events, such as family vacations, first days of school, or holidays. Family rituals such as family dinners, birthdays, holidays, special meals, and religious observances are significant ways in which families actively create frameworks for joint memory and narrative among family members and in which families can provide a degree of coordination between their actual lives and their idealized sense of how families should be (Fiese, 2006; Gillis, 1996a, 1996b).

Shared narratives are subject to both contestations and agreements. Individual members may have very differing memories of an empirically shared event. By conversing about them, members of the family can weave the discrepancies into a single coherent and generally accepted narrative. These specific narratives then serve as important markers that help draw the family's territories of inclusion and exclusion. The family congeals itself within the boundaries of its own narratives that fasten a sense of belonging. While serving as open and negotiated channels to a shared past, the narratives also reinforce the frontiers between the family as a private, organic mini-universe and the social world surrounding it. In short, memory narratives provide the family with a sense of identity and warrant the use of an emphatic "we": "We, the Johnsons" or "We, the Camachos."

Narrative, as it is most widely used, refers to an account of connected events or experiences. It is a story with a beginning and an end that is placed in specific time and space. It may or may not concern events the storyteller has personally experienced and thus uniquely embodies a sliding scale between episodic and semantic memories (Cappelletto, 2003). Such narratives are what James Wertsch (2008; see also Wertsch, Chapter 11, this volume) deems "specific narratives." Narrative can also refer to what Wertsch calls a "schematic narrative template." The theory of schemata and their relationship to memory was first formulated by Frederic Bartlett (1932/1995). He argued that "schema refers to an active organization . . . of past experiences, which must always be supposed to be operating in any well-adapted organic response" (p. 201). Schemata, according to Bartlett, undergird patterned behavior and thinking, regulating the relationship between distinct categories by which one's "well-adapted organic responses" are organized and executed (Bartlett, 1932/1995, p. 201; see also Wagoner, 2013, 2017).

Jerome Bruner (1990) has examined the role these schemata play in folk psychology. He contends that if mental schemata organize our thinking, behavior, and memories, what enables these mental processes and social practices to have meaning is our capacity to process them through a specific narrative frame. Narrative in Bruner's grip is not simply a story told and shared but also a structuring principle for our thoughts, experiences, and memories that is as canonical as it is diachronic.

The schematic narrative template refers to the models and patterns that structure and underpin the stories we tell. As Wertsch (2008) notes, these templates are not universal but, rather, culturally contingent. Neither are they modeled after any specific past event. "Instead," Wertsch writes, "each takes the form of a generalized schema that is in evidence when talking about any one of several episodes" (p. 123). This resonates strongly in how family memory narratives are structured. Shore (2009), for example, points out how in middle-class American family life the idea of economic upward mobility is often paralleled with the family's residential mobility, as well as generational dispersal. Ascending (or descending) the economic ladder becomes a narrative trope that structures American middle-class family narratives. The "chapters" of the American family narrative are often organized by houses and neighborhoods, indexing the family's changing economic fortunes. The middle-class American family narrative undergirds and gives shape to event-specific memories of residential relocations, children leaving home for college, or parents' change of jobs. It may also serve as a central trope for general life-theme memories. Consider the following example from Shore's fieldwork with middle-class families in Georgia:

> We were real blue collar. I grew up in middle class, lived in a little tiny brick house. Mother and Daddy worked hard, they were really, really hard workers. And gave me lots of things and I think the reason they did is because they grew up and didn't have a lot of things. (p. 100)

The structuring narrative schemata behind family narratives thus become like a meta-text that gives family identity its general orientation.

Memory narratives are not mere descriptions of the past. They offer an evaluative and explanatory view to the past whose meaning is relative to the circumstances surrounding the act of narrating, as well as to the narrator him- or herself. It is therefore not simply the fact of shared experiences within family that enhances the salience of family narratives but also the shared interpretative framework that makes those experiences meaningful. Developmental psychologists have shown keen interest in examining the relationship between family narratives and child development (Fivush, 2007). It has been established that active reminiscing between parents and children is causally linked to children's well-being, sense of self (Pratt, Norris, Hebblethwaite, & Arnold, 2008), development of their autobiographical memories (Edwards & Middleton, 1988; Farrant & Reese, 2000), and development of young adults' social skills (McLean, 2005). Fiese and Marjinsky (1999), for example, contend that the qualitatively positive narratives parents tell their children about their own childhoods and families help ground the children's disposition to relate to their surrounding world. The qualifiers embedded in and

the meanings attributed to recounted memory narratives therefore play an important role in the family's internal dynamics. However, they also serve as fertilizer
and building material for the younger family members' developing identities and
accruing memories.

NARRATIVE IN PRACTICE

When, and on what kinds of occasions, do family narratives surface? We make
a distinction between those instances in which families internally reminisce
about their own past and those in which the past is shared with outsiders (see
also Favart-Jardon, 2002). Although the narratives in both scenarios can be substantially the same, their function varies slightly. Internally shared family narratives are centripetally orchestrated; they foster inclusivity. This inclusivity is
not, however, necessarily predicated on consensual and uniform understandings of the shared past. One of family memory's distinguishing characteristics is
that it materializes in a space that actively promotes negotiation.[3] However, the
environment—the family—in which this negotiation takes place is normally characterized by relatively stable kinship relations. Discrepancies in family narratives
do not necessarily threaten the basic integrity of the family but, rather, keep the
family's memory of itself in perpetual motion. Family narratives told to outsiders,
in turn, tend to present a more fixed version of a given narrative, congealed, as it
were, in some kind of factual format. Their meaning is less subject to negotiation
because they serve the purpose of reifying the idea of family in a way that makes
clear its boundaries of inclusion and exclusion. The emphatic "we" is thus vested
with a sense of identity that marks it to the outside world as a social unit synonymous with belonging.

Internally shared family narratives take place in a myriad of situations in which
the family is gathered together, be it on a special occasion or in a very quotidian
context (Gillis, 2002). Most of us can think of an event spent with our family—for
example, an anniversary, a wedding, or Christmas or other religious holiday—
during which at some point the conversation was geared toward the past, turning
into a polyphonic reminiscing that substantiates the present. Intrafamilial memory narratives and narrative practices have been studied particularly in the context of family dinnertime conversations[4] (Bohanek et al., 2009; Fiese & Marjinsky,
1999; Fivush, 2007). Although the focus in these studies is on the effect of the
narratives on child development, they also suggest the particular kinds of narratives that are shared. Bohanek et al., for example, discovered that contrary to the
assumption that dinnertime narratives would mostly concern mundane, everyday
events, a considerable part of them also included memories pertaining to a more
remote past. In other words, families actively share stories that encompass a depth
of time that is not limited to the most recent past but also delves into past times
that exist both within and beyond the family members' organic memory.

Memory narratives are in constant flux. Just as the memories they articulate,
narratives are shaped by the circumstances in which they are told and by the

people who tell and listen to them. Although narratives express memories and infuse them with meaning, they can also alter the memories themselves. This renders family memory an inherently emergent process. It materializes in instances of communication and in the narratives that glue memories onto the present. Yet it is not only the memories that materialize in narratives but also the very idea of the family as a memory community. One of the undergirding motives for intrafamilial reminiscing, we argue, is to reify the idea of the family as a concrete entity that cultivates belonging while also harboring a promise of continuity. The existence of this collectively experienced sense of unity is contingent upon the instances in which it is communicated. Family memory becomes a memory object insofar as it is collectively shared, and its durability is tied to the length of the instances of sharing.

COMMEMORATIVE PRACTICES

The onset of the industrial era introduced a new spatiotemporal organization in traditional family life. This novel sense of time was also reflected in the family calendar, which began to revolve around marked dates for birthdays, christenings, weddings, Christmas, and so on. These traditions, whose history Gillis (2002) traces no further back than the Victorian era, have become the primary sites for the family not only to imagine itself but also for a brief moment to experience itself as it is imagined.

Following Gillis (2002), we suggest that the spatiotemporal reorganization of the family laid the foundations for present practices and imaginations of family memory. Families began to remember themselves through the lens of nostalgia while actively creating occasions for both present and future reminiscence. These occasions, usually highly ritualized, may fit Nora's (1989) definition of *lieux de mémoire*. Yet rather than environments devoid of what Nora called "true remembering," families' commemorative practices can also be seen as a historically reinvented way of remembering. Significant events marked on the family calendar create temporal memory environments that encourage revisiting the past in ways that make the family feel concrete, real, and perpetual in the present. The particular ritual structure of these events, comprising customs and practices to which the family members have been habituated since childhood, ensures their relative stability. That sense of stability, in turn, allows for the family to think of and commemorate itself as a unit with certain social and temporal fixity.

Think of Thanksgiving, the quintessential American family celebration. Thanksgiving is for Americans a rite of reincorporation, in which a normally dispersed family reaggregates and takes stock of itself as a fragile ongoing corporation. Similarly, in most Christian areas of the world, Christmas is celebrated not only as a religious holiday but also as an occasion for family members to come together as the family they do not necessarily live *with* but live *by* (Gillis, 2002). The scripts such family occasions often follow provide the event with structural organization that undergirds the recounting of stories and reminiscing they cultivate. Similarly, these scripts underpin practices, such as cooking, sitting at the dinner table, or gift exchanges, that are powerful family mnemonics.

PROSPECTIVE MEMORY

Commemorative occasions and the practices they entail are not just past-oriented, memory-laden environments that prompt the emergence and materialization of family memory in the present. They are also important sites for the making of anticipated future memories. David Sutton (2008) has examined this so-called prospective memory in the context of Easter fasting and the preparation of the Easter feast in Greece. The discussions about the feast while the fast is still occurring, and the preparation of the meal itself, conceal a deliberate planning to make the occasion memorable enough for it not to be forgotten in the future by the younger generations. It is thus less the feast itself than its planning and preparation that seamlessly weave together the past, the present, and the anticipated future. Prospective social memory points to a family's conscious need and desire to ensure the group's future memorability. Family memory in this sense escapes the confines of a past-oriented, often nostalgic framework created within the present and becomes a proactive process aiming to guarantee continuity.

Prospective social memory in the family context is not limited to commemorative occasions, despite these being particularly fertile sites for manufacturing future memories. Kerry Daly's (2001) research on "family time" analyzes the deliberate production of future memories as a key element also in the more ordinary moments families spend together and the time parents make for their children. Daly writes that time, as it is experienced in families, has a strong dialectical quality. It is at once intersubjective, a "socially created reality that shapes activity and action in the world" (p. 284), and also normative, a reality that is socially constrained and filled with organizational demands pertaining to schedules and family timetables. The intersubjective dimension of family time features strongly in families' idealizations of how they would like to spend their time together. Moreover, these idealizations are often conditioned by memories (or idealized versions) of the past that the parents themselves have lived and wish to have their children experience as well.

Daly's (2001) findings suggest that the way (American) families try to make time for themselves is strongly guided by parents' desires to instill future memories in their children. Dictated by working parents' hectic schedules, the time that families do spend together unfolds as a fragmented race against time itself. The often unfulfilled desire to spend more time together as a family is then compensated by an equally strong desire to provide stability and continuity for the idea of family in the future. In that sense, making time for the family as a planned effort implies the shaping of the family as a memory community for future purposes.

One of the most significant ways of immortalizing the present in the service of the future is through photography. As modernity took its toll on the traditional family unit, introducing a novel dimension of distance and absence, photography arrived at its rescue. The growth of children, landmark events in family history, and the family's absent members were increasingly memorialized on photographic film and paper. Photography became an inseparable feature of important family occasions, a witness that would verify and attest to the perpetuity of those occasions and, by extension, of the family itself. Whether kept in messy drawers, hung on walls, or compiled in family albums, photographs reminded families of their dispersed relatives, as well as the past they shared (Sontag, 1977). Although photographic practice has undergone considerable changes since Kodak's introduction of the Brownie, families' tendency to document their lives has, if anything, become easier, quicker, and cheaper. What remains to be further studied is how the onset of the digital era has changed the practices of *viewing* images and whether image-saturated technological devices have effectively made images less conducive to reminiscing, especially in the familial sphere.[5]

FAMILY MEMORY AND TRAUMA

It would be misleading to conceptualize family memory only in terms of the sense of unity and belonging it can cultivate. Family memories can be punctured by past disruptions and challenges, or shattered by experiences of trauma, whether collective or individual. Family narratives can serve as important mediators of these past disruptions, enabling family members collectively to make sense of their past difficulties (Denham, 2008). Often, however, memories of past challenges in general, and traumatic experiences in particular, are enveloped in a taut silence. This not only torpedoes collective efforts to come to terms with such troublesome memories but also inhibits their incorporation into the wider family narratives. And yet past traumatic events can seep into individual family members' own memories and be transmitted just like any other, more explicitly shared memory narratives.

How traumatic memories are intergenerationally transmitted has been the subject of considerable interest, especially among clinical psychologists. Holocaust survivors' children and grandchildren have been found to bear the sequelae of their parents' (and grandparents') traumatic experiences, even when—or perhaps precisely because—these experiences have not been explicitly discussed within the family (Fossion, Rejas, Servais, Pelc, & Hirsch, 2002). The impression that an "unspeakable" event has left in the individual may manifest itself, for example, in dysfunctional parenting behavior, such as overprotectiveness, or impaired sense of intimacy (Kellermann, 2001). Children whose upbringing has been marked by the tacit presence of the parents' past trauma may come to manifest sentiments of guilt or compensatory safety for their parents that stem from the vicariously absorbed parents' memories (Cohen, Brom, & Dasberg, 2001). In this vein, psychologists have also studied the mechanisms that render post-traumatic stress disorder (PTSD) potentially heritable. Children's long-term exposure to the parents' symptoms of PTSD can make them susceptible to assimilating these to a degree to which the children themselves begin to manifest symptoms of psychosocial distress (Kellermann, 2001, 2013). Dysfunctional behavior models or intergenerational symptoms of PTSD may not represent explicit recollections. However, their presence can become intrinsically woven into the many forms in which family memory is embodied.

Family memory of past trauma and loss poignantly illustrates the conflicting dynamics between forgetting and remembering. Parents' proactive attempts to forget their own experiences of trauma may reflect in the children's heightened necessity to know more about it. Marianne Hirsch (2008) calls the second generation's need to know and understand its parents' past "postmemory." The implicit presence of the first generation's ineffable past seeps into the children's imagination. This leads to the parents' recollections merging with the children's own memory. Although qualitatively different from real recollections, these "imagined" memories nevertheless harbor a sense of realness for their second-generation porters. These memories may not be topics of intrafamilial narration, let alone reminiscing, but they can be powerful anchors in the family's mnemonic horizon that explain and structure its identity.

Purposive silencing of a difficult past may not always engender negative consequences. Janet Carsten (1995), for example, has studied the importance of forgetting among immigrant families in Malaysia. Having been deleted from family narratives, the families' past trajectories were gradually erased from family memory. Families in this context actively cultivate an attitude that is first and foremost future oriented, thereby reducing the importance of the past that the generations beyond the living had experienced. Although silence regarding a problematic past has often been deemed negative, especially within the Western therapeutic framework, its potentially positive implications merit further research. It may well be that a family's coping mechanisms with regard to past distressing experiences by one or many of its members are cultural and context specific, thereby challenging paradigms that privilege voice over silence (Kidron, 2009).

ON MEMORY AND PLACE

It is easy to evoke a mental image of some particular place, such as a childhood home, that immediately kindles strong memories. Moreover, going to such places can trigger a plethora of sensory-based recollections that quickly cohere into more intelligible remembrances. The intimate relationship between memory and place is not only a function of ordinary lived experience. It has also been harnessed in the form of commemorative sites, memorials, and other physical places with the explicit aim of imparting and eliciting elements, images, and experiences from the past. As previously mentioned, Pierre Nora (1989) illustrates the spatial constitution of collective memories through his famous distinction between *les lieux* and *milieux de mémoire*. Modernity, he argues, has confined memory to specific, special purpose sites where "memory crystallizes and secretes itself" (p. 7). These sites of memory have replaced what Nora calls the "real environments of memory."

John Gillis (2002) suggests that modernity has changed what Nora calls memory's real environments by infusing them with a past- and future-oriented sense of time and space. In the preindustrial era, the family household defined the family's existence and served as the primary locus of the family's being. The household existed, Gillis writes, "without much sense of its own past or future, with a profound sense of being, but little sense of becoming" (p. 3). The arrival of modernity reorganized the family's spatiotemporal configuration by placing its existence on a linear timescale with a much wider horizon of both past and future. In so doing, it transformed the household from a locus of being to a locus of memories and dreams. The family home, then, gradually turned into the family's lived archive. It became a place to store and exhibit its past through material culture, as if to reconfirm its existence. And rather than simply housing the family in real time and space, the home became the material repository of the family's memory—a site that provided it with an illusion of stability and permanence while harboring dreams for continuity and persistence (see also Bachelard, 1958/1994).

The modern Western family's tendency toward spatial dispersion has conferred a special aura of nostalgia on the idea of the family household. As a physical place that once existed—the childhood home—it grounds remembrances and images we cultivate of the family. As a space inhabited in the present, it often houses material elements from the family's history, serving as a memorious map that describes and explains the family's genealogy and narratives of its past. The family household features distinctive spaces that organize mnemonic content according to its specific functions. The predominant spatial configuration in Western homes divides the layout into areas meant for more public use (e.g., the living/dining room) and spaces that are more personal and private (e.g., bedrooms). This spatial stratification is also reflected in the placement of memory objects. Mementos and images placed in the public areas of the house tend to symbolize those family relationships or salient moments from the family's past that are deemed appropriate for public consumption. Objects kept in the more private areas tend to embody family members' more intimate memories. In bedrooms, for example, items kept on dressers or bed stands have an ambiguous status as public–private memory objects. Although private, they are nonetheless suitable for display. On the other hand, memory objects with the potential of being embarrassingly personal tend to be kept hidden in drawers or closets (Petrelli & Whittaker, 2010).

In terms of the family home's spatial configuration, the kitchen often sets itself apart. A space with a particular function, it rarely serves as a public display room for the family's memorabilia. Yet perhaps more than other areas of the house, the kitchen is a particularly memorious space, harboring the potential to be, in Nora's (1989) words, a "real environment for memory." Cooking is often noted as a conduit of memory transmission, an embodied practice that transfers not only skill and technique but also distinct recipes or particular uses and understandings of ingredients and flavors that may have existed in the family for generations (Collings Eves, 2005; Sutton, 2008; Sutton & Hernandez, 2007; see also Seremetakis, 1993). Although cooking can create an environment for active reminiscing, the practice itself allows for the past to be enacted and transmitted in the present.[6]

MATERIAL CULTURE

Material objects can serve as powerful conduits for memory. Whether heirlooms that have stayed within the family for generations or mementos purchased as souvenirs during a holiday trip, material items can become strong memory objects that crystallize family memory in its strongest sense (FM3). Heirlooms, just like the narratives that explain and concretize different meanings attributed to them, are important indexical symbols of family memory. They are tangible objects that support and mediate ideas of the family's shared heritage and present identity while sustaining social relations as they are bequeathed from one generation to another (Odom et al., 2012). The older the heirloom, the greater the durability. The intergenerational circulation of these objects defines kin groups' boundaries, as well as power relations (Curasi, Price, & Arnould, 2004).

Family heirlooms are often noted for their capacity to serve as transmitters of memories. They attract the resuscitation and reconstruction of the past through the stories and reminiscing they can evoke. The meaning material objects contain is not intrinsic. It is created, activated, and bestowed upon the object through narratives that may unlock the item's mnemonic potential. The meaning is also produced by the object's application or consumption (Miller, 1987). By serving as *aides mémoires*, objects lend themselves to discursive interpretation while facilitating past-oriented reminiscing and nostalgia. Their capacity to serve as vehicles of family memory transmission is multilayered, composed of both narrative and embodied practices. Kidron (2009), for example, posits that material culture and the practices revolving around it speak in parallel with storytelling. A spoon that a Holocaust survivor has kept from Auschwitz and then used to feed her own children becomes a powerful mnemonic object that is used to enact and convey memories of survival through its application in the everyday life (Kidron, 2009).

Often, heirlooms are treated as objects of such value that their use is limited to special occasions. Items of specific religious significance are rescued from their storage for religious celebrations; the four-generation-old silverware or inherited jewelry see the light of day during weddings or other important festivities. Although such objects can have a significant market price, their value is primarily defined through their long-term presence and ownership within the family. In contrast to family heirlooms of more ordinary use, the special quality conferred on objects that are less quotidian sets them aside as *lieux de mémoire* (Sokolova, 2013). Their mnemonic capacity reveals itself ceremoniously in family rituals that accentuate their significance. That significance, in turn, stems from and is re-created through a shared knowledge and understanding of the family's past and familial relationships.[7]

The range of material culture embodying family memory is not limited to heirlooms. Mementoes whose time depth in the family's mnemonic horizon may not be so far-reaching (e.g., souvenirs from past holidays), and that have not yet become heirlooms, can also strengthen a sense of shared past. Perhaps more than any other memory object, family photographs are a particularly important material component of and contributor to family memory. A visual testament to that which has existed, photographs are not only repositories of memory but also sites for "performances of memory" (Kuhn, 2010).

Photographs are discursive objects whose mnemonic affordances materialize in the narratives and storytelling they evoke. In most societies, family photography has become commonplace, creating a cumulative archive of visual material that testifies to the family's past experiences. Just like many other memory objects, family photographs afford their viewers and/or exhibitors a sense of visual ownership of their past. The capacity of photographs to evoke the past is more pronounced for their beguiling (yet somewhat deceptive) lack of mediation. Rather than serving as metaphors, or being necessarily subject to interpretation, photographs appear as direct, albeit two-dimensional effigies of past moments, experiences, or people.

Family photographs are alluring because they stimulate remembrances and imaginative reconstructions of the past. The room they leave for imagination and interpretation is restricted by familiarity, or their quality as something familial. We look at our own family photographs with a status of an insider; we recognize a plethora of implications present in a family photograph, even if the image was taken much before our birth. This insider's gaze is what Marianne Hirsch (1997) calls the "affiliative look." The examined photograph allows for the viewer to inhabit the image and the narratives it evokes, while the image and its associated stories are at the same time incorporated into the viewer's family narrative.[8] Family photographs, whether of a past family gathering some years back or of great-grandparents now long gone, are effectively direct evidence of the past. But more important, they are visual, material "certificates of presence" (Barthes, 1981) that illustrate and enable the validation and reconfirmation of the family as a memory community.

Whereas singular photographs serve as powerful sites for memory performances through the narratives they elicit, family albums tend to entail an additional dimension of memory work. According to Martha Langford (2001, 2006), the show-and-tell performance that family albums tend to trigger is underpinned by the narrative organization of the albums. Langford (2006) suggests that family albums speak of their compilers' "expression of autobiographical and collective memory through image selection, annotation and organization" (p. 227). In other words, an album is the compiler's deliberate creation of specific, visual memory narratives that organize the family's past according to the compiler's criteria of relevance. The family album reveals itself as an object meant for future reanimation of the past with a predetermined narrative form.

Although heterogeneous memory objects continue to figure prominently as repositories of and catalysts for memory, family memory's material dimension has also become increasingly colonized by digital technology. Families often face the question of what to do with their deceased members' personal technology that may contain important tokens of the past, such as photographs or videos. Research, however, shows that rarely do these devices—computers, mobile phones, and so on—acquire the status of memory objects or keepsakes for future generations (Petrelli & Whittaker, 2010). They are considered as less valuable and heterogeneous than physical mementos that have traveled within the family across generations. The increasing obsolescence of particular digital devices due to the rapidity of innovation has weakened their status as objects with which individuals can personally identify. Moreover, their function is considered purely mediatory, which renders the technological devices in themselves less important. Massimi and Baecker (2010) have confirmed this in their study of how technologies are used by bereaved families and of family members' attitudes toward the digital devices they have inherited. Unlike a keepsake, such as a personal memento, a piece of jewelry, or even a postcard, digital devices are seemingly devoid of their past user's personal imprint.

SENSORY BASES OF MEMORY

The fact that some memory objects have powerful mnemonic affordances, whereas others, such as digital devices, do not raises the question of the sensory bases of family memory. Memory has been classified into the following distinct sensory modalities: haptic memory, encoded through touch and body movement; olfactory memory, the encoding of smells in memory associations (Schab, 1991; Schab & Crowder, 1995); iconic memory, the short-term recall of visual imagery; and echoic memory, the memory of auditory signals, particularly important in verbal imitation and recall (Ardila, Montanes, & Gempeler, 1986). Although all these sensory modalities play an important role in the human memory system, what often stand out, especially in terms of family memory, are the olfactory and gustatory dimensions of sensory memory.

Nadia Seremetakis' (1994) work on the sensory landscapes of memory is illustrative of the connections among the senses, practices of commensality, and memory. Memories, she suggests, are inscribed in the senses through specific practices, such as eating and sharing food, that bind generations together. David Sutton (2008), echoing Seremetakis, has conducted extensive research on food and practices revolving around eating in Greece. According to Sutton, food is a particularly fertile site for examining memory. Eating is a profoundly private act in that the senses at play are experienced purely on an individual level. At the same time, eating across societies is one of the most basic social acts that brings people together. It serves as a context for communication, and, especially in the case of families, forges unity in their shared sensory landscape. The taste of grandmother's meatballs or father's barbeque does not conjure up mere sensory traces of the past but, rather, a plethora of associations with family relationships, family members, or past time periods. Food, akin to other material aspects of family memory, is one of family memory's most faithful porters. It marks family's identity by channeling memories through the gustatory and olfactory cues with which it is saturated.

CONCLUSION

Our journey through the landscape of family memory has sought to explore the complex intersection of memory and family. Although not a structurally distinct form of memory, family memory is nonetheless a distinctive memory system by virtue of its universal centrality in the development of personal and social identity. A subset of autobiographical memory, family memory represents the entirety of one's autobiographical memory during the crucial developmental years of infancy and early childhood, and it remains for most humans throughout their lives an irreplaceable dimension of selfhood.

We have stressed the dual status of family memory as an important feature of individual memory and as a central component of the collective memory of kin groups. Given its status as both a cognitive and a social fact, we have been at pains to characterize family memory in relation to literatures from cognitive psychology, on the one hand, and from anthropology, sociology, and history, on the other hand—literatures that are not generally brought into direct relation with one another and that often support very differently framed accounts of memory.

In our journey through the landscape of family memory, we have traversed several different scholarly domains, including cognitive science, social science, and the humanities. The study of family memory lends itself particularly well to this sort of bridging of academic fields. We conceptualize family memory as a memory system in which individual and collective memories converge, and thus any adequate conceptualization of family memory necessitates an integrated appreciation of both its cognitive and its social/historical character.

In treating family memory as a form of collective memory, we have sought to problematize the meaning of "collective," acknowledging that remembering in the strict sense of the term is something inevitably done by individuals. And yet, recalling Halbwach's seminal insight that all memory is influenced in some way by social relations and contexts, we have distinguished three kinds of family memory (FM1, FM2, and FM3), proposing a triad defining three degrees of collectivity of family memory. These differences in the degree to which family memories can be called "collective" are mediated by family memory objects such as stories, photos, and heirlooms and by the degree to which they are acknowledged and actually shared by family members. In treating social memory, we have considered an important body of work on "transactive memory" that treats memory work by groups as distributed cognition and socially divided labor. We have also highlighted the important differences between individual abilities to effectively shape what is remembered and forgotten by family members in the course of their conversational interactions. In family groups, not all memories and not all rememberers have equal weight in determining what gets included as family memory. Finally, we have noted the important differences in the intrinsic affordances for joint remembering of different memory objects and spaces. Joint remembering is a highly contingent process.

Family memory is much more than a collection of the family members' individual memories. A complex memory system, at once cognitive and social, extending beyond living memory, family memory contains mnemonic content forever subject to negotiation, and it possesses the capacity to materialize in both narratives and a wide range of other memory objects. Although embodied in specific things, memorable individuals, and particular events, family memory is best understood not as a thing but as a process, a perpetual weaving and reweaving of family members' threads of memory. It is remembrance in perpetual motion, problematically shared and inherently emergent. And yet, in the face of all this inevitable contingency, when its collective life is embodied in shared memory artifacts, "a family" takes shape as a remembered community—a community with the power to generate an unmistakable and primal conviction of belonging.

NOTES

1. For a similar distinction, see Olick (1999).
2. On the concept of ad hoc categories, see Barsalou (1983).
3. This is not always the case. An active negotiation is highly dependent on the internal dynamics in the family. Families with strong authoritarian figures, for example, are more likely not to converse about the past in a negotiating manner but, rather, adhere to versions imposed by the chief narrator (Hirst et al., 1997).
4. These studies have usually been conducted with middle-class American families.
5. See van Dijck (2007) for an excellent analysis of the effects that the use of digital cameras has on the production of memories.
6. The kitchen as a space and cooking as a practice that defines it have also been examined as sites for gendered memory transmission, with the kitchen often viewed as a sociopolitical space that marks it as predominantly feminine (Inness, 2001a, 2001b). In the American kitchen, women are often the custodians of the everyday history of the family embodied in generations of recipes kept in boxes or books and also in the history of family activities inscribed in the calendar.
7. In the anthropology of gift exchange, heirlooms often take the form of traditional exchange valuables such as the armbands and necklaces of the *kula* exchange (Malinowski, 1922) or the mats woven by women in the Pacific Islands (Weiner, 1992). The value of these exchange goods is their capacity to embody social history. The older the good, the more it is valued.
8. See also Spitzer (1998).

REFERENCES

Aguirre, G., Zarahn, E., & D'Esposito, M. (1998). Neural components of topographical representation. *Proceedings of the National Academy of Sciences of the USA, 95*(3), 839–846.

Anderson, J. R. (1976). *Language, memory, and thought*. Hillsdale, NJ: Erlbaum.

Ardila, A., Montanes, P., & Gempeler, J. (1986). Echoic memory and language perception. *Brain and Language, 29*(1), 134–140.

Bachelard, G. (1994). *The poetics of space.* Boston, MA: Beacon. (Original work published 1958)

Barsalou, L. W. (1983). Ad hoc categories. *Memory & Cognition, 11*(3), 211–227.

Barthes, R. (1981). *Camera Lucida: Reflections on photography.* New York, NY: Hill & Wang.

Bartlett, F. C. (1995). *Remembering: A study in experimental and social psychology.* Cambridge, UK: Cambridge University Press. (Original work published 1932)

Bohanek, J., Fivush, R., Zaman, W., Lepore, C. E., Merchant, S., & Duke, M. (2009). Narrative interaction in family dinnertime conversations. *Merrill–Palmer Quarterly, 55*(4), 488–515.

Bohanek, J., Marin, K., Fivush, R., & Duke, M. (2006). Family narrative interaction and children's sense of self. *Family Process, 45*(3), 39–54.

Brown, N. R. (2005). On the prevalence of event clusters in autobiographical memory. *Social Cognition, 23*(1), 35–69.

Browning, O. (1892). The evolution of the family. *Transactions of the Royal Historical Society, New Series, 6,* 87–107.

Bruner, J. (1990). *Acts of meaning.* Cambridge, MA: Harvard University Press.

Caldwell, R. L. (2005). At the confluence of memory and meaning—Life review with older adults and families: Using narrative therapy and the expressive arts to remember and re-author stories of resilience. *The Family Journal, 13*(2), 172–175.

Cappelletto, F. (2003). Long-term memory of extreme events: From autobiography to history. *Journal of the Royal Anthropological Institute, 9*(2), 241–260.

Carsten, J. (1995). The politics of forgetting: Migration, kinship and memory on the periphery of the Southeast Asian state. *Journal of the Royal Anthropological Institute, 1*(2), 317–335.

Cohen, M., Brom, D., & Dasberg, H. (2001). Child survivors of the Holocaust: Symptoms and coping after fifty years. *Israel Journal of Psychiatry and Related Sciences, 38*(1), 3–12.

Collings Eves, R. (2005). A recipe for remembrance: Memory and identity in African-American women's cookbooks. *Rhetoric Review, 24*(3), 280–297.

Coman, A., Brown, A. D., Koppel, J., & Hirst, W. (2009). Collective memory from a psychological perspective. *International Journal of Political Culture and Society, 22*(2), 125–141.

Conway, M. A. (1997). The inventory of experience: Memory and identity. In J. Pennebaker, D. Paez, & B. Ramé (Eds.), *Collective memory of political events* (pp. 21–45). Mahwah, NJ: Erlbaum.

Conway, M. A., & Pleydell-Pearce, C. W. (2000). The construction of autobiographical memories in the self-memory system. *Psychological Review, 107*(2), 261–228.

Conway, M. A., & Williams, H. L. (2008). Autobiographical memory. In J. H. Byrne et al. (Eds.), *Learning and memory: A comprehensive reference.* Oxford, UK: Elsevier.

Csikszentmihalyi, M., & Beattie, O. V. (1979). Life themes: A theoretical and empirical exploration of their origins and effects. *Journal of Humanistic Psychology, 19*(1), 45–63.

Curasi, C. F., Price, L., & Arnould, E. (2004). Ritual desire and ritual development: An examination of family heirlooms in contemporary North American households. In C. Otnes & T. Lowrey (Eds.), *Contemporary consumption rituals: A research anthology.* Mahwah, NJ: Erlbaum.

Daly, K. J. (2001). Deconstructing family time: From ideology to lived experience. *Journal of Marriage and Family, 63*(2), 283–294.

Davis, J. N., & Daly, M. (1997). Evolutionary theory and the human family. *Quarterly Review of Biology, 72*(4), 407–435.

Denham, A. R. (2008). Rethinking historical trauma: Narratives of resilience. *Transcultural Psychiatry, 45*(3), 391–414.

Duke, M., Fivush, R., Lazarus, A., & Bohanek, J. (2003). *Of ketchup and kin: Dinnertime conversations as a major source of family knowledge, family adjustment, and family resilience.* Working Paper No. 26, Emory Center for Myth and Ritual in American Life, Atlanta, GA.

Edwards, D., & Middleton, D. (1988). Conversational remembering and family relationships: How children learn to remember. *Journal of Social and Personal Relationships, 5*(1), 3–25.

Farrant, K., & Reese, E. (2000). Maternal style and children's participation in reminiscing: Stepping stones in children's autobiographical memory development. *Journal of Cognition and Development, 1*(2), 193–225.

Favart-Jardon, E. (2002). Women's family speech: A trigenerational study of family memory. *Current Sociology, 50*(2), 309–319.

Fiese, B. H. (2006). *Family routines and rituals.* New Haven, CT: Yale University Press.

Fiese, B. H., & Marjinsky, K. A. (1999). Dinnertime stories: Connecting family practices with relationship beliefs and child adjustment. *Monographs of the Society for Research in Child Development, 64*(2), 52–68.

Fivush, R., Bohanek, J., Robertson, R., & Duke, M. (2004). Family narratives and the development of children's emotional well-being. In B. Fiese & M. W. Pratt (Eds.), *Family stories and the life course: Across time and generations* (pp. 55–76). Mahwah, NJ: Erlbaum.

Fossion, P., Rejas, M., Servais, L., Pelc, I., & Hirsch, S. (2002). Family approach with grandchildren of Holocaust survivors. *American Journal of Psychotherapy, 57*(4), 519–527.

Fox, R. (1967). *Kinship and marriage: An anthropological reader.* New York, NY: Penguin.

Garvey, C. (1990). *Play.* Cambridge, MA: Harvard University Press. (Original work published 1977)

Geertz, H., & Geertz, C. (1964). Teknonymy in Bali: Parenthood, age-grading and genealogical amnesia. *Journal of the Royal Anthropological Institute of Great Britain and Ireland, 94*(2), 94–108.

Gillis, J. R. (1996a). *A world of their own making: Myth, ritual and the quest for family values.* New York, NY: Basic Books.

Gillis, J. R. (1996b). Making time for family: The invention of family time and the reinvention of family history. *Journal of Family History, 21*(1), 4–21.

Gillis, J. R. (2002). *Our imagined families: The myths and rituals we live by.* Working Paper, Emory Center for Myth and Ritual in American Life, Atlanta, GA.

Goldman, I. (1970). *Ancient Polynesian society.* Chicago, IL: University of Chicago Press.

Goldman, I. (1975). *The mouth of heaven.* New York, NY: Wiley.

Habermas, T., & Paha, C. (2001). The development of coherence in adolescents' life narratives. *Narrative Inquiry, 11*(1), 35–54.

Halbwachs, M. (1992). *On collective memory.* Chicago, IL: University of Chicago Press.

Hirsch, M. (1997). *Family frames: Photography, narrative, and postmemory.* Cambridge, MA: Harvard University Press.

Hirsch, M. (2008). The generation of postmemory. *Poetics Today, 29*(1), 103–128.

Hirst, W., & Echterhoff, G. (2008). Creating shared memories in conversation: Toward a psychology of collective memory. *Social Research, 75*(1), 183–216.

Hirst, W., & Manier, D. (1996). Social influences on remembering. In D. Rubin (Ed.), *Remembering the past* (pp. 271–290). New York, NY: Cambridge University Press.

Hirst, W., & Manier, D. (2008). Towards a psychology of collective memory. *Memory, 16*(3), 183–200.

Hirst, W., Manier, D., & Apetroaia, I. (1997). The social construction of the remembered self: Family recounting. *Annals of the New York Academy of Sciences, 818*(1), 163–188.

Inness, S. A. (2001a). *Dinner roles: American women and culinary culture.* Iowa City, IA: University of Iowa Press.

Inness, S. A. (Ed.). (2001b). *Kitchen culture in America: Popular representations of food, gender, and race.* Philadelphia, PA: University of Pennsylvania Press.

Kellermann, N. P. (2001). Transmission of Holocaust trauma: An integrative view. *Psychiatry: Interpersonal and Biological Processes, 64*(3), 256–267.

Kellermann, N. P. (2013). Epigenetic transmission of holocaust trauma: Can nightmares be inherited? *Israeli Journal of Psychiatry and Related Sciences, 50*(1), 33–39.

Kidron, C. (2009). Toward an ethnography of silence: The lived presence of the past in the everyday life of Holocaust trauma survivors and their descendants in Israel. *Current Anthropology, 50*(1), 5–27.

Kuhn, A. (2010). Memory texts and memory work: Performances of memory in and with visual media. *Memory Studies, 3*(4), 298–313. Retrieved from http://mss.sage-pub.com/content/3/4/298

Langford, M. (2001). *Suspended conversations: The afterlife of memory in photographic albums.* London, UK: McGill–Queen's Press.

Langford, M. (2006). Speaking the album: An application of the oral–photographic framework. In A. Kuhn & K. McAllister (Eds.), *Locating memory: Photographic acts* (pp. 223–246). New York, NY: Berghnan Books.

Lareau, A. (2003). *Unequal childhoods: Class, race, and family life.* Los Angeles, CA: University of California Press.

Malinowski, B. (1922). *Argonauts of the pacific.* New York, NY: Dutton.

Massimi, M., & Baecker, R. M. (2010). A death in the family: Opportunities for designing technologies for the bereaved. In *Proceedings of the SIGCHI Conference on Human Factors in Computing Systems* (pp. 1821–1830). New York, NY: ACM.

McLean, K. C. (2005). Late adolescent identity development: Narrative meaning making and memory telling. *Developmental Psychology, 41*(4), 683.

Miller, D. (1987). *Material culture and mass consumption.* Oxford, UK: Basil Blackwell.

Neisser, U. (1982). *Memory observed: Remembering in natural contexts.* San Francisco, CA: Freeman.

Nelson, K., & Fivush, R. (2004). The emergence of autobiographical memory: A social cultural developmental theory. *Psychological Review, 111*(2), 486–511.

Nora, P. (1989). Between memory and history: Les lieux de mémoire. *Representations, 29*, 7–24.

Odom, W., Banks, R., Kirk, D., Harper, R., Lindley, S., & Sellen, A. (2012). Technology heirlooms? Considerations for passing down and inheriting digital materials.

In *Proceedings of the SIGCHI Conference on Human Factors in Computing Systems* (pp. 337–346). New York, NY: ACM.

Olick, J. K. (1999). Collective memory: The two cultures. *Sociological Theory, 17*(3), 333–348.

Olick, J. K., & Robbins, J. (1998). Social memory studies: From "collective memory" to the historical sociology of mnemonic practices. *Annual Review of Sociology, 24*, 105–140.

Peterson, C. (2002). Children's long-term memory for autobiographical events. *Developmental Review, 22*(3), 370–402.

Peterson, C., Wang, Q., & Hou, Y. (2009). "When I was little": Childhood recollections in Chinese and European Canadian grade school children. *Child Development, 80*(2), 506–518.

Petrelli, D., & Whittaker, S. (2010). Family memories in the home: Contrasting physical and digital mementos. *Personal and Ubiquitous Computing, 14*(2), 153–169.

Piaget, J. (1962). *Play, dreams and imitation in childhood.* New York, NY: Norton.

Pratt, M. W., Norris, J. E., Hebblethwaite, S., & Arnold, M. L. (2008). Intergenerational transmission of values: Family generativity and adolescents' narratives of parent and grandparent value teaching. *Journal of Personality, 76*(2), 171–198.

Rubin, D. C. (2000). The distribution of early childhood memories. *Memory, 8*, 265–269.

Sahlins, M. D. (1963). Poor man, rich man, big-man, chief: Political types in Melanesia and Polynesia. *Comparative Studies in Society and History, 5*(3), 285–303.

Schab, F. R. (1991). Odor memory: Taking stock. *Psychological Bulletin, 109*(2), 242–251.

Schab, F. R., & Crowder, R. G. (Eds.). (1995). *Memory for odors.* Mahwah, NJ: Erlbaum.

Seremetakis, N. (1993). The memory of the senses: Historical perception, commensal exchange and modernity. *Visual Anthropology Review, 9*(2), 2–18.

Seremetakis, N. (1994). The memory of the senses, Part I: Marks of the transitory. In *The senses still: Perception and memory as material culture in modernity* (pp. 1–18). Boulder, CO: Westview.

Shore, B. (1996). *Culture in mind: Cognition, culture and the problem of meaning.* New York, NY: Oxford University Press.

Shore, B. (2008). Spiritual work, memory work: Revival and recollection at Salem Camp Meeting. *Ethos, 36*(1), 98–119.

Shore, B. (2009). Making time for family: Schemas for long-term family memory. *Social Indicators Research, 93*(1), 95–103.

Shore, B. (2012). Allocentric and egocentric perspective in cultural models. In R. Sun (Ed.), *Grounding social science in cognitive science* (pp. 89–125). Cambridge, MA: MIT Press.

Shore, B. (2014). A view from the islands: Spatial cognition in the Western Pacific. *Spatial Cognition in the Pacific, 42*(3), 376–397. [Special issue]

Sokolova, A. (2013). Jewish memory and family heirlooms (based on materials from field studies in St. Petersburg, 2010–11). *East European Jewish Affairs, 43*(1), 3–30.

Sontag, S. (1977). *On photography.* New York, NY: Picador.

Spitzer, L. (1998). *Hotel Bolivia: The culture of memory in a refuge from Nazism.* New York, NY: Hill & Wang.

Stanner, W. E. H. (1966). *On Aboriginal religion,* Oceania Monograph No. 11. Sydney, Australia: Oceania.

Stanner, W. E. H. (2011). *The dreaming and other essays.* Collingwood, Victoria, Australia: Black.

Sutton, D. (2008). A tale of Easter ovens: Food and collective memory. *Social Research, 75*(1), 157–180.

Sutton, D., & Hernandez, M. (2007). Voices in the kitchen: Cooking tools as inalienable possessions. *Oral History, 35*(2), 67.

Tulving, E. (1972). Episodic and semantic memory. In E. Tulving & W. Donaldson (Eds.), *Organization of memory* (pp. 381–403). New York, NY: Academic Press.

Tulving, E. (1983). *Elements of episodic memory.* Oxford, UK: Clarendon.

Tulving, E. (1985). How many memory systems are there? *American Psychologist, 40*(4), 385–398.

van Dijck, J. (2007). *Mediated memories in the digital age.* Stanford, CA: Stanford University Press.

Wagoner, B. (2013). Bartlett's concept of schema in reconstruction. *Theory & Psychology, 23*(5), 553–575.

Wagoner, B. (2017). *The constructive mind: Bartlett's psychology in reconstruction.* Cambridge, UK: Cambridge University Press.

Wegner, D. M. (1986). Transactive memory: A contemporary analysis of the group mind. In B. Mullen & G. R. Goethals (Eds.), *Theories of group behavior* (pp. 185–205). New York, NY: Springer-Verlag.

Wegner, D. M., Erber, R., & Raymond, P. (1991). Transactive memory in close relationships. *Journal of Personality and Social Psychology, 61*(6), 923.

Wegner, D. M., Giuliano, T., & Hertel, P. T. (1985). Cognitive interdependence in close relationships. In W. Ickes (Ed.), *Compatible and incompatible relationships* (pp. 253–276). New York, NY: Springer.

Weiner, A. (1992). *Inalienable possessions: The paradox of keeping-while-giving.* Berkeley, CA: University of California Press.

Welch-Ross, M. K. (1995). An integrative model of the development of autobiographical memory. *Developmental Review, 15*(3), 338–365.

Weltzer, H. (2005). *Grandpa wasn't a Nazi: The Holocaust in German family remembrance,* International Perspectives No. 54. New York, NY: American Jewish Committee.

Wertsch, J. V. (2008). The narrative organization of collective memory. *Ethos, 36*(1), 120–135.

Winograd, E. (1988). Some observations on prospective remembering. In M. M. Gruneberg, P. E. Morris, & R. N. Sykes (Eds.), *Practical aspects of memory: Current research and issues, Vol. 1: Memory in everyday life* (pp. 348–353). Oxford, UK: Wiley.

Zerubavel, E. (1996). Social memories: Steps to a sociology of the past. *Qualitative Sociology, 19*(3), 283–299.

Materiality of Memory

The Case of the Remembrance Poppy

KYOKO MURAKAMI ∎

In this chapter, I highlight the importance of materiality in memory studies by drawing on the case of the remembrance poppy, an artifact canonical to the practice of commemoration of war and conflict in Britain. Since 2014, a number of research and community projects as well as commemorative ceremonies have taken place to mark the 100th anniversary of World War I, which lasted from 1914 to 1918. The red poppy is one of many objects commonly considered as a means by which war memories are eloquently represented. The poppy is ubiquitous from mid-October through early November in the streets of the United Kingdom. It is a fascinating cultural artifact that stands for multiple values, beliefs, and feelings; however, its use in the commemorative practice is tightly scripted and regulated in the Remembrance Sunday ceremony. A traditional psychological approach to studying the artifact—singling out the poppy as the memory object and studying it alone as a decontextualized subject—resorts to a simplistic representational model of the object, making up or standing for a particular version of collective memory. The remembrance poppy connects people with different times and places in the acting and performing of the ceremony. When used in an art installation in an iconic heritage site, it creates a perceptual field of experiencing the past in an extraordinary manner.

Overall, I argue that when studying phenomena of collective remembering, such as a national commemorative practice, it is important to consider the interplay between discourse, materials/artifacts/ornaments, body, and the environment as an integrated whole. The proposed argument is underpinned by the material view of remembering articulated by Radley (1990). This discussion is followed by revisiting Vygotsky's (1978) concept of semiotic mediation to reappraise the cultural artifact's role for people performing cultural rituals such as the Remembrance Sunday ceremony. The significance of the artifact to the ritual performance is explained with Connerton's (1989) work on how societies remember. Finally, I discuss Valsiner's (2008) analysis of the ornamental world and meaning construction to address how the artifacts can create a semiotic field for meaning construction.

THE REMEMBRANCE POPPY FOR REMEMBRANCE SUNDAY

Remembrance Sunday is observed with ceremonies throughout the United Kingdom on the Sunday nearest to November 11. It is the day the armistice signed with Germany brought to an end the hostilities of World War I (also known as the Great War). The day memorializes the fallen British soldiers in all conflicts since the war. In contemporary time, it is the day "to commemorate the contribution of British and Commonwealth military and civilian servicemen and women in the two World Wars and later conflicts" (Grant & Javid, 2013). On November 11 at 11 a.m.—the exact time that the guns fell silent in World War I—the United Kingdom holds a 2-minute silence. Remembrance poppies are worn and displayed in accordance with a tradition inspired by the Canadian poet John McCrae's poem titled "In Flanders Fields." The poem became very popular due to his use of imagery. Consider the first line: "In Flanders Fields the poppies blow/Between the crosses, row on row/That mark our place." This imagery with contrasts and rhymes became a part of the collective memory of war. Interestingly, remembrance poppies were first adopted by the American Legion to commemorate American soldiers killed during World War I. Subsequently, the United Kingdom followed suit, via the then British Empire (Legion, 2015).

The physical appearance of the remembrance poppy is rather simple, consisting of three parts—two petals in red paper, a leaf in green paper, and a green plastic stem that holds the petals and leaf—with a black round plastic button to bundle all the parts. The poppy is worn on the lapel with a small needle pin holding it in place on the chest. Wearing the poppy is a signal or a symbolic gesture filled with multiple meanings (Figure 5.1).

The poppy can be seen as what Moghaddam (2002) calls a "carrier," which acts as a transporter for meaning. It is a container into which people load values, beliefs, faith, and sentiments: "Carriers are at once public and collective, private and individual. They are public and collective in the sense that they are present in public space and are collaboratively constructed through the contributions of many people over generations" (p. 225). By wearing it on a lapel, one can personally relate to the poppy; it aligns one with its symbolic meaning as it stands for a range of values and beliefs as well as the participation in the Remembrance Sunday commemoration exercise as part of a culture and collective memory. Anyone can wear the poppy whether or not one genuinely believes in the values or beliefs it represents. One does not have to subscribe to or know the history and culture it stands for. However, the poppy is essential to those participating in the Remembrance Sunday ceremony—that is, the ritual of collective remembering in

Figure 5.1 Remembrance poppy.

a given culture. Focusing on the poppy as a carrier, we can come to see not only a personal representation but also "the larger, shared, collaboratively constructed social world for explanation of human behaviour" (p. 225). It is this tension of collective and personal found in the poppy as a cultural artifact that is explored in this chapter.

The collective remembrance of the Great War has received scholarly attention by historians and sociologically inclined researchers (C. Winter, 2009, 2012; J. Winter, 1995). However, relatively little research attention has been given to the psychological aspects of the artifact, such as the remembrance poppy's significance to a national commemoration. The poppy is a symbolic cultural object that materializes absence (Hockey, Komaromy, & Woodthrope, 2010) and works as shorthand for signifying a mass of fatalities, loss, and destruction of human lives. In contemporary Britain, commemorative rituals and acts have been criticized because they have strayed from their original meanings and lost their focus on personal meanings; war monuments, memorials, and ceremonies have, for many, come to glorify war rather than to promote peace (Harrison, 2012). The emphasis for celebrating patriotism in the present subsumes the original meaning of somber reflection associated with the suffering and death of soldiers (Harrison, 2012). The artifact, such as the poppy, brings about an ideological dilemma (Billig et al., 1988) and irresolvable tensions of meanings at many different levels—the collective, personal, national–state, institutional, individual, moral and emotional, and so on (Brockmeier, 2010).

The poppy initializes another tension—that of having to remember the suffering and honoring the dead and to forget the traumatic nation's past. The poppy, as a polysemic object, holds many meanings and stories of experiences of those involved. Whereas some people may honor one meaning, other meanings are hidden, obscured, and masked, creating an artifact with ambivalence.

The commemorative narrative "restructures the past, creating its own version of historical time as it elaborates, condenses, omits, or conflates historical events" (Zerubavel, 2011, p. 239). The commemorative narrative is shaped and sustained by the very artifacts in use in the commemorative ceremony as ritual.

Despite its simple appearance, the history of the poppy is complex, involving the intersection of people, events, places, and serendipities. Iles (2008) conducted a thoroughgoing ethnography of various sites associated with the remembrance poppy, including Flanders. The ethnography traced the poppy being appropriated and reinvented by stakeholders in various sites, showing multiple networks of linguistic-discursive, cultural communities of memory practice, which evolved from and originated in McCrae's poem. In any given society's commemoration, people need objects to understand and perform aspects of selfhood and to navigate the terrain of culture more broadly (Woodward, 2007). Aligned with the material role of cultural memory, Woodward suggests ways of studying the material as culture with a particular interest in people–object relations and objects in action. The next section extends the discussion of the poppy as a cultural memory artifact in terms of these two suggested foci. As acknowledged widely in cultural studies and other social sciences and humanities, no object has a single interpretation; "objects are always polysemous and capable of transformations of meaning across time and space contexts" (Woodward, 2007, p. 27). Understanding the social lives of objects (Kopytoff, 1986) is one of the keys to understanding culture and the processes in which people–object relations are underpinned. This focus presents us with the question as to how to frame the object in a given culture and formation of collective memory.

MATERIAL ARTIFACTS MEDIATING MEMORY

In the fields of cognitive and social psychology, the material world in the study of memory is, as yet, underexplored (Radley, 1990). Referring to Bartlett's (1932/1995; see also Wagoner, 2017) foundational work, memory studies in mainstream psychology have opened up a view that the study of remembering is a form of constructive activity. In other words, memory is much more than the retrieval of stored information in the brain. Rather, it is "the putting together of a claim about past states of affairs by means of described memory as a constructive act 'inside the head' of the social individual" (Radley, 1990, p. 46). Radley's move was to make a critical evaluation of social psychological research, relating to "remembering in a world of things—both natural, and products of cultural endeavor—where it concentrates upon memory as a product of discourse" (p. 46). The current chapter follows this interpretation, "redirect[ing] our view away from the remembering subject to social practices in which people engage with the material world" (p. 47). In seeking to understand the people's engagement with material worlds, such as the national commemoration of the Great War, discursive psychologists might have pursued this argument in examining the role of artifacts in social life as well as addressing how they are implicated in the way people go about establishing individual and collective pasts (Radley, 1990). The methodological move is for them to enquire into the discourses produced in establishing the significance of the collective and individual pasts by those discourse participants (interlocutors). There still remains, however, an area of inquiry beyond the discourses that encompasses other aspects of the *act* in the practices of national (and international) commemoration:

> The argument that signification within memory is inadequately understood by reference only to a cognitive ordering of neutral or passive objects: How and what we remember is also objectified in material forms which are sometimes (but not always) arranged to embody categories and thereby mark out the objects' significance. (p. 47)

To further address this question, I consult the work of social remembering, which I believe is clearly in line with a materialist view. A number of present-day memory researchers began by taking an account of materiality of memory within social psychology and beyond. For instance, Radley suggests,

> A social psychology of remembering is that one must look beyond the idea of a single cognitive faculty which people have in common to the proposition that their ways of remembering may be different depending upon their relationship to their community, including the world of objects it produces and preserves. (p. 49)

Likewise, Middleton and Brown (2005) advanced the material argument by incorporating a range of psychological, sociological, and philosophical perspectives of Vygotsky, Bartlett, Halbwachs, and Bergson and kneaded them into their interdisciplinary approach to remembering and forgetting as socially constituted activities (see also Brown & Reavey, Chapter 7, this volume).

One of the theoretical conundrums in terms of formulating the material argument for memory studies is the issue of how artifacts (culturally and historically significant memory objects) are used in the practice of collective remembrance, including the commemoration of war, disasters, conflict, and tragic events, as well as in the way personal meaning is made and retained or modified in the course of annual rituals. Vygotskian and cultural–historical psychology offers semiotic mediation as a key concept for understanding the role of artifact in commemoration rituals and related forms of collective remembering (Wertsch, 2002). This branch of psychology recognizes the importance of the concept of mediation through cultural artifacts as the foundation of human mental and emotional activity (Holland & Cole, 1995). People in a given society remember a past event jointly together via cultural tools such as narratives (Wertsch, 2002; see also Wertsch, Chapter 12, this volume). An image of the past in the form of a master narrative is communicated and sustained by ritual performances (Connerton, 1989). While acknowledging collective remembering (Middleton &

Edwards, 1990) as something that relies on the use of language as discourse, Radley (1990) reminds us of the significance of materiality in everyday practices of remembering, as well as in national and international commemorative practices. Succinctly stated, "Remembering is something which occurs in a world of things, as well as words, and that artifacts play a central role in the memories of cultures and individuals" (p. 57). This reflects on Vygotsky's (1978) concept, semiotic mediation, in its well-known illustration of a person tying a knot in his handkerchief as a reminder. Vygotsky argues that "human beings actively remember with the help of signs" and "humans personally influence their relations with the environment and through that environment personally change their behavior, subjecting it to their control" (p. 51). The concept of semiotic mediation helps us to understand the poppy's significance to cultural memory in the United Kingdom in relation to World War I and subsequent wars. In incorporating the concept of semiotic mediation into the discussion of the practice of national commemoration, there appears to be a need to further understand the ritual nature of the practice.

THE COMMEMORATIVE RITUAL ACT

The poppy is central to the commemorative ceremony of Remembrance Sunday. The material aspect of collective memory, according to Connerton (1989), is remembering as an act, a bodily movement—people do things with artifacts such as the remembrance poppy, with which people experience collectively what it is like to remember the Great War with others. Connerton insists that bodily social memory is an underresearched area of bodily social memory in reference to the practices of a non-inscribed kind of transmission of tradition. He argues that "images of the past and recollected knowledge of the past are conveyed and sustained by (more or less ritual) performances" (p. 40) and that performative memory is bodily.

War commemorations are part of a broader phenomenon of ritual action. Connerton (1989) highlights materiality in the ritual process. The ritual refers to the "rule-governed activity of a symbolic character which draws the attention of its participants to objects of thought and feeling which they hold to be of special significance" (p. 44). Connerton explains:

> Rites are not merely expressive. It is true that they are expressive acts rather than instrumental acts, in the sense that they are either not directed to a strategic end, or if they are so directed, as with fertility rites, they fail to achieve their strategic aim. But rites are expressive acts only by virtue of their conspicuous regularity. They are formalised acts, and tend to be stylised, stereotypical and receptive. Because they are deliberately stylised, they are not subject to spontaneous variation, or at least are susceptible of variation only within strict limits. They are not performed under inner momentary compulsion but are deliberately observed to denote feelings. (p. 44)

Connerton suggests that rites are held to be meaningful not just personally but also collectively. They have significance with respect to a set of further nonritual actions, to the whole life of a community. Rites such as the Remembrance Sunday commemorative ceremony "have the capacity to give value and meaning to the life of those who perform them" (p. 45). The body as the site of commemoration emphasizes how ideology and the moral order of victory and defeat are inscribed into the flesh of combatants (Middleton & Brown, 2005). However, this kind of memory depends on the longevity of the survivors. In their passing, the memory of war also dies; there is a need for succession of the memory to others, who might not have direct experience of the wars and conflict commemorated. Middleton and Brown state that "the commemoration of conflict is achieved also by creating objects that are meant to sustain and preserve certain kinds of relationship" (p. 137). Following this point, we come to see an enduring material effect in having to remember and never forget. This material effect is seen in how the remembrance poppy is worn by those who participate and act in the commemoration regardless of the experience of war and/or conflict. Collective remembering lies in the way in which the poppy brings people together across all walks of life; generations; and geographic, cultural, social, and political ideological boundaries. This relationship is emergent within the very commemorative ritual and not pre-given and static. In the following, it is the performance and acting within the ritual that I focus attention concerning the ritual process and how persons use the poppy with regard to war memorials and monuments. War memory is inscribed within artifacts and becomes objectified. Such material forms of objectification play an important role in prolonging the past into the present.

I now present two illustrative examples in order to develop my material argument for the important role of the artifact, the remembrance poppy. I first consider the ritual and bodily (Connerton, 1989) and then discuss collective remembering in the ornamental world (Valsiner, 2008). Here, I sketch my methodological approach to the illustrative examples. These recalled examples are far from what can be called data. They are episodic, simply drawn from my personal reflection on my living experiences of the commemoration ceremonies as a denizen in a community in Greater London and from a visit to a commemorative installation exhibition on November 1, 2014. On these occasions, I did not intend to write about these episodes for research purposes. My approach to discussing these episodes is comparable to an ethnography of experience, which conveys the intricacy, complexity, and detail of the knowledge that the ethnographer obtained from the fieldwork experience with the language that is sensitive to the thoughts, feelings, and lived realities of ethnographic subjects (Marcus & Fischer, 1986). Such ethnography includes the voice of "the ethnographer qua normal human being" (Walton, 1993, p. 381). What is crucial to this approach is "self-reflexivity and a close scrutiny of the research process itself" (Walton, 1993, p. 381). What follows is the ethnographer's/my attempt to advance the theories to explain those experiences of being involved in the commemoration practices.

Having lived in the United Kingdom for more than 15 years, I have, almost without fail, watched television coverage of the Remembrance Sunday event.

Every November 11 (or the nearest Sunday to this date), military and civilian veterans and professionals, royals, and political party leaders and representatives of the Commonwealth nations take part in the commemoration ceremony. As far as I can remember, the format of the ceremony has not changed. In Paul Connerton's (1989) sense, people perform the acts, such as the wearing of poppies; saluting to ceremonial participants and monuments, plaques, and tombs of the deceased; observing 2 minutes of silence; and reciting the "we will remember them" poem during the ritual/commemorative ceremony. All these performances at the commemorative ceremony can be considered as embodied actions of remembering. In relation to this embodied memory, Henri Bergson (1912/2004) calls it habit memory, consisting of obtaining certain automatic behavior by means of repetition. Habit memory is exemplified in rote learning, such as a poem or script learned by repeatedly reading the text. To some people, the Remembrance Sunday ceremony, being a highly scripted and staged ritual, may appear to be mechanistic, dry, and somber with repressed emotion. What is then the function of rituals? In the next section, I explore how the artifacts and bodies are an integral part of the commemorative practice—the making of a collective cultural memory.

In my view, the presence and use of an iconic artifact (the poppy) during the ritual of the commemorative ceremony on Remembrance Sunday holds a crucial role in the way people feel connected to the collective sense of nationhood and identity through the past, according to the cultural memory of the Great War, and subsequent wars. Social anthropologist Victor Turner (1969/1995) studied rituals in traditional, non-Western societies and theorized ritual and ceremony as spatially and temporarily arranged actions, involving several participants acting in concert, employing objects. Rituals are semiotic wholes, and it may be possible to produce grammars (rules of communication) that describe them (p. 94). Wearing the poppy entitles the participants of the ceremony and the participation framework to draw on Goffman's (1974) notion of "frame." Everyone wears the poppy at the ceremony, which is the ritual action. This is also akin to the participation framework of Halbwachs' approach, which highlights "social frameworks of memory" (Olick, Vinitzky-Seroussi, & Levy, 2011, p. 177). Through social frameworks, the individual finds him- or herself in the stories of his or her group, such as the narrative of nationhood through war, achieved by the Remembrance Sunday commemorative ceremony. Here, the participants in the ceremony, representing various groups as well as individuals, are constituted by the stories they tell, which in this case are rituals. Ritual is a performative storytelling, which sustains the national coherent narrative and the sense of collective identity.

In my discussion of the materiality of the poppy as a cultural memory artifact for commemoration, I have so far addressed how the cultural artifact is integral to performing the ritual of the national commemoration. Next, I direct attention to the effect of the environment on the ritual participants. To deal with this concern, I draw on the concepts of affective field and, in particular, hypergeneralized affective field (Valsiner, 2008) for accomplishing a shared experience of the past within the duration of the ritual.

POPPIES IN AN ORNAMENTED WORLD

Zooming in and out of the scene and actions performed during the Remembrance Sunday ceremony, one cannot help but notice the omnipresence of the poppy. It is indeed overwhelming. The commemorative ceremony is performed formally in the military fashion, in silence for the most part, except for the music and ceremonial signals. The gestures and movements of the ceremonial participants are equally important; therefore, the performance of the ceremony is multimodal using signs beyond spoken language. The ceremonial space is the discursive frame, in which the ritual action is performed by the participants in speaking, together with music and signals, as well as in silence. Within this space ornamented with the poppies, people perform in the most stylized manner of precision, leaving no room for individual diversion, variation, or improvisation according to the script and planned program. The poppies, the cenotaph, and the thoroughfare of Whitehall all constitute a semiotic field and a community of the commemoration. Valsiner's (2008) analysis of objects as constituting the ornamental world is helpful in supporting this observation. He argues that ornaments such as the poppy create cultural arenas of meaning construction:

> Patterns are constructed for a purpose—guiding the person encountering those towards some goal orientation. Most of these constructed cultural patterns are peripheral in their relating with our personal worlds—live among them rarely noticing them in the background. We even consider them "mere decorations"—or ornaments. (p. 67)

The poppy here is not a mere decoration. It serves an important psychological function. The abundance of poppies and the people moving and performing in concert with others and with other artifacts in the environment constitute a complex field for meaning-making. It creates a "semiotic" demand for activities, in which the participants in the commemoration ceremony act toward a meaning, suitable and appropriate to the norm and the moral order of the activity, obscuring the undesirable. Valsiner (2008) elaborates on the particular meaning of the ornamental world—for example, of the pilgrim, after a long journey, arriving at a cathedral and experiencing the imposing appearance of it: "The overwhelming impression of the grandiose pattern of abundantly decorated building feeds into the meaning-making facing the scene. . . . By proliferation of their pattern in space and time ornaments create an inescapable field structure" (p. 71).

To further illustrate Valsiner's (2008) point about the abundance of ornaments as cultural arenas of meaning construction, I refer to the 2014 art installation of the Tower of London as a case in point. The art installation is called *Blood Swept Lands and Seas of Red*. It was created by Paul Cummins in collaboration with the stage designer Tom Piper. The artist was inspired from an unknown World War I veteran's text describing the battlefields in the opening of the poem: "The blood-swept lands and seas of red, where angels fear to tread." The poem's opening was taken as the title of the installation.

Beginning on June 17, 2014, for nearly 4 months, five days per week, ceramic poppies were planted across the tower's grass-covered moat. The installation was completed November 11, Remembrance Day, when poppies in the exact number of the fallen soldiers filled the moat, rendering the cascading effect on the walls of the tower, sweeping out on the moat in their red, blood color. The installation of the poppies captured people's imagination. Visitor attendance was unprecedented in the history of Royal Palaces; they came to see the planting, as well as to witness the evening Roll of Honour call being read from within the moat. The installation's colossal scale reflects and honors the monumental toll of the war (Figure 5.2).

Having heard of the phenomenal success of the art installation, I myself made a visit to the Tower of London on the afternoon of November 1, 2016, approaching Remembrance Sunday. When I arrived at the surrounding site of the Tower of London, the atmosphere was palpably different from that of the streets leading to the Tower and the installation. An endless queue was formed; the crowds of visitors outside the moat trying to gain a view of the installation were blocked as if by a massive wall obscuring the spectacle of the installation. Struggling to find a vantage point, at last I managed to stand in the front of the queue; I was in a different field of experience. The inundation of the ceramic poppies, no longer individually identifiable from my viewpoint, and the moat filled with a carpet of the vivid color of red undoubtedly were associated with the blood of the fallen. This brought about my immediate reaction of speechless awe, and I was aware of the extraordinary nature of the experience—with

Figure 5.2 The installation titled *Blood Swept Lands and Seas of Red* in Tower of London.

my pounding heartbeat, deep breathing, and utter speechlessness. I was subsumed by the scale, intensity, and the complex whole, comprising the people (visitors, security guards, and staff), architecture (the Tower of London, streets, and nearby shops and facilities), the art installation, and objects that people were carrying.

Such a complex field of perception consisting of the artifacts (the art installation of the poppies), persons, and environment that I experienced may be comparable to what Valsiner (2008) calls "holistic patterning of our perceptual environment" (p. 70). It is in everything that surrounds us—architecture, textiles, wallpaper, monuments, and so on. Furthermore, the poppies were literally "right on our bodies"—not necessarily tattooed or painted (as in the examples of Valsiner's discussion) but publicly visible, creating a sense of unity and solidarity among the visitors and other people concerned, such as staff and attendants. I saw a variety of poppy products on visitors and their belongings. Obviously, the remembrance poppy was worn by default, but there were also individually unique forms of the poppy, such as hand-knitted poppies on hats, handbags, and backpacks or on people's jacket or coat lapels. "They envelope our immediate activity contexts" (Valsiner, 2008, p. 70)—in this case, the activity of commemorating the war and honoring the fallen to the Great War. The poppy, from the simplest form to the exaggerated art installation form, gives rise to the generalized whole—the patterning of the collective experience of commemorating the war in the very moment and place of the art installation.

In what sense does this complex whole afford meaning constructions and for or by whom? Being in this affective field did not necessarily enable me to articulate the experience into an intelligible story. It was one of those moments in which I was so struck that I was *without words*. The process of how people turn the experience into a story is a contentious area of memory research. In the post-visit stage, while trying to reflect on my own reactions to the visit and verbalize them, I resorted to reading various media articles (I googled and checked Twitter posts and posted photos I took on my Facebook page). This was a further attempt to make sense of an experience of the poppy in an extraordinary work of art as part of the national commemoration. I was searching for a discursive frame in which I sought words to explain to myself and others after the visit. In one of the articles (Treble, 2014), a yeoman (aka Beefeater) of the Tower was interviewed, saying "[I was] in awe. . . . I get goose pimples every time I walk by it." One of the production managers also commented,

If there is a bit of a wind going, you hear the tinkling of the poppies as they touch each other. Each poppy represents the life of a fallen soldier. To see them move, it's a bit like reveille in the morning—someone is waking them up.

The perceptual world created by the abundance of ornaments, the artifact of the poppy, triggers a semiotic demand setting. The semiotic demand setting is "the meaning structure that guides persons' feeling, thinking, and acting in their environments" (Valsiner, 2000). It guides how persons are expected to view what happens with them in their relating with the environment (Valsiner, 2003). The poppy installation sets up social guidance for making sense of the art installation through storytelling, such as that presented previously.

The aforementioned observation of the abundance of the poppies leads to another detail that Valsiner (2008) points to—the escalated tension within the exaggerated opposition A and non-A, leading to hyper-A, in the course of the resolving tension between A and the opposition of A. Valsiner explains:

> The latter can take the form of exaggeration of selected parts of the figure, or through proliferation of the redundancy—by repetition of the pattern of its ground that is ornamented. By manifold replicating, a simple element of an ornament covers the sensory field of the person in full, thus "keeping the person within the field." (p. 70)

Differences in the trajectories of resolving the tension between PLAIN (non-A) <> FANCY (hyper-A) in the construction of the exteriors of the building between different societies demonstrate the prevailing need to strategically regulate the activity fields of everyday public worlds (Valsiner, 2008). The sense or feeling of unity and solidarity with other visitors, even though they are total strangers, may be explained by the exact point of how the ornamented area afforded my own "being in the field." This is highly affective, according to Valsiner:

> The actor establishes the unity of the internal affective sphere with the external socially canalized activity frames. For example, the song to be sung while collecting honey among hunters–gatherers of the Nilgiri Hills (Demmer, 1997) catalyzes the personal meaningfulness of the activity. (p. 72)

My feeling of being completely subsumed by the art installation is the work of the abundance of the ornaments for meaning construction. What about the personal meaningfulness or sense-making for visitors, who do not have a direct cultural, familial connection to what the art installation signifies? Again, the signification of the installation is far from monolithic. I recall one moment during my visit when I overheard (eavesdropped) a conversation between a mother and a child, who were standing right beside me as I was contemplating the mass of ceramic poppies. The mother was explaining to the child that the ceramic poppies represent the fallen soldiers. The child was attentively listening, and the mother went on to comment on how the soldiers had contributed to keeping the country the way it was in the present time. The mother's conversational storytelling to the child was made in relevance to the collective memory that the art involves. This storytelling seems to parallel the singing of the honey collectors in the Nilgiri Hills in the aforementioned example. The episode was a further illustration of how personal meaning-making was made available to another person (and also a third who overheard it) in the context of the activity of commemoration, illustrating

Figure 5.3 The remembrance poppies tied to the fence of Tower of London for personal tribute (the photograph was taken while listening to a mother talking to a child).

that the collective and the personal/individual are intertwined in the materiality of the activity (Figure 5.3).

CONCLUSION

In this chapter, I considered the case of the remembrance poppy for the national commemoration as a broader phenomenon of cultural memory. I hope this chapter has provided insight into materiality in critical debates on memory and cultural studies and developed a more integrated view of collective remembering in the context of culture, artifacts, discourse, and cognition—aligning with Radley's material view of remembering. Drawing on Connerton's work, I then discussed the use of the remembrance poppy and explored the ritual nature of the cultural use of the artifact for the commemorative practice. Last, to further the discussion of the cultural use of the artifact and the emergence of meaning-making potentialities, I consulted Valsiner's work on ornaments and the concept of hypergeneralization through ornamental abundance for meaning construction. This chapter highlighted the interplay between discourse, materials/artifacts/ornaments, body, and environment as an integrated whole. This discussion, along with recent trends in material and affective turns in material culture and memory studies, highlights the importance of body and artifacts in understanding the phenomena of remembering and forgetting both at the collective (public) level and at the individual (personal) level.

REFERENCES

Bartlett, F. C. (1995). *Remembering: A study in experimental and social psychology.* Cambridge, UK: Cambridge University Press. (Original work published 1932)

Bergson, H. (2004). *Matter and memory* (N. M. Paul & W. S. Palmer, Trans.). Mineola, NY: Dover. (Original work published 1912)

Billig, M., Condor, S., Edwards, D., Gane, M., Middleton, D. J., & Radley, A. R. (1988). *Ideological dilemmas: A social psychology of everyday thinking.* London, UK: Sage.

Brockmeier, J. (2010). After the archive: Remapping memory. *Culture & Psychology, 16*(1), 5–35.

Connerton, P. (1989). *How societies remember.* Cambridge, UK: Cambridge University Press.

Demmer, U. (1997). Voices in the forest: The field of gathering among the Jenu Kurumba. In P. Hockings (Ed.), *Blue Mountains revisited: Cultural studies on the Nilgiri Hills* (pp. 164–191). Delhi, India: Oxford University Press.

Goffman, E. (1974). *Frame analysis: An essay on the organization of experience.* Cambridge, MA: Harvard University Press.

Grant, H., & Javid, S. T. R. H. M. (2013). *First World War centenary and national events and ceremonies (Appendix 2: Remembrance Sunday).* London, UK: Department of Culture Media & Sport. Retrieved from https://www.gov.uk/government/policies/marking-relevant-national-events-and-ceremonies

Harrison, T. (2012). *Remembrance today: Poppies, grief and heroism.* London, UK: Reaktion Books.

Hockey, J., Komaromy, C., & Woodthrope, K. (2010). Materialising absence. In J. Hockey, C. Komaromy, & K. Woodthrope (Eds.), *The matter of death: Space, place and materiality* (pp. 1–18). Basingstoke, UK: Palgrave Macmillan.

Holland, D., & Cole, M. (1995). Between discourse and schema: Reformulating a cultural–historical approach to culture and mind. *Anthropology & Education Quarterly, 26*(4), 475–489.

Iles, J. (2008). In remembrance: The Flanders poppy. *Mortality: Promoting the Interdisciplinary Study of Death and Dying, 13*(3), 201–221.

Kopytoff, I. (1986). The cultural biography of things. In A. Appadurai (Ed.), *The social life of things: Commodities in cultural perspective* (pp. 64–91). Cambridge, UK: Cambridge University Press.

Legion, T. R. B. (2015). *The story of the poppy.* Retrieved from http://www.britishlegion.org.uk/remembrance/how-we-remember/the-story-of-the-poppy/?gclid=CMjmieLOtM4CFcgp0wodHKgBHA

Marcus, G. E., & Fischer, M. M. (1986). *Anthropology as cultural critique: An experimental moment in the human sciences.* Chicago, IL: University of Chicago Press.

Middleton, D., & Brown, S. D. (2005). *The social psychology of experience: Studies in remembering and forgetting.* London, UK: Sage.

Middleton, D. J., & Edwards, D. (Eds.). (1990). *Collective remembering.* London, UK: Sage.

Moghaddam, F. M. (2002). *The individual and society: A cultural integration*. New York, NY: Worth.

Olick, J. K., Vinitzky-Seroussi, V., & Levy, D. (Eds.). (2011). *The collective memory reader*. New York, NY: Oxford University Press.

Radley, A. (1990). Artefacts, memory and a sense of the past. In D. Middleton & D. Edwards (Eds.), *Collective remembering* (pp. 46–59). London, UK: Sage.

Treble, P. (2014, October 9). In the tower, the poppies flow: Inside an extraordinary art project. *Maclean's*. Retrieved from http://www.macleans.ca/multimedia/photo/in-the-tower-the-poppies-flow-inside-an-extraordinary-art-project

Turner, V. W. (1995(1969)). *The ritual process: structure and anti-structure*. New York: Aldine de Gruyter.

Valsiner, J. (2000). *Culture and human development*. London, UK: Sage.

Valsiner, J. (2003). Sensuality and sense: Cultural construction of the human nature. *Human Affairs, 2*, 151–162.

Valsiner, J. (2008). Ornamented worlds and textures of feeling: The power of abundance. *Critical Social Studies, 1*, 67–78.

Vygotsky, L. S. (1978). *Mind in society: The development of higher psychological processes* (M. Cole, V. John-Steiner, S. Scribner, & E. Souberman, Eds. and Trans.). Cambridge, MA: Harvard University Press.

Wagoner, B. (2017). *The constructive mind: Bartlett's psychology in reconstruction*. Cambridge, UK: Cambridge University Press.

Walton, S. P. (1993). Jean Briggs' *Never in Anger* as an ethnography of experience. *Critique of Anthropology, 13*(4), 379–399.

Wertsch, J. V. (2002). *Voices of collective remembering*. New York, NY: Cambridge University Press.

Winter, C. (2009). Tourism, social memory and the Great War. *Annals of Tourism Research, 36*(4), 607–627

Winter, C. (2012). Commemoration of the Great War on the Somme: Exploring personal connections. *Journal of Tourism and Cultural Change, 10*(3), 248–263.

Winter, J. (1995). *Sites of memory, sites of moruning: The Great War in European cultural history*. Cambridge, UK: Cambridge University Press.

Woodward, I. (2007). *Understanding material culture*. London, UK: Sage.

Zerubavel, Y. (2011). Recovered roots: Collective memory and the making of Israeli national tradition. In J. K. Olick, V. Vinitzky-Seroussi, & D. Levy (Eds.), *The collective memory reader* (pp. 237–241). Oxford, UK: Oxford University Press.

Approaches to Testimony

Two Current Views and Beyond

KOTARO TAKAGI AND NAOHISA MORI ■

Q. The same as in memory, as you said, you wanted to do for memory what Gibson did for perception, but there was no theoretical revolution.
A. Yes, that's right. But I did something in that area. I managed to get a real good start for studying memory under natural conditions. A lot of people are doing that and that's Gibson's influence. But there isn't an underlying theory, an underlying changed kind of world view for memory that Gibson represented for perception. Once you start asking what's the information in the light instead of asking what mental representations are involved, that's a real shift, not just in method but in goal. Nothing as dramatic as that has happened in memory. You're not transforming the study of memory with that, you're just contributing to it. Whether it will ever happen, I don't know. We'll have to wait on somebody getting a better idea than I ever had about it.

—SZOKOLSZKY (2013, p. 196)

INTRODUCTION

Although Neisser is known as one of the leading researchers in cognitive psychology, in 1978 he manifested his criticism against it (Neisser, 1978). His criticism was accepted, and many researchers removed memory from the laboratory and began to study it in various natural conditions. This new line of research is called "everyday memory studies." Eyewitness testimony has been one of the most successful areas in everyday memory study since Elizabeth Loftus and colleagues' seminal works were published (Loftus, 1979; Loftus & Ketcham, 1991). However, Neisser did not just aim to get memory studies out of the laboratory, as he stated in the interview in his later life that was cited at the beginning of the chapter. He was really looking for a new theory of memory instead of the cognitive approach, which has been dominant in studies of eyewitness testimony. In this chapter, we follow Neisser's direction and propose a new theory that he was longing for—that is, a Gibsonian or the ecological approach to memory in a research field of confession and testimony.

Testimony is one form of mnemonic practice in our everyday lives. In this chapter, we first briefly analyze the nature of this practice and review the history of the research that psychology has been concerned with throughout more than a century of research. In recent decades, two approaches to testimony have been dominant: the cognitive approach and the discursive approach. However, when appropriately studied, both approaches are problematic. A hint of this new theory exists in Neisser's (1982) study of "John Dean's memory." His concept of "repisodic memory" is a key. Neisser roughly defined this concept as representatives or common characteristics of a series of events, in contrast to "episodic memory" (Tulving, 1972), which refers to the representation of a single event. We closely examine the concept and integrate it with Gibson's (1979) ecological perspective of perception and Bartlett's (1932) schema theory in a synthesis that combines these two approaches. Then we propose a new approach that Neisser would have hoped to develop. We next demonstrate the validity of our new theory by referring to the practical and experimental studies that we have been carrying out. Finally, we reconsider how and where testimony occurs from our new perspective.

TESTIMONY AS SOCIAL PRACTICE

In judicial procedures and investigations of criminal cases, eyewitnesses and suspects are required to verbally explain criminal events from their past. In this practice, referred to as testimonies (or statements or confessions), social and institutional constraints different from the daily recall of past experiences can be observed.

First, witnesses cannot choose either the events that must be explained or their methods of explanation. Witnesses must remember events selected as necessary to clarify the facts of an incident in accordance with the legal system; moreover, they must verbalize them in the style allowed by that legal system. Second, the explanation of events must be composed based on information derived solely from witnesses' own memories. Information obtained from various media, hearsay from third parties, and witnesses' inferences and imaginings must be excluded from the explanation. Third, the explanation must reflect the criminal event's content in detail, as precisely as possible. For such detail, a word-for-word explanation is emphatically demanded. In court, witnesses who intentionally give false explanations might be accused of perjury. Last, witnesses' explanations are not received unconditionally by the interviewer: Their credibility is strictly examined. Therefore, witnesses are not simply required to explain their experiences but must also attempt to provide a credible explanation that persuades listeners to believe them. To satisfy these constraints, witnesses and suspects are pressured both directly and indirectly. In Japanese criminal courts, for instance, witnesses must respond only to questions from interrogators, and explanations that deviate from these questions, in principle, are not allowed. In addition, referring to memos or other evidence on the witness stand is forbidden; only when strictly necessary can this be done, with an authorization obtained from the judge.

In legal proceedings, based only on memory, a rememberer must recall events designated by others and produce as accurate and detailed a verbal explanation as possible, which is then evaluated by others. This same structure occurs in interaction between participants and psychologists in memory experiments. In most experiments on memory, the event to be recalled has already been selected by researchers. Participants must retrieve information from their memory and report the results. Even if the retrieval fails, participants cannot refer to information not included in the experimental design. Finally, in memory experiments, researchers analyze and evaluate participants' performances.

Of course, testimony and memory experiments have important differences. One is the purpose of remembering. In testimony, the interviewer intends to clarify an original event through verbal statements by a witness, victim, or suspect. In an experiment on memory, however, the purpose is to understand the system or function of human memory through the subject's performance. Another difference is accessibility to the original event. With eyewitness testimony and confession, no one has an accurate grasp of the original event's actual nature. Even eyewitnesses and perpetrators perceive no more than a portion of the event. And of course, memories can be distorted. The police and lawyers, who have not directly experienced the event themselves, can only make assumptions on the basis of the evidence provided. Decisions of judges and juries do not constitute an accurate explanation of the event itself but, rather, are a product of inference based on the evidence provided—in other words, representations of a socially agreed understanding of the event. In regard to testimony, all players participate in an interaction on the premise of inaccessibility to the original event, aiming to understand its details. Inaccessibility to the original event is not only the nature of testimony but also the nature of people's everyday practice of remembering.

By contrast, in memory experiments, privileged observers—psychologists— can access the original event (Mori, 1995). By obtaining the right to determine events that participants should remember, psychologists avoid the problem of inaccessibility to the original event. On the other hand, participants take part in an experiment without the right to access the original event. Working within this asymmetric relationship, psychologists aim to understand the mechanism of memory underlying subjects' performances. Invisible psychological mechanisms can be inferred through differences between the original event, which psychologists determine and manage, and subjects' verbal explanations about it.

Dissociation of memory experiments from the everyday practice of remembering, including testimony, has come under repeated criticism in terms of "ecological validity" (Neisser, 1978). Such criticisms indicate the difference between experiments and everyday practice—for example, the nature of the event to be remembered, the time span between the original experience and its retrieval, and the motivation for retrieval of such memories. These differences can be overcome by proper experimental techniques. In contrast, however, the psychologist's accessibility to the original event bears on elemental presuppositions of memory experiments and might constitute a fundamental difference from everyday memory practice (including testimony), in which nobody has access to the original event.

THE CLASSICAL APPROACH

Notwithstanding this fundamental difference, repeated attempts have long been made for experimental research on memory to contribute to the credible assessment of testimony. We can trace this attempt to the dawn of scientific psychology (Binet, 1900; Cattell, 1895; Münsterberg, 1908; Stern, 1902). For example, in 1895, J. M. Cattell conducted an experiment in which 56 students were asked a list of questions, including questions concerning memory, and published the results in the journal *Science*. The questions posed included, for example, "What was the weather a week ago?" In reply, 16 students answered "clear," 12 "rain," 7 "snow," 9 "stormy," 6 "cloudy," and another 6 "partly stormy and partly clear." Connecting these research findings and the credibility of witnesses' testimony, Cattell stated the following:

> It seems that an average man with a moderate time for reflection cannot state much better what the weather was a week ago than what it will be a week hence. Yet this is a question that might naturally be asked in a court of justice. An unscrupulous attorney can discredit the statement of a truthful witness by cunningly selected questions. The jury, or at least the judge, should know how far errors in recollection are normal and how they vary under different conditions. (p. 761)

Münsterberg (1908) also indicated the frailty of witness testimony, drawing on individual anecdotes and numerous experiments. The most striking example is a staged event, conducted as an experiment by criminologist Professor Franz von Liszt. During a lecture, as von Liszt referred to one book, a student shouted, "I wanted to throw light on the matter from the standpoint of Christian morality!" In reaction, another student interjected, "I cannot stand that!" The two became involved in a heated debate, upon which the older student, who had spoken first, drew a pistol. The other student "rushed madly upon him" as though driven out of his senses. Von Liszt, asking other students in the lecture hall to stay calm, explained that the entire event had been scripted as an experiment and asked them to describe in writing, as accurately as possible, the event they had just witnessed.

In analysis, students' recollections were divided according to the script's 14 headings, and errors such as omission, incorrect addition, and alteration were counted for each heading. Students who produced the most accurate version of the event were mistaken in 26% of their descriptions. Participants who produced the most errant versions were mistaken in 80% of their descriptions. Errors were more apparent in information on the second, more heated, half of the proceedings as opposed to the first. Reflecting on these findings, Münsterberg warned how easily witness testimony can be wrong:

> In the life of justice trains are wrecked and ships are colliding too often, simply because the law does not care to examine the mental color blindness of the witness's memory. And yet we have not even touched one factor which, more than anything else, devastates memory and plays havoc with our best intended recollections: That is, the power of suggestion. (pp. 68–69)

Münsterberg was one of the first researchers who propounded to a general audience that psychology's scientific findings should be employed in courts of law. However, Münsterberg's claims were exaggerated to some extent and overly assertive; this drew strong criticism from jurists. In particular, jurist J. H. Wigmore (1909) wrote an acerbic statement to the effect that psychologists' expertise was insufficiently trustworthy to serve in the courtroom. Münsterberg failed to respond publicly to this criticism, and this led, in part, to a long-standing lack of interchange between lawyers and psychologists in the United States (Sato, 1996).

Pioneering psychologists attempted to establish, on the basis of experiments and examples, how easily prone to error witness testimony is and to arouse the concern of both lawyers and the general public. One could term this a project of forensic psychology, intending to set definite constraints on inferences of judges and juries who must evaluate witness testimony's credibility where access to the original event is impossible. For such intervention, psychological findings obtained in experimental settings, in which psychologists have privileged access to the original event, could play an effective role. Errors in witness testimony, while raising important and interesting research questions in the psychology of memory, are also a serious problem in legal practice, with potentially highly undesirable outcomes such as false charges. Pioneer psychologists thought of witness testimony as an ideal field for demonstrating the reliability and usefulness of psychology—a science as yet barely born.

THE COGNITIVE APPROACH

Experimental psychological research on testimony finally began to build close connections with the world of law courts in the 1970s, when cognitive psychology was developing at a rapid pace (Buckhout, 1974; Loftus, 1974, 1979). Unlike the research undertaken by pioneering psychologists, in the 1970s a novel approach was employed that, rather than seeking simply to find examples of how easily mistakes in remembering are made by witnesses, emphasized underlying factors of such mistakes and clarified cognitive processes by which information is processed. For example, Loftus and Palmer (1974) conducted the following experiment on the influence of post-event misinformation on witness memory. First, they showed 100 subjects a movie of a car crash. They then asked, "About how fast were the cars going when they smashed?" Other subjects were asked, "About how fast were the cars going when they hit?" A week later, they had the subjects return for an unscheduled interview, asking all of them, "Did you see any broken glass?" No car's glass had been broken in the movie; however, the group that had been asked the question containing the word "smashed," with the misguidance of violent collision, gave significantly more incorrect answers compared to the group that had been asked the question containing the more neutral word "hit." Findings from this experiment suggested that the slightest fragment of verbal information could significantly affect witnesses' memories. These results also have an important practical implication: They strongly suggest the importance of investigators and lawyers choosing their words carefully when questioning witnesses.

Groundbreaking research undertaken by Loftus and others in the 1970s (e.g., Loftus, 1974, 1979) had a major impact on memory researchers; albeit more gradually, they also found acceptance in the courtroom as scientific experts who could not be ignored (Loftus & Ketcham, 1991). The cognitive approach to eyewitness testimony went global, rapidly gathering a body of further findings into factors affecting the credibility of witness testimony. To assess the extent of "general acceptance" of various eyewitness research findings within the psychological community, Kassin, Tubb, Hosch, and Memon (2001) chose 30 well-known psychological findings concerning eyewitness testimony and asked 64 psychologists from 13 countries to evaluate the reliability of such findings on a 7-point scale. The majority (>80%) of researchers accepted the reliability of post-event misinformation effect, along with other findings, such as wording of questions, child suggestibility, weapon focus, and unconscious transference.

A framework has also been proposed for organizing these factors systematically. Wells (1978) suggested classification of factors into estimator variables and system variables. Estimator variables refer to factors over which investigators and lawyers have no control. These include the exposure duration of an event; the gravity and complexity of a crime; and the race, gender, age, and so on of the criminal and the witness. System variables refer to those factors over which investigators and related individuals can have control. These include the time elapsed from witnessing to identification, suggestive questions, the structure of questions, and so on.

Whereas the framework Wells (1978) proposed reflects the actual on-the-ground context of investigative intervention in crime, Loftus, Greene, and Doyle (1989) proposed a framework that corresponds to the information-processing process in the human brain. First, underlying factors related to event perception and its memory encoding are further categorized into two factors: one associated with the event, such as illuminance level, exposure duration, and weapon focus effect, and the other associated with the witness, such as gender, age, and stress.

Second, there are factors related to retention of information in memory storage, including forgetting, distortions of memory, post-event misinformation, and so on. Finally, there are factors related to memory retrieval, including how questions are framed, use of hypnotism, and so on.

Energetic efforts are also underway to develop interview techniques that can yield more reliable witness testimony. One such proposal is the cognitive interview (Geiselman et al., 1984), in which the following four questioning strategies are used to facilitate witness retrieval of memory: (1) "mental reinstatement of context," in which the witness is required to remember the context of the event witnessed; (2) the "report everything" strategy, in which the witness is required to retrieve all available information about the event, no matter how trivial; (3) the "change order" strategy, in which the witness is required to retrieve the event in various time orders; and (4) the "change perspective" strategy, in which the witness is required to retrieve the event from different perspectives than that at the time of the event. This interview technique has been further developed as the enhanced cognitive interview, in which a social component is included to facilitate communication in the interview (Fisher & Geiselman, 1992). In addition to interview techniques for adult witnesses, interview techniques for child witnesses and victims are also being developed and applied to legal practices (Lamb, Orbach, Hershkowitz, Esplin, & Horowitz, 2007; Ministry of Justice, 2011).

Furthermore, in recent years, the focus has been widening from witnesses to research on the extent to which the general public, jury members, and so on grasp underlying psychological factors affecting witness testimony (Neal, Christiansen, Bornstein, & Robicheaux, 2012; Read & Desmarais, 2009; Schmechel, O'Toole, Easterly, & Loftus, 2006; Wise, Safer, & Maro, 2011). This approach is born of practical necessity, under conditions in which psychologists' expert statements on eyewitness testimony are rejected by jurors on the basis of "common sense," which often does not align with scientific evidence (Loftus, 2013). There are also moves to apply the findings of neuroscience to research on witness testimony. For example, Okado and Stark (2005) used neuroimaging to clarify mental mechanisms at work in creating the misinformation effect. Loftus (2005) expects that in the future, the application of techniques such as these might make it possible to judge whether memory-related information is based on the original event or on misinformation (see also Frenda, Nichols, & Loftus, 2011).

Thus, the cognitive approach to eyewitness testimony has made important strides from the 1970s to the 2010s, and it has become a provider of expertise that cannot be ignored in legal practice. Münsterberg's dream of a century ago is now becoming a reality. Loftus (2013) declares the following regarding this achievement:

Today, expert testimony has an easier time being admitted. Courts are more favorably commenting on our science. This slow-to-start, but exponentially growing, collaboration between psychologists, legal professionals, and others has done a great deal to change the justice landscape for people accused of crimes (Steblay & Loftus, 2013). Who could ask for a more rewarding payoff for decades of cumulative work? (p. 557)

This "victory declaration" reaffirms the cognitive approach's effectiveness on eyewitness testimony, in which psychologists establish privileged access to the original event; produce scientific knowledge on memory distortions; and use this knowledge to constrain credibility assessment of testimony in the legal context in which, in principle, nobody can access the original event. In the history of psychology, this achievement—more than 100 years in the making—is an extremely rare example of successful collaboration between experimental research and social practices.

JOHN DEAN'S MEMORY

The cognitive approach to testimony has achieved great success both in its practical applications and as empirical research on memory. However, is this the only approach to testimony? In fact, at the dawn of cognitive research on testimony, there was one case study that could have potentially led research on testimony in a very different direction. This was a study by Neisser (1982) on the memory of former counsel John Dean, who testified to President Nixon's involvement in crime during the Watergate scandal's investigation.

Dean was deeply involved in the cover-up of the wiretapping incident perpetrated by Nixon's camp. However, after the scandal was uncovered, he reversed his position and gave testimony that substantiated the president's personal involvement to the Senate Watergate Committee. His testimony was incredibly detailed, and it provided specific exposition of exchanges between Nixon and his staff in the Oval Office. However, an audiotape recording of the conversation that occurred in the Oval Office was subsequently discovered, and it became apparent that some content in Dean's testimony did not coincide with what actually happened. For example, in his statement written 9 months after his meeting with President Nixon on September 15, 1972, the day the federal grand jury reached a verdict, Dean stated that when he visited the president's office that day, the president asked him to sit down. However, the president never actually said anything like that. Moreover, Dean testified that the president said he had received a report about his work from a close associate; however, the recording could not confirm this statement. Furthermore, Dean also testified that he had responded humbly to praise from the president, saying, "It isn't my own personal achievement," but this statement did not exist in the recording. Initially, the detailed nature of Dean's testimony surprised people, but in actuality, it included much inaccurate information compared to the verbatim recording, and it was also clearly inaccurate about the gist of the event.

However, Neisser (1982) asserted that Dean's testimony was accurate according to a different standard than providing a verbatim account or the gist of the event. Dean intended to recount word for word his remembering of the September 15,

1972, event. However, Neisser asserted that what Dean actually remembered was not details from that day but, rather, characteristics shared by several meetings he repeatedly experienced while working on the cover-up. Neisser proposed that information remembered as representative of a series of events should be called a "repisode" as opposed to an "episode" that refers to a single event:

> I think that he extracted the common themes that remained invariant across many conversations and many experiences, and then incorporated those themes in his testimony. His many encounters with Nixon were themselves a kind of "repisode." There were certain consistent and repeated elements in all those meetings; they had a theme that expressed itself in different ways on different occasions. Nixon wanted the cover-up to succeed; he was pleased when it went well; he was troubled when it began to unravel; he was per-fectly willing to consider illegal activities if they would extend his power or confound his enemies. John Dean did not misrepresent this theme in his testimony. (p. 159)

Neisser's (1982) concept of a repisode could potentially have brought about a different analytic perspective for credibility assessment of testimony. This per-spective differed fundamentally from the cognitive approach taken by Loftus that examines the possibility of errors (compared with a word-for-word record or gist of the original event) being mixed into testimony. Unfortunately, how-ever, Neisser did not subsequently refine this concept adequately. As Neisser recalls (Szokolszky, 2013), his "ecological approach" to memory during the 1980s largely promoted memory research conducted under natural conditions (Neisser, 1978), but it did not provide "an underlying theory, an underlying changed kind of world view for memory" (Szokolszky, 2013, p. 196). For this reason, Neisser's (1982) analysis of Dean's testimony was referenced as only one classical study that observationally examined testimony under natural conditions.

THE DISCURSIVE APPROACH

Edwards and Potter (1992) praised Neisser's (1982) study of Dean's testimony for succeeding in being a welcome departure from conventional cognitive approaches for the following reasons: (1) It observed recollection in a natural context, (2) it focused on functional aspects of remembering in communication (e.g., control-ling one's own position through remembering), and (3) it focused on accuracy of memory rather than on its distortion. At the same time, however, they criticized Neisser's study for lacking sufficient attention to the testimony's discursive nature, especially its pragmatic organization, and emphasized the necessity of a social and discursive approach to testimony.

Neisser (1982) treated the audiotape recording's transcription as a definitive record that accurately reflected original events in the Oval Office and examined its consistency with Dean's testimony as a verbatim account, as the gist of events, and as a repisode. According to Edwards and Potter (1992), this approach resembles the cognitive approach, insofar as it first establishes a description of the "truth" of original events that is beyond dispute, and then it uses this as a criterion to assess objectively the remembering's accuracy. They observed that obtaining a single description of the original event beyond dispute is fundamentally difficult because even when the original event has been audio or video recorded, certain aspects are inevitably selected and others omitted in the recording process. When a word-for-word transcription of an audio or video recording is created, the extent to which breath sounds and hesitations are included in a description remains the transcriber's decision. In this sense, even records that psychologists create as privileged observers are just a single descriptive version of the original event. Similarly, the transcription that Neisser used is also a single descriptive version of past events in the Oval Office.

Upon identifying these fundamental difficulties in describing original events, Edwards and Potter (1992) asserted that approaches to testimony should not focus on the corresponding relationship between descriptions of original events and their rememberings but, rather, on the discursive process whereby people create and negotiate an acceptable descriptive version of past events. This process includes negotiation of explanations or selections of materials that provide a basis of "truth," and it also includes negotiations for a functional purpose—for example, "I will make the president guilty, and I will not become a scapegoat." A concrete example is Edwards and Potter's (1992) research, an analysis of the controversy surrounding the "off-the-record" briefing for journalists by Nigel Lawson, British Chancellor of the Exchequer. The controversy involved whether Lawson had said to alter benefits payable to old age pensioners. In the analysis, Edwards and Potter examined what Lawson and the journalists selected as the "record of the truth" and how they used it, what rhetoric was used to describe the event as truth, and how they explained error of remembering. Other examples of research based on this same approach are Lynch and Bogen's (1996) analysis of Lieutenant Colonel North's testimony related to the Iran-Contra affair and the series of studies by Drew regarding court testimony in criminal trials (Atkinson & Drew, 1979; Drew, 1990, 1992).

A discursive approach does not evaluate the credibility of testimony based on the original event. Rather, it emphasizes the necessity of understanding testimony as situated within the process by which people construct social meaning of a past event. This approach made very important progress because it enabled understanding of a wide variety of social practices concerning testimony. At the same time, however, this approach detaches testimony from the original event and understands testimony as a phenomenon produced and given meaning in current social interactions. Consequently, these studies come to completely ignore important questions concerning witness "experience," such as the type of events the witness has actually encountered and how this is reflected in testimony. In other words, this approach invalidates questions on the credibility of testimony that psychology has explored for more than 100 years, and it also abandons attempts to contribute practically to the judicial system. Judges and juries do not aim to understand the process of lawyers and witnesses constructing social meaning but, instead, look for support in determining whether testimony is based on actual experiences.

REPISODIC MEMORY REVISITED

As has been explained to this point, modern psychological approaches to testimony can be broadly classified into the cognitive approach, which focuses on the relationship between original events and testimony, and the discursive approach, which focuses on the social negotiation process. The cognitive approach has succeeded in responding to the judicial system's requirements, but it faces a fundamental difficulty in being unable to establish firmly a description of original events that can be used as a criterion to assess the credibility of testimony. On the other hand, the discursive approach has succeeded in understanding testimony within its social context, but in so doing, it abandons any response to the judicial system's practical requirements. In this way, studies of testimony are split into two camps, and both face fundamental difficulties. This is a situation that Vygotsky (1997) referred to as a "crisis." How can we overcome the deadlock? Required here is a new approach that avoids fundamental difficulties concerning original events without abandoning practical contributions to the courtroom through credibility assessment of testimony. For this pursuit, critical re-examination of various psychological concepts related to witness experience is inevitably required.

Despite Edwards and Potter's (1992) criticism, the repisode could potentially become a "welcome departure" toward a new approach. Edwards and Potter criticized Neisser's (1982) focus on the repisode because it examined the corresponding relationship between original events and testimony in the same way that verbatim or gist did so. Certainly, Neisser explained repisodes as common characteristics of events the rememberer repetitively experienced. He then contrasted this with audiotape recording transcripts taken to be true records of original events. Interestingly, although Neisser applied a common analytic method with the cognitive approach, he also rephrased the term repisode as "invariants" of a series of events, using the terminology of J. J. Gibson's (1966, 1979) ecological theory of perception. Neisser stated,

> What I learned, at least, is that being "right" is not a simple notion. Even when Dean was entirely wrong about the course of a particular conversation, he could be giving an essentially true account of the facts lying behind that conversation—of long run, invariant states of affairs that had manifested themselves in many individual episodes. Combining information from several points in time may indeed lead to error, and it is not what witnesses are supposed to do. Nevertheless, it is often a good way to establish the real facts of the matter—the ones that are worth remembering. (p. 139)

I think that he extracted the common themes that remained invariant across many conversations and many experiences, and then incorporated those themes in his testimony. (pp. 158–159)

Gibson's "invariants" are apparently incompatible with the cognitive approach, and Neisser never further investigated his idea's ecological implications. We believe that refining the concept of the repisode based on Gibsonian theory opens possibilities for developing a new approach to testimony. This is our argument hereafter.

Gibson's concept of invariants can be explained as follows (Reed, 1996): When an animal searches its environment, the arrangement pattern of information perceived in that environment (e.g., the optical arrangement) is transformed. However, a pattern of information is also stably maintained without change, despite this transformation. This is an invariant. For example, a person waving a stick can still somewhat accurately perceive its length (the distance between the hand and the tip of the stick) even if he or she cannot directly see the stick (Solomon & Turvey, 1988). By waving the stick, the person explores and "picks up" information (inertia tensor) that makes it possible to perceive the stick's length as an invariant existing in the transformation of the haptic sensory pattern.

Then, how do we reinterpret the repisode using the concept of invariants? In the Watergate case, for example, the details and gist of the meetings among Dean, Nixon, and other close associates differed at each meeting. Therefore, repeated participation in these meetings led to a transformation of information pattern that constitutes the gist and details of these events. Dean picked up his repisode as the invariant that was consistently distinguishable from the transformation throughout this series of events. For example, what is picked up from waving the stick is information that specifies the stick's length but not common elements of how the stick was repeatedly waved. Similarly, the repisode Dean recalled did not consist of elements that multiple meetings shared but, rather, the invariant that indicated "intensity" or "qualities" that differed from the summary of the repeated event in which he participated.

The invariant of events that is picked up as a repisode is not an objective special characteristic that exists in a vacuum with the rememberer. Small children and adults move their hands in different ways, at different speeds, even if they wave the same stick. However, both children and adults can specify the stick's length similarly because of the invariant they pick up through their different motions. This is also the situation with regard to repisodes. The manner in which Dean participated in these meetings was naturally different from the way the president and other close associates did so. However, the invariant Dean picked up through repeated participation appropriately reflected the events' quality from his perspective. Repisodes as a form of invariant do not merely reflect characteristics of certain events but, rather, reflect the relationship between the rememberer and the event. This is believed to be the reason for Dean's repisode being connected to his attitude, expectations, and stance with regard to the meetings and the cover-up.

In remembering a repisode, the exploration of environment is conducted in a mode different from perception. According to Gibson (1979), perceptual exploration of the environment by animals is not a neutral gathering of information but, rather, always coupled with their own actions. Animals explore their environments by including possibilities for their own actions—for example, "Can I walk in this location?" "Can I climb this?" and "Can I eat this?" Gibson referred to this as the "duality" of the "self" and the "environment" in the mode of perceptually exploring the environment. Reed (1994) and Sasaki (1996) attempted to expand this idea to memory. According to Reed, remembering is also a mode through which animals explore their environment. However, remembering differs from perception insofar as the duality it creates is between "past" and "present." When animals explore the environment using this mode, they grasp their current environment by relating it to events they have experienced in the past, not by relating it to their own actions. For example, an exploration is perceptual when someone walking on a road reaches a dead end and perceives that this means he or she "cannot go any further" based on the relationship between the current environment and his or her own actions. On the other hand, if the person perceives the dead end based on a relationship between past and present, thinking something like "I thought I could get through here before" or "This has been a dead end for a long time," that is an exploration of the environment as a form of remembering. Accordingly, perceptual exploration inevitably precedes recollection. Remembering is repetition of animals' exploration of the environment that includes a change of modes (Sasaki, 1996).

The mode of remembering has several types of exploration of environment. Takagi (2014) classified remembering into four categories based on the pattern of duality between past and present:

1. Recognition: I again encounter the object that I encountered in the past.
2. Recall: I fail to encounter again the object that I encountered in the past.
3. New event: I encounter a new object that I have not encountered in the past.
4. Non-existence: I fail to encounter a new object that I have not encountered in the past.

Based on these categories, testimony would be considered recall in which target events are detected as absent from the present environment. In recall, rememberers attempt to repeat perceptual exploration they conducted in the past. This type of exploration inevitably produces discrepancies between actions and the environment. We detect the absence of an event due to these discrepancies. Accordingly, a repisode as an invariant explored through recall differs from invariants picked up through perceptual exploration, and a repisode cannot be directly picked up in the current environment because environments that make it possible to pick up invariants perceptually have already ceased to exist.

Assuming that a repisode (as a form of invariants) is absent from the current environment, how should we approach testimony? The primary target of analysis by both cognitive and discursive approaches is semiotic representations of past events. The cognitive approach has investigated the possibility that semiotic representations produced by witnesses do not coincide with original events. The discursive approach has emphasized the necessity of focusing on people's negotiation process concerning proper representations of past events. In contrast, the ecological approach primarily focuses on the act of remembering itself as an exploration of the environment. Thus, this approach analyzes testimony not by examining "what the witness is explaining" about the past but, rather, by focusing centrally on "how the witness explores past events" in the current environment.

By focusing on remembering as an exploratory action of the current environment, how can we approach witness experience? As previously mentioned, in recall, perceptual exploration of previous events is repeated in a different mode of exploration in the current environment in which events no longer exist. The ecological approach presupposes that through this repetition of exploration, past experiences are connected with current actions. Bartlett's (1932) concept of "schema" helps us more clearly understand this idea. Although cognitive psychologists have interpreted schema as the structuring framework of the brain's memory representations, schema is more appropriately understood as related to a process in which past experience dynamically connects with present action through the repetition of actions. Northway (1940a, 1940b) first indicated this, and in more recent years, Mori (2009) and Wagoner (2013, 2017) again noted its importance. According to Bartlett, when a player takes a stance to hit a ball in tennis or cricket, the stance is not a perfect repetition of one taken in the past. However, it is not a completely unrelated, new stance compared with those taken for past hits. A player hits the ball by flexibly adjusting past hitting stance to suit the current situation. In this way, hitting a ball in cricket or tennis repeats a past action but at the same time creatively produces a present action. In a similar manner, remembering repeats a past exploratory action but at the same time creates present exploratory action. The concept of schema refers to such flexible, repetitive organization, which can be observed in the act of remembering.

In the ecological approach to testimony, we focus on the process by which a witness reactivates schema in the present environment, explores invariants of past events, and fails to pick it up. In this approach, it seems that exploration of invariants, which is nonexistent in the current environment, involves clumsiness or instability of action, like reproducing a former hit when the ball is not actually being pitched. In many cases, language mediates this type of exploration. Semiotic representations generated during this exploration are analyzed not as descriptions of past events but, rather, as clues to understand the unstable movement of schema that explores absent invariants of a past event.

We believe that taking the ecological approach will enable understanding witness experience differently from the cognitive and discursive approaches. In memory studies, some researchers have also proposed an interesting approach to the rememberer's experience, using a Bergsonian concept of duration (Brown

& Reavey, 2014; Middleton & Brown, 2005). The ecological approach could also be a promising alternative. Subsequent sections of this chapter, using some legal cases as examples, show how this new approach explores witness experience while responding to the judicial system's practical demands and bringing the discursive process of testimony into view.

THE ECOLOGICAL TURN OF CONFESSION AND TESTIMONY

Remembering starts with the reactivation of schema, which means, in our ecological perspective, the perceptual exploration of environment is being shifted to another mode of exploration (Mori, 2008, 2009; Reed, 1994; Sasaki, 1996). This means a quality of duality on which our cognition relies starts to change. Perception relies on the duality of self and environment. In perception, we identify objects in the present environment (exteroception) as well as our own conditions (proprioception). This type of duality, which can be called "spatial duality," no longer succeeds to explore the environment when we realize something that we once encountered is now absent. At this moment, another kind of duality, which in contrast can be called "temporal duality," is applied to explore it. The environment surrounding us is temporally being extended, and it is in this environment that different parts of subenvironments—the past and the present environment—are nested. The same process of extension and differentiation is simultaneously occurring on our self. Our self becomes temporally dual to be differentiated into the past and the present self. In remembering, we try to construct the twofold—spatial and temporal—duality. The present and the past selves—environments in the twofold duality—are different but identical. The past self that once encountered the past environment (some objects or events) no longer exists in the present in which they have already gone. The contradictory nature of this kind in the twofold duality is supported by the exploration and discovery of invariants in time that specify once occurred but now absent events. In summary, successful remembering means the discovery of such invariants to achieve the twofold duality. Remembering is newly defined as the exploration and discovery of invariants that secure this twofold duality of the past self-environment/the present self-environment. So it is not necessary to pick up the past environment separately from the present one, as Bartlett (1932) states:

> When I make a stroke I do not, as a matter of fact, produce something absolutely new, and I never merely repeat something old. The stroke is literally manufactured out of the living visual and postural "schemata" of the moment and their interrelations. I may say, I may think that I reproduce exactly a series of text-book movements, but demonstrably I do not; just as, under other circumstance, I may say and think that I reproduce exactly some isolated event which I want to remember, and again demonstrably I do not. (p. 202)

Sole reproduction of each event is probably an illusion produced by experimental procedures of the cognitive approach, in which each event is separately presented and the person is requested to recall item by item.

Specification and report of the invariants to be explored are realized in various forms. One of them is Neisser's reposides, and other appears in forms of action during remembering, such as narrative styles. In general, these forms of action appear not on *what* is remembered but on *how* it is remembered. This resonates with Bartlett's (1932) distinction between the "matter" and the "manner" of recall. Examples of this are presented later. After such a conceptual turn, the credibility of confession and testimony has to be assessed by determining whether or not invariants that secure the twofold duality of the past self-environment/the present self-environment are being explored during those activities.

Sumio Hamada can be considered a pioneer of this new approach in Japan. Hamada by himself reached a similar position to ours without referring to the work of Bartlett or Gibson, and he devised his own credibility assessment techniques. His techniques are simple: Statement records by the police and public prosecutors are arranged following their dates,[1] transitions of their contents concerning an alleged crime are identified, and possible reasons are attributed to these transitions. When they are considered normal for true criminals to show (e.g., memory decay with the passage of time, temporal absent-mindedness, and lies to conceal their guilt), no problem is claimed. Otherwise, other kinds of exogenous factors from suspects' attributes are suggested (e.g., pressure to confess and misleading questions by interviewers and interrogators). Hamada's techniques to examine transitions among records reminds us of Bartlett's (1932) famous "method of repeated reproduction." As Bartlett attempted to find different kinds of force—cultural and personal—that change remembered contents, Hamada tried to find in transitions of records the involvement of interviewers who lead suspects to false confession. Hamada's techniques do not directly find traces of the exploration of invariants but, instead, negatively prove nonexistence of them by identifying interviewers' factors described previously.

Hamada's works inspired us to organize the Tokyo Confession Research Group, in which we started to assess the credibility of confession and testimony of possible false accusation. We moved beyond Hamada, developing a new approach to confession and testimony—the schema approach (Mori, 2009; Ohashi, Mori, Takagi, & Matsushima, 2002)—and thus opening a door to an ecological approach to remembering. The schema approach switches attention from what is remembered or narrative contents to how it is remembered or narrative styles and, more generally, bodily actions during remembering. It also indicates that different styles and actions in remembering reflect different qualities of experience. In the reliable assessment of a defendant's confession of a murder in the case known as the Ashikaga case (for details, see Mori, 2009), we made it clear that some correlation appeared between qualities of experience and narrative styles (Hara, Takagi, & Matsushima, 1997; Mori, 2009; Ohashi et al., 2002). Hara et al. found that when the defendant talked about his real experience,[2] he often applied a particular narrative style called "agent alteration" by which the defendant switched between a subject "I" and "others (things)," sentence by sentence (i.e., I . . ., other . . ., I . . ., other . . ., etc.). His report of the domiciliary search by a policeman is cited here (as quoted in Ohashi et al., 2002):

> Well, the policeman said, "Are you Mr. S?" and I responded, "Yes, I am." Then he said, "Can I come in and see your room?" So, I let him come. And he said, "Will you show me the inside of the closet?" then I opened the closet and a small box appeared. The policeman said, "Can I see it?" and I took it to him, then he said, "What is this inside of this box?" and I said, . . . (pp. 48–49)

This style suggests his contacting experience to the past environment including other people and things he encountered. This trend was scarcely found when he talked about the murder he allegedly committed. He applied chiefly a different style called "agent succession," in which the defendant uttered his own actions but hardly mentioned those of the victim. The victim could have been one of the most important parts of his past environment that belongs to the duality to be achieved during his confession if he had committed the murder. Ohashi et al. concluded that different narrative styles tell what kinds of environment—that can differentiate into the twofold duality or not, for example—are explored during remembering and can be attributed to different qualities of experience.

The new conception of remembering was further justified by an experimental examination performed by Mori (2008). He found similar phenomena to what the defendant in the Ashikaga case showed: Different narrative styles reflect different qualities of experience. When the participant talked about her experience contacting the environment, she described multifaceted objects, called them by different names, and attributed them to her motive for action. These characteristics in her real remembering suggest the physical environment in which she had been surrounded and had moved. However when she remembered her experience originating from hearsay information from others, these particularities of the physical environment did not appear.

These practical and experimental findings pushed remembering to its new ontology. A brain that is assumed to store memories is replaced by a body that can explore the twofold duality to find invariants. Thus, when assessing remembering, our focus of examination should be placed on bodily actions such as narrative styles rather than narrative contents because the former can reflect the exploration process of invariants. The cognitive approach is overcome by arguing that past experience is not stored in nor retrieved from a brain but, rather, realized through the exploration of invariants in the twofold duality between the past self-environment and the present self-environment. In contrast, the discursive approach retreats when we pay attention to the exploration of invariants in the duality at issue instead of the construction process and contents of semiotic representations of past events.

LES LIEUX (REALMS) OF EXPLORATION

When we consider remembering the exploration of invariants in the twofold duality of the past self-environment/the present self-environment, analysis of present environments in which testimony is produced—an investigation room and a court—is needed. What kinds of environmental factors influence witnesses' exploration of invariants in the twofold duality?

Pierre Nora (2002) states that oblivion of the past is resisted by the construction of *lieu de mémoire* (realms of memory) that maintain and facilitate remembering after *milieu de mémoire* (groups of memory) no longer exist. In a court or an investigation room, no one but a suspect/defendant and an eyewitness can access a past event (crime) at issue, assuming they were really engaged in it. Participants in a court or an investigation room, including police officers, prosecutors, judges, and juries, should construct realms of memory in which a suspect/defendant and an eyewitness are facilitated in expressing themselves to remember targeted events and to suppress misremembering such as distorted testimony or false confession.

Because we have replaced a concept of "memory" with "remembering as exploration of invariants in the twofold duality" after the ecological turn, the following discussion focuses on how proper environments, such as a court or an investigation room, set conditions on a suspect/defendant or an eyewitness for performing the exploration of invariants. This discussion contributes to forensic psychology because innovations of our testimony-gathering interview technique are expected. Moreover, it gives the cultural psychology of remembering another perspective in addition to the cognitive one.

An investigation room and a court are sociocultural environments to explore, in which several aspects can be identified as constraints to remember, such as dominance of verbal activities, limited resources, and disparity of power.

Interdependency between Physical and Verbal Environments

Environments in which experience and remembering are carried out are physical as well as verbal (semiotic). We have experience with being surrounded by many physical objects, which are also semiotically differentiated. We can name almost all things around us. Witnesses have to remember by referring to physical resources in response to interviewers' questions that orient and specify what and how to remember. They are requested to report to-be-remembered events in linguistic ways—use of common language and legally intelligible words—and to reach the representation of experience called "facts." Such a type of environment has already been suggested by Bartlett's (1932) concept of "organised setting" and has the characteristic of "interdependency" (Brockmeier, 2002; Middleton & Brown, 2005) between the physical and the verbal.

Note that the ecological approach stresses the difference between the experience of contacting a physical world, on the one hand, and the experience of a verbal one heard from others and generated by imagination, on the other hand. We acknowledge the interdependency of environments surrounding us and at the same time examine which aspect of environmental exploration is occurring in remembering. Mori (2008) showed that physical characteristics are more dominant in remembering when the participant talks about the experience she really had compared to when she pretends to have had a physical contact experience but in actuality is basing her narrative on information heard from others. If remembering is only verbal transformation of memory traces, as the cognitive approach assumes, how did such a difference occur? The discursive approach might attribute it to some rhetorics of past narrative, but the participant's description of environments she really encountered was beyond a linguistic plane. Her description suggested structures of environments rather than simply being based on verbal associations or imaginations.

Mori (2008) also noted that repeated verbal expression of real experience to be explored and communication of it with an interviewer reduce its physical characteristics and make different qualities of the experience unclear. He referred to the former as "intrapersonal conventionalization" and to the latter as "interpersonal conventionalization," following Bartlett's (1932) terminology. In contrast to Bartlett, who stressed forces of culture in conventionalization, Mori attended to verbal pollution of physical aspects of experience and the gradual tendency of real and confabulated remembering to resemble one another.

Another kind of penetration by language to experience was identified by Hamada (2009) when he examined victims' statements of *chikan*. *Chikan* is a kind of molestation that often happens in crowded trains (especially commuter trains) and is probably particular to Japanese society. It is an obscene crime mostly committed by men against women, who are often touched on their buttocks. Hamada noted that unrealistic statements of victims are often given. They are unrealistic because too many details of being touched are reported. Hamada pointed out the low sensitivity of buttocks, citing classical findings of psychophysics, and argued that victims' statements are probably based more on their imagination than the real experience. Hamada insisted that real victims do not report so many details of being touched and instead admit that they do not know such details. In actuality, victims talk about more than they experienced because of investigators' requests to provide more details. Worse, judges do not know that many details in cases of *chikan* are unrealistic. All participants in investigations and courts are often ignorant of characteristics of the real experience in environments and mistakenly identify it with imagination constructed within a linguistic space.

Limited Resources

Resources for the exploration of invariants in the twofold duality are constrained by laws and customs for criminal investigation. Also, their use is often open to investigators' decisions. Police officers and prosecutors tactically and cleverly present evidence and question accounts in order to challenge alibis, to remind suspects and witnesses of critical memories, and to point out contradictions in testimony. Investigators' arbitrary use of resources has been criticized for its possible elicitation of memory distortion, false memory, and false confession (Loftus, 1979; Loftus & Ketcham, 1991). Biased sample construction (including a suspect with others who are known to be innocent) in an identification book (Tomita, 1991) and in lineups (Wells, 1978) sometimes increases the probability of false identification. Presenting mug shots before lineups is criticized because of the high possibility to mislead (Itsukushima, Naka, & Hara, 2003). The defendant's false confession in the Ashikaga case was generated from several resources introduced by the investigators: leading questions, pieces of physical evidence, eyewitness testimony, and so on. The defendant was only exploring a hypothetical environment verbally fabricated by these resources. Misuse and abuse of investigative resources are criticized in our context for their potential to lead witnesses to perform inappropriate exploration of the duality, instead of as a possible memory distortion.

Resources that rememberers produce by themselves are safer. Remembering often proceeds with gradual verbalization of invariants in which targeted events in addition to their relevant information are differentiated. These self-produced resources in the microgenetic process of remembering can facilitate the exploration of invariants in the twofold duality. They are labeled "performatory activities" (Reed, 1996) in the ecological approach, which makes environments more appropriate to explore invariants, securing the twofold duality through their modification. In the context of memory research and mnemonic development studies of children, such modification of environments is identified when people use a paper string around a finger, making physical cues to remember (Flavell, 1970; Rogoff & Mistry, 1985; Vygotsky, 1978; Wellman, Ritter, & Flavell, 1975). Cognitive and forensic interview studies (Milne & Bull, 1999; Shepard, 2007) are also relevant if they are viewed in the new light of self-produced resources used for exploration of environments during remembering. Investigators and interrogators should not frequently intervene when rememberers are providing their account; rather, rememberers should be given enough chances to generate self-produced resources. Questioning procedures in PEACE (Shepard, 2007), for example, are well organized for rememberers to access their past. They are allowed to give free narrative at the beginning as well as during the course of investigation. In this kind of environment, their production of resources is maximized.

Power Relations

Note that power relations among participants in an investigation room and a court are influential in exploring invariants in the twofold duality. Although a suspect/defendant and a witness are obliged to behave and talk under conditions constrained by power relations, they and even investigators and judges are often not aware of it, as many studies of institutional talk have shown (J. M. Atkinson & Drew, 1979; P. Atkinson, 1995; Bogoch & Danet, 1984; Edwards & Mercer, 1987; Makitalo & Saljo, 2002; Mehan, 1979; Philips, 1984; Waitzkin, 1991).

As discussed at the beginning of the chapter, investigators are dominant over a suspect/defendant and a witness during investigations. They allow the latter participants to talk about a crime just in response to their questions concerning items of criminal law. Neither counterquestions nor requests to talk about what they want are often accepted. Because of their passivity, their exploration in the twofold duality is not free; as a result, they morph their past according to the influence of criminal law.

Remembering of *mens rea* (criminal intent) that is necessary to confirm in criminal cases is especially problematic. Although people often find it difficult to decide whether they had intent when they performed some action, the system of criminal law forces suspects/defendants to decide the presence or the absence of intent of their criminal actions.

In the context of the discursive approach, intent is often inferred retrospectively or from the viewpoint of the third person (Mills, 1940). If the position of discursive approach is right and is reworded in terms of the ecological approach, criminal intents cannot be specified in the past but are formed in the present environment. Criminal intents are not the production of remembering in the twofold duality but of perception in the present environment. On the other hand, the cognitive approach would insist that criminal intents were there in the past and stored in memory. If intents existed in the past experience, the ecological approach tries to pick them up as part of invariants in the twofold duality. Regardless of their presence or absence in the past experience, the ecological approach can provide a different view of intent compared to the cognitive and discursive approaches. This discussion on intent is tentative and has to be further supported by future studies, but we believe it is a possible and promising direction.

In investigations in the criminal justice system in Japan, suspects/defendants are asked if they have regrets about crimes they committed and to apologize to victims. This is due to "Japanese culture of criminal justice" (Sasaki, 2007, chapter 6), which gives some forgiveness and mercy to criminals who have regrets for their commitment of crimes and who apologize to their victims (and for their circumstances). Actually, the criminal laws of Japan allow quite a wide range of punishment. Murder, for example, can be punished with a 5-month sentence or the death penalty, following Section 199 of the criminal code. Suspects are sometimes not prosecuted when their crimes are not very severe, and defendants can also be given a stay of execution by judges, according to their regrets and apologies (and their circumstances). In these situations, some paternal relationships are also constructed between suspects/defendants and police officers/prosecutors/judges (Foote, 1999). Once they admit their guilt, investigators set them in a frame of criminality and easily overlook their possible innocence that would appear in gaps between their confession and pieces of evidence and in unnatural transitions of statements. The disparity of power in paternal relationships between them sometimes leads innocent suspects/defendants to false confession, as found by

Hamada (1992) and Ohashi et al. (2002). Power relations can influence suspects'/defendants' exploration and make them fabricate narratives concerning a crime at issue. The ecological approach should ask what exploration suspects/defendants perform under various power relations and discriminate between real remembering and fake remembering.

By considering confession and testimony as exploration of self/environment, the ecological approach can realize the importance of the design of an investigation room and a court as environments to explore. However, studies following this approach have just begun. First, the designs of an investigation room and a court have to be studied to clarify how they influence people who are required to explore their self/environment in the realms of exploration. Based on many cognitive studies, it is well known that inappropriateness of repetitive and leading questions should be criticized and that permission of free narrative and open questions should be introduced. We have taken a step forward to some theoretical reconsideration of these phenomena from the ecological standpoint, departing from the mere collection of data.

CONCLUSION

We have already demonstrated the effectiveness and usefulness of the ecological approach to the credibility of confession and testimony (Mori, 2008, 2009, 2010; Ohashi et al., 2002; Takagi, 2014). Remembering including confession and testimony are reconceptualized as the "exploration" in the "twofold duality" of "self/environment" in order to pick up "invariants" as hints of past events at issue. It has resulted in a minor success but for which the other two approaches—cognitive and discursive—have never reached: "Experience" and "time" essential to remembering are returned to psychology. The ecological approach not only contributes to forensic psychology but also provides a new perspective to cultural psychology. Our project has just begun, but we believe it is promising.

ACKNOWLEDGMENT

Naohisa Mori was partially supported by the 2012 Sapporo Gakuin University Research Support Grant SGU-S12-198008-05.

NOTES

1. In Japan, suspects are often repeatedly asked about their alleged engagement to a crime at issue during the investigative interview, and some of their statement records contain the same topics concerning the crime.
2. It is impossible to access original events, of course, but we can identify the kinds of events that occurred by various means, such as official documents of the police,

physical evidence, and agreement among several people. "Real experience" here is used with such implications.

REFERENCES

Atkinson, J. M., & Drew, P. (1979). *Order in court: The organizations of verbal interaction in judicial settings*. London, UK: Macmillan.

Atkinson, P. (1995). *Medical talk and medical work*. London, UK: Sage.

Bartlett, F. C. (1932). *Remembering: A study in experimental and social psychology*. Cambridge, UK: Cambridge University Press.

Binet, A. (1900). *La suggestibilité*. Paris, France: Schleicher.

Bogoch, B., & Danet, B. (1984). Challenge and control lawyer–client interaction: A case study in an Israeli Legal Aid office. *Text, 4*, 249–275.

Brockmeier, J. (2002). Remembering and forgetting: Narrative as cultural memory. *Culture & Psychology, 8*, 15–43.

Brown, S. D., & Reavey, P. (2014). Vital memories: Movements in and between affect, ethics and self. *Memory Studies, 7*, 328–338.

Buckhout, R. (1974). Eyewitness testimony. *Scientific American, 231*, 23–31.

Cattell, J. (1895). Measurements of the accuracy of recollection. *Science, 2*, 761–766.

Drew, P. (1990). Strategies in the contest between lawyer and witness in cross-examination. In J. Levi & A. G. Walker (Eds.), *Language in the judicial process* (pp. 39–64). New York, NY: Plenum.

Drew, P. (1992). Contested evidence in courtroom cross-examination: The case of a trial for rape. In P. Drew & J. Heritage (Eds.), *Talk at work: Interaction in institutional settings* (pp. 470–520). New York, NY: Cambridge University Press.

Edwards, D., & Mercer, N. (1987). *Common knowledge: The development of understanding in the classroom*. New York, NY: Routledge.

Edwards, D., & Potter, J. (1992). The chancellor's memory: Rhetoric and truth in discursive remembering. *Applied Cognitive Psychology, 6*, 187–215.

Fisher, R. P., & Geiselman, R. E. (1992). *Memory-enhancing techniques for investigative interviewing: The cognitive interview*. Springfield, IL: Charles C. Thomas.

Flavell, J. H. (1970). Developmental studies of mediated memory. *Advances in Child Development and Behavior, 5*, 181–211.

Foote, D. H. (1999). Looking back on my lecture on comparative studies of criminal justice between Japan and USA [Nichibei hikaku keijishiho no kougi wo frikaette]. *Jurist, 1148*, 165–173. (In Japanese)

Frenda, S. J., Nichols, R. M., & Loftus, E. F. (2011). Current issues and advances in misinformation research. *Current Directions in Psychological Science, 20*, 20–23.

Geiselman, R. E., Fisher, R. P., Firstenberg, I., Hutton, L. A., Sullivan, S., Avetissian, I., & Prosk, A. (1984). Enhancement of eyewitness memory: An empirical evaluation of the cognitive interview. *Journal of Police Science and Administration, 12*, 74–80.

Gibson, J. J. (1966). *The senses considered as perceptual systems*. Boston, MA: Houghton Mifflin.

Gibson, J. J. (1979). *The ecological approach to visual perception*. Boston, MA: Houghton Mifflin.

Hamada, S. (1992). *A study of confession [Jihaku no kenkyu]*. Tokyo, Japan: Sanichi-Shobo. (In Japanese)

Hamada, S. (2009). *I, others and narrative worlds* [*Watashi to tasya to katari no sekai*]. Kyoto, Japan: Minerva-Shobo. (In Japanese)

Hara, S., Takagi, K., & Matsushima, K. (1997). Psychological analysis on the communication style of the accused in trial (II)—A murder case at Ashikaga. *Surugadai University Studies, 14*, 109–176. (In Japanese)

Itsukushima, Y., Naka, M., & Hara, S. (2003). *The psychology of eyewitness testimony.* [*Mokugeki shogen no shinrigaku*]. Kyoto, Japan: Kitaooji-Shobo. (In Japanese)

Kassin, S. M., Tubb, V. A., Hosch, H. M., & Memon, A. (2001). On the "general acceptance" of eyewitness testimony research. *American Psychologist, 56*, 405–416.

Lamb, M. E., Orbach, Y., Hershkowitz, I., Esplin, P. W., & Horowitz, D. (2007). Structured forensic interview protocols improve the quality and informativeness of investigative interviews with children: A review of research using the NICHD Investigative Interview Protocol. *Child Abuse and Neglect, 31*, 1201–1231.

Loftus, E. F. (1974). Reconstructing memory: The incredible eyewitness. *Psychology Today, 8*, 116–119.

Loftus, E. F. (1979). *Eyewitness testimony.* Cambridge, MA: Harvard University Press.

Loftus, E. F. (2005). Searching for the neurobiology of the misinformation effect. *Learning & Memory, 12*, 1–2.

Loftus, E. F. (2013). 25 Years of eyewitness science . . . finally pays off. *Perspectives on Psychological Science, 8*, 556–557.

Loftus, E. F., Greene, E. L., & Doyle, J. M. (1989). The psychology of eyewitness testimony. In D. C. Raskin (Ed.), *Psychological methods in criminal investigation and evidence* (pp. 3–46). New York, NY: Springer.

Loftus, E. F., & Ketcham, K. (1991). *Witness for the defense: The accused, the eyewitness, and the expert who puts memory on trial.* New York, NY: St. Martin's.

Loftus, E. F., & Palmer, J. J. (1974). Reconstruction of automobile destruction: An example of the interaction between language and memory. *Journal of Verbal Learning and Verbal Behavior, 13*, 585–589.

Lynch, M., & Bogen, D. (1996). *The spectacle of history: Speech, text, and memory at the Iran-contra hearings.* Durham, NC: Duke University Press.

Makitalo, A., & Saljo, R. (2002). Talk in institutional context and institutional context in talk: Categories as situated practices. *Text, 22*, 57–82.

Mehan, H. (1979). *Learning lessons: Social organization in the classroom.* Cambridge, MA: Harvard University Press.

Middleton, D., & Brown, S. D. (2005). *The social psychology of experience: Studies in remembering and forgetting.* London, UK: Sage.

Mills, C. W. (1940). Situated actions and vocabularies of motive. *American Sociological Review, 5*, 904–913.

Milne, R., & Bull, R. (1999). *Investigative interviewing: Psychology and practice.* Chichester, UK: Wiley.

Ministry of Justice. (2011). *Achieving best evidence in criminal proceedings: Guidance on interviewing victims and witnesses, and guidance on using special measures.* Retrieved from https://www.cps.gov.uk/publications/docs/best_evidence_in_criminal_proceedings.pdf; accessed December 31, 2015

Mori, N. (1995). The function of remembering and the nature of a group in joint remembering. *Japanese Psychological Review, 38*, 107–136. (In Japanese)

Mori, N. (2008). Styles of remembering and types of experience: An experimental investigation of reconstructive memory. *Integrative Psychological and Behavioral Science*, *42*, 291–314.

Mori, N. (2009). The schema approach. In J. Valsiner, P. Molenaar, N. Chaudhary, & M. Lyra (Eds.), *Handbook of dynamic process methodology in the social and developmental sciences* (pp. 123–140). New York, NY: Springer.

Mori, N. (2010). Remembering with others: The veracity of an experience in the symbol formation process. In B. Wagoner (Ed.), *Symbolic transformation: The mind in movement through culture and society* (pp. 142–158). London, UK: Routledge.

Münsterberg, H. (1908). *On the witness stand: Essays on psychology and crime.* New York, NY: Doubleday, Page.

Neal, T. M. S., Christiansen, A, Bornstein, B. H., & Robicheaux, T. R. (2012). The effects of mock jurors' beliefs about eyewitness performance on trial judgments. *Psychology, Crime and Law*, *18*, 49–64.

Neisser, U. (1978). Memory: What are the important questions? In M. M. Gruneberg, P. E. Morris, & R. N. Sykes (Eds.), *Practical aspects of memory* (pp. 3–24). London, UK: Academic Press.

Neisser, U. (1982). John Dean's memory: A case study. In U. Neisser (Ed.), *Memory observed: Remembering in natural contexts* (pp. 139–159). New York, NY: Freeman.

Nora, P. (N. Nagai, Trans.). (2002). Entre mémoire et histoire: La problématique des lieux. In P. Nora (Ed.) (translation supervised by M. Tanigawa), *Les lieux de mémoire* [*kioku no ba*] (pp. 29–56). Tokyo, Japan: Iwanami-Shoten.

Northway, M. L. (1940a). The concept of "schema": Part I. *British Journal of Psychology*, *30*, 316–325.

Northway, M. L. (1940b). The concept of "schema": Part II. *British Journal of Psychology*, *31*, 22–36.

Ohashi, Y., Mori, N., Takagi, K., & Matsushima, K. (2002). *Psychologists meet trials.* Kyoto, Japan: Kitaooji-Shobo. (In Japanese)

Okado, Y., & Stark, C. E. L. (2005). Neural activity during encoding predicts false memories created by misinformation. *Learning & Memory*, *12*, 3–11.

Philips, S. U. (1984). The social organization of questions and answers in courtroom discourse: A study of changes of plea in an Arizona court. *Text*, *4*, 225–248.

Read, J. D., & Desmarais, S. L. (2009). Lay knowledge of eyewitness issues: A Canadian evaluation. *Applied Cognitive Psychology*, *23*, 301–326.

Reed, E. S. (1994). Perception is to self as memory is to selves. In U. Neisser & R. Fivush (Eds.), *The remembering self: Construction and accuracy in the self-narrative* (pp. 278–292). New York, NY: Cambridge University Press.

Reed, E. S. (1996). *Encountering the world: Toward an ecological psychology.* New York, NY: Oxford University Press.

Rogoff, B., & Mistry, J. (1985). Memory development in cultural context. In M. Pressly & C. J. Brainerd (Eds.), *Cognitive learning and memory in children: Progress in cognitive development research* (pp. 117–142). New York, NY: Springer.

Sasaki, M. (1996). A note on the "nature" of remembering [Souki no "shizen" ni stuite no oboegaki]. In M. Sasaki (Ed.), *Fields of remembering* [*Souki no field*] (pp. 31–67). Tokyo, Japan: Shinyou-Sha. (In Japanese)

Sasaki, T. (2007). *Japanese culture of criminal justice* [*Nippon no shihou bunka*]. Tokyo, Japan: Bungei-Shunj.

Sato, T. (1996). Development of psychology of testimony in Europe, America, and Japan [Oubei to nippon ni okeru shougenshinrigaku no tenkai]. *Gendai no esupuri, 350*, 135–142. (In Japanese)

Schmechel, R. S., O'Toole, T. P., Easterly, C., & Loftus, E. F. (2006). Beyond the ken? Testing jurors' understanding of eyewitness reliability evidence. *Jurimetrics, 46*, 177–214.

Shepard, E. (2007). *Investigative interviewing: The conversation management approach.* London, UK: Oxford University Press.

Solomon, H. Y., & Turvey, M. T. (1988). Haptically perceiving the distances reachable with hand-held objects. *Journal of Experimental Psychology: Human Perception and Performance, 14*, 404–427.

Steblay, N. K., & Loftus, E. F. (2013). Eyewitness identification and the legal system. In E. Shafir (Ed.), *The behavioral foundations of policy* (pp. 145–162). Princeton, NJ: Princeton University Press.

Stern, W. (1902). Zur Psychologie der Aussage. *Zeitschrift für die gesamte Strafrechtswissenschaft, 22*, 315–370.

Szokolszky, A. (2013). Interview with Ulric Neisser. *Ecological Psychology, 25*, 182–199.

Takagi, K. (2014). *Remembering as exploration of "absence": An approach to "experience" in the context of criminal justice.* Paper presented at the 4th Congress of the International Society for Cultural and Activity Research, Sydney, Australia.

Tomita, T. (1991). A psychological study of the credibility of identification of criminals with photos. *Hougaku Seminar, 441*, 126–128. (In Japanese)

Tulving, E. (1972). Episodic and semantic memory. In E. Tulving & W. Donaldson (Eds.), *Organization of memory* (pp. 381–403). New York, NY: Academic Press.

Vygotsky, L. S. (1978). *Mind in society: The development of higher psychological processes.* Cambridge, MA: Harvard University Press.

Vygotsky, L. S. (1997). The historical meaning of the crisis in psychology: A methodological investigation. In R. W. Rieber & J. Wollock (Eds.), *The collected works of L. S. Vygotsky. Volume 3: Problems of the theory and history of psychology* (pp. 233–343). New York, NY: Plenum. (Original work published 1927)

Wagoner, B. (2013). Bartlett's concept of schema in reconstruction. *Theory & Psychology, 23*, 535–575.

Wagoner, B. (2017). *The constructive mind: Bartlett's psychology in reconstruction.* Cambridge, UK: Cambridge University Press.

Waitzkin, H. (1991). *The politics of medical encounters: How patients and doctors deal with social problems.* New Haven, CT: Yale University Press.

Wellman, H. M., Ritter, K., & Flavell, J. H. (1975). Deliberate memory behavior in the delayed reactions of very young children. *Developmental Psychology, 11*, 780–787.

Wells, G. L. (1978). Applied eyewitness-testimony research: System variables and estimator variables. *Journal of Personality and Social Psychology, 36*, 1546–1557.

Wigmore, J. H. (1909). Professor Münsterberg and the psychology of testimony. *Illinois Law Review, 3*, 399–444.

Wise, R. A., Safer, M. A., & Maro, C. M. (2011). What U.S. law enforcement officers know and believe about eyewitness factors, eyewitness interviews and identification procedures. *Applied Cognitive Psychology, 25*, 488–500.

Rethinking Function, Self, and Culture in "Difficult" Autobiographical Memories

STEVEN D. BROWN AND PAULA REAVEY ■

The psychology of memory appears to be entering a phase of transformation, at least with regard to autobiographical memory (AM). The role of others, of the cultural landscape, is no longer confined to the peculiar interests of the social psychologist, cultural theorist, or anthropologist. And in contemporary AM work, the individual and culture are now to become ever more conceptually and empirically unified (Boyer & Wertsch, 2009), and there are now greater numbers of psychologists wishing to conceptually and empirically demonstrate the link between private mentation and the collective cultural landscape out of which such memorial activities emerge (Conway & Jobson, 2012; Nelson & Fivush, 2004).

As social psychologists, it is perhaps unsurprising that we welcome this move toward examining remembering in cultural context with unreserved enthusiasm. Understanding the social and cultural processes that "make" remembering is at the center of our work on how people experience, and make sense of, difficult memories (e.g., sexual, physical, and emotional abuse, adoption, incarceration, and disasters) (Brown & Reavey, 2015). It is with these "vital memories" (in that we argue they are "vital" to a sense of self in the present) in mind that our aim in this chapter is to open up a dialogue regarding the manner in which certain key aspects of autobiographical memory have been conceptualized. In particular, we provide an alternative way in which to conceptualize three key elements: memory function, culture, and self. Specifically, we draw on the idea of what we call the *expanded* model of memory (Brown & Reavey, 2014, 2015) to explore how memory function, culture, and self require situating beyond the boundaries of private mentations (even if influenced by culture) and are threaded into, and afforded by, the material world (Ingold, 1996, 2013). We also explore the idea that discrepancies or ambiguities in memory can serve *productive* purposes for the ongoing negotiation of self, as it unfolds in the present. The self, thus, is never fully complete but, rather, involved in constant negotiation and meaning-making. This approach will, we hope, assist in illustrating further the productive links between memory function, culture, and self that currently circulate in the AM literature.

THE ORIGINS OF AUTOBIOGRAPHICAL MEMORY: FUNCTION, CULTURE, AND SELF

Work on AM is increasingly concerned with how recollections of the past are shaped by the ongoing needs and projects of the present self and with the cultural communities that shape its emergence and development (Conway & Loveday, 2015; Nelson, 2006; 2009; Rubin, 2012). This focus on the *functional significance* of memory—that is, the role of the past in creating and/or maintaining current self and identity—treats memory as a reflexive activity that moves with the concerns of the present. As Bluck (2003) summarizes,

> the primary concern is not with how much or how well humans remember their personal past (although those features often play some role), but instead with *why and how* humans remember both mundane and significant life events. What functions does it serve people to remember, reflect on, and share with others, the experiences of their lives? (p. 113)

One answer to the "how" question comes from Martin Conway's influential cognitive psychological model of AM and the self-memory system. This posits that our memories of particular events are shaped by our current concerns as they are cognitively organized by the "working self" (Conway & Pleydell-Pearce, 2000). The working self is responsible for organizing event-specific, as well as general, knowledge and is functionally oriented toward current goals and identity maintenance. In short, we typically recall events and feelings that help support our present views about who and what we are and that also help us solve problems that are relevant to us in the present time and help anticipate likely futures (Pasupathi, 2001).

This functional approach builds on evidence from developmental studies that AM emerges as a critical developmental skill during approximately the third or fourth year of life (Fivush, 2011). Early interactions can lead to the shaping of recollections in a number of significant ways, including enduring gendered styles of remembering, in both children and adults (Fivush, 1998). Conversational exchanges have been studied in detail to examine the instructional and pedagogical cues delivered by parents that direct the meaning focus of children's recollections (Nelson & Fivush, 2004), assist children in distinguishing their own private memories from the memories of others, as well as assist them in identifying themselves as the directive agent in their recollections. In childhood, "reality monitoring" can be subject to error, with recurrent source confusions, including the confusion between self-memory or episodic memory and general episode memory. This suggests that how we come to learn about ourselves over time, mainly through the medium of recollection, can be entangled with the stories of others (Roberts & Blades, 2000) and with broader cultural narratives (Nelson, 2003).

Function in Relation to the (Cultural) Self

The embedding of the psychological in sociocultural frameworks seems crucial to addressing how AM emerges as a human capacity (Nelson & Fivush, 2004). But it further seems to be of central importance to understanding the "why" question. Pillemer (1998) points to the value of recounting AMs for maintaining social ties. Telling stories of one's involvement in past events "serves a significant social–cultural function; the acquisition of such sharing means that the child can enter into the social and cultural history of the family and community" (Nelson, 1993, p. 178). Autobiographical memory provides the means for offering a self-narrative of belonging and membership with the people and groups around us (Nelson, 2006).

However, the implications of the functionality of AM can be pushed still further. Perhaps our very sense of "self" is bound up in an emergent capacity to tell stories of our personal past. Katherine Nelson and Robyn Fivush have argued for a social constructivist approach to AM in which self and memory become entwined through the construction of a "life narrative" (see Nelson & Fivush, 2004). This involves both the kind of autonoetic awareness (mentally placing ourselves or traveling back in time) described by Tulving and the reflexive ability to do what Bartlett (1932) described as "turning around on one's own schemas" or, simply stated, telling stories from memory about ourselves to others. This principle of *constructing* meaning via interrelationships with others does not only hold sway for children but also plays a role in identity formation in adulthood. Memories are thus a result of both actual experience and the social construction of those experiences, through joint interaction with others (Pasupathi, 2001).

Remembering thus becomes an act of self and meaning-making for the individual. It serves as a foundation for identity across time (Baddeley, 1988). If this is so, then as Conway (2005) observes, the strict accuracy or "correspondence" of a given recollection needs to be considered in relation to its "coherence" with other recollections and the rememberer's self-beliefs. In many cases, then, coherence is more important than correspondence. In a remarkable statement, Conway and Loveday (2015) argue for what they call a "modern view of human memory," in which what is remembered as AM is a selective construction that may compress time, mix together events, and engage with imaginative leaps:

> In the modern view of human memory memories are . . . transient constructions and although they may to some degree accurately represent the past they are time-compressed and contain many details that are inferred, consciously and non-consciously, at the time of their construction. Thus, all

memories are to some degree false in the sense that they do not represent past experience literally. . . . One of the main functions of memories is to generate meanings, personal meanings that allow us to make sense of the world and operate on it adaptively. Memories are, perhaps, most important in supporting a wide range of social interactions where coherence is predominant and correspondence often less central. (p. 7)

Critics of the cognitive–experimental psychology of memory have often accused its practitioners of being obsessed with matters of accuracy and of being ignorant of the wider social practices in which remembering is enacted (Edwards & Potter, 1992; Middleton & Brown, 2005). Conway and Loveday's summary of the modern view of memory dramatically closes the supposed gap between cognitive and social–discursive approaches. Both, we can belatedly recognize, are principally concerned with the constructive nature of remembering, the social functions it performs, and the generation of personal meanings that allows for the enactment of self-identity.

We welcome entirely the acknowledgment of the convergence of cognitive and social approaches on a shared set of problems. Going forward, the task will be, we believe, to develop these mutual problems without lapsing back into distracting debate around methodological or epistemological differences. There are three principal issues, which, for us, seem to define the cognitive–sociocultural problem space of AM. We outline these while specifically speaking to a set of issues that inform our work on vital memories.

The first issue concerns the functionality of memory. If AM is functionally oriented—that is, remembering personal memories accomplishes something in the here and now—then how are we to understand the recollection of "difficult" or "painful" events that are disruptive of current self and actions? The common position taken is that certain kinds of experience are so extreme (i.e., childhood abuse, witnessing violence, or catastrophic events) that memory distortions arise to protect the working self from subsequently having to engage with them, or the working self may itself be disrupted due to some deficit (i.e., an underlying psychiatric disorder) such that it becomes unconstrained by the need to create coherence or correspondence in AM (Conway & Loveday, 2015).[1] However, this is to assume a prior normative set of values by which different kinds of recollections might be distinguished. One of the characteristics of distressing memories is often that the person recollecting finds it difficult to arrive at judgments as to whether they are wholly "bad" or may, perhaps, contain elements that are of value (Reavey & Brown, 2007). Establishing the meaning and value of a difficult memory is part of the process of recollection, and it may indicate that complex sociocultural functions are being enacted.

This leads us immediately to the second issue. It is difficult to establish exactly what functions may be served by a given recollection, however incoherent or lacking in veridicality it may be, without first analyzing the practical contexts in which it is produced (e.g., in a therapy session or at a family meeting). Our relationship to distressing aspects of our personal past is often ambiguous and shaped considerably by the practices and setting in which it is recollected. Moreover, even recollections that have good fit with "normative" life stories (e.g., starting a new job and getting married) may be told in very different ways depending on the interactional contexts in which they become relevant (e.g., conversations between either a present or past partner). Setting and practice are then crucial sites where the relationship between culture and the individual is mediated.

Third, the useful distinction made by Conway (2005) between correspondence and congruency in AM shifts attention to the nature of the "self" processes through which the congruency of a given recollection is established. The "conceptual self" described by Conway, Singer, and Tagini (2004) is composed of culturally prescribed self-images, beliefs, and life stories. But if these memories that inform these representations and narratives are "transient constructions," then how stable is the conceptual self through and around which they cluster? Is it appropriate to speak of a self as a "thing" at all (however schematically) rather than as an ongoing process or project? In what ways is it best to conceive of stability and change in relation to self? We address some of these issues by turning to what we refer to as an expanded model of memory to examine the link between function, culture, and self further and also its emergence in material settings.

EXPANDING THE DOMAIN
OF AUTOBIOGRAPHICAL MEMORY

Conway and Jobson (2012) offer the following as an example of what they call "broken memories" to differentiate between individuals who possess stability (and thus coherence) and those who do not. Largely their differentiation appears to be based on a separation of those who experience trauma or those diagnosed with a psychiatric disorder and the remainder of the population. According to Conway and Jobson, then, broken memories (belonging largely to the former) are instances in which there is disruption to AM processes brought about by extreme events or extant underlying pathologies. The examples they provide are meant to analytically frame the normal functioning of AM by illustrating its potential malfunctions (what is usually called a "deviant case"). They describe the following:

> One patient, for example, had been sexually abused by his grandfather from ages of 4 to 12. He had a persistent and intrusive flashback in which he was naked in a bathroom being pushed against the radiator by his naked grandfather. In this intrusive fragment he saw himself from an observer perspective as he was now, a balding 35-year-old, and saw in the memory his grandfather as a frail 70-year-old. In fact it became clear during therapy that he had been 6 at the time and his grandfather was in his 40s. The false (coherence) memory served the function of obscuring the fact that he had been a helpless victim. (p. 7)

For Conway and Jobson, there are two issues with this memory. It is seen from the position of the observer rather than as the one who experienced the event, and it transposes the patient's[2] and the abuser's current ages with their chronological ages at the time the event was thought to have occurred. The shift in perspective is treated as a normal distortion, but the swapping around of ages is taken to indicate the falseness of the memory in terms of its overall coherence. It is worth noting that contra to the way that "false memory" scholars such as Elizabeth Loftus[3] might deal with such an example, Conway and Jobson do not question the overall correspondence of the recollection (i.e., that it refers to something that actually occurred), nor doubt that the recollection may have some function for the patient—namely that of masking his victimhood—and they do not seize upon the context in which it was produced as further evidence of the malfeasance of therapeutic professionals in co-producing false memories. However, we would view the function of the memory in slightly different terms. The substitution of the ages, for example, might be seen as not so much masking victimhood but, rather, as an explicit (although not necessarily deliberate) turning around on it. The recollection renders the original event ambiguous in a number of ways. There is a reversal of power. The powerful adult becomes a weak, elderly man. The powerless child is transformed into the man the patient is now. This may reflect the contemporary relationship between the patient and the abuser—perhaps it is the grandfather who is now vulnerable and unable to defend himself. In transforming the event in this way, the recollection proposes that powerlessness in the past need not determine relations of power in the present. In fact, in the original account of the case in Conway et al. (2004), we learn that the patient had continuously "updated" his age in the recollection throughout his adult life to "make him seem as adult as he could be" (p. 529).

Questions of agency can also be posed differently through the substitution of ages. Victims of child sexual abuse can experience difficulties in separating their adult conceptions of what constitutes agency from those of a child when they reflect back on their experiences (Haaken, 1999; Lamb, 1996; Reavey, 2010; Reavey & Brown, 2006). It is common in most therapeutic practices to encourage survivors not to misattribute adult notions of choice to their child self. This appears to be what was done in the course of the cognitive therapy in which the previously discussed patient participated and which resulted in what were deemed to be good therapeutic outcomes (Conway et al., 2004). But settling matters of agency, arriving at a clear sense that one did not have a choice about what happened, can also be very problematic because it carries with it the implication that past victimhood may determine one's current sense of agency (Reavey & Brown, 2006, 2009). Moreover, it can mean denying ambiguous feelings—albeit ones that are often challenging and threatening—that were part of the experience. In the original account, it is stated that the patient recollects feelings of sexual arousal during the later years of the abuse, which led him to believe that he was "at fault and an equal participant in the activity" (Conway et al., 2004, p. 529). Although we can be utterly clear that legally and morally this was not the case, there may nevertheless be some value in exploring these feelings further (this might have been a starting point had the patient been enrolled in a different kind of therapeutic practice) because they offer an alternative to what Janice Haaken (1999) calls a "master narrative of abuse." Substituting the ages in the recollection potentially keeps questions of choice open, which may be of some benefit to the patient in his or her long-term struggles to accommodate the experience into his or her changing version of self (i.e., not simply in terms of the short-term goals of the cognitive therapy, important as they are) (see also Reavey, 2010). Responsibility and accountability are thus rendered ongoing rather than complete and finite.

Finally, from the details given in both papers (Conway et al., 2004; Conway & Jobson, 2012), it is not clear whether or not the abuse has been subsequently acknowledged by the grandfather or others or subject to legal measures (although, as in the vast majority of cases, the abuser silenced the child at the time with threats of the consequences of disclosure). Responsibility for what happened may not have been either informally or formally addressed. The recollection thematizes some of the key issues that might have been "live" for the patient at the time of its production: Is my grandfather in his current state still culpable for his actions? What might it say about me, as an adult, that I need this elderly man, who is close to death, to be punished? Are we different, as middle-aged men, him, then and me, now? A very important detail here is that it was the patient, as a 12-year-old, who ultimately put a stop to the abuse when he was "physically strong enough to retaliate" (Conway et al., 2004, p. 529) rather than any of the adult carers who were present during his childhood. Perhaps the switching of selves is speaking to a very powerful idea—this is someone who has always had to be "the grownup" and take responsibility for his own fate while being let down by the adults around him who have so woefully neglected or abused their own duties of care.

Overall, we think this example offers some very different suggestions about how to treat functionality in AM. It is very difficult to establish which functions a given recollection of personal experience may be serving in isolation from other details of the person's life. In the previous example, the current relationship between the patient and his family, including the grandfather, is highly relevant to understanding what this recollection may be doing. The swapping of ages could be a way of resisting a victim narrative, or it could be a vivid way of thematizing an ongoing sense of injustice. Indeed, there may be several identity-relevant functions being performed simultaneously. Functions can also "misfire." They can accomplish some social acts but also have significant unintended consequences. In the example, the patient's continuous updating of his age in the recollection seems to have brought with it a sense of being active rather than passive as a child, which may have been of value to him in his struggles in adult life. Over time, however, this has come at the colossal cost of increasingly attributing agency to his past self, which has become increasingly problematic. We cannot then treat the potential functions of AM in any clear-cut way—they are likely to be multiple, sometimes contradictory, contextually bound, and rarely unitary in their effects (Brookfield, Brown & Reavey, 2008; ;Reavey & Brown, 2009).

Expanding Cultural Selves

Many contemporary accounts of AM hold that social conventions, in the form of culturally generated life scripts (e.g., marriage, attending college, buying a house, and having a child), help organize AMs by providing the basis for life narratives, beliefs, and values (Berntsen & Bohn, 2009; Conway & Jobson, 2012). These in turn influence the structuring of goals, which are organized hierarchically (Conway, 2005). One of the difficulties that the patient in Conway and Jobson's example doubtless confronts is that his experiences of childhood sexual abuse do not map onto the kinds of cultural life scripts that are normatively valued. The patient faces the challenge of trying to produce a coherent life story using sociocultural narrative resources that do not help to articulate his lived experiences. It is not then surprising that the outcome is what Conway and Jobson call a "false (coherence) memory."

But is coherence—the sense of there being an order, stability, and meaning to our recollected past experiences—an achievable goal, not just for the particular patient discussed in Conway and Jobson (2012) but also more generally within AM? As Nelson (2003) observes, the very idea that we have unique life histories to narrate is a comparatively recent historical construction and is subject to considerable cultural variation and social change. What constitutes "coherence" depends greatly on local sociocultural standards and practices. There are, for example, cultural representations and life narratives of "survivorship" following child abuse and neglect that have emerged in the past two decades, which the previously mentioned patient may or may not have been able to access. However, to view coherence as the outcome of applying external representational frameworks to one's own experiences is to reach for a quite static conception of culture as a stockpile of preexisting narrative themes, norms, and collective representations. This contrasts with the view of culture typically expressed in contemporary social anthropology and related disciplines such as archeology, in which culture is treated not as a "thing" that is transmitted *to us* from on high but, rather, a process, in continual negotiation, with attendant contradictions and potential resistance by members of that culture (Cole, 2005). Meaning and value are outcomes rather than inputs into the sociocultural work of mobilizing the past in the present. Our personal pasts are, to some degree, interpretively open, and the cultural resources we may draw upon to engage in the work of establishing current significance very rarely offer the means of clearly fixing what a given event means in the present. The term "culture" names this live, contextually bound process of mobilizing the past "on the ground," so to speak, in our interactions with others and in our relations with the settings of the material world. Thus, materiality is as integral to function, culture, and self as language or script. It is out of these diverse settings that the function of memories shifts accordingly.

The Relevance of Setting

The previous discussion suggests the need for analysis of the specific settings, persons, and materials that are involved in the personal work of recollection. It is important that the recollection in the previously discussed example was given during the course of a therapeutic encounter and that this therapy was provided following the patient's engagement with an "educational group workshop on borderline personality disorder" (Conway et al., 2004, p. 529). Remembering is shaped by the nature of the practice and setting through which it occurs. For instance, if the patient had been making a legal witness statement about the same event, it is likely that matters of correspondence and coherence would have been jointly managed very differently by the professionals concerned. We recollect stories about our personal experiences differently, depending on the interlocutors to whom the story is told and with an awareness of what the likely implications could be of how the story might subsequently be acted upon. In this case, the outcome of telling the event with ages transposed in cognitive therapy was that the patient was encouraged to reformulate his recollection to restore correspondence with likely ages at the time. A different kind of therapy might have sought to work on the memory in another way. If the process had been legal, rather than therapeutic, it is likely that during the time between the initial statement and the court proceeding, the patient would have been guided to refine his recollection to fit with the requirements of clear evidence.

Both correspondence and coherence in personal memory are not just up to us, as individuals, to constitute and sustain. They are jointly accomplished with others in the settings in which they are relevant, drawing on the sociocultural and material resources that are at hand. Questions of bias are not really relevant here. If, as Conway and Jobson (2012) assert, there is no literal representation of past experience, then what is available for analysis are occasioned, setting-specific acts of recollection that are fashioned in the moment from available cultural resources. From this, it follows that cognition has to be treated as a set of processes that are embedded in the world. As John Sutton and colleagues argue, remembering engages both "internal" and "external" resources in a relation of complementarity (Sutton, Keil, & Barnier, 2010; Harris, Sutton, & Barnier, 2010). Their "distributed-scaffolded" approach is richly suggestive of possible ways of thinking about relationships between "in-the-head" and "environmental" resources. Or as Clark (1997) states, cognition comprises a "heterogeneous assembly of brains, bodies, artifacts and other external structures" (p. 77). In Conway and Jobson's example, the patient draws upon neural resources while recollecting (as indeed we all do in all forms of cognition), and it may or may not be relevant that the patient's deployment of his neural resources is mediated by a prior history of "smoking large amounts of cannabis" and possibly also by use of prescription psychoactive medication. However, these neural resources constitute but one component of a broader, distributed set of loosely coupled resources that are brought together within the setting-specific production of their recollection.

Expanding the meaning of the term cognition in this way offers an interesting challenge for conceptualizing AM: If remembering is the outcome of distributed processes, then in what sense do our memories *belong* to us? In Conway's work, it is the role of the "working self" to organize episodic memory through threading together its contents with culturally derived knowledge. This model draws upon classic work in social–cognitive approaches to memory, such as that of Neisser (1994), in positing distinctions within self-knowledge. Neisser distinguished no less than five sources of self-knowledge, ranging from information provided by direct perception (the "ecological self") to higher-level material such as internalized cultural beliefs (the "conceptual self"). However, this kind of theorizing arguably leans too much on the assumptions of early cognitive science, in which the problem to be explained is how information from the environment gets "inside" the cognitive system. By contrast, contemporary cognitive science that builds on Clark's "extended mind" hypothesis (see Clark & Chalmers, 1998) expands the cognitive system beyond the boundary of the brain and skin into communicative and material relations. Consequently, what counts as "the self" or "self knowledge" includes relations with others, material artifacts, and external cognitive technologies.

The shift from early to contemporary cognitive approaches implies that the basic premise of AM requires rethinking. Instead of attempting to understand the way that culture "gets inside" the person to form the conceptual self, the problem is rather that of explaining how a sense of selfhood and personal continuity emerges from the shifting arrangement of materials (e.g., brain, bodies, artifacts, and settings) that make up the distributed cognitive system. For instance, when Conway and Jobson (2012) place the example under the heading "broken memories," they are suggesting that continuity in selfhood is the default, which is compromised by memories associated with extreme events, against which the "working self" seeks to protect itself. However, if the "self-memory system" is a distributed system, along the lines suggested by Clark (1997), then the problem is reversed: How is the felt continuity of self extracted from the diverse materials out of which it is constituted?

There are extant philosophical resources that may assist in developing this problem. Alfred North Whitehead (1978), for instance, offers a whole conceptual framework for treating personal experience as an ongoing process that gathers together varied materials to create "actual occasions" or "drops" of experience. Whitehead argues that the flow of awareness is composed of continuously forming "events," which fold together diverse entities into a "feeling." Each drop of experience conditions the next in such a way that although we can speak of our "self" as being composed of the kind of heterogeneous assembly that Clark (1997) describes, there is nevertheless a form of continuity that emerges as the conditioning of successive drops creates a pathway or general tendency over time. Whitehead then allows us to conceive the way in which "your personal experience does not happen 'in' your mind; your mind simply *is* the flow of your experience" (Mesle, 2008, p. 96). Autobiographical memories could then be treated as "chreods" or emergent patterns that persist through the successive conditioning of experience rather than as internally generated mental representations.

VITAL MEMORIES

Our work has explored personal memories concerning distressing or painful events (see Brown & Reavey, 2015). We have treated these as a subset of autobiographical memory that we refer to as "vital memories." The principal characteristics of these memories are that they offer considerable challenges for accommodation into a coherent life narrative because they often refer to life-changing events. As such, they cannot be readily dismissed and are often treated as central to self-definition. It is important to state that although many of the participants in our studies have engaged with therapeutic practices, we avoid recourse to notions of trauma or pathology. Rather than draw upon some kind of "deficit" model that conceptualizes painful pasts as necessarily resulting in psychological disturbance, we prefer to treat participants as ordinary people who have undergone extraordinary events, either directly or vicariously, and who have developed, with the assistance of others, ways of living with the past that are, for the most part, fit for purpose (although without discounting the sometimes high levels of distress associated with them).

Theoretically, our work was initially derived from the social remembering framework developed in discursive approaches to psychology (Middleton & Edwards, 1990). This treatment of memory emphasizes that remembering is a social act that is interactionally performed to mobilize a version of the past to accomplish some purpose in the present. Function, rather than correspondence, is the dominant concern in this work (Edwards & Potter, 1992). Memories are descriptions or accounts that are constructed and offered to "do things" in the present. This line of thinking has led contemporary researchers in discursive psychology to dismiss the idea of inner mentation as being relevant to analyzing the public performance of psychological phenomenon (e.g., remembering, feeling, and arguing) (Tileagă & Stokoe, 2015). According to this perspective, experience is the lived engagement with the world around us, primarily enacted in talk-in-interaction, with all its richness and complexity, rather than some inner kernel of being (Potter, 2012).

Although there is much in this work that continues to inspire us, the notion that all that is worth saying about the psychological can be found in empirical analysis of interaction seems overly restrictive. At the core of experience is a felt sense of continuity—that we have a personal history and are living at a particular time within specific places. Now this continuity is subject to continuous variation. We are not stable "things" that *endure* through time but, rather, collections of changing personal qualities whose unique temporal trajectories of activity, or *perdurance*, define our being (Ingold, 2013). We are not made of talk alone. The psychological is constituted through the material world by way of the artifacts and features of the settings in which they dwell and also by the complex biochemical constitution of the bodies by means of which we feel and act. The rethinking of "cognition" in terms of distributed arrangements of resources and capacities to act seems to offer a productive way forward.

We briefly state what we view as points of connection with Conway's model of AM. The resources out of which personal recollections are built (i.e., the autobiographical knowledge base) are distributed within a given setting, across persons, materials, and practices, and typically offer the possibilities for a number of versions of the past, some of which are contradictory. In this sense, all autobiographical remembering is collectively enacted, although it is typically attached to us as persons (i.e., we are taken to be the authors of the recollected experience). Correspondence is a setting-specific accomplishment that draws on the practices and norms that are operant within the setting (e.g., courts of law, therapy, and family conversations). Coherence is an aspiration rather than a settled matter, and it reflects our ongoing, situated efforts to turn around on our personal past. Our sense of self (i.e., the conceptual self) is both spatially and temporally extended. What we think we are depends on others and the resources of the settings we inhabit. We are also never, in a strict sense, existing in the present moment because our current concerns reach back into the past, seeking meaning, and push forward into likely futures, exploring possible implications (Pasupathi, 2001). The self is then best thought of as an ongoing project that consists of a shifting array of elements (Ingold, 2013). We next illustrate this further by describing how some of our work relates to the three themes of function, culture, and self.

The Functionality of Ambiguity

All autobiographical recollections have some function; they are remembered in the course of social structured activity (even if that activity is solitary). The functions served by vital memories tend to be somewhat ambiguous. Difficult or painful experiences may contain multiple layers of contradictory meaning and a range of complex feelings. This is particularly so in AMs of child sexual abuse (Haaken, 1999). There can be considerable time compression, with multiple episodes of abuse condensed into particularly vivid scenes; shifts in perspective; and ambivalence around feelings and intentions (Reavey & Brown, 2006). Over time, these features of vital memories are likely to become more, rather than less, diffuse as they are repeatedly considered upon retelling. Sorting out "what happened" and "what it means now" can remain lifelong concerns.

In one example, Lorna described a recollection of being sexually abused by her older brother in a room in their family home. Lorna described how the ambivalent feelings that she recalls from that event, which included some elements of pleasure, have been an ongoing source of distress to her throughout her adult life. For her, a crucial aspect of the abuse is whether her brother was acting on the basis of naive curiosity or with the active intention to sexually abuse his much younger sister. She recalls how during several episodes, he removed the handle from the door to the room in which the abuse occurred, thereby ensuring it was locked from inside. Lorna takes the act of locking the door to be an indicator of his active intentions, which leaves her unable to excuse her brother for what he did (for further details, see Reavey & Brown, 2009).

Here, we can see Lorna turning around on her memory to establish correspondence and infer motives. The scene she recollects with the arrangement of the siblings around the door seems to suggest or "propose" two very different statements: The brother either acted with or acted without conscious awareness of what he was doing. As long as the door remains unlocked, then both statements can be in play, and Lorna does not have to "settle" either her relationship with her brother or the meaning of the contradictory feelings she experienced. But if she chooses to believe that the detail of the door being locked is correct, then the brother is an abuser, she is a victim, and her feelings are a source of guilt—because in cultural terms, real victims should never enjoy aspects of their abuse.

In this recollection, it seems that it is the ambivalence over correspondence that it is functional. As long as Lorna does not have to settle "what actually happened," she can accommodate the vital memory into her sense of adult self in different ways. To use Conway and Jobson's (2012) terms, maintaining uncertain correspondence enables higher and more flexible coherence. On this basis, we suggest that the switching of ages by the patient in their example may have accomplished something similar, up to a certain point. The broader point here is that the "propositions" that emerge from vital memories (i.e., statements about what happened and their significance for the present) are inherently neither true nor false but, rather, are realized as such in how we dispose of ambiguity and thereby settle on how we ought to orient to the recollection in question (e.g., "He meant to do it," "I am a victim," and "I cannot forgive him").

Often, the work of either maintaining or settling ambivalence in vital memories is done in concert with others. For example, in a study of the strategies that adoptive parents maintain to preserve the early memories of their adopted children (Brookfield, Brown & Reavey, 2008; Brown, Reavey, & Brookfield, 2013), parent C describes a dilemma she was faced with in relation to her young adopted daughter. In the recent past, the daughter had developed what C refers to as an "obsession" with fire. She and her partner had addressed this by buying her age-appropriate toys such as a firefighter's play costume. However, C is concerned by her daughter's "pyromanic" interest because she knows—and she believes her daughter does not yet know—that her daughter's adoption came about because her birth mother set fire to their family flat while under the influence of alcohol and drugs, for which she subsequently received a prison sentence. The dilemma here is that if C attempts to steer her daughter away from pursing her fascination with fire, she may be accused by her daughter, at some point later in life, of trying to hide or dispose of her early life. However, by colluding in this interest, she risks premature disclosure of the personal history at an age when she judges her daughter to be insufficiently equipped to manage the details.

This example is slightly unusual because it concerns what Marianne Hirsch (1997) calls a "vicarious memory." The daughter currently appears not to remember the fire; however, there is good reason to suppose that in later life the account of the fire—which C is adamant that her daughter has the right to know about when she appears to be ready to hear the details—will form part of her life story, and the retellings will constitute AMs in their own right. Currently, C is acting as custodian of the potential memories, in effect managing her daughter's access to her own personal past. Parent C does this by maintaining ambivalence. The daughter can explore her "obsession" with fire within the safety of the relations of care of the adoptive family. We might say that the story of the fire is "hidden in plain sight," awaiting the time of its eventual discovery by the daughter, who will

then find a place for that episode in her life story, which has already been anticipated by its careful management by parent C.

Setting Specificity

The example of parent C and her daughter demonstrates that the knowledge that
we draw upon in constituting autobiographical memory is distributed across our
relationships with others (see studies of older couples' joint autobiographical recollections by Harris, Barnier, Sutton, & Keil, 2014). This raises ethical questions
about what our memorial responsibilities are to one another. For example, what
are our duties in relation to what we hold of the personal experiences of others?
Do they obtain merely within close personal relationships, or do they extend to
broader social and professional relationships? Conversely, are we entitled to refuse
to speak of or even to dispose of what we know of other's lives as and when we
see fit? These kinds of questions indicate a point of passage between the focused
study of AM per se and broader social and political questions of the kind posed
within what has come to be called cultural memory studies (Erll & Nünning,
2008; Wagoner, 2011).

In our work, the intermediate point at which psychological and broader ethi-
copolitical questions come together is in the study of specific settings in which
remembering is performed. If there is broad agreement within the "modern" or,
as we term it, "expanded" view of memory that in principle distinctions between
truth and falsity of recollections are not meaningful to make, then this does not
mean abandoning the search for veracity. It simply means acknowledging that
the "truth" of a given memory depends on the particular practice and setting in
which the recollection is subject to evaluation and the criterion that are in play.
For example, had the patient from Conway and Jobson's (2012) example offered
his recollection as part of a legal case against the grandfather, the success of the
prosecution would probably be in doubt. In therapy, however, the switching
of ages does not undermine the veracity of what is recalled and perhaps even
increases its believability because it fits with therapeutic expectations about managing traumatic experience.

Our approach to vital memories addresses settings (e.g., professional practices
and sites, institutions, and families) as crucial sites where the resources for constituting and evaluating personal memories are located. We can make a notion of
culture operant here as the ways in which we collectively assemble and mobilize
versions of the past in accordance with the extant practices of the setting. For example, the Reminiscence Museum based in the Humanitas care home in Rotterdam
is a somewhat unique space of memory (Bendien, 2009, 2013; Bendien, 2010;
Bendien, Brown, & Reavey, 2010). Constructed in the basement of the care home,
it consists of a series of rooms arranged with the décor and household objects of
homes in the Netherlands during the period 1930–1950. The museum includes
a living room, two kitchen spaces, bedrooms, a child's nursery, a workshop, and

several adjoining spaces that are full of period objects. The museum is open to visitors, along with elderly clients of the home, and provides a space for viewing the collected objects, entertaining visiting families, or simply reflection. As might be imagined, the museum is extraordinarily successful at facilitating AM, even among visitors who are just beginning to experience memory problems, and a whole series of museums have opened throughout the country.

Two short stories from the museum demonstrate its power. A group of elderly visitors were discussing a washing tub with one of the museum staff, telling stories of how "wash days" were organized domestically when they were children. One member of the group offered a recollection of being 8 or 9 years old and having to carry a bucket filled with scalding hot water up the stairs from the communal water heater to the family apartment. On another occasion, a different elderly client was in the kitchen with her adult daughter, who was visiting. The mother appeared unimpressed with much of what was on display until they looked at an old mechanical washing machine. On viewing this, the mother spoke in quick succession of her teenage school years and early married life, her now adult son who had recently died, and, finally, told a story about the son as a young boy that involved him coming into danger when playing near the exposed machine parts of a similar washing machine.

In both of these cases, we argue that it is the arrangement of the setting that affords the recollection. These AMs likely have been discussed on other occasions and for other purposes. However, the specific form they take when recollected in the museum appears to be fitted to the particular circumstances of the visit. In the first story, the collective talk with regard to the washing tub elaborates a shared history among the women. What is not explicit in the brief details we have provided is that the way they talk indicates that they all grew up in Rotterdam during the 1930s and 1940s. What they are describing is the city as it was before its partial destruction during World War II and the difficult times of the *Hongerwinter* (famine or "hunger winter") that occurred toward the end of the war. To talk of wash days is then also to acknowledge the loss of that world and the difficult period that ensued. Interestingly, the way the story about carrying the water is narrated emphasizes not the danger but, rather, the resilience of the woman as a young child. The implication of this story is that if she could do such things at a young age, then one should not assume that her current age makes her vulnerable or infirm.

The second story equally seems to be addressed as much to current circumstances as to the past. The elderly mother initially takes their joint viewing of the antiquated kitchen appliances as an opportunity to emphasize the difference between her early adult life and that of her daughter. This shifts into a memory of a recent loss that then segues into a recollected episode in which the mother was able to shield her then young son from danger. Much is occurring here: The mother is comparing her life with those of her children, emphasizing the difficulties that women of her age faced, and showing how she confronted adversity in the past. All of this, which is accomplished in a matter of minutes, speaks to her current circumstances and the state of her relationship with her daughter as she is passing into the challenges of later life. This recollection, like the one before, seems to be uniquely afforded by the very particular sets of resources on offer in the setting at that moment—the specific objects they are viewing, the interaction between the visitors, and the current life circumstances of the person remembering.

The Reminiscence Museum appears to support coherence in AM, and authorizes elderly visitors to show the relevance of their personal past to an understanding of the present. However, there are settings in which precisely the opposite appears to be the case. We have researched the experiences of patients in medium-security forensic psychiatric units (Brown, Reavey, Kanyeredzi, & Batty, 2014). These are psychiatric hospital units within the United Kingdom's National Health Service in which persons who have been either charged or convicted of criminal offenses are transferred following a mental health diagnosis that renders them as either having "diminished responsibility" for their "index offense" or as unsuited to prison committal. Patients on the unit remain detained under the guidance of a section of the Mental Health Act ("sectioned") until such time as a tribunal agrees to their release, which is typically 3–10 years, depending on the severity of the initial offense and their compliance with psychiatric intervention.

One might imagine that, as a therapeutic space, a concern with the original index offense and with the circumstances that led to its occurrence would be central to the practices of the unit. In fact, the opposite is the case. Forensic psychiatric care primarily aims at "stabilizing" a patient's condition until he or she is judged to be well enough to return to long-term outpatient care within the community. As such, patients are discouraged from talking about their life prior to entering the unit because this is taken to be irrelevant to the practice of supporting their current self-management of their condition. Brown et al. (2014) found that patients typically spoke in vague, euphemistic terms of their recent past life (e.g., "I was very unwell") and indicated that they had been made aware that dwelling on this was counterproductive to successful progression on the unit (e.g., "You don't want to get deeper into your illness"). Whereas the Reminiscence Museum facilitates coherence, the secure units seem to actively disrupt or suspend coherence and emphasize the need to dispose of AM, if only for the time of seeing out one's section.

What we want to draw attention to by way of the previous examples is that coherency in vital memories and, by extension, among other kinds of AMs is not accomplished by the person alone. It necessarily depends on the settings in which we participate and the relations that are afforded there. Authorship of our life stories may, in the final instance, be attributed to each of us alone. However, the composition of those stories, the resources out of which they are built, and the opportunity to rehearse them are a collective, setting-specific process. And although we draw upon broader cultural narratives and values, they are mediated through the specific practices that define the setting in question.

Self as Ongoing Project

There are almost unbearably weighty philosophical issues involved in conceptualizing self in relation to memory (Bergson, 1933/1992; Ricoeur, 1990; Stiegler, 2009). In the same way that the consensus on memories themselves has shifted from treating memories as "traces" or "things" that are stored within the cognitive system to the notion of them being transient constructions that are assembled in the here-and-now to accomplish some purpose, so it may be that the challenge ahead is to offer compelling conceptual "non-foundational" descriptions of "self" as an ongoing, reflexive process rather than a structure or a system that is located somewhere or other (e.g., in the brain, society, or the interaction that lies between them) (Brown & Stenner, 2009; Reavey, 2010).

Our own contribution to these emerging debates is to elaborate upon a notion of self as spatially and temporally extended. What we are emerges from the relationships we have with others and from the diverse heterogeneous materials through which we act. If the term cognition can be plausibly extended to these distributed arrangements of materials, then there is some meaning in considering whether "self" can be similarly dislodged from its tradition location "in the head" and into a process unfolding in the world. Indeed, one of the concerns regarding "digital memory" that has emerged in media studies and elsewhere (Garde-Hansen, Hoskins, & Reading, 2009; Hoskins, 2011) is with the vulnerabilities and potential fragility of self that arises when so much of our personal memories are resourced by networked electronic media whose technical formats and proprietary arrangements do not necessarily guarantee its longevity. Think of how much of "you" would be compromised by losing your smartphone or by your Facebook profile being made inaccessible.

We have argued elsewhere (Brown & Reavey, 2015) that temporal extension is best considered using metaphors of flow. Although we divide our lives according to various sociochronological conventions, our personal experience is continuous and indivisible. There are no preexisting markers that clearly demarcate our lives into constituent parts. We live not so much in the present moment as in a flow in which past and future meet and in which both are ceaselessly responding to the unfolding of events. Our past is never really over—it is reworked and reconstructed as we go along—and our anticipation of the future is correspondingly shifting. In this sense, "self" names a project—a work in progress subject to endless revision, hesitation, and reflection.

Vital memories provide vivid illustrations of the contingency and potential difficulties of this project. For example, survivors of the July 7, 2005 (7/7), London bombings found that their lives were irrevocably altered in the space of a few hours (Allen, 2015; Brown, Allen, & Reavey, 2015). Some survivors suffered life-changing injuries that meant that there could be no possibility of a return to the life and the aspirations they had had before the bombings. Other survivors found that they were immediately caught up in the fast-developing media and political story. John Tulloch, for instance, was photographed leaving the Aldgate underground tube station in a state of distress, with bandages around his head injuries and his face covered in blood. During the time of his extensive recuperation from his injuries, he discovered that his image had been used (without his consent) by a national UK newspaper in a front-page editorial supporting increased antiterrorism legislation. As he stated, he was faced with the task of reconstructing himself at the same time as he was being reconstructed by the broadcast media in completely different ways and in support of a political project to which he profoundly disagreed.

Tulloch eventually wrote an account of his experiences, in part to rescue his own project of remaking himself from competing versions that were in circulation in the media. Rachel North, who was on the Piccadilly line train, where the largest number of fatalities occurred, also wrote a book in an effort to reclaim her personal experiences. North had begun writing online posts about what had happened to her on the day of the bombings, and she had been invited by the BBC to maintain a blog about the events. This led to her engaging with the media and subsequently becoming active in support groups for fellow survivors and in campaigning for an enquiry into the official response to the bombings. As a consequence, North's account of her experiences became widely circulated. Her book is an attempt to situate that relatively short period of time in relation to her broader life story and, in particular, to link her distress and recovery from the bombings to a previous period in her life in which she was a survivor of a serious sexual assault (North, 2007). Both Tulloch and North have found that their lives have been irrevocably fractured by the 7/7 bombings, and they have faced the challenge of having their experiences reconstructed in multiple ways by others (including so-called 7/7 "truthers," who deny that the events happened at all), as well as having to try to accommodate what happened into their own project of (re)making themselves.

Tulloch's and North's projects of self-making have been unusually complex because of the highly public nature of the events in which they were caught up. However, their experiences are exemplary of many other kinds of vital memories. What happened to them was an irrevocable change that shifted the flow of their lives thereafter and became central to their self-definition. Although the significance of the event was clear, the meaning of it and the ways in which it ought to be accommodated into their evolving project of self was uncertain. In a sense, both Tulloch and North will always be there, on the trains, in the immediate aftermath and confusion of the bombings. Everything that they aspire to be, that they can be, will have to be routed through this indelible rupture in their lives.

CONCLUSION

In the early 1990s, critics of experimental psychology could confidently assert that the mainstream psychology of memory had a woefully underdeveloped conceptualization of the sociocultural contexts in which remembering was performed. Such critiques are certainly not pertinent today. Research on autobiographical memory is one of the most vibrant and progressive areas within the psychology of memory. Through the efforts of researchers such as Katherine Nelson and Robyn Fivush, the idea that telling culturally derived and sanctioned stories about one-self is a "critical developmental skill" has been successfully embedded. Martin Conway's recent reformulations of his model of the "self-memory system," which has near hegemonic status within the field, clearly demonstrate a willingness to take "culture" on board as a critical component of autobiographical memory. At the same time, recent developments in "extended," "enactive," and "distributed" cognition explored by researchers such as John Sutton and others are beginning to revise some of the fundaments of cognitive science in ways that close the gap sig-nificantly with constructionist approaches to psychology, not least because they converge on shared problems regarding how to conceptualize the role of external material resources and technologies in psychological functions.

It seems to us that the time has come to put aside squabbles about fine-grained philosophical distinctions and methodological (in)securities and recognize a shared convergence on a set of problems. In this chapter, we proposed that one starting point for seeking a way forward is to reflect on the key issues of function, culture, and self in relation to autobiographical memory. Our particular concern is with a subset of autobiographical memories that refer to painful or distressing events, which we call "vital memories." It is important to us that these memories are not treated as in some way outside of normal functioning or as pathological in any way. The participants with whom we have worked—including people who have been given mental health diagnoses and who are currently "sectioned"— seem to us to be doing their best to creatively produce a form of coherency in their life stories using the resources available to them. It seems to us that one should not depart too far from the practice and the setting in which the recollec-tion was occasioned in one's theorizing. Thus, in our repeated citing of Conway and Jobson's example, we have been keen to place it back in what we take to be its original context rather than view it as a jumping off point for abstraction.

The most pressing agenda, as we see it, is to build upon Conway and Jobson's distinction between correspondence and coherence in autobiographical memory. It is to be celebrated that the frankly ludicrous obsession with correspondence as the principal evaluative criterion for personal memories, much promoted by Elizabeth Loftus and colleagues, has been superseded with a concern for how recollections of personal experiences are fitted into a broader conception of self. However, treating correspondence and coherence as dimensions that can be plot-ted together to create a kind of 2×2 problem space of remembering does not really do justice to the setting- and practice-specific nature of recollection. We propose that the way forward is to view both correspondence and coherence as setting-level accomplishments that are indexed to the practices that are operant in the setting in question. We further propose that clarity and ambivalence are not normative criterion but are themselves relative to our participation in the settings in which our autobiographical memories are made relevant. Sometimes we need to settle matters. Other times, it works best for us to leave them open. It beggars belief that we, as analysts, would dare to assume that we have, in principle, defini-tive answers to such highly contextual and situated problems.

NOTES

1. These can be termed the "extremity" and "deficit" models of memory (Brown & Reavey, 2015).
2. We use the term "patient" to reflect the description used by Conway and Jobson, not because we think this is the most appropriate way in which to refer to individuals using services, unless they are de facto patients in a hospital setting.
3. Elizabeth Loftus and colleagues' work has claimed to be able to provide a recipe for the creation of false memories and is a generalized model of how false memory operates, regardless of context or type of memory. Using data from experiments designed to implant benign false memories (being lost in a mall or a balloon rise) in the general population (i.e., nonspecified research participants), this research lays claim to a generalizable model of all false memory, via suggestion, false feedback, and visualization. According to this model, the individual can become convinced that the false event was personally experienced, using these well-established techniques. Loftus (2003) remarks, "At this point, the individual might merely believe that the event is true but have no sense of recollection. But with guided imagination, with visualization of the stories of others, and with suggestive feedback and other sorts of manipulation, a rich false memory can occur" (p. 871). Pertinent to this approach is that all false memories follow a similar pathway. This false memory approach thus starts with the general and then tries to work its way down a quasi-causal pathway to the particular, such that benign memories can then also be used to explain false traumatic and/or vital memories, such as being sexually abused as a child.

REFERENCES

Allen, M. J. (2015). *The labour of memory: Memorial culture and 7/7*. London, UK: Palgrave Macmillan.

Baddeley, A. (1988). Imagery and Working Memory. Cognitive and Neuropsychological Approaches to Mental Imagery. Volume 42 of the series NATO ASI Series pp 169–180.

Bartlett, F. C. (1932). *Remembering: A study in experimental social psychology*. Cambridge, UK: Cambridge University Press.

Bendien, E. (2010). From the art of remembering to the craft of ageing: A study of the Reminiscence Museum at Humanitas, Rotterdam. Rotterdam: Stichting Humanitas Huisdrukkerij.

Bendien, E. (2013). The last stitch in the quilt. *Gender, Work and Organization, 20*, 709–719.

Bendien, E., Brown, S. D., & Reavey, P. (2010). Social remembering as an art of living: Analysis of a "reminiscence museum." In M. Domenech & M. Schillmeier (Eds.), *New technologies and emerging spaces of care* (pp. 149–167). Surrey, UK: Ashgate.

Bergson, H. (1992). *The creative mind: An introduction to metaphysics* (M. L. Andison, Trans.). New York, NY: Citadel. (Original work published 1933)

Bernsten, D., & Bohn, A. (2009). Cultural life scripts and individual stories. In P. Boyer, & J. V. Wertsch (Eds.), *Memory in mind and culture*. Cambridge: Cambridge University Press.

Bluck, S. (2003) Autobiographical memory: Exploring its functions in everyday life. *Memory, 11*(2), 113–123.

Boyer, P., & Wertsch, J. V. (Eds.). (2009). *Memory in mind and culture.* Cambridge, UK: Cambridge University Press.

Brookfield, H., Brown, S. D., & Reavey, P. (2008). Vicarious and post memory practices in adopting families: The construction of the past in photography and narrative. *Journal of Community and Applied Social Psychology, 18*(5), 474–491.

Brown, S. D., Allen, M. A., & Reavey, P. (2015). Remembering 7/7: The collective shaping of memories of the London bombings. In A. L. Tota & T. Hagen (Eds.), *Routledge international handbook of memory studies.* London, UK: Routledge.

Brown, S. D., & Reavey, P. (2014). Vital memories: Movements in and between affect, ethics and self. *Memory Studies: Remembering in Context, 7*(3), 328–338. [Special issue]

Brown, S. D., & Reavey, P. (2015). *Vital memory and affect: Ethics, agency and self.* London, UK: Routledge.

Brown, S. D., Reavey, P., & Brookfield, H. (2013). Spectral objects: Material links to difficult pasts for adoptive parents. In P. Harvey, E. Casella, G. Evans, H. Knox, C. McLean, E. Silva, . . . K. Woodward (Eds.), *Objects and materials: A Routledge companion* (pp. 173–181). London, UK: Routledge.

Brown, S. D., Reavey, P., Kanyeredzi, A., & Batty, R. (2014). Transformations of self and sexuality: Psychologically modified experiences in the context of forensic mental health. *Health, 18*(3), 240–260.

Brown, S. D., & Stenner, P. (2009). *Psychology without foundations: History, philosophy and psychosocial theory.* London, UK: Sage.

Clark, A. (1997). *Being there: Putting brain, body, and world together again.* Cambridge, MA: MIT Press.

Clark, A., & Chalmers, D. (1998). The extended mind. *Analysis, 58*(1), 7–19.

Cole, M. (2005). *Cultural Psychology: A Once and Future Discipline.* Cambridge: Harvard University Press.

Conway, M. A. (2005). Memory and the self. *Journal of Memory and Language, 53,* 594–628.

Conway, M. A., & Jobson, L. (2012). On the nature of autobiographical memory. In D. Berntsen & D. C. Rubin (Eds.), *Understanding autobiographical memory: Theories and approaches* (pp. 54–69). Cambridge, UK: Cambridge University Press.

Conway, M. A., & Loveday, C. (2015). Remembering, imagining, false memories & personal meanings. *Consciousness & Cognition, 33,* 574–581.

Conway, M. A., & Pleydell-Pearce, C. W. (2000). The construction of autobiographical memories in the self-memory system. *Psychological Review, 107,* 261–288.

Conway, M. A., Singer, J. A., & Tagini, A. (2004). The self and autobiographical memory: Correspondence and coherence. *Social Cognition, 22*(5), 491–529.

Edwards, D., & Potter, J. (1992). *Discursive psychology.* London, UK: Sage.

Erll, A., & Nünning, A. (Eds.). (2008). *Cultural memory studies: An international and interdisciplinary handbook* (pp. 109–118). New York, NY: de Gruyter.

Fivush, R. (1998). Children's recollections of traumatic and non-traumatic events. *Development and Psychopathology, 10,* 699–716.

Fivush, R. (2011). The development of autobiographical memory. *Annual Review of Psychology, 62,* 559–582.

Garde-Hansen, J., Hoskins, A., & Reading, A. (Eds.). (2009). *Save as . . . digital memories*. London, UK: Palgrave.

Haaken, J. (1999). "Heretical texts: *The Courage to Heal* and the incest survivor movement." In S. Lamb (Ed.), *New versions of victims: Feminists struggle with the concept* (pp. 13–41). New York, NY: New York University Press.

Harris, C. B., Barnier, A. J., Sutton, J., & Keil, P. G. (2014). Couples as socially distributed cognitive systems: Remembering in everyday social and material contexts. *Memory Studies, 7*(3), 285–297.

Harris, C. B., Sutton, J., & Barnier, A. J. (2010). Autobiographical forgetting, social forgetting, and situated forgetting: Forgetting in context. In S. G. Della Salla (Ed.), *Forgetting* (pp. 253–284). London: Psychology Press.

Hirsch, M. (1997). *Family frames: Photography, narrative and postmemory*. Cambridge, MA: Harvard University Press.

Hoskins, A. (2011). From collective memory to memory systems. *Memory Studies, 4*(2), 131–133.

Ingold, T. (1996). *Perceptions of the environment: Essays on livelihood, dwelling and skill*. London, UK: Routledge.

Ingold, T. (2013). *Making: Anthropology, archaeology, art and architecture*. London, UK: Routledge.

Lamb, S. (1996). *The trouble with blame*. Cambridge, MA: Harvard University Press.

Loftus, E. F. (2003). Make-believe memories. *American Psychologist, 58*, 867–873.

Mesle, C. R. (2008). *Process-relational philosophy: An introduction to Alfred North Whitehead*. West Conshohocken, PA: Templeton Foundation Press.

Middleton, D., & Brown, S. D. (2005). *The social psychology of experience: Studies in remembering and forgetting*. London, UK: Sage.

Middleton, D., & Edwards, D. (1990). *Collective remembering*. London, UK: Sage.

Neisser, U. (1994). Multiple systems: A new approach to cognitive theory. *European Journal of Cognitive Psychology, 6*(3), 225–241.

Nelson, K. (1993). The psychological and social origins of autobiographical memory. *Psychological Science, 4*, 7–14.

Nelson, K. (2003). Self and social functions: Individual autobiographical memory and collective narrative. *Memory, 11*(2), 125–136.

Nelson, K. (Ed.). (2006). *Narratives from the crib*. Cambridge, MA: Harvard University Press.

Nelson, K. (2009). *Young minds in social worlds: Experience, meaning and memory*. Cambridge, MA: Harvard University Press.

Nelson, K., & Fivush, R. (2004). The emergence of autobiographical memory: A social cultural developmental theory. *Psychological Review, 111*, 486–511.

North, R. (2007). *Out of the tunnel*. London, UK: The Friday Project.

Pasupathi, M. (2001). The social construction of the past and its implications for adult development. *Psychological Bulletin, 127*, 651–672.

Pillemer, D. B. (1998). What is remembered from early childhood events. *Clinical Psychology Review, 18*, 895–913.

Potter, J. (2012). How to study experience. *Discourse & Society, 23*, 576–588.

Reavey, P. (2010). Spatial markings: Memory, narrative and survival. *Memory Studies, 3*, 314–329.

Reavey, P., & Brown, S. D. (2006). Transforming past agency and action in the present: Time, social remembering and child sexual abuse. *Theory and Psychology*, *16*(2), 179–202.

Reavey, P., & Brown, S. D. (2007). Rethinking agency in memory: Space and embodiment in memories of child sexual abuse. *Journal of Social Work Practice*, *21*(4), 5–21.

Reavey, P., & Brown, S. D. (2009). The mediating role of objects in recollections of adult women survivors of child sexual abuse. *Culture & Psychology*, *15*(4), 463–484.

Ricoeur, P. (1990). *Time & narrative* (Vol. 2). Chicago, IL: University of Chicago Press.

Roberts, K. R., & Blades, M. (2000). *Children's source monitoring*. Sussex, UK: Psychology Press.

Rubin, D. C. (2012). The basic system models of autobiographical memory. In D. Berntsen & D. C. Rubin (Eds.), *Understanding autobiographical memory: Theories and approaches* (pp. 11–32). Cambridge, UK: Cambridge University Press.

Stiegler, B. (2009). Teleologics of the snail: The errant self wired to a WiMax network. *Theory, Culture & Society*, *26*, 33–45.

Sutton, J., Harris, C. B., Keil, P. G., & Barnier, A. J. (2010). The psychology of memory, extended cognition, and socially distributed remembering. *Phenomenology and the Cognitive Sciences*, *9*(4), 521–560.

Tileagă, C., & Stokoe, E. (Eds.). (2015). *Discursive psychology: Classic and contemporary issues*. London, UK: Sage.

Wagoner, B. (2011). Meaning construction in remembering: A synthesis of Bartlett and Vygotsky. In P. Stenner (Ed.), *Theoretical psychology: Global transformations and challenges* (pp. 105–114). Toronto, Ontario, Canada: Captus Press.

Whitehead, A. N. (1978). *Process & reality* (corrected ed.). New York, NY: Free Press.

PART III

Memory Through the Life Course

The Cultural Construction
of Memory in Early Childhood

KATHERINE NELSON ∎

This chapter explores the role of culture in the development of memory from infancy through early childhood to school age, the period that builds the foundations of memory structure and functions in mature life. Cross-cultural differences in aspects of memory, including in its early development, have been widely explored in recent decades (Wang, 2013). The discussion here is more general and basic, asking in what way cultural exposure and experience during the early years of the human lifespan may be an essential contributor to cognitive development, including specifically memory development. Here, the focus is on different *levels* of culture that may be accessible to the young child at different ages and through different kinds of socially supported experiences, as well as through the child's own action. The concept of culture here is essentially a dynamic one, reflecting changes over time, in evolution and through history, continuing into the present. Development of human memory is also of course a dynamic process on the individual level, specifically here the time between birth and approximately 5 years of age. Despite radically different timescales, the two constructs—culture and individual development—intersect in ways that are critical to each.

Specifically, the construct of multilevels of culture assumed here is first considered in relation to developmental issues, drawing broadly on Merlin Donald's (1991, 2001) proposals, with the focus on how such levels may be accessed by the child at different developmental periods. Next, I consider kinds of memory and what we now know about their development, focusing especially on the emergence of autobiographical memory. The research that supports the cultural levels accessibility proposal is reviewed with its implications for better understanding of the developmental processes involved in what appears to be a major change across many areas of behavioral and conceptual organization, including or depending on memory, between 3 and 5 years of age.

LEVELS OF CULTURE AND MIND EMERGING OVER TIME

Merlin Donald's (1991, 2001; see also Chapter 1, this volume) account of the emergence of the "modern human mind" begins with the assumption that cultural activity and communication emerged in the pre-human hominid line, as evidenced in the archeological record of advanced toolmaking by the species *Homo erectus*. Donald proposed that these relatively advanced hominids developed mimetic means of interaction and communication, based in "body language" for purposes such as hunting; keeping track of food sources and tool materials; signaling to other members in cooperative tasks; and even widely sharing group activities through mimetic practices such as dancing, drumming, and perhaps singing. This view that mimetic social–cultural practices are essential bases for the emergence of spoken language utilizing human vocal abilities has gained many adherents since Donald proposed it. The action-based cognition and cultural foundation referred to as *mimetic* constitutes the first level in the advanced cognition and communication within the human line, viewed as a critical forerunner to a truly symbolic linguistic system. Through its means, participants can move beyond the socially aware interactions, but still strictly individual mind and perspective, that other primates (and all other animals) are confined to and toward the wider cultural perspective available through language use.[1]

The mimetic level of cognition and culture did not disappear with pre-human species but continues as a major component of our cultural and social lives today, evident in the practice of sports, dance, theater, everyday greetings and intimate signals, among others. Important to the developmental story unfolding here, the mimetic cultural level is the primary level that is *accessible* to the nonverbal infant and child. Social exchange through mimetic practices, as in games such as peek-a-boo or in everyday activities of feeding, going to bed, and so on, is typical in infant care. Mimetic practices executed in play and daily routines serve as the primary context of the very young for exploring the outside world with social partners. Much has been made in typical developmental accounts of the infant's exploration of the world through individual action, but a large proportion of the time, most infants are in close contact with their caregivers and other adults and older children. Accounting for the influence of pervasive social interaction on cognitive development in infancy has until recently been a somewhat neglected topic but one of great importance.

As verbal language emerged as a medium of communication in early human societies, major cultural change in social practices, knowledge systems, and institutions followed (Donald, 2001). Summarily speaking, mimetic culture fostered the emergence of vocal language, which in turn supported new kinds of cultural knowledge and practices. Oral language use depends on cooperative exchange of symbolic signs (Tomasello, 2008) that convey agreed-upon meanings[2] within the larger language community. Symbolic use of this kind implies radical change in human cognition and its development (Deacon, 1997; Donald, 2001; see also Donald, Chapter 1, this volume). Social exchange through language reflected the changing cultural systems (in practices, shared knowledge, and institutions).

Oral language culture is largely organized in narrative terms, exemplified in the myths of many ancient as well as contemporary cultures. Narrative structures reflect multiple causal relations as well as interactions among actors with different interests.

In brief, this model involves the individual mind open to changing interactions with the world; cultural accumulations of practices, knowledge, and institutions; and social interactions serving as "carriers" of culture for each other and specifically as mediators for the young initiate in the cultural world. In its historical context, the broad dynamic network just sketched (culture ↔ social ↔ individual) both required and supported further changes in mental content, symbolic format, and organization and, as Donald demonstrated, continued (and continues) to do so. In its developmental context, it supports the child in coming to understand and share the concepts, constructs, and practices that are critical to taking part in and growing within this ever-changing dynamic system. An essential part of this process is the development of complex cognitive structures, including the memory system described in the sections that follow.

The overall result is the human mind as a layered system, like the culture, including at first mimetic symbols and practices overlaid by oral language practices (especially face-to-face communication but also later through telephone, radio, theater, etc.). A third layer of culture and mind was initiated through the development of written alphabetic language, extending the limited temporal representation of messages and providing a mode for recording and sharing complex narratives and arguments, as well as documents required by legal, economic, and government institutions. Prior to the availability of written texts, narratives such as the classical Greek and Roman myths and tales were memorized by individuals for presentation and maintenance over generations of listeners in groups. These practices continue today through speeches and lectures as well as everyday talk. The oral mental and cultural modes of knowledge were later supplemented with literate practices, making knowledge bases more widely accessible to government, economic, and social institutions.

Much has been documented about the changes wrought through literate practices in both individual mentality and the culture at large (Olson, 1994). Notable for the present account, participation in literate culture normally requires formal learning of the alphabetic and numeric systems of notation, usually accomplished through educational institutions beginning in mid-childhood. The level of mentality associated with literate practices is also associated with changes in representation in the brain. Although lexical and grammatical systems for oral language are located in specific areas of the left hemisphere of the brain, there is no specific space for alphabetic writing (e.g., non-literate individuals do not have an empty module waiting to be filled in with letters and printed words). Such a system must be constructed anew for each individual, made possible by the plasticity of the human brain. Such additional representational modes may be established in either the immature or the adult organism. Systems of reading, writing, and arithmetic must be learned in practice; once established, they change the operations of conscious and unconscious mental processes.

For more than two millennia, literacy was mostly confined to a small learned class who possessed the tools for engaging in its practices at high levels of governing and business or in literary, philosophical, or religious study with access to the limited availability of texts. Still a fourth level of culture gradually emerged following the invention of the printing press in the 16th century of the current era. As Donald and others have argued, as printed works became widely used, they affected memory practices that were adapted to the wide availability of texts and their endurance over time, thus facilitating the sharing of knowledge across large segments of the population. Modern science emerged in the 18th century as a complex practice that requires social networks operating at a distance, with accepted rules, extensive scholarship in institutions, and experience with relevant tools and activities. It cannot take place in either a strictly mimetic culture or a solely oral culture, nor by solitary scholars working alone, but requires the tools of a literate and knowledge-oriented society. An individual growing up in a solitary or oral community without access to these cultural advantages could not take part in the practice of science nor have full access to its knowledge base.

Widespread distribution of printed texts also encouraged the emergence of popular literary works such as the novel, partially replacing the group practices of sharing narratives in recitation and singing. Interestingly, although this meant that more such tales could be enjoyed by wider audiences, it also made possible private and solitary reading. A likely consequence was widespread knowledge consumption accompanied by a kind of increased individualism (Eakin, 1999; Nelson, 2003). Other individual literary practices, such as autobiography and diary-keeping, emerged and became common. By the 20th century in the modern era, literate cultures supported science, scholarship, higher levels of education, journalism, and related industries for the production and distribution of printed material.

Thus, the complex mixed culture we live in, think in, work and play in, and communicate in today is layered with mimetic practice, oral language practice, everyday written materials such as letters and shopping lists, and widely available complex literate works. We can speculate that the middle level of this mixture is disappearing into the digital world, still dependent on language but not for the many written uses that were important only a decade or two ago. How these novel changes may affect our cognition is another question that will likely not be answerable for many decades to come.[3]

In summary, the argument here, following Donald (1991, 2001; see also Chapter 1, this volume), is that culture and mind evolved together, first in biological evolution, then through the combination of cultural change and cognitive construction. Cultural change over historical time has had a major impact on the complexity and organization of individual human minds in conjunction with the complexities involved in the extensively expanded cultural knowledge base. The resulting adult mind is an intricate mix coherent with the cultural complexity of mimetic, linguistic, literate, and widely shared and distributed components. The implication of this account of evolving language practices and concomitant population-wide cognitive change is that development of these structures in childhood is essential for their effective operation over the lifespan and for responding to changing social–cultural conditions. These developments in early childhood are as dependent on cultural and social support as on basic cognitive structures and inherent constructive processes.

The assumption here is that the processes necessary for this development to succeed at the basic mimetic and spoken language levels take place in the context of families and communities through the cultural practices and social interactions typical of human societies. Because all levels of the culture surround children from the beginning, they are typically exposed to many aspects of both oral and literate culture, and over time they come to utilize more and more aspects of these levels. However, the first level of culture fully accessible to the maturing infant includes mimetic practices, artifacts, and interactions with the social figures of their lives in varied scenes and routine activities. Infants are experts at understanding the recurrent routines of their lives, including the roles and messages directed by parents and other caretakers and familiar interactors. These activities are the mimetic contents of their social experience, and toward the end of the first year they begin to participate more actively in this social–cultural milieu through gesture (e.g., pointing), action games, and other means. They also begin to use these communicative acts to interpret some of the verbal components of their shared activities, using these as a springboard into the use of verbal language themselves.[4] Together with these practices is the ubiquitous use of oral language among people in the social surround, including verbal messages directed to the child. Years of practice are required to gain the comprehension skills of oral language use sufficient to fully engage in the cultural practices at that level (Nelson, 2007). These achievements occupy the first 5 years of the child's life. During this period of early childhood, children's cognitive systems undergo extensive expansion and structural organization through interaction with the linguistic world.

Infants may well become aware of the artifacts of the third level of culture—writing and print—which are pointed out to them by parents and literally litter their lives in papers, books, and the endless machinery of the written world, including its digital components. Nobody shelters the child from these materials; indeed, the adult world goes out of its way to introduce them to it.[5] However, formal schooling is a virtual requirement for participation at the literary level and is an add-on now almost universal across societies. It typically begins during the 5- to 7-year shift in cognitive functioning resulting from earlier cultural experience. The topic explored here is how this cultural and cognitive experiential complex is involved in the development of the cognitive process of memory in infancy and early childhood.

DEVELOPING MEMORY KINDS IN CULTURAL CONTEXT

Consider memory as the content of the mind—content that, by the process posited here, is derived from individual activity and social interaction in cultural context. Memory also refers to the vast brain systems that organize and utilize acquired contents of experience in the world and enable conscious access to this content over short or long periods of time. Memory may result from conscious experience in the world, from deliberate learning by self or through teaching, or from conscious individual thought processes, including imagination and problem-solving (see discussion in Nelson, 2007). Unconscious learning such as habits and behavioral conditioning or biased attitudes may affect aspects of cognition and are long-lasting but often are not accessible to conscious recall. The critical period in this account of memory development is the years of first language acquisition and use as the child moves into the narrative-rich oral language cultural environment. The central question here is how memory development is affected by the onset of language and its use between the child and others during this period. The *kinds of memory* that are evident among children at different points in this process provide the framework for this analysis.

The general memory literature distinguishes several distinct memory systems: a first cut is made between *procedural* memory as distinct from *declarative* memory. Procedural memory is typically "how to" knowledge, involving action, and it is generally activated in specific contexts. A typical example is bicycle riding, but for the period in focus here it applies to all skills of infancy, such as crawling, walking, feeding with a spoon, and so on.[6] Within declarative memory, which is accessible to conscious recall, *episodic* and *semantic* memory are distinguished. Semantic memory is best thought of as knowledge, typically referred to as "factual" (but see discussion to follow). Semantic memory is to a large extent derived from the cultural knowledge base shared with other community members. Much of its content has a source in language, but the cognitive system also derives concepts and contents from individual and social experience in the world independent of external representation of any kind, including language.

Episodic memory has two distinctive features: (1) It involves the *self* in experience (2) of a *past* event (Tulving, 1983). Tulving (1993) emphasizes the self-relevant aspect in the term *autonoetic* (self-knowing). Although by definition memory retains some parts of past experience, recognition of the past time of a specific event is the hallmark of episodic memory. Episodic memory may be fleeting and incomplete or long-retained and highly detailed—an ongoing record of the personal past or, in Damasio's (1999) terms, an internal narrative. The construct of episodic memory is now a topic of interest to psychologists and philosophers on both theoretical and empirical grounds (Mahr & Csibra, 2017; Perrin & Rousset, 2014; Tulving, 2005).

Autobiographical memory is a fourth memory kind, combining both episodic and semantic content. It is distinctively long-lasting (for years or, in some cases, for decades). Episodic memories about meaningful events in specific place and time in the past predominate in autobiographical memory, typically including other participants, scenes, and motivations in semi-narrative form. Semantic information about the past relevant to the self and self-memories also exists in autobiographical memory (e.g., the house in which one once lived).

Questions arose early in investigations of infant memory as to whether it is entirely procedural or may include declarative memory even though infants lack communicative systems for making declarations (for history and details, see Bauer, 2007). Donald (1991) proposed that the first important move toward the unique human mentality was the appearance of *deliberate conscious recall* out of the context of its learning, the hallmark (although unobservable) of declarative memory. Some scattered evidence that infants younger than age 12 months recalled specific aspects of previously experienced events appears to support the claim of infant declarative memory[7] (Bauer & Mandler, 1989; Fivush, 1994; Moscovitsch, 1984; Perlmutter, 1980; Rovee-Collier, 1997).

Several lines of research are available for testing these claims using delayed imitation tasks. They indicate that infants in the latter half of the first year retain information from a one-time experience of watching a three-part action sequence after the retention period increases gradually; by 2 years it may extend as long as a year (Bauer, 2007). This evidence supports earlier observations that some 1- to 2-year-olds refer through action or words to experience from 6 months or even 1 year in the past. There is no evidence (to my knowledge) of any such reports being remembered again much later in childhood, although Cleveland and Reese (2008) have documented recall of 2-year-old memories recalled at age 5½ years. It can thus be stated with some confidence that older infants and toddlers give evidence of both procedural and declarative memory, the latter revealed primarily in actions rather than in language, as would be expected at this age. However, whether this is episodic or some version of semantic memory, or a more generic kind, is not clear.

Specifically, do infants and toddlers (1½–3 years) have memory with the distinctive characteristics of episodic memory: autonoesis and temporal reference to a specific past time? Because these concepts are difficult to assess without the aid of language, the issue remains unsettled (but see further discussion in the next section).[8] As the child becomes more proficient with language, a third area of inquiry emerges—the question of the *source* of the memory, whether from personal experience or based on social and cultural narratives conveyed through stories or conversations or other semiotic sources. There is good evidence (Roberts & Blades, 2000) that in general, the source of acquired knowledge is rarely registered by children younger than age 4 or 5 years, thus potentially confounding possible distinctions in memory between cultural knowledge and personal experience memory.

Autobiographical memory—combining aspects of semantic and episodic memory—is the last major memory system to be developed in early childhood. Autobiographical memory was first brought into focus by a memory phenomenon that has remained a point of inquiry for more than 100 years, namely adult *infantile amnesia*, the inability of adults to recall specific episodic memories from the first 3 years of their lives. William James (1890/1950) took note of this peculiarity, and Freud (1924) made it a key part of his theory of the unconscious. The first systematic study of "first memories" was obtained through a questionnaire reporting the average age of the earliest childhood memory as 3 years (Miles, 1893). An individual adult may report a first memory from slightly earlier than 3 years, and often only from somewhat later—as late as 6 or 7 years—but the mean age for European and American adults has not significantly changed from a range of 3 to 3½ years during more than 100 years of investigations (Bauer, 2007; White & Pillemer, 1979). This age has withstood numerous replications of these investigations for more than a century, as well as disbelief on the part of some psychologists (and a few individuals who maintain that they have a distinct memory from infancy, even from the birth process).

If infants and young children do not retain episodic memories over a long period, is this the case for their semantic memory? Clearly, even very young infants have memory of the familiar people, places, and things of their lives, and as work by Rovee-Collier (1997) has demonstrated, they retain memory for their own unique action–object relations over several months. Semantic memory for the places, scenes, people, and things from late infancy, like episodic memory, appears to last for months, as indicated by nonverbal cues, but these memories appear inaccessible to recall later in life. In other words, something like the semantic system of general knowledge must exist in infancy, but like the events of infancy, it is lost to recall in later years.

The absence from adult memory of early memories of all kinds strongly implies that children younger than 3 years of age do not yet have an autobiographical memory system that preserves significant memories of events involving the self and also that such memory emerges gradually sometime between ages 4 and 7 years for most children. Despite reports of occasional memories from earlier ages, a realistic age range for the onset of autobiographical memory is 5–7 years, both in terms of numbers of events recalled by adults and in terms of the proportion of adults who report memories from these ages (Nelson & Fivush, 2004). It is interesting that, this period coincides with the widely noted "5 to 7 shift" in numerous aspects of cognitive and social functioning (White, 1965, 1996). Reports on research in a number of areas in the 1996 volume edited by Sameroff and Haith included neurological transitions (culminating changes that had been taking place during the previous years), cognitive shifts in representation, theory of mind, and self, among others relevant to school performance, including memory. In their report on neurological transitions during this period, Janowsky and Carper (1996) specifically connected the neurological changes in memory functions located in the prefrontal lobes to the reports of children's personal memory accounts and the emergence of autobiographical memory during this period. It has long been established that basic neurological systems involved in memory are completed at this age (for a detailed account, see Bauer 2007). The burden of the evidence for this shift implicates interconnections between developmental processes and outcomes among what are considered to be separately developing areas of function. This supposition applies specifically to memory, theory of mind, and self-concept, as discussed later in this chapter.

Autobiographical memory has been characterized here in terms of its onset. What, if anything, distinguishes it from episodic and semantic memory? Is it simply a combination of the two? On one view, it consists of all those memories (both episodic and semantic) that are retained over the long term into adolescence and adulthood, with some memories lasting into the late years of life. The memories are both personally significant and specific to a temporal period of life, if not to a specific date. From another view, autobiographical memory constitutes a kind of life story or autobiography, not a simple collection of interesting episodes but a meaningful record, including generalized knowledge of what an era in a lifespan involved, with a focus on the self in experience.

Important to the characterization of autobiographical memory is the fact that people vary considerably with regard not only to its onset time but also in the frequency of memories from any period of the lifespan and the overall number of memories retained. Some individuals with excellent semantic memory have very few autobiographical memories from earlier periods, and those with little detail. Others retain enough to feel able to reconstruct in detail whole segments of their lifespan. Their memories are very narrative-like. In addition, some memories long forgotten reappear in old age. There is no generally established explanation for such wide variations that are not apparently predicted by other characteristics such as education, intelligence, or achievement. One presumption is that such variations point to the central role of the construction of self in memory, or specifically to the cultural self developing over the lifespan, and to variations on the dimension of self-construal (see papers in Moore & Lemmon, 2001; Sani, 2008). This aspect of AM is considered in the section on the social–cultural context of memory development.

CHILDREN IN COMPLEX CULTURE DEVELOPING COMPLEX MEMORY

Let me clarify the constructive view of memory taken here, which was outlined in an early form in Nelson (1993). It begins with the assumption that the basic function of memory in any animal, including humans, is to support action in the present and in possible re-encounters with elements from the past by the accumulation of information about the experienced world. Thus, the evolution of the long-term memory function of the brain might be traced from the simple neuronal model that Kandel (2006) studied in the giant marine snail *Aplysia* to the modern complexities of human memory. Tracing its development over the human lifespan is a different matter that has been addressed in terms of its basic brain processes (for a summary, see Bauer, 2007). The division into "kinds" of memory just discussed is a related but incomplete approach. Keeping in mind that the basic evolved function is to guide present and future activity (rather than to reminisce about the past) helps to interpret the apparent course of development revealed through studies of memory in infants and young children. The present argument is that in humans social and cultural conditions have repeatedly *required* new applications of memory and have supported the development of these through elaborations of the basic memory processes, eventuating in the different "systems" or "kinds" that are now recognized.

From the perspective of memory development in its cultural context, we can think of the first year as largely organized around *event knowledge* (Nelson,

1986) based in mimetic social–cultural context. Infants seem specially tuned to track and remember new activity sequences, even those that do not involve themselves, as Bauer's innovative research on the delayed imitation of action sequences revealed (Bauer, 2007; Mandler, 2004). This knowledge is derived from the repeated coordinated action of self and other. It typically involves other actors and materials and also a *sequence* of actions. To some degree, such sequences may be considered procedural memory, or action knowledge. However, it is not confined to the child's actions: It includes the actions and responses of other actors. Examples are games such as pat-a-cake and routines such as bedtime. Event knowledge is no doubt based on very basic memory processes not different from those of other species, although with different social–cultural content. Event knowledge has the potential, however, for supporting further memory developments (Nelson, 1993, 1996).

Event knowledge is knowledge of how the world works in its dynamic forms, in addition to its non-temporal characteristics. It is basic to adult functioning in the world as well as to infants, as originally proposed by Schank and Abelson (1977) and studied extensively by social psychologists in terms of scripts (Abelson, 1981). In infancy, it is socially and culturally supported through the daily routines of caretakers and child rather than derived solely from the infant's individual exploration. However, an aspect of such routine knowledge is that it is also always changing, especially during the period of rapid growth in infancy, during which parents inevitably change the methods and contents of meals, for example, as well as such routines as naps and bedtime. Infants must be flexible enough to override old routines with the new; memory must be deletable. However, beginning in the second year, as parents know, toddlers may resist changes in established routines, perhaps indicating a new value of self-direction rather than adult dependence. This resistance may also indicate a new implicit understanding on the child's part of the importance of this kind of knowledge for participating in the surrounding social–cultural life.

The knowledge of everyday events and the materials that are used in them later supports more complex cultural knowledge systems, such as categories of foods, clothes, and tools (Lucariello, Kyratzis, & Nelson, 1992; Lucariello & Nelson, 1987; Nelson, 1986). These studies suggested the hypothesis that the beginnings of organized semantic memory categories are established through social routines prior to the learning of language, then aiding in language acquisition, and in the further development of a language-based semantic system. In other words, they imply that there is a rather smooth continuity between the establishment of a protosemantic system prior to language and that of the later semantic system that becomes expressed and remembered in language formats. This proposal is reasonable inasmuch as similar materials and activities are available from one period to the next. However, the language system also imposes its own organization on the terms for familiar materials, resulting in a mixture of the child's self-organized categories and those of the culture (Mandler & McDonough, 2000; Nelson, 1996).

Early studies of general event knowledge suggested that such knowledge might preempt memory for specific episodic events early in development. For example,

3-year-old children who were asked to respond to questions about either "what [usually] happens" (e.g., at a birthday party) or "what happened at a [specific] birthday party" that the children had attended answered both the *specific* and the *general* event questions in the present tense form and with the same routine information (e.g., "We have a cake and presents"). There was no discernible differentiation between the two. This was true for everyday events such as having dinner at home as well as for more exceptional ones. In effect, the event knowledge studies indicate an early development of a kind of generalized semantic event memory but not a differentiated episodic memory. Differentiation of functions is an important developmental principle, as delineated in Heinz Werner's orthogenetic theory (Werner & Kaplan, 1963); thus, the emergence of memory for specific episodes would indicate an important advance.

Specific people and the self may be "actors" with specific roles to play in the child's general event accounts, but because the very young child's event knowledge favors generic repeated events rather than one-time narratives, specific motivations or uncertain intentionality are not an issue in them and are not mentioned. These matters only slowly become incorporated within the language period that follows. Consistent with such findings, Bogdan (2010) argues that the young child's conception of self is first as actor and interactor and not from the outset as "mindful." This position does not reject the now widely accepted evidence of "self-consciousness" by age 2 years, as measured by the "mirror test" of self-recognition, or the related use of personal pronouns for self and other (Lewis, 1997). Such early consciousness of self, it is argued, is confined to the whole body self as a distinct actor among actors. Such consciousness does not necessarily imply all of the "mindfulness" of self and others that the concept implies for adult actors and thinkers.[9] Early self-consciousness is clearly a start on the path toward a more mature conception of persons, just as two-word "sentences" of this period are a start toward full linguistic competence. Both require experience in the world of social language exchange to fulfill their promise[10] (Bogdan, 2010; Nelson, 2007).

Entering into Oral Language and Narrative Culture

As young children participate with parents and others in the oral language world, they become more alert to speech accompanying everyday activities, as adults highlight aspects of play and routines that they may not have attended to or understood previously. Many other uses of language come into focus in the year between the second and third birthdays for many children: accounts of events to come, choices of activities, and, importantly, storytelling and story reading, as well as personal accounts of "what we did together," "what we'll do," or "where I went and why." In these ways, children are introduced to the cultural world of narrative, both personal—about other people, times, and places—and imaginative. Even the simplest narratives incorporate and make explicit temporal relations, causes and results, and often the actions and motivations of third persons with effects on other actors.

Hutto (2008) has strongly argued that narrative experience and understanding lie behind the child's understanding of the intentionality of other persons, an argument that I believe extends not only to "theory of mind" but also to many other aspects of social understanding in the preschool years and ultimately to the construction of autobiographical memory. Personal storytelling about self and others (often gossip) is a pervasive use of language in all cultures. At the present time, its growing understanding by young participants in the narrative culture is understudied. (The exception is memory talk by parents with their 3- and 4-year-old children discussed later in this section). The potential value of such research is indicated in the study of the private "crib speech" of 2-year-old Emily in conjunction with her parents' bedtime talk (Nelson, 1989a, 1989b). We found that in her private crib talk, Emily first focused on the routine events of her life, but approaching her third birthday she produced a true original narrative about a shopping expedition (for analysis, see Nelson, 2015; for a related analysis, see Bruner & Lucariello, 1989). This child's language was quite advanced for her age, and we can assume that this achievement was also early and would not be expected until a later age for most children.

The hypothesis that event knowledge from infancy and later is a memory platform for first language learning and use, as well as for entry into the complexities of narrative cultural experience, is supported by this research. Event knowledge aids the initial comprehension of simple narratives in stories and personal tales that elicit focus on specific happenings, such as swimming in the ocean, a visit to an amusement park, or a painful accident. These episodes may then be remembered in part, sometimes for as long as 6 months or a year. As noted previously, specific memories of this kind by 2- and 3-year-olds have been reported by parents (Hudson, 1990; Nelson & Ross, 1980). Children vary widely in the pace of their acquisition of language, as well as in their experience with social partners. Therefore, variability in progress toward the narrative basis of episodic memory, and a unique self-perspective, is also to be expected.

Episodic memory is the most intensively studied memory development of this early period of language use, but development of semantic memory is certainly as affected. The difference between the two within the cognitive domain may not, in fact, have been established in the early years, although I am not aware of studies that speak specifically to this point. Previously, it was noted that specific episodes were not distinguished from general event knowledge early in development. The implication is that two differentiations must be made: general versus specific and episode versus known fact. It is a reasonable hypothesis that distinguishing in memory between personal experience and socially imparted information (including others' personal memories) is another specific differentiation and developmental achievement. This distinction may well depend on experience with language used to talk about different episodes. It may in fact be the case that the most basic distinction is between personal knowledge of all kinds (episodic and general) and knowledge gained from other sources, with semantic and episodic kinds subordinate to each of the two divisions. I know of no existing persuasive evidence to illuminate the developmental course of these differentiations.

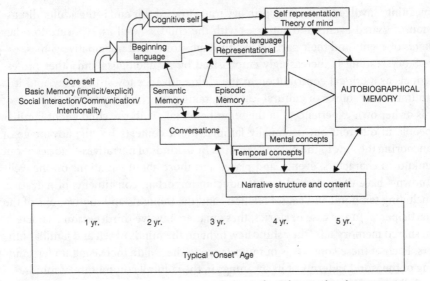

Figure 8.1 Contributing sources to the emergence of autobiographical memory in preschool years. The developmental sequence moves from left to right in the diagram. Arrows indicate interactions among sources over time. Individual developments are above the central arrow with social contributors below. Original publication in Nelson and Fivush (2004).

At this point, it may be helpful to complement Figure 8.1 with a developmental sketch of the varying achievements and social–cultural influences presumed to eventuate in the establishment of autobiographical memory. Figure 8.1 is replicated from Nelson and Fivush (2004) (see also Nelson, 2013). Achievements of the child are noted above the main arrow in the figure, with social experiences presumed important to those below it. Note that all are interactive with arrows pointing in both directions; achievements are dependent on experiences, and the effect of experiences depends on prior achievements.

THE SOCIAL–CULTURAL CONTEXT OF DEVELOPMENTAL CHANGES IN MEMORY AND CONCEPTUAL ORGANIZATION

As previously argued, children younger than age 3 years are significantly tuned to the everyday routine events of their lives, enabling them to take their parts in these events with confidence and assurance that things will be carried through "as they should be" or always are. This knowledge base not only supports participation in routines but also provides a base for imaginative play, for taking part in variations on familiar events, and for interpreting simple stories, often with some guidance from adults or older peers. Simple language ability enhances participation in these activities and opens the way to deeper understanding of the shared meanings involved in them. A primary route toward this end is the adults' discussion of shared events and activities with the child, as well as exposure to other *kinds* of events and their participants through stories and imaginative games.

Story reading is increasingly emphasized by psychologists and other professionals as a critical contribution to the child's advance toward literacy, and it is an important source of cultural learning, taking the child beyond the bounds of his or her own experience. On the other hand, talk with the child about familiar people in different but personally familiar event contexts has the advantage of anchoring the new to the old and familiar. Both kinds of narratives—stories about unknown characters, events, and places and those about variations on the well-known—have the potential for introducing important constituents of narrative, including temporal and causal relations and the thoughts and motivations of the participants. In the case of stories, these matters involve third-person characters; in shared memory talk, they shine new light on the minds of self and familiar others. Each of these contexts is of importance to the child's increasing understanding of the world in terms of its meanings in the cultural community of minds.

Talk about the ongoing activity and about the past by parents with their young children has been particularly enlightening with regard to these developments. Recordings of mother-child talk with their 2- to 4-year-old children were originally gathered in the process of studying children's event knowledge, as discussed previously (Nelson, 1986). Mothers were enlisted as more capable than researchers of eliciting information from children of this age. Some of the first recordings of parent–child talk specifically about the past were Judy Hudson's records of her talk with her 3-year-old daughter about their shared past experiences (Hudson, 1990). Additional recordings of this period included mother–child talk with 2-year-olds during daily activities (Lucariello & Nelson, 1987), mother–child talk about the past with a longitudinal sample of children during a 6-month period in the latter part of the second year (Engel, 1988), and records of 3-year-olds talking together (Nelson & Gruendel, 1979).

These studies were all critical to understanding the first phases of children's entry into the adult world of reminiscing, but they also indicated that children younger than age 3 years were typically unable to contribute much to such accounts and often seemed not to understand them. On the other hand, there were indications that mothers' talk was relevant to what a 2- or 3-year-old child might later remember from a shared experience (Haden, Ornstein, Eckerman, & Didow, 2001; Tessler & Nelson, 1994), an important indication that entering the narrative cultural world of language may reshape and certainly expands the child's memory.

Robyn Fivush and colleagues took this work in an important new direction, in an extensive program of research on the characteristics and effects of mothers' talking about the past with their 3- or 4-year-old children (for a review, see Fivush, 2010). They first identified different typical styles of mother talk, termed *elaborative* and *factual* (Fivush & Reese, 1993). Elaborative style picks up on contributions of the child to the talk and elaborates on it, extending the part of the event that the child seems to have focused on and producing more of a narrative.

Fact-focused mothers tend to extend their conversations with requests for specific facts about the experience from the child (e.g., "What color was the car?" or "Where did we have breakfast?"). Next, with a longitudinal sample of mothers and their 3-year-old children, the Fivush group showed that mothers' style at 3 years predicted the children's number of details in memory from earlier experiences a year later (Reese, Haden, & Fivush, 1993). These results have been extended and replicated many times and in different laboratories (for an overview, see Nelson & Fivush, 2004).

The significance of these studies for the social–cultural account of memory development in the 2- to 4-year-old period is beyond question. At the very least, they point to the critical role of social interaction in the child's memory during this period. They also point to the social role of narrative-making with children, and its variability in different social and cultural contexts. Cross-cultural studies comparing American mother–child pairs with their counterparts in East Asia (China, Korea, and Japan) have found both memory talk and the age of first memories in recall by older children and adults to vary across these cultures in important ways, in both content and style (for a review of an extensive research base, see Wang, 2013). Wang's work also shows the effects of such differences on the younger children's recall, emphasizing the role of self-action among American children in contrast to the more frequent mention of social partners among the other groups.

The many studies of parent–child memory talk suggest that experience with narrative talk as well as storytelling and story reading may have significant effects on the emergence of autonoetic episodic memory from the more general declarative memory system. As Fivush and colleagues have shown, children's specific event memories increase between ages 3 and 5 years, and relate significantly to their experiences with maternal memory talk. However, 3-year-old children do not for the most part give evidence of the kind of self-oriented autobiographical memory that is typical of older children and adults in Western cultures. With growing competence in using language and understanding narrative during the fourth year (3 to 4 years of age), children may begin to share memories that have the characteristics of episodic memory and the potential for entering into autobiographical memory.

A major component of autobiographical memory is the autonoetic component of episodic memory—that is, its orientation around self experience. Of course, all of the child's experience and memory from the beginning may be considered "self experience." What is new in the language-using culture is the distinction of self from *other* sources, social and cultural, and the focus on the self as experiencer in distinction from other persons. This requires the distinction between memory acquired by the self or imagined by the self and that reported—and remembered as such—by another person or story character. Children's susceptibility to reporting another's experience as their own (Miller, Potts, Fung, Hoogstra, & Mintz,1990) and their susceptibility to acceptance of others' suggestions or false reports of their own experience (Ceci & Bruck,1993; Goodman, Ogle, McWilliams, Narr, & Paz-Alonso, 2013) indicate that the strong identity of "my own experience"—implied in the definition of autonoetic memory—is weak or non-existent for children 3 years of age or younger.

Very little research has been devoted to the issue of the awareness or the attribution of memory source—for example, whether from a story or a personal experience. Thus, strong evidence with respect to when during the period between infancy and the end of the preschool period such a distinction may be made within the memory system is lacking. Clearly, the autonoetic component of episodic memory is relevant to this issue, as is the concept of self and other in all its course of development. It is a reasonable hypothesis that a major distinction between self and other sources of memory is made toward the end of the preschool period, in line with other developments during that period, such as theory of mind. The first major division in memory, following post-infancy development, would then be between semantic and episodic and secondarily between own and other source of each kind. Such a hypothesis, however, remains to be empirically explored.

Other persons are no doubt present in memory from the outset, but the perspectives of self and other are not initially distinguished or emphasized. Achieving perspectival distinctions is one of the hallmarks of the early childhood period and is accompanied by the gradual development of the concept of the interior self (in addition to awareness of the self-in-the-world; see Lewis, 1997). As the philosopher Bogdan (2010) has argued persuasively (see also Nelson, 2007), awareness of the concept of the interior self develops in response to (primarily adult) talk about thoughts, feelings, and knowledge of self and the child. Much of this talk occurs in the course of discussing narratives of third persons and their motivations. As Hutto (2008) has argued, narratives of this kind are critical to the child's understanding of the concept now termed "theory of mind," roughly the idea that persons act on the basis of beliefs about states of the world and intentions related to goals. In line with Bogdan's conception, bringing this perspective into the conscious interactive space between adult and child enables the reciprocal consciousness of the child's own mind and previously unaware contents related to self and other.

The development of the conscious sense of self is that of self within the social culture, reflective of the cultural understanding of this concept that varies among other values along the lines of the independence of the individual within the social group. Variation in this value between East Asia cultures and Western European or American cultures has been widely documented (Markus & Kitayama, 1991; Wang, 2004), including its relevance for memory development in children. This research suggests that a major problem for the child may be to differentiate the personal from the cultural perspective—to maintain a sense of individual memory, knowledge, and perspective as different from that of others in their shared world. This suggestion may be counterintuitive, given many views of the self-concept as a strong component of children's thought at least from the age of 2 years, but it is consistent with the social cultural approach and the research cited here.

In summary, I suggest that episodic memory emerges from generalized declarative memory between 3 and 5 years of age with a distinctive self component. Other people's narratives are not included in episodic memory but, rather, in a narrative component of semantic memory; semantic memory then has a narrative as well as a categorical or paradigmatic base. What distinguishes episodic memory is its autonoetic self experience component. Lasting episodic memories become the primary content of autobiographical memory. Others' narratives belong to semantic (established) memory/knowledge. It is this component that is expanded in the literacy/school period and subjected to different demands and strategies.

Entering the Community of Minds

A large literature exists on topics related to children's development of theory of mind (ToM), from its presumed beginnings in infancy (Baillargeon, Scott, & He 2010) to notions of the intentionality of others (considered critical to the interpretation of language by Tomasello (2008) and others) and passing the "false belief" tests at age 4 years or later (Astington, Harris, & Olson, 1988). Its relevance to issues involved in the development of autobiographical memory lies in the common concern with the concepts of mind, self, and other in cultural context. A constructive developmental view of this literature assumes that the social experiences of infancy provide the basis for interpreting actions and intentionality at 2 years of age (Bogdan, 2003; Nelson, 2007). Furthermore, understanding the perspectives and motivations of third persons is a later development that depends on cognitive understanding of the mind concept, which develops in the course of discourse with others, especially on problematic situations in complex narratives (Hutto, 2008; Nelson, 2007). These situations do not, I believe, need to be the classical stories cited by Hutto but, rather, may be gossip or games, tales of deception in the real world, and so on. As children gain experience in interpreting such narrative discourse, they begin to understand the construct referred to as "mind" and to attribute such an entity to themselves as well as to others. Coming into this understanding is what I and my students have referred to as "entering the community of minds" (Nelson, 2005; Nelson et al., 2002).

This concept was initially put forth in relation to our studies of children's understanding of the false belief test (Nelson, Henseler, & Plesa, 2000; Nelson et al., 2002) and was elaborated specifically in relation to language development (Nelson, 2005, 2007). The crux of the idea is that the problem for the child is much broader than the interpretation of the meanings and intentions of the familiar other in a one-on-one encounter, generally thought to be established in late infancy. Here, familiarity with the actions, emotions (revealed in facial and body expression), and typical goals of the other may support the very young in understanding intentions in both action and language. They also provide a basis for simple perspective-taking. However, faced with unfamiliar others' accounts of actors in different situations and activities, one-to-one understanding can easily fail, leading to attempts to comprehend on a higher level, namely the broader social–cultural level of third-person narrative based on motivations and causes as well as situations. To understand the actions of unfamiliar others in unfamiliar situations requires entering into the interpretive framework of the narrative of third persons and their presumed intentions and beliefs. In other words, it requires the construct of mind attributed to both the other and the self.

The relevance of this account of ToM to the construction of the mental self and to the development of autobiographical memory as self history may be obvious.[11] In brief, it implies that the initial sense of self emerges from social experience. Its more complex interior form of self-consciousness derives from cultural ways of viewing what the self is or should be—whether, for example, independent of others' views or dependent on the relationships and good opinions of other persons, a self within a community of selves. The path toward this achievement involves mastering the cultural constructs of knowing, thinking, intending, and feeling, among others. These are not simple acquisitions of words and their meanings; rather, in mastering these concepts, children are mastering cultural knowledge and values held in the community of minds that they are in the process of entering.

CONCLUSION

The focus of this chapter is the relation of culture, language, and memory in early human development. It began with a sketch of the layered nature of culture in relation to different ways of using language as they emerged over the millennia of human existence and to contingent changes in mental functions and processes. The construct of the layered "modern mind" (Donald, 1991) was adapted to describing cognitive development in relation to the aspects of culture accessible to children from infancy through the early stages of language acquisition and use. Specifically, successive memory kinds develop during the period from infancy to 5 years of age, reflecting different modes of learning and knowing before and during the years of language acquisition and use within a supportive social and cultural environment. The specific role of social experiences with narrative use and understanding was related to the emergence of autonoetic episodic memory and to lifelong retention of such episodes in autobiographical memory.

The treatment of these relations here reflects the assumption that memory is not simply part of a learning process but, rather, is at the center of cognition, cognitive change, and developmental construction (Nelson, 2007). Of course, change is the heart of development, and its results are the basis for grounding succeeding levels of cognitive operations. In the case of 5- and 6-year-old children, this grounding enables successful entry into the complexities of the literate level of human cognitive operations and its vast cultural knowledge systems. The main import of this assessment is that the pieces (biological, social, and cultural) cannot be disentangled in the developmental process because they are interdependent. Any effort to disentangle these parts—for example, to suppose that nature and nurture are competing for direction of development, that culture is a kind of "add-on" that differentiates some developmental contexts and contents from others, or that language follows cognitive development but does not change it—is simply misleading.

This account is concerned with what can be referred to as "non-deliberate" and "non-strategic" memory. Rather than deliberate or strategic, the early developing cognitive system is designed to organize and retain experiential content that is *meaningful* to the system (Nelson, 2007). Many other studies of memory, beginning in the period of early childhood, cover the topics of strategic learning, which is called upon in varying ways in educational contexts. Most memory tasks used in laboratory experiments are of this kind. These contexts are organized around the cultural level of literacy practices, take many forms, and cover topics that are beyond the concerns of this chapter, although they obviously also must be considered in a complete account of the social and cultural contexts of memory. A major investigation of the relations between memory contexts and demands during the period from entry into elementary school to adolescence reported that "overall, individual differences in verbal memory develop very early in life and are relatively unaffected by differences in educational experience" (Schneider, Knopf, & Stefaneck, 2002, p. 751). The relation between experiential memory (which continues of course throughout the lifespan) and explicit memory demands in school contexts is not yet clear, as this conclusion implies. Although not clearly treated as such, these later demands and uses of memory appear to represent a specifically "higher" level of cognitive functioning, much like literacy itself. Indeed, Donald's (1991) discussion of this level implied such a distinction. Still, how memory organizes content and functions from ordinary interactions in the social–cultural world appears to be basic and important to all that follows in this domain, which this chapter has aimed to illuminate.

NOTES

1. Although other primates live in social groups, they do not use signs to communicate or to cooperate in tasks (Tomasello, 1999, 2012), and they do not develop cultural practices that endure over generations.

2. I use the term *meaning* (or *meanings*) in the broad sense discussed in Millikan (2004). The general agreement on the meaning of a mimetic signal or a word does not imply that all individual or shared interpretations of its use are necessarily the same.

3. I acknowledge that this brief account in—of its focus on language and communication has neglected the material side of the culture. The material side is of course essential and has generated enormous advances that accompanied and supported cultural changes in communication and knowledge and its distribution. For example, the explosion of innovation in transportation and communication across distance (telephone and telegraph, radio, and television) followed the widespread availability of written works. Consideration of the material world in relation to this account is a complicated story for another time and place, however. Another serious neglect here is the realm of graphic representations of the world and their contents and meanings, including signs and symbols and pictorial media of all kinds. A full account of these is not possible here.

4. There are fewer studies of language comprehension in this period compared to those of language production, but comprehension is more important both for ongoing development and for predicting further progress.

5. In the United States, parents are urged to read books to their young from birth, and most educated adults seem to make little distinction between oral language and the written or printed word.

6. Of course, motoric skills such as crawling and walking are to a large extent biologically programmed and not generally thought of as requiring memory. However, something like motor memory must be involved; crawling is a pattern that cannot be easily recovered by the older child or adult—it is lost to the recall system. Walking must be "relearned" after a long period of inability. These skills then appear to require memory of some kind. Only if we think of memory as a general function of the cognitive system as a whole rather than a special repository of some kind can we make sense of these various "kinds" of acquisition and retrieval.

7. Karmiloff-Smith's (1992) proposal of representation levels is, in my view, related to these studies of declarative versus procedural memory, but to my knowledge the connection is not generally made and is not directly related to the issues discussed here.

8. Studies of episodic memory in other animals (e.g., scrub jays) have focused on relative temporality and in my view are of little relevance to the developmental issues.

9. The conception of self and other in terms of actors rather than persons may explain the child's long continuing acceptance of animal characters as equivalent to humans; that is, no specific interiority of mentality is involved for either.

10. Many otherwise knowledgeable scholars appear to assume that when a child uses a word or appears to make a distinction that emanates from a complex conception in adult thinking, the child "has" this same conception in his or her cognitive repertoire. Such an assumption emerges from the unacknowledged notion that a word has a given "meaning" that is the same for all users in all contexts. Regardless of the linguistic and philosophical arguments on this position, it is blatantly false for first language acquisition by young children. I share the position that it is false in general but certainly so for early language users who acquire many words with only vague understanding of their meanings as used by adults. Indeed, they use these words to support their further understanding of the concepts in question.

11. This approach has much in common with those of social theorists from the past, such as G. H. Mead (1934). What is different in the contemporary discourse is the focus on the child's concept of mind and, here, the focus on the specific model of culture and mind derived from Donald's work.

REFERENCES

Abelson, R. P. (1981). Psychological status of the script concept. *American Psychologist*, 36, 715–729.

Astington, J., Harris, P., & Olson, D. R. (1988). *Developing theories of mind*. New York, NY: Cambridge University Press.

Baillargeon, R., Scott, R. M., & He, Z. (2010). False-belief understanding in infants. *Trends in Cognitive Science*, 14, 292–305.

Bauer, P. J. (2007). *Remembering the times of our lives: Memory in infancy and beyond.* Mahwah, NJ: Erlbaum.

Bauer, P. J., & Fivush, R. (2014). *The Wiley handbook on the development of children's memory.* New York, NY: Wiley-Blackwell.

Bauer, P. J., & Mandler, J. M. (1989). One thing follows another: Effects of temporal structure on one- to two-year-olds' recall of events. *Developmental Psychology, 25,* 197–206.

Bogdan, R. J. (2003). *Interpreting Minds.* Cambridge, MA: MIT Press.

Bogdan, R. J. (2010). *Our own minds: Sociocultural grounds for self-consciousness.* Cambridge, MA: MIT Press.

Bruner, J. S., & Lucariello, J. (1989). Monologue as a narrative recreation of the world. In K. Nelson (Ed.), *Narratives from the crib* (pp. 73–97). Cambridge, MA: Harvard University Press.

Ceci, S. J., & Bruck, M. (1993). The suggestibility of the child witness: A historical review and synthesis. *Psychological Bulletin, 113,* 403–439.

Cleveland, E. S., & Reese, E. (2008). Children remember early childhood: Long-term recall across the offset of childhood amnesia. *Applied Cognitive Psychology, 22,* 127–142.

Damasio, A. (1999). *The feeling of what happens: Body and emotion in the making of consciousness.* New York, NY: Harcourt.

Deacon, T. W. (1997). *The symbolic species: The co-evolution of language and the brain.* New York, NY: Norton.

Donald, M. (1991). *Origins of the modern mind.* Cambridge, MA: Harvard University Press.

Donald, M. (2001). *A mind so rare: The evolution of human consciousness.* New York, NY: Norton.

Eakin, P. J. (1999). *How our lives become stories: Making selves.* Ithaca, NY: Cornell University Press.

Engel, S. (1988). *Learning to reminisce: A developmental study of how young children talk about the past.* Unpublished PhD dissertation, City University of New York Graduate Center, New York.

Fivush, R. (2010). The development of autobiographical memory. *Annual Review of Psychology, 62,* 21–24.

Fivush, R. (2014). Maternal reminiscing style: The social cultural construction of autobiographical memory across childhood and adolescence. In P. J. Bauer & R. Fivush (Eds.), *The Wiley handbook on the development of children's memory* (Vol. 2, pp. 568–585). New York, NY: Wiley-Blackwell.

Freud, S. (1924). *A general introduction to psychoanalysis* (G. S. Hall, Trans.). New York, NY: Horace Liveright.

Goodman, G. S., Ogle, C. M., McWilliams, K., Narr, R. K., & Paz-Alonso, P. M. (2013). Memory development in the forensic context. In P. Bauer & R. Fivush (Eds.), *The Wiley handbook on the development of children's memory* (pp. 920–941). New York, NY: Wiley-Blackwell.

Haden, C. A., Ornstein, P. A., Eckerman, C. O., & Didow, S. M. (2001). Mother–child conversational interchanges as events unfold: Linkages to subsequent remembering. *Child Development, 72,* 1016–1031.

Hudson, J. A. (1990). The emergence of autobiographic memory in mother–child conversation. In R. Fivush & J. A. Hudson (Eds.), *Knowing and remembering in young children* (pp. 166–196). New York, NY: Cambridge University Press.

Hutto, D. D. (2008). *Folk psychological narratives: The sociocultural basis of understanding reasons.* Cambridge, MA: MIT Press.

James, W. (1950). *The principles of psychology.* New York, NY: Dover. (Original work published 1890)

Janowsky, J., & Carper, R. (1996). Is there a neural basis for cognitive transitions in school-age children? In A. J. Sameroff & M. M. Haith (Eds.), *The five to seven year shift* (pp. 33–62). Chicago, IL: University of Chicago Press.

Kandel, E. R. (2006). *In search of memory: The emergence of a new science of mind.* New York, NY: Norton.

Karmiloff-Smith, A. (1992). *Beyond modularity.* Cambridge, MA: MIT Press.

Lewis, M. (1997). The self in self-conscious emotions. In J. G. Snodgrass & R. L. Thompson (Eds.), *The self across psychology* (pp. 119–142). New York, NY: New York Academy of Sciences.

Lucariello, J., Kyratzis, A., & Nelson, K. (1992). Taxonomic knowledge: What kind and when? *Child Development, 63,* 978–998.

Lucariello, J., & Nelson, K. (1987). Remembering and planning talk between mothers and children. *Discourse Processes, 10,* 219–235.

Mahr, J., & Csibra, G. (2017). Why Do We Remember? The Communicative Function of Episodic Memory. *Brain and Behavioral Sciences.*

Mandler, J. M. (2004). *The foundations of mind: Origins of conceptual thought.* New York, NY: Oxford University Press.

Mandler, J. M., & McDonough, L. (2000). Advancing downward to the basic level. *Journal of Cognition and Development, 1,* 379–405.

Markus, H. R., & Kitayama, S. (1991). Culture and the self: Implications for cognition, emotion, and motivation. *Psychological Review, 98*(2), 224–253.

Mead, G. H. (1934). *Mind, self, and society.* Chicago, IL: Chicago University Press.

Miles, C. (1893). A study of individual psychology. *American Journal of Psychology, 6,* 534–558.

Miller, P. J., Potts, R., Fung, H., Hoogstra, L., & Mintz, J. (1990). Narrative practices and the social construction of self in childhood. *American Ethnologist, 17,* 292–311.

Millikan, R. G. (2004). *Varieties of meaning.* Cambridge, MA: MIT Press.

Moore, C., & Lemmon, K. (2001). *The self in time: Developmental perspectives.* Mahwah, NJ: Erlbaum.

Moscovitsch, M. (1984). *Infant memory.* New York, NY: Plenum.

Nelson, K. (1986). *Event knowledge: Structure and function in development.* Hillsdale, NJ: Erlbaum.

Nelson, K. (1989a). Monologue as representation of real-life experience. In K. Nelson (Ed.), *Narratives from the crib* (pp. 27–72). Cambridge, MA: Harvard University Press.

Nelson, K. (Ed.). (1989b). *Narratives from the crib.* Cambridge, MA: Harvard University Press.

Nelson, K. (1993). The psychological and social origins of autobiographical memory. *Psychological Science, 4,* 1–8.

Nelson, K. (1996). *Language in cognitive development: The emergence of the mediated mind.* New York, NY: Cambridge University Press.

Nelson, K. (2005). Language pathways to the community of minds. In J. W. Astington & J. Baird (Eds.), *Why language matters to theory of mind* (pp. 26–49). New York, NY: Oxford University Press.

Nelson, K. (2007). *Young minds in social worlds: Experience, meaning, and memory.* Cambridge, MA: Harvard University Press.

Nelson, K. (2013). Sociocultural theories of memory development. In P. J. Bauer & R. Fivush (Eds.), *The Wiley handbook on the development of children's memory* (Vol. 1, pp. 87–108). New York, NY: Wiley-Blackwell.

Nelson, K. (2015). Making sense with private speech. *Cognitive Development, 36.* [Special issue]

Nelson, K., & Fivush, R. (2004). The emergence of autobiographical memory: A social cultural developmental theory. *Psychological Review, 111,* 486–511.

Nelson, K., & Gruendel, J. M. (1979). At morning it's lunchtime: A scriptal view of children's dialogues. *Discourse Processes, 2,* 73–94.

Nelson, K., Henseler, S., & Plesa, D. (2000). Entering a community of minds: A feminist perspective on theory of mind development. In P. Miller & E. S. Scholnick (Eds.), *Toward a feminist developmental psychology* (pp. 61–84). New York, NY: Routledge.

Nelson, K., Plesa, D., Goldman, S., Henseler, S., Presler, N., & Walkenfeld, F. (2002). Entering a community of minds: An experiental approach to theory of minds. *Human Development, 41,* 7–29.

Nelson, K., & Ross, G. (1980). The generalities and specifics of long term memory in infants and young children. In M. Perlmutter (Ed.), *Children's memory: New directions for child development* (pp. 87–101). San Francisco, CA: Jossey-Bass.

Olson, D. (1994). *The world on paper.* New York, NY: Cambridge University Press.

Perlmutter, M. (Ed.). (1980). *Children's memory: New directions for child development.* San Francisco, CA: Jossey-Bass.

Perrin, D., & Rousset, S. (2014). The episodicity of memory: Current trends in philosophy and psychology. *Review of Philosophy and Psychology, 5,* 291–312.

Reese, E., Haden, C. A., & Fivush, R. (1993). Mother–child conversations about the past: Relationships of style and memory over time. *Cognitive Development, 8,* 403–430.

Roberts, K. P., & Blades, M. (Eds.). (2000). *Children's source monitoring.* Mahwah, NJ: Erlbaum.

Rovee-Collier, C. (1997). Dissociations in infant memory: Rethinking the development of implicit and explicit memory. *Psychological Review, 104,* 467–498.

Sameroff, A. J., & Haith, M. M. (1996). *The five to seven year shift: The age of reason and responsibility.* Chicago, IL: Chicago University Press.

Sani, F. (2008). *Self continuity: Individual and collective perspectives.* New York, NY: Psychology Press.

Schank, R. P., & Abelson, R. P. (1977). *Scripts, plans, goals, and understanding.* Hillsdale, NJ: Erlbaum.

Schneider, W., Knopf, M., & Stefaneck, J. (2002). The development of verbal memory from the beginning of elementary school to late adolescence. *Journal of Educational Psychology, 94,* 751–761.

Tessler, M., & Nelson, K. (1994). Making memories: The influence of joint encoding on later recall. *Consciousness and Cognition, 3,* 307–326.

Tomasello, M. (1999). *The cultural origins of human cognition.* Cambridge, MA: Harvard University Press.

Tomasello, M. (2008). *The origins of human communication*. Cambridge, MA: MIT Press.

Tulving, E. (1983). *Elements of episodic memory*. New York, NY: Oxford University Press.

Tulving, E. (1993). What is episodic memory? *Current Directions in Psychological Science, 2*, 67–70.

Tulving, E. (2005). Episodic memory and autonoesis: Uniquely human? In H. S. Terrace & J. Metcalfe (Eds.), *The missing link in cognition: Origins of self-reflective consciousness* (pp. 3–56). New York, NY: Oxford University Press.

Wang, Q. (2004). The emergence of cultural self-constructs: Autobiographical memory and self-description in European American and Chinese children: *Developmental Psychology, 40*, 3–15.

Wang, Q. (2013). The cultured self and remembering. In P. J. Bauer & R. Fivush (Eds.), *The Wiley handbook on the development of children's memory* (Vol. 2, pp. 605–625). New York, NY: Wiley-Blackwell.

Werner, H., & Kaplan, B. (1963). *Symbol Formation*. New York: Wiley.

White, S. H. (1965). Evidence for a hierarchical arrangement of learning processes. *Advances in Child Development and Behavior, 2*, 187–220.

White, S. H. (1996). The child's entry into the "age of reason." In A. J. Sameroff & M. M. Haith (Eds.), *The five to seven shift* (pp. 17–32). Chicago, IL: University of Chicago Press.

White, S. H., & Pillemer, D. B. (1979). Childhood amnesia and the development of a socially accessible memory system. In J. F. Kihlstrom & F. J. Evans (Eds.), *Functional disorders of memory* (pp. 29–74). Hillsdale, NJ: Erlbaum.

Memory in Life Transitions

CONSTANCE DE SAINT LAURENT AND TANIA ZITTOUN ■

Why do we attach so much importance to the memories of our own life—enough to keep them in diaries and books, share them with others through anecdotes and pictures, or worry that, in time, we might forget them? In this chapter, we explore how such memories help us overcome changes, transitions, and challenges in life by allowing us to make sense of what has happened and to imagine what could come next. To do so, we adopt a pragmatic stance that highlights three main functions of autobiographical memory: its role in the construction of the self, in relating with others, and in directing our actions toward the future. By connecting the last, directive function to scholarship on imagination, we propose a dynamic and pragmatic model of autobiographical remembering as a sociocultural act unfolding in time. This model allows us to retrace the development of autobiographical memory over the life-course and follow the transformation of its uses. Finally, we apply this model to the longitudinal case study of a teenager and discuss its implications for further research.

AUTOBIOGRAPHICAL MEMORY

There are probably as many ways to define autobiographical memory as there are researchers working on the topic. We adopt the view that it is made up of the "personal memories of the events of our lives" (Nelson, 2007, p. 184) and that it is distributed along four main dimensions, which we describe next.

First, and quite unsurprisingly, autobiographical memory concerns what one remembers about one's own past. The main point here is not so much that it is about what happened to oneself in the past but that it is remembered as such— that is, a memory of an event affecting the self. This specific quality of autobiographical memory is called *autoneotic consciousness* (Tulving, 2002). This means that, for instance, remembering that the word for "butterfly" in Spanish is "mariposa" is not quite the same as remembering that one learned it from a story told by one's mother about a failed Spanish exam—although both actually refer to the same event in one's life. The first formulation is just a memory of a fact; the second one refers to a personal life event—that is, one's personal experience of being told a story by one's mother.

Second, autobiographical memory is more than the mere accumulation of past life events; it involves at least a partial semiotic, semantic, or narrative integration. The degree of this integration varies, leading to more or less general memories—from the *episodic memories* of single events to a *personal memory* encompassing general principles about self, values, and beliefs. Multiple episodes of one's life can be brought together by giving them similar meanings (Habermas & Bluck, 2000), organizing them along a coherent timeline (Bluck & Alea, 2008), relating them to the stories of others (Fivush, Bohanek, & Duke, 2008), or making them fit into cultural autobiographical narratives (Berntsen & Rubin, 2002).

Third, these integrations are supported by a rather wide array of cultural tools—narrative structures, conventional ways of telling one's life, lay normative models of development, and so on, up to language—shaping the way we talk about our past, link it to the present, and make sense of it (Fivush, 2011), to the point that, as McAdams (2001), states,

> stories live in culture. . . . [Indeed, they] are born, they grow, they proliferate, and they eventually die according to the norms, rules, and traditions that prevail in a given society, according to a society's implicit understandings of what counts as a tellable story, a tellable life. (p. 114)

Fourth, remembering one's past is a social activity, often done together with others and thus involving multiple perspectives (Nelson, 2008). Indeed, social interactions are necessary for the development of memory: It is through their conversations with adults that children learn to remember the past and organize it in narratives that can be communicated to others (Nelson, 2007; see also Nelson, Chapter 8, this volume). Moreover, reminiscence is a cultural activity (Fivush, 2011); not only do our social environments shape the way we talk about our past but also they are often an important source of autobiographical demands. This may be especially true in Western societies, in which performing an auto-biographical narrative is required from children quite early on (through activities such as retelling one's weekend, etc.). These specific demands may be linked to certain representations of the "healthy" self as an independent and coherent whole (Nelson, 2008).

Taking these four aspects into consideration, a more thorough definition of autobiographical memory thus considers it as "that uniquely human form of memory that moves beyond recall of experienced events to integrate perspectives, interpretation, and evaluation across self, other, and time to create a personal history" (Fivush, 2011, p. 560). This implies that autobiographical memory changes throughout the life: It depends on the experiences a person had, the ability she has to reflect upon them, the cultural tools she masters, and her interactions with others. This development has rarely been studied beyond childhood. In this chapter, we examine the development of memory in the life course, focusing on the moments of catalyzed change that we call transitions (Kadianaki & Zittoun, 2014). To do so, we propose taking a pragmatic stance on memory.

A PRAGMATIC STANCE ON MEMORY

Pragmatism invites us to move away from abstract considerations about the true value of a notion or the a priori examination of its value to concentrate on what can be done with it. From a pragmatist stance, a notion is useful or good enough if it allows one to see the world in a more intelligible way, to explain a phenomenon otherwise not understood, or to act upon it. Pragmatism also invites us to examine what people do with the entity designated by the notion discussed (James, 1904). In our case, it implies to focus not only on what autobiographical memory is but also mainly what it is used for (Pillemer & Kuwabara, 2012).

Life stories are not told in a vacuum: They are part of conversations with others and often with the self; have a developmental history; and take place in specific social, historical, and cultural contexts. Then, what do we do when we talk about our past in these contexts? Why do we tell stories about ourselves? What does a personal history bring that other forms of memory would not provide already? To answer these questions, Susan Bluck has proposed dividing the functions of autobiographical memory into three main categories: self, social, and directive (Bluck, 2003; Bluck, Alea, Habermas, & Rubin, 2005). Following these three functions, we explore what is known about the development of memory.

Autobiographical Memory and the Self

First, and quite unsurprisingly, we use autobiographical memory to define who we are (Fivush, 2011). Life is full of ruptures and changes, and we also tend to assume different roles and positions depending on the sphere of experience we are in. By sphere of experience, we mean the following (Zittoun & Gillespie, 2015a):

> A configuration of experiences, activities, representations and feelings, recurrently occurring in a given type of social (material and symbolic) setting—it is one of the various regular, stabilized patterns of experience in which a person is likely to engage on a regular basis. (p. 8)

Even if the me-at-home and the me-at-work are not similar, both are part of who I experience I am. Thus, each "self" is a set of multiple identities or "identity positions," interacting with each other and evolving in time—a sort of "society of minds" (Hermans, 2002). But if it is so, how do we achieve a coherent sense of who we are? Through organizing past events into a narrative, we establish a sense of continuity (Erikson, 1959). By causally and temporally linking different parts of our lives (Fitzgerald & Broadbridge, 2012), we develop "narrative identities," which are "stories people construct and tell about themselves to define who they are" (McAdams, Josselson, & Liebich, 2006, p. 4).

This ability to connect past and present selves has a long developmental history, from infancy to early adulthood. Indeed, although children are able to produce personal stories that are chronologically organized from approximately the age of 8, it is not until they are 10 years old that they can integrate several proximal events into a single narrative (Habermas, 2012). More global coherence, causally and thematically linking multiple personal events, does not appear until the age of 12 (Habermas & de Silveira, 2008). It seems, however, that people start to tell full life stories only during adolescence, when the necessary and previously mentioned cognitive skills are fully developed and when it becomes an "age-specific requirement" to define one's identity (Habermas & Bluck, 2000, p. 753). Indeed, it is expected from teenagers to develop a stable identity (Erikson, 1968), and in Western societies, in which being a "unique being" is particularly valued (Nelson, 2008), personal narratives are an especially efficient way to achieve such an aim (Habermas & Bluck, 2000).

Life stories also require the mastery of various norms and expectations that surround the narration of one's life (Bruner, 2003)—what Habermas (2007) termed mastery of "the cultural concept of biography" (p. 1). These cultural norms can also be represented in the form of life-scripts or "culturally shared representations of the timing of major transitional life events" (Berntsen & Rubin, 2004, p. 427). In any case, the idea is that to tell one's life "is a form of cultural activity and as such is individually and culturally specific to the local and cultural forms of social interaction from which it is shaped" (Fivush, 2011, p. 561). Although children start to use culture-specific story forms to tell personal events starting at approximately 5–7 years of age, using frames borrowed from myths and tales to structure their stories (Nelson, 2003), it is not until adolescence that individuals fully master normative life-scripts. Research has shown that a peak is attained at approximately 16 years old, followed by a decrease until the age of 20 and remaining quite stable for the rest of the life course, probably because "adults [convey] a more realistic variation in the life course than adolescents [do], whose depiction [is] highly stereotyped" (Habermas, 2007, p. 4). However, the mastery of these normative cornerstones is necessary to be able to tell a life story: Even if one's path always deviates from what is expected to happen in life, they help us choose which elements to include—especially those that are culturally considered as relevant— and which ones deserve explanation—typically those that differ from the norm (Schütze, 1984, as cited in Habermas & Bluck, 2000, p. 750).

In addition, memories change together with the ideas one has about the self (Habermas, 2012) and are constantly reinterpreted from the perspective of the present. Thus, the relation between autobiographical memory and self is bidirectional (Conway, 2005), and as Cameron, Wilson, and Ross (2004) expressed it, "People fashion identities that fit their memories and memories that fit their identities" (p. 208). Periods of transitions and changes lead to more conscious efforts to reconstruct a meaningful and coherent narrative (Bluck & Alea,

2008). Moreover, periods during which important aspects of one's identity are defined tend to be remembered more, or at least made more salient (Fitzgerald & Broadbridge, 2012): If we remember more events that occur during the 10- to 30-year-old age period than during any other—the "reminiscence bump" (Rubin, Wetzler, & Nebes, 1986)—it is because these events play the major role in our identity (Rathbone, Moulin, & Conway, 2008).

Finally, having a personal story implies being able to make a distinction between one's own past and the memories of others (Fivush, 2011), and thus between self and other (Nelson, 2008). It also involves being able to recognize memory as perspectival—what I remember about an event may not be what you remember about it—which children are not able to do until the end of the preschool years (Fivush et al., 2008). By taking part in reminiscing conversations with adults whose perspectives on the past may diverge, children move away from a memory perceived as a copy of what happened to understanding their memories as their own subjective version of the past (Nelson, 2008).

What happens to the development of autobiographical memory beyond childhood? If one function of autobiographical memory is to establish a sense of who we are, then any events that are likely to question who we are, or change our definition of ourselves, can also demand some new elaboration of autobiographical memories. From a lifecourse perspective, it is typically moments of crises, bifurcations, or transitions that question our sense of integrity and self-continuity and usually call upon our memories (Erikson, 1959; Sato, Yasuda, Kanzaki, & Valsiner, 2013; Zittoun et al., 2013). Adolescence, becoming a parent, moving to a different country, and changing job or partner usually question who we are, for oneself and for others. The notion of transition designates the processes of readjustment in which a person engages when or after she perceives a rupture; these usually involve identity transformations, learning (acquiring new skills, knowledge, or ways of doing), and sense-making (Zittoun, 2006). As discussed later, transitions are quite likely to engage memory work, precisely because of the various functions of memory.

Autobiographical Memory and Interactions

The second function autobiographical memory serves is *relational*. By conversing about the past, people create converging accounts of what happened, thus developing a shared representation of the past that facilitates collective action (Hirst, Cuc, & Wohl, 2012). However, life stories also have the potential to locate us in time and in the social world by connecting our lives with those of others (Fivush et al., 2008): Developing a narrative about one's childhood, for instance, also locates one relative to siblings, parents, and so on. Moreover, because much of autobiographical memory is actually memory of past relations (Habermas, 2012), it "provide[s] a framework for interpreting current relationships" (Fivush, 2011, p. 575) and "serve[s] to create and maintain social and emotional bonds with others through reminiscing and through representations of relationships" (p. 574). Other people's narratives also participate in this function, especially those of family members, which have the potential to create a sense of connection and cohesion with the rest of the family (Fivush et al., 2008).

The links between social relations and autobiographical memory are not limited to the latter sustaining the former: Accounts of the past are also forged through social interactions. Indeed, remembering is a social activity, and what we recall and forget depends on with whom we are remembering (Halbwachs, 1950). Elements that are made salient by others will be more easily recalled, whereas what others silence will eventually be forgotten (Hirst & Echterhoff, 2012). Moreover, the stories we tell are forged through past reminiscing episodes. Very rehearsed narratives, for instance, can become surprisingly stable through the years, as in the case of flashbulb memories (Baddeley, 2012), whereas stories of difficult events may be transformed each time they are told until a form of closure is found (Habermas, 2012). In any case, "acts of recall must be viewed as having a social history" and are created in conversation with others (Hirst & Echterhoff, 2012, p. 63).

Social interactions also play a central role in the development of autobiographical memory. As discussed in the previous section, it is through social interactions that children realize the perspectival nature of memories (Nelson, 2008). In addition, during conversations about the past, parents scaffold children's accounts "by specifically supporting those aspects of life narratives which children and adolescents are about to acquire next" (Habermas, Negele, & Mayer, 2010, p. 348). They also "convey that there are certain ways to tell these kinds of stories, focusing not just on what happened but why it was interesting, important, and emotional" (Fivush, Habermas, Waters, & Zaman, 2011, p. 324). Through this, children acquire biographical concepts to the point that they master the life stories of others before they can build their own (Habermas & Bluck, 2000). Thus, "the ways in which parents, and especially mothers, structure conversations about past events with their preschool children have strong and enduring influences on how children come to construct their own narrative life history" (Nelson & Fivush, 2004, p. 497). Moreover, different cultural and historical contexts will also give more or less importance to reminiscing and will shape what is expected in an autobiographical account (Habermas, 2011). School activities such as telling what one did for the holidays, a tradition favored in Western societies, teach children not only how to tell a story but also that they are expected to do so (Nelson, 2008).

Again, it is quite likely that as people move through life, the meeting of new others will also convoke autobiographical memories: To fulfill their relational function, memories are quite likely to be revisited every time people establish new significant relationships—friends, partners, and children. These might typically occur during transitions but not only during these times. Many social situations, which can be connected to transitions, require the elaboration of an autobiographical account: a job postulation, creating a blog, a family celebration, and so on.

Autobiographical Memory and Imagination

The third function of autobiographical memory is *directive*. By this, we mean that it has the potential to direct actions. The notion of "directive function" has been used to designate its role in guiding, planning, or motivating future actions on the basis of the past (Pillemer, 2003). This directive function has variations.

First, it allows us to act in the present based on what we learned from past experiences. Singer and Blagov (2004), for instance, showed that "self-defining memories"—vivid and emotional memories that are repeatedly recalled—are able to guide action in the present based on past experiences, which is why people remember them so often. When faced with decisions about their lives or difficulties to overcome, people can use memories of past similar events to choose a path of action.

Second, by organizing the past into a narrative and linking it to the present (Fivush, 2011), autobiographical memory also gives a direction to one's life (Habermas, 2012). Indeed, if narratives follow culturally shared story lines, it also means that we come to expect, or anticipate, what comes next and how things should end (e.g., think of the much anticipated endings of many Hollywood movies). Some authors have thus called this "prospective memory," the process of "remembering to perform an action at a future point in time in the absence of an external prompt" (Mattli, Schnitzspahn, Studerus-Germann, Brehmer, & Zöllig, 2014), and have studied it in the workplace (McDaniel & Einstein, 2007).

Third, autobiographical memory allows us to imagine possible futures. Similarly, imagination allows us to explore what could or might be and, on this basis, enables us to choose a path toward what we view as desirable (Zittoun & de Saint-Laurent, 2015). Memory not only provides the "material" from which the future can be imagined (Vygotsky, 2004) but also, by giving us a sense of who we are, gives us a sense of what we could be and what we may want to be. Such observations have led many researchers to argue that autobiographical memory is primarily oriented toward the future (Fivush, 2011) and that its directive function is the most important one (Dudai & Carruthers, 2005; Schacter & Addis, 2007). We could indeed argue that memory feeds forward into the future; it is what has been called a "proleptic" function (Cole, 2007; Valsiner, 2014).

However, research rarely explores the directive function of memory, and when asked why they remember, people refer to the self and social functions much more often than they refer to the future (Bluck et al., 2005); however, the self-report method might be responsible for these results (Pillemer, 2003). Although the importance of the directive function is still to be explored, there is compelling evidence that autobiographical memory and imagining the future are deeply linked. Indeed, the underlying neurological processes seem be the same (Berntsen & Bohn, 2010) or at least to rest on similar abilities (Mullally & Maguire, 2014); memory deficits and losses are usually accompanied by difficulties in imagining future situations and in telling fictitious stories (D'Argembeau, 2012). Moreover, these two functions develop during the same period (D'Argembeau, 2012), and children acquire a sense of past and future at the same time, during the preschool years (Nelson, 2008). Finally, both remembering the past and imagining the future rely on cultural scripts that help one move away from the present (Berntsen & Bohn, 2010). For instance, the amount of details given is identical for periods that are similarly distant from the present, whether they are located in the future or in the past (D'Argembeau, 2012).

The directive function of memory is likely to be triggered in transitions. In many cases, it is when the taken for granted is questioned that new options have to be imagined; these explorations of possibility rely on re-examining one's past in light of the future, and defining possible futures in light of one's past, through the present (Zittoun & Gillespie, 2015b). Similar to the previous two functions, the directive function can be normatively triggered; again, career choices or job interviews typically demand people to be able to show how their past experiences led them to a clear future path.

What may be lacking, then, is a model that fully integrates remembering and imagining. Although some proposals have been presented, such as Tulving's (2002) idea of mental time travel, few attempts have been made to link scholarship on memory and on imagination (for some notable exceptions, see Bartlett (1995) or Mullally & Maguire (2014)). This lack of articulation may be due to the fact that most memory research is considered to be about the reality of the past, whereas most studies of imagination consider it as focused on the non-real. However, the directive function of memory encourages us to further examine the link between these two processes.

Imagination is the process of distancing from the here and now of experience, a move that draws on past experiences and a diversity of resources while allowing us to explore alternative and future possibilities, which in turn transform the present and may guide immediate action (Vygotsky, 1931/1994, 2004; Zittoun & Gillespie, 2015a). Previously, we proposed to represent this process as a loop of consciousness. These loops can vary in a three-dimensional space according to their temporal orientation (i.e., they are about past or future events), their generality (i.e., they concern a specific event, such as fixing a bookshelf, or general matters, such as making the world a better place), and their (im)plausibility (e.g., in a northern European town in 2014, imagining that one could receive a fine for parking one's automobile poorly, which is a plausible event; or imagining one could sunbathe on Mars, which is less likely to happen) (Figure 9.1).

Elsewhere, we have shown how imagination can play an important role in the creation of new life paths during periods of transition (Zittoun & de Saint-Laurent, 2015). Here, we highlight the mutual dependency of thinking about the past and thinking about the future, of memory and imagination. These two orientations are part of the same movement of thinking, typically in transitions, when the future has to be defined on the basis of the past. Conversely, examining how people imagine the future reveals much about how they imagine the past. In fact, these processes are so closely related that, at times, remembering can appear as a way of imagining the past. On the other hand, imaginations of the future become forms of remembering when engaged in regularly, particularly during

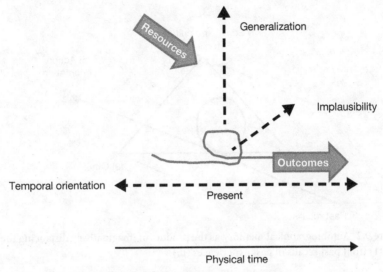

Figure 9.1 Loop of imagination in a three-dimensional space.
SOURCE: Zittoun and Gillespie (2015a).

adolescence. Considering these two processes within a unified framework, we can draw on literature related to both imagination and remembering in order to overcome the limits of each. More precisely, adopting a developmental perspective, we use this framework to understand the development of autobiographic memory in the life course.

A PRAGMATIC MODEL
OF AUTOBIOGRAPHICAL MEMORY

We propose an integrative model that, in a dynamic way, accounts for the three functions of memory identified so far—that is, its role in the definition of self, in relations with others, and in defining possibilities and the future. Figure 9.2 integrates the existing literature and defines autobiographical remembering as an oriented sociocultural act (de Saint-Laurent, 2017).

In this model, the "self" pole of the triangle refers to both the fact that remembering is done by a socially and culturally located self and the fact that such a self is constructed through autobiographical remembering (the self function). The "other" pole designates the audience in relation to which the self remembers, which can be physically or imaginatively present, as well as the relation that is maintained through recall (the relational function). The "social and cultural resources" are the social, cultural, and material elements that are used for recall and those developed through remembering, which range from cultural narrative frames and concepts to social scaffoldings by others. This notion is left deliberately large: What people can use to remember is, in the end, infinite. It can be material

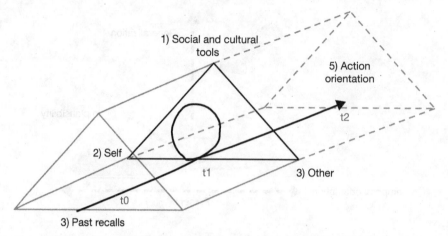

Figure 9.2 Autobiographical memory as the product of imaginatively distancing the self (t1) from past recalls of past experiences (t0).

(e.g., a diary or a notebook), social (e.g., using a past conservation with a friend to enrich one's story), or semiotic (e.g., using a metaphor to convey meaning about one's past). What matters here is that remembering is not something done "in the mind" (Wagoner, 2015) but, rather, is distributed across material, social, and symbolic dimensions. In Figure 9.2, the arrow going from "past recalls" to "action orientation" refers to both the history of recalling—how the self remembered this event in the past—and the fact that remembering is part of an activity oriented toward an aim (the directive function), in a pragmatist sense.

In addition, the model represents the movement of remembering as an imaginative "loop" borrowed from models of imagination (see Figure 9.1). It suggests that remembering demands imaginatively distancing oneself from past experiences through interaction with others and the use of cultural resources that give these experiences meaning, narrative shape, and relate them with other periods of one's life, eventually leading to the production of a life narrative. Finally, we also integrate a temporal dimension into the model, showing that remembering always occurs along a line of other instances of remembering or imagining (t0, t1, and t2 in Figure 9.2)—hence the triangular-shaped "Toblerone"-like model (see also Bauer & Gaskell, 1999).

This integrative model thus proposes to contribute to the literature on autobiographical memory. First, it postulates that it is the triangular relation between self, other, and tools that opens the symbolic space necessary for autobiographical memory (see also Nelson, Chapter 8, this volume). On the one hand, social and cultural tools are what make the (re)organization of past events, beyond the chronological retelling of single episodes, possible in the first place. On the other hand, it is through the interaction with the perspective of others that we can both understand our memories as being subjective and specific to ourselves—Tulving's *autonoetic consciousness*—and distance ourselves from them to construct alternative interpretations. Second, autobiographical memories must be understood as the product of a double history: the history of the past recalls of the specific event(s) remembered and one's history of remembering in general, as it participates in the construction of the "pool" of resources one can use to remember. Third, the central role of imagining is highlighted as an active process of construction partaking in remembering and its inherent future orientation. Fourth, autobiographical memory is part of a larger ongoing action, and the functions memory may serve are constrained by the resources and interlocutors available, as well as one's history of recall.

This conceptualization allows understanding why memories are so sensitive to cultural norms, media, and other people's discourses. In effect, telling one's story is a process of narrative imagination, which demands selection and creation and which is fed by "'second-hand' resources as books, movies, and other media—that are at once highly influential in shaping the process of autobiographical understanding but of which one may remain largely unaware" (Freeman, 2007, p. 139). Issues about children testimony (Jensen, 2005; Takagi & Mori, Chapter 6, this volume) or the reliability of past events in oral history (e.g., former Wehrmacht soldiers tend to use images and events from recent films when they tell their past war experiences; Welzer, Moller, & Tschuggnall, 2002/2013) can thus be explained by the fact that remembering is closely linked to imagining, being always a creation that combines both personal experiences and the resources at hand. In this way, the imaginative processes of memory can lead to practices that can actually change social relations and situations.

THE DEVELOPMENT OF AUTOBIOGRAPHICAL MEMORY IN THE LIFE COURSE

As the functional approach has shown, there is much at stake in the development of autobiographical memory. First, it is by developing a narrative explaining who they have been through time that people acquire a coherent sense of self. Second, through reminiscing together, people redefine and reinforce social relationships. Third, by integrating multiple life events into a single narrative, people can give direction to their lives and imagine what may come next. But how do these functions develop during the life course?

Adolescence and Memory

As discussed previously, little is known about the emergence of these functions (Fivush, 2011). Memory researchers do consider the self "as a continuous individual person with a past and a future [which] emerges during the early childhood period" (Nelson, 2008, p. 13). Then, most existing models draw on Erikson's intuition that the ability to tell one's life story appears during adolescence (Erikson, 1968) and consider that these functions develop during this period (McAdams, 2001; Reese, Yan, Jack, & Hayne, 2010). Adolescence—classically, the period that follows biological puberty—is thus considered one of the most important periods to understand the development of memory, and the development of autobiography can be linked to a more general developmental process.

There seems to be a consensus that it is during adolescence that people are faced with the tremendous task of developing a stable identity, a purpose that is best served by reaching a global and coherent life narrative (Bluck & Habermas, 2000). Indeed, memories of adolescence tend to become central to one's story once an adult and also to be linked to important aspects of the self (Rathbone et al., 2008). That "task" of defining a stable identity is set both by psychological needs and by relational and social expectations.

Adolescence appears to be the period during which many of the cognitive abilities necessary for autobiographical memory are developed (Fivush et al., 2011). In a review of the existing literature on the development of autobiographical memory in adolescence, Habermas and Bluck (2000) regrouped the abilities necessary to attain global narrative coherence in a life story into four main categories. The first one is temporal sequencing, or the organization of stories around timelines, which does not fully develop until late childhood (Friedman, 1992). The second one is mastery of the cultural concept of biography—that is, the local understanding of how a life story should be organized. As noted previously, it is not until mid-adolescence that people fully master these life-scripts (Habermas, 2007), and it is not until late adolescence to early adulthood that they can use these in a flexible and realistic manner (Habermas & de Silveira, 2008). The third one is causal coherence, which links multiple events and emotional states with one another. Although children can achieve local coherence from late childhood, only by mid-adolescence do teenagers begin to make connections between long periods of time and to explain their life in terms of personality and developmental trajectory. Also, it is not until late adolescence that they begin to explain change and people's behaviors in terms of past experiences (Feldman, Bruner, Kalmar, & Renderer, 1993). The fourth one is thematic coherence, which establishes a global coherence between several episodes of one's life through tools such as metaphors or cultural maxims. This ability develops slowly during adolescence through the capacity to summarize stories, interpret them, and question existing interpretations and knowledge (Bluck & Habermas, 2000).

Adolescence is the period during which young people progressively become independent from their parents and families (Grotevant & Cooper, 1986; Hofer, 2004; Steinberg & Silverberg, 1986) and the importance of horizontal relationships—those with friends, intimates, and partners—increases (Collins, Gleason, & Sesma, 1997; Laursen & Collins, 2011; Meeus, Branje, van der Valk, & de Wied, 2007). As a consequence, the role of parents in supporting consistency and information in the construction of memories (Habermas, 2012; Fivush et al., 2008) may progressively diminish, especially with regard to recent memories. Socializing outside the home, young people create new memories and new groups with which they can remember. Adolescents may thus develop new understandings of their past, which may foster what has been called "autobiographical reasoning." This is the "process of self-reflective thinking or talking about the personal past that involves forming links between elements of one's life and the self in an attempt to relate one's personal past and present," the basis of life narratives (Bluck & Habermas, 2000, p. 749).

Finally, the need for identity definition is set socially as people enter the life period during which they define studies, career paths, or life trajectories—a period whose ending has been largely debated (Arnett, 2006; Hendry & Kloep, 2007; Zittoun, 2007). This raises the important need to understand autobiographical memory in adolescence within a broader lifecourse perspective.

A Case Study

Despite its richness for the topic of autobiographical memory, adolescence has rarely been explored by researchers interested in this topic. We previously investigated the development and transformation of imaginative processes during adolescence (Zittoun & de Saint-Laurent, 2015) using the longitudinal documentary *Romans d'ados* (*Teens Novels*) (Bakhti, 2010).[1] This documentary follows the parallel evolution of seven young people (four young women and three young men, all middle class), who live in a midsize French-speaking town in Switzerland, from their 11th to their 18th birthday. They are visited regularly by the documentary crew at their homes, at school, at the workplace, or when they are with their friends. Although the documentary is scripted and edited according to the interests of the director, it gives good access to the evolution of these young people's close relationships, vocational choices, and general orientations.

The focus of this initial exploration was on the imaginative loops in which adolescents engage (see Figure 9.1) and their contribution to developing a life trajectory (Zittoun & de Saint-Laurent, 2015). In doing so, however, the teenagers also drew on the past, showing how memory feeds into imaginative processes. This can be seen, for instance, in the case of Rachel, aged 15, who reflects on her active role in supporting her mother at a time of major crises between her mother and her stepfather (Figure 9.3). Discovering one day her desperate mother left alone by her companion after a violent quarrel, Rachel engaged in the following reflection (Bakhti, 2010; as quoted in Zittoun & de Saint-Laurent, 2015, p. 68):

> I thought about it. [I went into my room, I thought about it]. [I told myself that I would] take the matter into my hands. I didn't want my family to break up like this. I wanted to help my mother and my sister the best I could. (Rachel, 15, DVD 2)

Rachel also tells that this episode put at stake her own future: Because her father left the house when she was 2 years old, "I felt as if I was losing my second father. In case of another divorce, I thought I could never trust a man again. And that my relationships with men were going to be very complicated" (Rachel, 15, DVD 2) (Bakhti, 2010; as quoted in Zittoun & de Saint-Laurent, 2015, p. 68). Finally, she

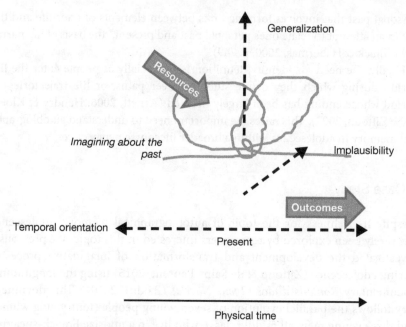

Figure 9.3 Rachel's memory and imagination.

explains how, during that time, she was drawing on the memory of her grandfather Bakhti, 2010; as quoted in Zittoun & de Saint-Laurent, 2015, p. 67):

> I've always been very proud of my grandfather. I had a very special relationship with him even when I was little. I really have the impression that he taught us many things, and that it is thanks to him that I am as I am. And I was always impassioned by his culture, and his charisma, and his good mood. I constructed myself with his image, and I always have been really really proud of the relationship I had with him. I feared that when he would die the family would turn to dust. It is thanks to him that the family is so united, that's his work. I think that that's why he came on earth, I think it was in that role, because really . . . for me thanks to him family is sacred. (Rachel, 14, DVD 2)

Rachel seems to engage in a complex imagination loop. Given the current situation, her parents' crisis, she imagines the close and distant futures, based on her childhood: Like her father, the stepfather may leave, but if so, she will grow up as a woman who cannot trust men. She then loops back into the past to draw on the memories of her grandfather and, finally, focuses on doing her best to help her parents through the current crisis. Hence, through this imagination loop, drawing on her past, she helps to shape her own future or—the other way around—in shaping her future, she can draw on her memories. This also helps her to build new relations with her family by creating a sense of continuity between her grandfather, her mother, and herself.

In the following discussion, we draw on the same data source (*Romans d'ados*) to explore the developmental dynamics of autobiographic memory along the life course, using our unified model of autobiographical memory (see Figure 9.2). Specifically, following our pragmatic stance, we focus on the transformation of remembering along the three functions discussed in this chapter—self, social relations, and directive. If we can show that the same person's remembering acts vary along these three aspects, we will have shown the development of remembering. We thus turn to a new case study, that of Thys, another young person followed for 7 years by Bakhti (2010).

Thys' story starts when he is 12 years old, living with his mother and older brother. He is not very talkative, and most of his life seems to revolve around "being an old couple" with his mother, something she jokes about, and visiting his father on weekends, who teases him frequently. In the following conversation, his mother asks him what he did with his father over the weekend (Bakhti, 2010, DVD 1):

MOTHER: How are you doing, Thyssou? The weekend went well?

THYS: Yes.

MOTHER: What did you do?

THYS: Well, we came Friday . . .

MOTHER: Yes.

THYS: We watched TV for a bit . . .

MOTHER: Yes.

THYS: And after, well Saturday we went . . . well, in the morning we went to Jean-Claude's . . .

MOTHER: Saturday morning you went out? Ah, good, well, ok.

THYS: Yes. Well . . . after we did lunch there . . . well, after we went to see the show . . .

MOTHER: So you had lunch and dinner at Jean-Claude's? The Auntie was there?

THYS: No, she was not there.

MOTHER: Ah, it was only the two of you?

THYS: Yes! Us, us three.

MOTHER: Ok.

THYS: There was also Christiane.

MOTHER: Ah, she came?

THYS: Yeah.

This conversation seems quite typical of late childhood reminiscing: The mother scaffolds her child's recall, which becomes organized into a small local narrative, as illustrated in Figure 9.4. Thys, in a conversation with his mother, reconstructs what happened, with the mother supporting this process (Fivush, 2011). His

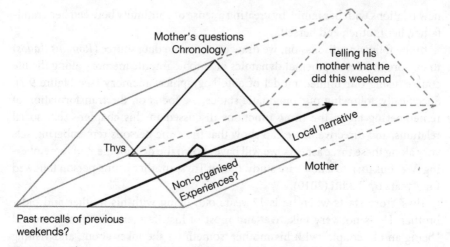

Figure 9.4 Thys, age 12 years, remembering his weekend with his mother.

mother's questions as well as basic chronological rules—starting the story with Friday evening, for instance—help him organize his story into a narrative, albeit a limited one. This is a transformation of the past because it is very likely that it had not been told to anyone yet: The conversation takes place just after Thys returned home. However, it is extremely likely, although we do not see it in the documentary, that it is not the first time that Thys, upon returning home, is asked by his mother what he did during the weekend; this segment is thus a probably quite well-rehearsed conversation, in which he can build on previous recalls to satisfy his mother's demands. The remembering episode is strongly guided by the local routines and is based on the use of quite simple resources that allow for the production of a local and limited narrative but that is sufficient to satisfy the demands of the situation.

Let us examine this episode in terms of the three functions. First, in terms of self-identity, Thys' voice is quite absent. He presents what he has been asked to do, using a "we" including him and his father, as well as other persons. None of the activities—watching TV, eating, and visiting the father's friend—seems to have a personal implication. Second, regarding social relations, we observe here the importance of the role of the mother, who is both a support for the recall and at the origin of the request. Also, the narration itself could be seen as reinforcing the relation between mother and child because the episode with the father appears to be relatively dull. Third, in terms of the directive function, the remembering, modestly turned to the immediate past, comes to the present but does not explore any possible futures, as the modest loop in Figure 9.4 suggests—unless, of course, it announces a very similar disappointing next encounter with the father.

A few years later, however, we find Thys, aged 15 years, having a quite different type of conversation with his mother (Bakhti, 2010, DVD 2):

FILMMAKER: So, you're still like an old couple?

MOTHER: But exactly. We are an old couple. It's totally that. So, we'll have to take the tricks. That's why sometimes it's a bit hard, isn't it, Thys? Actually, is it hard for you or not? I say that it's hard for me, but what about you?

THYS: When you yell for nothing, yes.

MOTHER: I yell for nothing, you think I yell for nothing? I yell straight away . . . but well . . . not that much.

THYS: As soon as she realizes that she is wrong, as soon as she believes that she is right, although it's not true, she starts raising her voice and oh, careful.

MOTHER: You too you throw words at me.

THYS: Ah yes, but . . .

MOTHER: You don't realize you're getting angry. You tap . . .

THYS: Neither do you . . .

MOTHER: You tap your feet, and all. You get up, you get upset. Yes, no, still a bit. But it's true that it is not violent. We are not violent, anyway, are we? We are not breaking things yet. Or well . . . yes, did we break anything yet? No, it's your brother who used to do that, not us.

Although it is still his mother who includes him in the conversation and pushes him to talk about the recurring past, his answer here is of a quite different tone compared to the previous episode. He challenges his mother on her depiction on their life together, and he uses memories as arguments to defend his position on how she is, as shown in Figure 9.5. He does so by generalizing multiple experiences, showing a beginning of autobiographical reasoning. It seems that Thys generalizes from past experiences using the recurring chronology of past events to extract general statements about his mother.

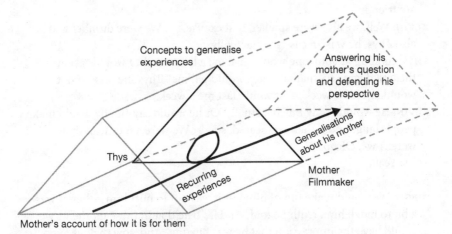

Figure 9.5 Thys, age 15 years, challenges his mother's representation of their relationship.

Interestingly, all the teenagers in the *Teens Novel* documentary similarly start creating new accounts of the past by challenging their parents' summaries of recurring past experiences. Here, however, both Thys and his mother settle on a version of the past in which neither is better. But, temporarily at least, Thys contradicts his mother on her understanding of the past, and a symbolic space to reinterpret memories is open: New interlocutors are available—the change from "you" to "she" when he talks about his mother to the new other that is the filmmaker is noticeable—and new resources appear. Old resources are used in new ways: Thys already used knowledge of chronological order to narrate his weekend in the previous intercept. Here, however, he uses recurring chronologies not only to generalize from experience but also to attribute motivations to the actions of his mother: If she yells, it is because she is afraid to be wrong.

Regarding the three functions, we could thus say that due to his wider uses of resources, Thys achieves different results. First, in terms of identity definition, Thys starts to differentiate himself from his mother—most of his utterances are formulated in "you"; his position is that of someone having his own perspective. Second, in terms of relations, Thys uses the established relation to triangulate and question the relation to the mother, who becomes "she." Third, and this is where we need to be careful, it seems that by identifying a current pattern in their relationship, Thys timidly suggests that another mode of relation could be wished for or possible.

A year later, Thys transforms from a shy boy mocked at school to a more social teen with new friends who, in fact, happened to be his past bullies. He explains (Bakhti, 2010, DVD 3):

THYS: Diego, Kevin, and other people in the class, we didn't really get along, actually. In 7th grade, I even went to see the school mediator because they would provoke me and . . . I, I hated them. And now, that's just it, we are friends.

KEVIN: Well, we also were smaller, first excuse. . . . We were dumber and also Thys, he was an easy prey, actually.

THYS: As soon as someone would give me a little insult, I would take it at the first degree so that's it. They would tell me "Thys the piss" and it would last me a week . . . it would last me a week.

KEVIN: He wouldn't say much, actually. Or he would say, but he would make people laugh more than feel scared, so. . . . We were a bit mean then, weren't we, Diego?

THYS: Yeah.

[. . .]

DIEGO: We would make fun of him but it was not to hurt him either. It was a bit to mock him, truth be told. And it's true that in these moments we would have the impression that he was hurting. And now that we are

here and we laugh with him, well it's less hurtful for him, well, it's not to
hurt him actually.

THYS: I changed a bit and then I came with them and I managed to talk and
talk. Well yeah, it was super cool, actually.

Here, Thys, with the help of his new friends, creates a new account of the past, as
shown in Figure 9.6. What he used to interpret as being bullied in the first year of
the documentary (Bakhti, 2010, DVD 1) becomes the product of his overreaction
and their global immaturity (Kevin's "first excuse"). He discovers new perspectives on the past, which leads to its reinterpretation, although previous resources
are still present (generalization). His interlocutors, however, also refer to what
we may call "lay theories of development" or common-sense concepts about the
maturation of the person. This allows Kevin to explain his previous behaviors as a
product of a lack of maturity and as something quite acceptable for a young teenager. What is notable here is that the story Thys, Kevin, and Diego are telling is a
co-construction in which the past is reinterpreted—one was overreacting and the
others were "dumb," in their words—to link it to current social interactions: They
can now be friends because they have changed and matured. By remembering
with his new friends, Thys gains new insights on the situation, has access to new
tools, and is thus given a new space to understand his past.

In this case, the functions of memory are very clear. First, Thys starts to have
an autobiographic narrative that his is own—a story of development and more
maturity. Second, in terms of relationships, we observe the radical change of the
others with whom memory is build and with whom memory allows to establish
a relationship. Third, this autobiographic reasoning that goes further in the past
allows to enrich the present—which is now "super cool"—and perhaps allows to
open new options.

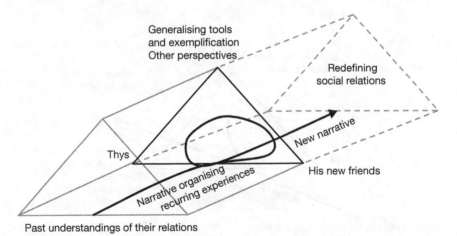

Figure 9.6 Thys, age 16 years, reinterpreting his past with his new friends.

Finally, 2 years later, the filmmakers confront Thys with his early statements about his father (Bakhti, 2010, DVD 4):

THYS (AGE 12 YEARS): Well, it was difficult. Even, once my daddy, he was . . . when they were not together anymore, I overturned a full wardrobe for him to come. I was very sad, yes, I . . . angry. . . . I wondered what was going on.

THYS (AGE 18 YEARS): I used to want to, before . . . to have more relations with my father, share like other would and all. I also idealized a lot to have my father . . . yeah, I idealized a father, all that. But now, I'm passed this stage.

In this intercept, analyzed in Figure 9.7, Thys completely reinterprets his relation with his father. Where he used to view his father's absence as the result of his parents' divorce, he now follows a version favored by his brother much earlier in the documentary: His father just did not really behave like one. But to make sense of this change of perspective on the past and link it to the present, Thys makes use of a resource his friends introduced in the previous intercept: the idea that to different ages in life correspond different ways, more or less mature, to interact with others.

Here we see the most drastic changes in uses of memory. First, in terms of identity and position, Thys is reflecting on his former attachment and ideas, and he is positioning himself as having "passed a stage"—that is, having gone through a transition. Second, as mentioned previously, using his internalized friends, he is now using memories to distance himself from his father. Third, for the first time, he opens new options for the future, where he will no longer expect the impossible from his father.

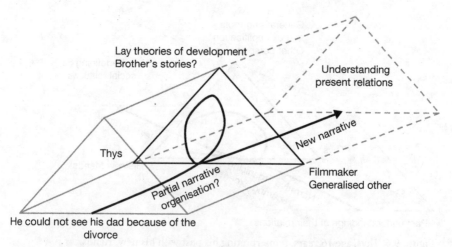

Figure 9.7 Thys, age 18 years, reinterpreting his relation with his father.

We have thus seen that Thys, during his adolescence, does indeed become more independent from his mother's accounts of the past, which gives him the space necessary for a more personal interpretation of his past. However, the role of others in scaffolding remembering does not end here: New relations introduce him to new ways of thinking about his past. Also, as the years go by, he indeed becomes familiar with new tools that allow him to think of his past further and differently. As a result, this allows him to move away from an orientation to the past—what was and what could have been—to a possible future—now that this stage is over. Interestingly, however, new resources do not always seem to be required for new forms of memory to emerge: New challenges and new desires, such as challenging one's mother, may bring one to use old resources in new ways.

CONCLUSION

As we move through life, we live new experiences and engage in new relationships, all of which can question who we are or, at least, invite us to reflect on our past or to share some memories. But how does autobiographical memory evolve though the life course?

In this chapter, we proposed to understand the development of autobiographical memory as the process through which one learns to "rework" and reinterpret the past in a way that is relevant to the current situation of the self. We considered this movement as being one of distancing the self from the exactitude and details of past experiences, to organize them into stories that can be told to others, and to generalize them into concepts about oneself or turn them into lessons to be learned.

Our attempt here consisted in drawing on the developmental literature and expanding it beyond childhood. We have for this privileged a pragmatic stance and have proposed an integrative model of remembering, which highlights the social, cultural, and imaginary nature of remembering. Our proposition is that remembering, like any other complex social and cultural psychological dynamic, is a socially situated activity that demands the mastery of specific cultural tools and uses diverse resources.

Because remembering draws on previous recalls through time, it is subjected to more general developmental processes. In effect, as with any other modality of experience, memory is mediated by language and social norms, and in spheres of experience that are frequently shared, nourished, and elaborated, memories can become increasingly more differentiated. In addition, some experiences can be moved from one sphere of experience to another (e.g., when one's musical success can support one's academic expenses; Zittoun, 2012). Finally, some other memories can diffuse across spheres of experience and be generalized into general principles or personal life philosophies or allow more abstract contemplation (Baldwin, 1915/2009; Vygotsky, 1931/1994; Werner & Kaplan, 1963; Zittoun et al., 2013).

Hence, teenagers who start to narrate their childhood to their close friends actually start to create the vocabulary and the grammar of the autobiographical memories in a given sphere of experience, which can then become the values that may govern their future choices in other spheres. Conversely, the fact that older people's stories lose details but convey more meaning can be understood as a result of such forms of generalization rather than a form of memory loss (Fitzgerald & Broadbridge, 2012).

However, the developmental literature tends to focus on the early development of the capacity to remember; then, as life passes and one has defined who he or she is, autobiographical memory appears generally as nonproblematic. Of course, the question of autobiographical memory and its fate appears in different studies—for example, clinical research examining the way in which people narrate themselves and, at times, develop more functional autobiographical accounts (Gonçalves & Ribeiro, 2012a, 2012b); studies on aging, which emphasize progressive transformation or losses of memory due to organic transformation (Balota, Dolan, & Duchek, 2000); or more general considerations of our sense of time and memory (Draaisma, 2004).

If every occurrence of autobiographical reasoning is one element in a long chain of remembering, then it can evolve with experience, become more abstract and generalized, and be part of the many processes that constitute who we are. Thus, it both allows and constrains our capacity to reinvent ourselves. In this sense, autobiographical memory is suspended between past and future because it is a variation of a loop of imagination. Just as does imagination, it distances itself from experience to produce new and unique compositions. Remembering one's life is, in that sense, an imagination of the past that uses a diversity of resources and that will have a variety of outcomes (Zittoun & Gillespie, 2015a). Indeed, if memory is a way to mentally travel through time (Tulving, 2002) and to defy the laws of irreversibility of time, then memory is an imagination oriented toward the past.

ACKNOWLEDGMENTS

We thank Beatrice Bakhti for allowing us to use the transcripts of the documentary she directed, as well as Vlad Glaveanu for his reading of a previous version of the text.

NOTE

1. Longitudinal documentaries, as specific genre following people over a longer period of time (Kilborn, 2010), offer an interesting source of data for developmental research—a strategy that we have used and justified elsewhere (Gillespie & Zittoun, 2010; Zittoun & de Saint-Laurent, 2015; Zittoun & Gillespie, 2012).

REFERENCES

Arnett, J. J. (2006). *Emerging adulthood: The winding road from the late teens through the twenties* (new ed.). Oxford, UK: Oxford University Press.

Baddeley, A. D. (2012). Reflections on autobiographical memory. In D. Bernsten & D. C. Rubin (Eds.), *Understanding autobiographical memory: Theories and approaches* (pp. 70–88). New York, NY: Cambridge University Press.

Bakhti, B. (2010). *Romans d'ados*. Documentary, Troubadour Films.

Baldwin, J. (2009). *Genetic theory of reality* (J. Valsiner, Ed.). New Brunswick, NJ: Transaction Publishers. (Original work published 1915)

Balota, D. A., Dolan, P. O., & Duchek, J. M. (2000). Memory changes in healthy young and older adults. In E. Tulving & F. I. M. Craik (Eds.), *The Oxford handbook of memory* (pp. 395–409). New York, NY: Oxford University Press.

Bartlett, S. F. C. (1995). *Remembering: A study in experimental and social psychology*. Cambridge, UK: Cambridge University Press.

Bauer, M. W., & Gaskell, G. (1999). Towards a paradigm for research on social representations. *Journal for the Theory of Social Behaviour, 29*(2), 163–186.

Berntsen, D., & Bohn, A. (2010). Remembering and forecasting: The relation between autobiographical memory and episodic future thinking. *Memory & Cognition, 38*(3), 265–278. doi:10.3758/MC.38.3.265

Berntsen, D., &Rubin, D. C. (2002). Emotionally charged memories across the life span: The recall of happy, sad, traumatic, and involuntary memories. *Psychology of Aging, 17*, 636–652.

Berntsen, D., & Rubin, D. C. (2004). Cultural life scripts structure recall from autobiographical memory. *Memory & Cognition, 32*(3), 427–442. doi:10.3758/BF03195836

Bluck, S. (2003). Autobiographical memory: Exploring its functions in everyday life. *Memory, 11*(2), 113–123. doi:10.1080/741938206

Bluck, S., & Alea, N. (2008). Remembering being me: The self continuity function of autobiographical memory in younger and older adults. In F. Sani (Ed.), *Self continuity: Individual and collective perspectives* (pp. 55–70). New York, NY: Psychology Press.

Bluck, S., Alea, N., Habermas, T., & Rubin, D. C. (2005). A TALE of three functions: The self-reported uses of autobiographical memory. *Social Cognition, 23*(1), 91–117. doi:10.1521/soco.23.1.91.59198

Bruner, J. S. (2003). *Making stories: Law, literature, life*. Cambridge, MA: Harvard University Press.

Cameron, J. J., Wilson, A. E., & Ross, M. (2004). Autobiographical memory and self-assessment. In D. R. Bleike, J. M. Lampinen, & D. A. Behrend (Eds.), *The self and memory* (pp. 207–226). New York, NY: Psychology Press.

Cole, M. (2007). Phylogeny and cultural history in ontogeny. *Journal of Physiology (Paris), 101*(4-6), 236–246. doi:10.1016/j.jphysparis.2007.11.007

Collins, W. A., Gleason, T., & Sesma, A. (1997). Internalization, autonomy, and relationships: Development during adolescence. In J. E. Grusec & L. Kuczinsky (Eds.), *Parenting and children's internalization of values: A handbook of contemporary theory* (pp. 78–99). Hoboken, NJ: Wiley.

Conway, M. A. (2005). Memory and the self. *Journal of Memory and Language, 53*(4), 594–628. doi:10.1016/j.jml.2005.08.005

D'Argembeau, A. (2012). Autobiographical memory and future thinking. In D. Bernsten & D. C. Rubin (Eds.), *Understanding autobiographical memory* (pp. 311–330). New York, NY: Cambridge University Press.

de Saint-Laurent, C. (2017). Memory acts: A theory for the study of collective memory in everyday life. *Journal of Constructivist Psychology*, Online first. doi: 10.1080/10720537.2016.1271375

Draaisma, D. (2004). *Why life speeds up as you get older: How memory shapes our past.* Cambridge, UK: Cambridge University Press.

Dudai, Y., & Carruthers, M. (2005). The Janus face of Mnemosyne. *Nature, 434*(7033), 567–567. doi:10.1038/434567a

Erikson, E. H. (1959). *Identity and the life cycle: Selected papers.* New York, NY: International Universities Press.

Erikson, E. H. (1968). *Identity: Youth and crisis.* London, UK: Faber & Faber.

Feldman, C., Bruner, J., Kalmar, D., & Renderer, B. (1993). Plot, plight, and dramatism: Interpretation at three ages. *Human Development, 36*(6), 327–342. doi:10.1159/000278220

Fitzgerald, J. M., & Broadbridge, C. L. (2012). Theory and research in autobiographical memory: A life-span developmental perspective. In D. Bernsten & D. C. Rubin (Eds.), *Understanding autobiographical memory: Theories and approaches* (pp. 246–266). Cambridge, UK: Cambridge University Press.

Fivush, R. (2011). The development of autobiographical memory. *Annual Review of Psychology, 62*(1), 559–582. doi:10.1146/annurev.psych.121208.131702

Fivush, R., Bohanek, J. G., & Duke, M. (2008). The intergenerational self: Subjective perspective and family history. In F. Sani (Ed.), *Self continuity: Individual and collective perspectives* (pp. 131–143). New York, NY: Psychology Press.

Fivush, R., Habermas, T., Waters, T. E. A., & Zaman, W. (2011). The making of autobiographical memory: Intersections of culture, narratives and identity. *International Journal of Psychology, 46*(5), 321–345. doi:10.1080/00207594.2011.596541

Freeman, M. (2007). Autobiographical understanding and narrative inquiry. In J. Clandinin (Ed.), *Handbook of narrative inquiry* (pp. 120–145). London, UK: Sage.

Friedman, W. J. (1992). Children's time memory: The development of a differentiated past. *Cognitive Development, 7*(2), 171–187. doi:10.1016/0885-2014(92)90010-O

Gillespie, A., & Zittoun, T. (2010). Studying the movement of thought. In A. Toomela & J. Valsiner (Eds.), *Methodological thinking in psychology: 60 years gone astray?* (pp. 69–88). Charlotte, NC: Information Age Publishing.

Gonçalves, M. M., & Ribeiro, A. P. (2012a). Narrative processes of innovation and stability within the dialogical self. In H. J. M. Hermans & T. Gieser (Eds.), *Handbook of dialogical self theory* (pp. 301–218). Cambridge, UK: Cambridge University Press.

Gonçalves, M. M., & Ribeiro, A. P. (2012b). Therapeutic change, innovative moments, and the reconceptualization of the self: A dialogical account. *International Journal for Dialogical Science, 6*(1), 81–98.

Grotevant, H. D., & Cooper, C. R. (1986). Individuation in family relationships: A perspective on individual differences in the development of identity and role-taking skill in adolescence. *Human Development, 29*(2), 82–100. doi:10.1159/000273025

Habermas, T. (2007). How to tell a life: The development of the cultural concept of biography. *Journal of Cognition and Development, 8*(1), 1–31. doi:10.1080/15248370709336991

Habermas, T. (2011). Autobiographical reasoning: Arguing and narrating from a biographical perspective. *New Directions for Child and Adolescent Development, 2011*(131), 1–17. doi:10.1002/cd.285

Habermas, T. (2012). Identity, emotion, and the social matrix of autobiographical memory: A psychoanalytic narrative view. In D. Bernsten & D. Rubin (Eds.), *Understanding autobiographical memory: Theories and approaches* (pp. 33–53). Cambridge, UK: Cambridge University Press.

Habermas, T., & Bluck, S. (2000). Getting a life: The emergence of the life story in adolescence. *Psychological Bulletin, 126*(5), 748–769. doi:10.1037/0033-2909.126.5.748

Habermas, T., & de Silveira, C. (2008). The development of global coherence in life narratives across adolescence: Temporal, causal, and thematic aspects. *Developmental Psychology, 44*(3), 707–721. doi:http://dx.doi.org/10.1037/0012-1649.44.3.707

Habermas, T., Negele, A., & Mayer, F. B. (2010). "Honey, you're jumping about"— Mothers' scaffolding of their children's and adolescents' life narration. *Cognitive Development, 25*(4), 339–351. doi:10.1016/j.cogdev.2010.08.004

Halbwachs, M. (1950). *La mémoire collective*. Paris, France: Albin Michel.

Hendry, L. B., & Kloep, M. (2007). Conceptualizing emerging adulthood: Inspecting the emperor's new clothes? *Child Development Perspectives, 1*(2), 74–79. doi:10.1111/j.1750-8606.2007.00017.x

Hermans, H. J. M. (2002). The dialogical self as a society of mind. *Theory & Psychology, 12*, 147–160. doi:10.1177/0959354302122001

Hirst, W., Cuc, A., & Wohl, D. (2012). Of sins and virtues: Memory and collective identity. In D. Berntsen & D. C. Rubin (Eds.), *Understanding autobiographical memory* (pp. 141–159). New York, NY: Cambridge University Press.

Hirst, W., & Echterhoff, G. (2012). Remembering in conversations: The social sharing and reshaping of memories. *Annual Review of Psychology, 63*, 55–79. doi:10.1146/annurev-psych-120710-100340

Hofer, M. (2004). The role of discourse in the transformation of parent–adolescent relationships. In A.-N. Perret-Clermont, C. Pontecorvo, L. Resnick, T. Zittoun, & B. Burge (Eds.), *Joining society: Social interaction and learning in adolescence and youth* (pp. 241–251). Cambridge, UK: Cambridge University Press.

James, W. (1904). What is pragmatism. In *A new name for some old ways of thinking*. New York, NY: The Library of America. Retrieved from http://www.marxists.org/reference/subject/philosophy/works/us/james.htm

Jensen, T. K. (2005). The interpretation of signs of child sexual abuse. *Culture & Psychology, 11*(4), 469–498. doi:10.1177/1354067X05058588

Kadianaki, I., & Zittoun, T. (2014). Catalysts and regulators of psychological change in the context of immigration ruptures. In K. R. Cabell & J. Valsiner (Eds.), *The catalyzing mind* (pp. 191–207). New York, NY: Springer.

Kilborn, R. (2010). *Taking the long view: A study of longitudinal documentary*. Manchester, UK: Manchester University Press.

Laursen, B., & Collins, W. A. (2011). *Relationship pathways: From adolescence to young adulthood*. Thousand Oaks, CA: Sage.

Mattli, F., Schnitzspahn, K. M., Studerus-Germann, A., Brehmer, Y., & Zöllig, J. (2014). Prospective memory across the lifespan: Investigating the contribution of retrospective and prospective processes. *Aging, Neuropsychology, and Cognition, 21*(5), 515–543. doi:10.1080/13825585.2013.837860

McAdams, D. P. (2001). The psychology of life stories. *Review of General Psychology, 5,* 100–122.

McAdams, D. P., Josselson, R., & Liebich, A. (2006). Introduction. In D. P. McAdams, R. Josselson, & A. Liebich (Eds.), *Identity and story: Creating self in narrative* (pp. 3–11). Washington, DC: American Psychological Association.

McDaniel, M. A., & Einstein, G. O. (2007). *Prospective memory: An overview and synthesis of an emerging field.* Thousand Oaks, CA: Sage.

Meeus, W. H. J., Branje, S. J. T., van der Valk, I., & de Wied, M. (2007). Relationships with intimate partner, best friend, and parents in adolescence and early adulthood: A study of the saliency of the intimate partnership. *International Journal of Behavioral Development, 31*(6), 569–580. doi:10.1177/0165025407080584

Mullally, S. L., & Maguire, E. A. (2014). Memory, imagination, and predicting the future: A common brain mechanism? *The Neuroscientist, 20*(3), 220–234. Retrieved from http://doi.org/10.1177/1073858413495091

Nelson, K. (2003). Narrative and self, myth and memory: Emergence of the cultural self. In R. Fivush & C. A. Haden (Eds.), *Autobiographical memory and the construction of a narrative self: Developmental and cultural perspectives* (pp. 3–28). Mahwah, NJ: Erlbaum.

Nelson, K. (2007). *Young minds in social worlds: Experience, meaning, and memory.* Cambridge, MA: Harvard University Press.

Nelson, K. (2008). Self in time: Emergence within a community of minds. In F. Sani (Ed.), *Self continuity: Individual and collective perspectives* (pp. 13–26). New York, NY: Psychology Press.

Nelson, K., & Fivush, R. (2004). The emergence of autobiographical memory: A social cultural developmental theory. *Psychological Review, 111*(2), 486–511. doi:10.1037/0033-295X.111.2.486

Pillemer, D. B. (2003). Directive functions of autobiographical memory: The guiding power of the specific episode. *Memory, 11*(2), 193–202. doi:10.1080/741938208

Pillemer, D. B., & Kuwabara, K. J. (2012). Directive functions of autobiographical memory: Theory and method. In D. Berntsen & D. C. Rubin (Eds.), *Understanding autobiographical memory* (pp. 181–202). New York, NY: Cambridge University Press.

Rathbone, C. J., Moulin, C. J. A., & Conway, M. A. (2008). Self-centered memories: The reminiscence bump and the self. *Memory & Cognition, 36*(8), 1403–1414. doi:10.3758/MC.36.8.1403

Reese, E., Yan, C., Jack, F., & Hayne, H. (2010). Emerging identities: Narrative and self from early childhood to early adolescence. In K. C. McLean & M. Pasupathi (Eds.), *Narrative development in adolescence* (pp. 23–43). New York, NY: Springer.

Rubin, D. C., Wetzler, S. E., & Nebes, R. D. (1986). Autobiographical memory across the lifespan. In D. C. Rubin (Ed.), *Autobiographical memory* (pp. 202–222). Cambridge, UK: Cambridge University Press.

Sato, T., Yasuda, Y., Kanzaki, M., & Valsiner, J. (2013). From describing to reconstructing life trajectories: How the TEA (trajectory equifinality approach) explicates context-dependent human phenomena. In B. Wagoner, N. Chaudhary, & P. Hviid (Eds.), *Cultural psychology and its future: Complementarity in a new key* (pp. 93–105). Charlotte, NC: Information Age Publishing.

Schacter, D. L., & Addis, D. R. (2007). Constructive memory: The ghosts of past and future. *Nature, 445*(7123), 27–27. doi:10.1038/445027a

Singer, J. A., & Blagov, P. (2004). The integrative function of narrative processing: Autobiographical memory, self-defining memories, and the life story of identity. In D. R. Bleike, J. M. Lampinen, & D. A. Behrend (Eds.), *The self and memory* (pp. 117–138). New York, NY: Psychology Press.

Steinberg, L., & Silverberg, S. B. (1986). The vicissitudes of autonomy in early adolescence. *Child Development*, *57*(4), 841–851. doi:http://dx.doi.org/10.2307/1130361

Tulving, E. (2002). Episodic memory: From mind to brain. *Annual Review of Psychology*, *53*(1), 1–25. doi:10.1146/annurev.psych.53.100901.135114

Valsiner, J. (2014). *An invitation to cultural psychology*. London, UK: Sage.

Vygotsky, L. S. (1994). Imagination and creativity of the adolescent. In R. van der Veer & J. Valsiner (Eds.), *The Vygotsky reader* (pp. 266–288). Oxford, UK: Blackwell. (Original work published 1931)

Vygotsky, L. S. (2004). Imagination and creativity in childhood. *Journal of Russian and East European Psychology*, *42*(1), 7–97.

Wagoner, B. (2015). Collective remembering as a process of social representation. In *Cambridge handbook of social representations*. Cambridge, UK: Cambridge University Press.

Welzer, H., Moller, S., & Tschuggnall, K. (2013). *Grand-père n'était pas un nazi:. Nationalsocialisme et Shoah dans la mémoire familiale*. Paris, France: Gallimard. (original German edition published 2002)

Werner, H., & Kaplan, B. (1963). *Symbol formation: An organismic–developmental approach to language and the expression of thought*. New York, NY: Wiley.

Zittoun, T. (2006). *Transitions: Development through symbolic resources*. Greenwich, CT: Information Age Publishing.

Zittoun, T. (2007). Symbolic resources and responsibility in transitions. *Young: Nordic Journal of Youth Research*, *15*(2), 193–211.

Zittoun, T. (2012). Life course. In J. Valsiner (Ed.), *Handbook of culture and psychology* (pp. 513–535). Oxford, UK: Oxford University Press.

Zittoun, T., & de Saint-Laurent, C. (2015). Life-creativity: Imagining one's life. In V. P. Glǎveanu, A. Gillespie, & J. Valsiner (Eds.), *Rethinking creativity: Contributions from cultural psychology* (pp. 58–75). New York, NY: Routledge.

Zittoun, T., & Gillespie, A. (2012). Using diaries and self-writings as data in psychological research. In E. Abbey & S. E. Surgan (Eds.), *Emerging methods in psychology* (pp. 1–26). New Brunswick, NJ: Transaction Publishers.

Zittoun, T., & Gillespie, A. (2015a). *Imagination in human and cultural development*. London, UK: Routledge.

Zittoun, T., & Gillespie, A. (2015b). Integrating experiences: Body and mind moving between contexts. In B. Wagoner, N. Chaudhary, & P. Hviid (Eds.), *Integrating experiences: Body and mind moving between contexts* (pp. 3–49). Charlotte, NC: Information Age Publishing.

Zittoun, T., Valsiner, J., Vedeler, D., Salgado, J., Gonçalves, M., & Ferring, D. (2013). *Human development in the life course: Melodies of living*. Cambridge, UK: Cambridge University Press.

Memory in Old Age

A Lifespan Perspective

DIETER FERRING ∎

Demographic change, involving perpetual low fertility, on the one hand, and steady increase in life expectancy that may result in over-aging societies, on the other hand, poses a problem in many developed countries (United Nations, 2013). The phenomenon is currently most apparent in Japan as well as in Europe, where pronounced effects of population aging on public expenditures, economy, employment, education, and health care—to name just the most prominent criteria—are expected by 2030.[1] "Getting older" describes the individually and collectively shared experience of the aging process that, for most of human history, has been conceptualized as a unidirectional sequence leading to decline and death. Although this still represents a significant part of the human life course, several factors have changed. Until the 1970s, old age seemed to be a comparatively short period of life whose predominant characteristics were declines in the physical and functional domains leading to death. This line of thought has changed because one can now clearly differentiate between the Third Age as a phase of comparatively fewer impairments and deficits that may also be compensated and the Fourth Age, which has a heightened probability of losses in learning potential and cognitive plasticity and a heightened prevalence of neurodegenerative disorders and functional impairments in general (Baltes & Smith, 2003).

Based on population estimates, the beginning of the Fourth Age is approximately 80–85 years in developed countries. The individual-based differentiation highlights that the transition between the Third Age and the Fourth Age may occur at different chronological ages given that the maximum individual life span may last up to 120 years (Zittoun et al., 2013, Chapter 10). There is considerable variability in human aging, and the often cited statement by Rowe and Kahn (1998) that *aging is universal but not uniform* describes this perfectly. Aging is a multidimensional process—involving physical, mental, cognitive, and social factors—and differential forms of aging exist depending on which domains of aging are considered (Thomae, 1963). One 80-year-old may thus show severe physical decline as indicated by multimorbidity, but he or she may have excellent morale as well as outstanding cognitive capabilities, whereas another person of the same age may show severe cognitive and mental deficits while having a robust physical constitution. Explaining aging processes thus always implies the explanation of interindividual differences in intraindividual change processes.

Memory performance in old age—as an often used indicator of the cognitive capacity—is linked to the previously mentioned declines in learning potential and cognitive plasticity. Since Alois Alzheimer described loss of memory, delusions, and sleeping troubles as the major symptoms shown by Auguste Deter—the world's first officially diagnosed Alzheimer patient—in 1901,[2] deteriorations in working memory performance have been considered early indicators of Alzheimer's disease (AD). Within the category of neurodegenerative diseases, AD takes a prominent role given that an estimated 24 million people worldwide have dementia, with the majority of these cases assumed to be AD (Ballard et al., 2011). Memory thus has crucial importance in several domains and is the object of different perspectives and conceptualizations. The general public considers memory loss as a threatening major functional decline in advanced age (Anderson, Day, Beard, Reed, & Wu, 2009; Wortman, Andrieu, Mackell, & Knox, 2010), which reflects the fact that AD is often diagnosed in the mild dementia stage, in which memory functioning and daily activities are observably impaired (Ferring, 2015). Research in basic as well as applied psychology studying specificities of the aging memory process is speeded up by the eminent motivation to identify early symptoms of neurodegenerative diseases and to develop programs that will help postpone the onset of the disease. This area of research is best characterized as cross-disciplinary because medical science, biology, biochemistry, and neuroscience are involved here as well.

In this chapter, memory is considered from a lifespan perspective combining a geropsychological as well as a lifespan developmental view. Characteristics of such a view are outlined for developmental outcomes in general and memory in particular. Then, central concepts describing memory functioning in a developmental perspective are described and aligned with theories of self-regulation. Memory is thus considered with a focus on identity formation and self-regulation. Following this, the chapter discusses the interaction between memory in old age and culture, seen as assistive culture or as a semiotic frame.

AGING AND MEMORY FUNCTIONING FROM A GEROPSYCHOLOGICAL AND LIFESPAN PERSPECTIVE

In the following account, I use the term "memory functioning" as a comprehensive concept to substitute the more general term of memory. In this view, memory functioning covers the perception, storage, and retrieval of information and is subject to both explicit and implicit attention processes. Thus, using memory always implies a sensorial and perceptual contact with the outside world. I further elaborate this first conceptual clarification in the subsequent section. The purpose of this discussion is to introduce a geropsychological and a lifespan perspective on memory functioning in particular as well as developmental outcomes in general. Such an approach explains changes in memory and other domains of human functioning by the interplay of genetics and culture as well as individual habits and lifestyles.

The dynamics underlying genetics and epigenetics explain changes and specificities of human metabolism directly affecting the functioning of the human brain and its various functions. During the past few decades, the notion of epigenetics has received increased attention from several domains of developmental psychology, given the apparent and associated increase in the explanative power of developmental theories that the concept provides. Genetics thus constitute the hardware that is triggered or stopped by specific experiences in a given living context, resulting in a specific epigenetic structure. For instance, there is increasing evidence for the role of DNA methylation—as one motor of epigenetics—in explaining differences in cognitive functioning by having an impact on synaptic plasticity and memory formation (Coppieters & Dragunow, 2011; Levenson & Sweatt, 2005). Returning to the role that genetics play in human aging and in human memory in particular, one may use the metaphor introduced by Baltes (1997) when speaking of the incomplete architecture of the human lifespan. In a review of research findings, he concludes that "the genetic material, associated genetic mechanisms, and genetic expressions become less effective and less able to generate or maintain high levels of functioning. Evolution and biology are not good friends of old age" (p. 368).

This is why Baltes (1997) sees a heightened need for assistive culture with advancing age, although the efficiency of these resources declines with age as well. He defines culture as "the entirety of psychological, social, material, and symbolic (knowledge-based) resources that humans have generated over the millennia, and which as they are transmitted across generations, make human development possible as we know it today" (p. 368). In this view, the older a person becomes, the more he or she is in need of culture-based compensations to generate and maintain (high) levels of functioning. Thus, the availability of cultural resources adds, in many ways, to the description and explanation of differences in human ontogenesis in general and differences in memory functioning in particular. Raising public awareness about the link between memory problems and aging represents a first and quite evident sign of how Western culture, having to cope with a growing number of dependent older persons, deals with this threat. This is easily demonstrated by entering the terms "memory" and "old age" into Internet search engines, which will return approximately 70 million hits. Another example for this is the growing number of memory clinics established since the late 1970s aiming at the early diagnosis and treatment of people with dementia (Ramakers & Verhey, 2011; Wright & Lindesay, 1995). A third sign is the public discourse on neurodegenerative diseases—involving memory difficulties, decline, or loss as major symptoms—in the print media. Peel (2014) describes this discourse as a predominating "panic-blame" scenario depicting dementia in catastrophic terms (e.g., "tsunami" and "worse than death"), while also covering individualistic behavioral change and lifestyle recommendations to cope with the changed life situation. All this describes the second meaning of the culture concept that stands for the discourse of a given phenomenon and its possible consequences at the individual and the social levels, thus influencing the personal construals of the meaning that this disease may have.

Here, one may add that despite this emerging threat in public awareness, different views on human aging exist that reflect both negative and positive stereotypes at the individual level as well as within and between cultures. In general, I hold that age in its positive connotation is primarily linked to experience and knowledge of the older adult. In line with this and despite the threat of memory loss and increasing dependence, the aging person is also considered as a source of wisdom reflecting his or her life experiences, and this notion is elaborated, for example, in research programs focusing on wisdom as a resource in old age (Baltes & Staudinger, 2000). As a further illustration, refer to the book *30 Lessons for Loving* by Pillemer (2015), which uses life stories and views of older Americans on specific topics and highlights the importance of experiential knowledge of the older generations. An inspiring (and also often criticized) conceptual approach to modernization and aging states that the perception of age and aging changes during the transition from traditional rural–agricultural to industrialized and urbanized societies (see Cowgill & Holmes, 1972). Experiential knowledge—given its evident importance for life—and its bearers are much more appreciated in traditional societies that combine family life and production than in industrialized societies that focus on the capacities of productivity (especially in the younger generation) and separate family and production of goods. Cultures of economy and production thus exert an influence on the positive or negative perceptions of old age.[3] This is currently reflected in Western societies in a discourse debating the distribution of resources between the increasing number of older adults and the decreasing number of the young generation depicting a "war between generations" (Ferring, 2010; Gokhale & Kotlikoff, 2001).

Finally, habits and lifestyles are a third dynamic that influences the ways in which individuals age and thus help to describe, explain, and predict variability of developmental outcomes. In this view, habits that are formed across the individual life course have an effect on various developmental outcomes, including memory. An early definition by Andrews (1903) describes habits as mental processes of being "a more or less fixed way of thinking, willing, or feeling acquired through previous repetition of a mental experience" (p. 121) and as "a mode of mental functioning in which repeated processes are predominant in consciousness" (p. 122). This is contrasted by Hull's (1943) principles of behavior, in which habits and habit strength result from the number of reinforcements that an organism experiences. Building up habits starts early in development, and depending on the instrumental value of both overt and covert behavior, complex patterns of both mental and behavioral processes may develop that constitute lifestyles consistently shown across the lifespan. A child may thus learn that "loud weeping when frustrated" will lead to the positive result that the cause of frustration is removed. Repeated experiences may then lead to and feed a mental representation that will be activated in similar situations. The more the behavior proves to be adaptive, the more it will become a routine. In a lifespan view, one may assume that the adolescent and the adult person will still show variations of "weeping when frustrated" that conform to socially and culturally shared expectations of age-adequate behavior. Persons may thus show a consistent and stable behavior when frustrated, which is considered as a personality trait used in self-description ("I am a sensitive person and react quite emotionally") as well as in social ascriptions and even socially shared behavior regulations toward this person ("He/she has always been very sensitive; please be careful how you deal with him/her.").

Such a view gains an intuitive meaning if one considers the instrumental adaptive functions of such routine behaviors: Individuals adopt lifestyles because they allow them to safeguard physical as well as mental energy, and people adhere to these lifestyles as long as their adaptive value is not called into question. In this configuration, habits form lifestyles that are on a further level of abstraction considered as personality traits.

Thomae (1963) highlighted that the way in which a person copes with adjustment problems in early or middle adulthood is decisive for the degree to which the major problems of life in old age are resolved. In such an understanding, people may make use of memory in different ways across different life domains. This is illustrated, for instance, in the so-called "nun study" describing links between linguistic ability in young adulthood and cognitive function and AD in late life (i.e., approximately 58 years later) in a sample of religious sisters (Snowdon et al., 1996) or by studies analyzing the link between leisure time activities and habits with AD risk (Verghese et al., 2003).

I stress that patterns of mental and behavioral activity develop across the lifespan depending on their importance for individual adaptation, and they interact with both (epi)genetic mechanisms—leading to different gene expressions—and cultural resources. Thus, the interaction of genetics and lifestyles in culture explains development across the lifespan and differences in developmental outcomes. In such a scenario, specific genetic information will be triggered by specific experiences an individual has in a given environment resulting in a specific gene expression and leading to behavior—both mental and overt—that will become a habit and a lifestyle due to the instrumental adaptive value implied here. In such a way, the specific interactions that have taken place throughout the individual life reconstruct the apparent diversity in the developmental outcomes that will be observed in old age. Interactions are complex and challenge the logic of linear causal models across the involved disciplines here. Wagner (2004)[4] highlights the notion of interaction by succinctly stating,

The only proper word we have for what is going on in biology is interaction. Interaction means that the effect of a factor depends on many other so-called factors, and the dependency on context ensures that the explanatory currency drawn from measuring the effects of causal factors is very limited. (p. 1405)

Understanding the dynamics of memory functioning in a lifespan view will have to follow such a logic that puts the emphasis on interaction.

MEMORY FUNCTIONING AND ONTOGENESIS: CENTRAL CONCEPTS

As outlined previously, the conceptual meaning of the term memory is related to human information processing, where the term is used—in a narrow sense—for the processes and structures of storage and retrieval of sensory and conceptual information. These processes can involve explicit processing with explicit attention as well as the implicit processing of information, which highlights that memory and attentive processes are closely linked to one another. Processes that run under high attention focus and thus conscious awareness are considered as higher executive processes involving, for instance, volitional and decisional processes. Implicit processing involves habits in the previously mentioned sense that, due to repeated use, do not require implicit attention and thus no conscious awareness. Interestingly, ruptures in these processes trigger attentional processes that subsequently supervise the perception and memory processes with a higher level of consciousness, again highlighting the adaptive nature of human memory.

It seems that the memory process always starts with the process of perception— be it visual, auditory, tactile, olfactory, or taste—and it thus always implies a contact between the individual's inside and outside worlds. This contact can take the form of a bottom-up or data-driven process that assimilates information from the outside into the inner world, or it takes the form of a top-down or concept-driven process that processes information according to the representations and schemata available in individual memory structures. For the latter task, the terms "retrieval," "remembering," and/or "thinking" are used when the process requires explicit attention, but top-down processing runs mostly automatically without conscious awareness. All these processes involve the notion of a representation of the outer world; such a representation is constructed by perception as an (complex sensorial) experience, or it is an internal representation guiding the perception of the outer world. Memory processes thus include both internalization processes of encoding experiences with the outer world by meaningful signs and externalization processes producing signs in the world on the basis of a given memory content (Zittoun et al., 2013). Imagination plays a special and important role here because it uses memory contents and combines these to construct a concrete life situation (e.g., "Next weekend, I will go to Denmark") or an abstract, speculative, and/or fantastic image of life (e.g., "If I were a rock star, . . .").

In this context, "thinking" is imagination that is based on perceptual processes reflecting the accumulation of physical information that has been elaborated semantically. Depending on the acquisition and elaboration of such information, memory processing will lead to different contents and results. A person who does not see or does not hear properly will have a different way of processing sensory information and will therefore achieve a different structure of knowledge, which in turn will affect processes of thinking and imagination.

Associated with this is the question, "When does memory start in human onto-genesis?" The answer to this question will allow for rules of memory functioning across the lifespan to be identified. The discussion of memory in infancy is governed by the term *childhood amnesia*, which signifies that conscious memories before the age of 3 years are rare. An early study by Henri and Henri (1898) found contradictory evidence to support this, and Jack, Simcock, and Hayne (2012) prospectively showed that some children may reliably remember events that occurred before the age of 3 years. The question of when memory starts concerns additional notions besides the conscious use of memory contents: Attention, habituation, and adaptation play crucial roles here as well. Following an evolutionary perspective, one can assume that humans need memory functioning quite early in ontogenesis if they want to survive. An infant needs to habituate, for instance, to different noises and differentiate between his or her mother's voice and other voices that are not important for adaptation and survival. Infants thus build up internal neural representations used in the interaction with the external world that are additionally used in other interactions. This is convincingly demonstrated in experiments in which infants are confronted with a violation of expectation and that use attention span dedicated to novel and unexpected events as an indicator of memory functioning. In this type of experiment, infants view events that are consistent or inconsistent with their expectations. In a study by Wang, Baillargeon, and Brueckner (2004), 4-month-old infants watched a wide container disappear into a narrow container, and they showed a longer attention span to this event than in the consistent condition in which the narrow container disappeared into the wide container. Moreover, novel stimuli in general occupy more attention than familiar ones. These results indicate top-down processing using a mental representation that is needed to build up a violation of expectation (for further elaboration on childhood memories, see Nelson, Chapter 8, this volume).

Such a view highlights that memory is crucial for human functioning and adaptation, and I take the position here that the motive of "adaptation" underlies the development of memory. Adaptation basically means the satisfaction of basic and—with advancing development—acquired needs; the growing organism will easily comprehend by direct feedback from the environment which behavior is in this sense goal-directed and which is not. This will lead to specific cognitive–affective and behavioral links with the specific experience represented by neural substrates serving as a memory store. Habituation plays an additional significant role in this because it reduces the energetic load of the organism induced by the continued attention, and it will play a role in guiding the use of memory with advancing age. As soon as the organism has become familiar with specific stimuli, these will no longer require any further explicit attention, which guarantees parsimonious information processing. Habituation prepares a store of "knowledge" allowing for the matching of information in both the outside world and the inside

world. Habituation is thus also behind the formation of expectations—a violation
of expectation occurs only if there is no set of information allowing for the specific matching (Wang et al., 2004).

When using the term "memory store," I do not imply that knowledge is stored
and retrieved following a linear logic. "Knowledge" comprises dynamic information processing at different sensory levels using already stored information and is
open to elements of the current situation activating the specific knowledge structure. The concept of schema proposed by Bartlett as "embodied, dynamic, temporal, holistic, and social concept" may better reflect the complex and dynamic
quality of these knowledge representations (Wagoner, 2013, p. 553). Following this,
memory acquires and uses schematic representations that are comprehensively
described as declarative memory comprising semantic and episodic memory as
well as implicit or procedural memory (Squire, 2004). Tulving (1985) described
these systems as constituting a "monohierarchical arrangement" in which procedural memory at the lowest level uses semantic memory as its specialized subsystem and uses semantic memory containing episodic memory as its specialized
subsystem. Tulving states that "in this scheme, each higher system depends on,
and is supported by, the lower system or systems, but it possesses unique capabilities not possessed by the lower system" (p. 387). Moreover, he characterizes the
three systems by different levels of consciousness: anoetic (not-knowing) consciousness at the procedural memory level, noetic (knowing) consciousness at
the semantic memory level, and auto-noetic (self-knowing) consciousness at the
episodic level. This distinction reflects the different states of awareness.

As previously discussed, the motive of adaptation to a given life situation may
be considered as the leading principle in memory development; thus, the "construction" and the interplay of these systems start early in life. Anoetic, procedural
knowledge reflecting a refinement of reflexes is the first system, and with advancing language acquisition, it is then combined with noetic, semantic contents—that
is, the construction of meaning by the assignment of specific signs to phenomena
of the outside world. Recognizing the self, experiencing the difference to others, and reflecting the self as an object produce auto-noetic episodic evidence
that is accumulated across the lifespan. Squire (2004) highlights that declarative
and nondeclarative memory represent these different parts of the human memory, with the former comprising aspects of noetic and auto-noetic contents and
the latter covering the anoetic procedural components. As an example, Squire
explains that an aversive childhood event such as being bitten by a dog can lead to
a stable childhood memory as well as a long-lasting fear associated with autonomous reactions stored in the nondeclarative part of the human memory system.
Thus, the auto-noetic knowledge structure can be considered as being interlinked
with both noetic and anoetic knowledge. Specific life experiences (e.g., a dog
bite) find their neurological substrate eliciting reflexes and habits that have been
stored in the anoetic consciousness (e.g., autonomous excitation leading to flight
reflex) and are also represented as ego-relevant information in the auto-noetic
part (e.g., "I do not like dogs; I am afraid of dogs") that may be subject to interpretation using information from the noetic part of memory (e.g., there are different

ways to explain the dog's behavior). The more symbolic knowledge a person has acquired, the more different his or her evaluation of an event may be. Here, the link between memory stores and the self becomes quite evident.

MEMORY AND THE SELF

The concept of awareness of age-related changes by Diehl and Wahl (2010) refers "to all those experiences that make a person aware that his or her behavior, level of performance, or ways of experiencing his or her life have changed as a consequence of having grown older (i.e., increased chronological age)" (p. 340). The authors elaborate that differing states of awareness are triggered by experiences residing both within (e.g., subjective feelings of diminished capacity) and outside the person (e.g., reactions by others and social structural conditions). The awareness of age-related changes—reflecting the high probability of physical and functional impairments and losses associated with chronological age—sets the starting point for self-regulation theories that focus on old age. The aging organism loses physical strength, there are evident changes in visual appearance, physical speed and agility decline, and so on. Moreover, there is evidence of a decline in the speed of information processing and memory functioning. Salthouse (1996) described the degrading effects of reduced speed on cognitive performance that are already present in middle adulthood. According to Salthouse, slower processing impairs the successful execution of relevant operations (i.e., encoding, elaboration, search, rehearsal, retrieval, integration, and abstraction) due to limited time, and products of early processing may no longer be available when later processing is complete, which he denotes as simultaneity.

Models of self-regulation, describing the adaptive potentials of the aging self, state that despite these changes, individual life satisfaction and self-esteem are not (necessarily) affected, and they link this to the use of self-regulatory strategies. Several models specify such processes at the individual level, assuming that the older person actively selects goals, optimizes existing capacities, and compensates losses (Baltes, 1997). The dual-process model proposed by Brandtstädter and co-workers (e.g., Brandtstädter & Greve, 1994) supposes—in line with Piaget—that persons in general assimilate experiences into their cognitive schemata, thus confirming their view of the self and the world; if this is no longer possible, they immunize themselves against self-threatening experiences (e.g., by selective comparisons) or accommodate their cognitive schemata. The motivational theory of lifespan development proposed by Heckhausen, Wrosch, and Schulz (2010) highlights the differential use of primary and secondary control in the pursuit of developmental and personal goals across the lifespan, and the authors reconstruct individual adaptive capacity by the self-regulation of motivational processes.[5]

The use of memory in this context serves to validate, preserve, and enhance the self (see Brown & Reavey, Chapter 7, this volume). Awareness of aging requires the comparison of individual experiences with a mental standard of functioning.

If there is a divergence, for example, in the cognitive performance of retrieving action-relevant knowledge, the person may attribute this to personal factors not linked with age (e.g., tiredness) or to external factors (e.g., aspects of the task), or the person may attribute this to the fact that he or she is aging. In coming to this last conclusion, one has to use individual and culturally shared standards about functioning. Here, one may identify individual standards reflecting specific life-time experiences that also include standards of the social and cultural context. Age awareness can be considered as processing information under the threat of self-deprecating conclusions if one considers age and aging as a threat. The evaluation of aging and age reflects culturally shared meanings using biological, medical, economic, and other scientific aspects as well as stereotypical images with different affective valence attached to aging. On the other hand, culture not only provides the frame of evaluation but also offers resources to develop and promote memory functioning.

Memory and Culture

According to Valsiner (2007), the concept of culture implies a "constructive modification of the natural course of affairs" in a way that natural events are transformed into meaningful objects. In this understanding, cultural knowledge belongs to a person and is used in both intra- and interpersonal interaction and discourses. Valsiner elaborates that the meanings of objects have their own "cultivated value" and objects have their own "cultural biographies." In such an understanding, memory and memory functioning are subject to cultural construction resulting in different meanings depending on the specific cultural and historical context. The term memory is a cultural construction of a "natural course of affairs" describing the act of perceiving and associating specific phenomena with a term denoted as "memory." As an early illustration, I refer to Aristotle (340 BC), who described memory as follows:

> Memory is, therefore, neither Perception nor Conception, but a state or affection of one of these, conditioned by lapse of time. As already observed, there is no such thing as memory of the present while present, for the present is object only of perception, and the future, of expectation, but the object of memory is the past. All memory, therefore, implies a time elapsed; consequently only those animals which perceive time remember, and the organ whereby they perceive time is also that whereby they remember.[6]

Thus, the object of memory is the past, and the process of using memory includes perception of time. I use this quotation because I think that this logico-deductive understanding still underlies most definitions of memory that are shared both in the scientific and in the public use of the term. There are no memories of the future—and never will be, unless they are used as a play on words.

If one takes up the previously quoted notion proposed by Baltes (1997) that culture represents "the entirety of psychological, social, material, and symbolic (knowledge-based) resources that humans have generated over the millennia, and which . . . are transmitted across generations" (p. 368), one may reconstruct especially the assistive effect of culture on human memory in diverse and different ways. Here, I distinguish between technologies dedicated to this goal and symbolic resources aiming at the understanding and the construction of meaning underlying memory changes across the lifespan. In this, I also make a distinction between the transfer of declarative and mostly noetic information and the part of memory, including the nondeclarative part, involving anoetic and autonoetic information.

Education and Technology Promoting Memory Development and Performance

If one defines memory performance as the willing acquisition, storage, and retrieval of declarative knowledge, all educational and training activities serve memory development. Primary and secondary socialization set the frame for knowledge transfer between different generations, and this transfer will only work if the memory structure is open and willing to assimilate and accommodate the incoming information. Culture provides educational resources across the lifespan that help to build up knowledge and memory structures. This starts very early in life in the form of early childhood education and training, continues by means of educational programs into adulthood, and is then taken up by lifelong learning programs. In addition, culture provides technological and material means that help the storage and retrieval of information across the lifespan. Memory aides comprise different tools, including early childhood rhymes that help in learning language as well as technologies ranging from paper-and-pencil notes to complex electronic devices that help plan one's activities. In addition, assistive culture provides pharmacological means that support and aim to prevent weakening memory functions.

Demographic change and the growing prevalence of neurodegenerative disorders have further contributed to assistive efforts that will help to compensate or prevent memory loss as the symptom and predecessor of potential functional decline due to irreversible neurodegeneration. Some examples will illustrate these endeavors. Memory clinics and training programs are offered that address the preclinical stage of dementia when mild cognitive problems appear, thus serving as a means of secondary prevention. Evidence shows that the preclinical stage can be diagnosed up to a maximum of 10 years before the clinical stage of the disease (Buchhave et al., 2012), and such early psychosocial interventions should thus help to prevent or slow the disease outbreak as well as foster the delay of institutionalization. These early stage programs mostly include different constituents such as physical activation, social integration, and cognitive activation aiming at better memory performance. Evidence concerning their efficiency is mixed (Koivisto et al., 2016).

When dementia is diagnosed and one is in need of care, several additional approaches can be followed to compensate memory loss. Icons and pictures are used when language is no longer available. Home and other types of accommodations are reconstructed, thus possibly becoming "smart homes" that will supervise daily routines and help prevent accidents. In general, assistive technologies in old age have gained increasing importance both in research and consumer settings. It is assumed that technology can be used at all three levels of prevention—that is, primary, secondary, and tertiary—to improve quality of life and functioning of older adults who require different stages of support.

Two examples illustrate the rapid development of assistive technology during the past two decades. Gerontechnology is a "hybrid" discipline comprising gerontology and engineering and technology development aiming at the study of those factors that ensure an optimal technological environment corresponding to the needs of all older adults. Bouma, Fozard, Bouwhuis, and Taipale (2007) differentiate five domains of daily life in which gerontechnology can intervene: housing and daily living, mobility and transport, communication and information, work and leisure, and health and self-esteem (with this fifth domain combining physical and psychological health). These gerontechnological interventions should aim at four goals, namely (1) enhancement and satisfaction, (2) prevention and engagement, (3) compensation and assistance, and (4) care support and organization. Reflecting the increasing need for and development of this discipline since its inception in 2001, the journal *Gerontechnology* offers publications on the diverse aspects of technology use.[7] The European Commission has implemented the Active and Assistive Living (AAL) program, which has provided funding for "projects in public–private partnership in the field of information and communication technology (ICT) for active and healthy ageing since 2008."[8] The goals of this program are twofold: to enhance the quality of life of older adults at the individual level and to strengthen the industrial base in Europe through the use of ICT at the societal level. All these activities aim at assisting a person in his or her daily life to preserve a physical and functional status thus allowing an autonomous life for as long as possible.[9]

Culture in its notion as assistive culture thus provides a range of knowledge and technology resources that will help by offering material resources and assistance to adapt to the changing life situation in old age. The central question underlying the use of assistive technology, however, is how to motivate older adults to use a given technology because technology solutions do not receive unequivocal acceptance by potential end users or may be used in different ways, thus serving different motivational functions (Leist & Ferring, 2011). At first glance, the use of technologies seems to be evident because a given technology is "assistive" and, in being so, it serves the purpose of compensating and supporting a person. On the other hand, accepting an assistive technology requires a person to admit that he or she is in a position of dependence and need, which is certainly not so easily accepted. I present a case history to illustrate this point. An 84-year-old woman

living independently in her own apartment started experiencing vertigo: Her children asked her to use a telecare device in the form of a medical alarm bracelet
that contained a red button to be pressed in case of emergency that would set off
an alarm at a nearby community center. The use of this device as it was intended,
however, was limited because the woman did not wear it but, rather, displayed it
in her living room, proudly showing it to visitors and commenting that it was a
present from her children to show how much they care about her. The assistive
device thus received a completely different function and was not used in the way
it had been designed.

There is a further open question regarding technology use that touches on the
ethical issue of autonomy limitation. One example of this is the use of monitoring technologies in the context of progressed dementia. Applying a bracelet with
a sensor—such as those used in the penal system—clearly limits individual free
movement. On the other hand, it seems obvious that a person suffering from
dementia may become completely lost and run the risk of injury when moving
around. Measures such as video cameras or movement sensors, which may be
used in "smart" environments to allow people to live independently as long as
possible, also hold this ethical dilemma. The very act of observation renders the
person dependent and no longer capable of dealing with his or her own life situation. This may lead to confirmation of a self-view as dependent, which is counterproductive to the original goals of these technologies.

Symbolic Resources, Narratives, and Memory

Memory is crucial for "culture" because memory performance constitutes the
basis of storytelling, sharing information, and developing narratives that comprise the "collective memory" of social groups of families, clubs, or even nations
(see Shore & Kauko, Chapter 4, this volume; Wertsch, Chapter 11, this volume).
In this, memory and culture show a mutual interplay. Following this logic, what is
forgotten ceases to exist or has even never existed before. Oral history has become
written history in many societies, and using these resources defines what "reality" is in a given cultural context. Deleting memory is thus a process of reality
construction, and this is well described in George Orwell's (1949) *1984*, in which
the protagonist, Winston Smith, works in the Ministry of Truth destroying collective memories. Cultural knowledge as an intra- and interindividual resource
thus depends on the availability of memory contents and the ability to retrieve
and use these.

I use the notion of *symbolic resources* in a broad sense to cover the exchange of
signs and symbols that convey meaning to experiences that the individual and the
group share at a given time. In general, these resources are of high importance,
especially if experiences occur that are new or not expected by the person and/or
group (see de Saint Laurent & Zittoun, Chapter 9, this volume). Here, symbolic
resources serve to construct narratives that help establish meaning by describing
and explaining new experiences. Culture provides the frame for self-description

by providing a set of norms, values, practices, artifacts, and institutions that influence individual information processing and reasoning (Markus & Kitayama, 2010). In this, culturally shared signs of various kinds constitute memory contents via internalization as well as memory use by externalization. Moreover, a person constitutes his or her own private culture by selectively internalizing and externalizing cultural signs (Zittoun et al., 2013).

The topic of memory in old age has been accorded specific attention and has gained importance in both the public and the scientific discourse as an indicator of a larger cultural discourse in many societies. This is certainly due to the increased prevalence of dementia, but the process of aging itself is subject to socially shared stereotypes that link old age and growing old with deteriorating physical, functional, and cognitive status (Hummert, 1999). This may lead to stereotyping of older adults—both unconsciously and consciously—thus influencing behavior and communication toward them (Hummert, 1994), as well as self-stereotyping by older adults, leading to both worse general performance and worse memory performance (Levy, 2003).

Poor memory performance and the loss of specific memory contents are considered principal symptoms of cognitive decline leading to neurodegenerative disease. The causes of poor memory performance, however, are diverse and thus leave a certain interpretative space that may be used by the concerned older adult as well as his or her social network. Not knowing the objective causes of these diseases also characterizes this situation as not well-defined. As Weiner (1995) elaborated in his attribution theory approach, individual information processing follows a general model of linear causality that links causes to effects. Diseases with unknown causes or that have several causes with differing impact lead to uncertainty within social groups. Following such logic, the control of known causes may also control the outbreak of the disease. The need for control may thus lead persons to try to identify the causes of a specific disease even though these or their relative contribution are not known. This may then lead to blaming and stereotyping disease victims as responsible for their own fate without any evident objective causality.

Several diseases of which the causes are not well understood have challenged society and the individual, resulting in a symbolic reconstruction of the underlying causes. Tuberculosis or consumption, for instance, has thus become a part of music, literature, and films (Chalke, 1962). This is illustrated by Verdi's *La Traviata*, Puccini's *La Bohème*, and Thomas Mann's *Zauberberg*—three examples of cultural resources dealing with a phenomenon that comprises a threat to the individual and society. AIDS represents another illustration of how threats with unknown genesis are treated. In a 1997 book review, Robert Plunkett formulated the need for literary speculation in his introductory statement as follows:

> There are certain situations that are so dramatic, so filled with moral complexity, so much a matter of life and death that they become irresistible subjects for literary speculation. Some are acts of God; some are all too manmade. And some seem to come out of the blue, in unimaginable ways—like

AIDS. People have been writing novels about AIDS for the past 15 years; they will probably be doing it a hundred years from now.[10]

Cancer leaves interpretative space about its possible causes for both patients and their social context, resulting in different narratives about the disease (Ferring & Filipp, 2000). Finally, dementia "arrives" and poses new threats and questions, reflecting uncertainty about its causes. Again, it is interesting to follow how many cultural productions are created to help explain and deal with the phenomena. There are movies as well as novels describing the fate of persons and their families affected by these diseases. Productions such as these help the general public become acquainted with the development of symptoms and their progress while simultaneously offering role models for dealing with these challenges.

The "private culture" shared within a family also plays a significant role in perceiving and evaluating memory performance and the eventual loss of memory. Families share stories about diseases and how to deal with them, and they maintain ideas about age and aging as well. All this is based on the (selectively) remembered history of a family and is transmitted across family generations. Some events gain significance given their eminent effect on the whole family system, and they constitute an important part of the family history (see Shore & Kauko, Chapter 4, this volume). For example, there may be a story of a grandfather who suffered from dementia for many years in old age, thus requiring extensive care by family members as well as straining the financial resources of the family. All this is important because it may even threaten the existence of the family. Family members will contemplate how to prevent such a disease and may thus be more open to specific information. Moreover, they may also develop lay theories about why the person got the disease (e.g., genetics and lifestyle) that will have direct consequences for their own behavior, depending on their experienced instrumentality. Apparently, a family without such an experience will exhibit different behaviors to deal with aging, especially when the family history holds examples of persons living to a distinguished old age without any major impairments. Knowledge of such events is stored at the procedural, semantic, and—depending on the closeness of the experience—episodic levels, implying anoetic, noetic, and autonoetic consciousness in the sense proposed by Tulving (1985). This knowledge, when retrieved at the different levels, may thus trigger reactions and/or reflexes, semantic elaborations, or self-referential thoughts and behavior.

As dynamic systems theory (Zittoun et al., 2013) and systemic family therapy suggest, families tend to reproduce their identity, which is defined by the experiences that shape family life and that contribute to its "survival" across time. Family identity is nothing that is written down but, rather, is an autopoietic process serving to maintain identity by the interaction of family members. Generations within families thus share certain experiences (e.g., war, migration, and loss of a loved one), leading to values, practices, and even "family norms" for this specific generation if they prove to be adaptive. For instance, a family may learn that parsimoniousness guarantees survival, and this will be a value that is practiced and forwarded to future generations even though these future family members may miss the specific experience leading to this lifestyle. Sharing meaning within the family can be a process of willfully sharing information in the form of "oral history" elaborating semantics of an event with a message about how things were. But (mostly) the sharing of values and practices is also regulated by the interplay of acting and reacting within a given family at the anoetic level. These latter processes reflect the value system of a family, setting the frame for accepting and rewarding specific behavior or avoiding and even sanctioning it. Here, it becomes evident that families have a memory of their own that exerts its influence on their members even though most experiences leading to a certain memory store of values, norms, and practices may not be known at all by the younger generation.

This is of particular importance with regard to aging and old age, as mentioned previously. The adult son may thus help his mother find a misplaced key and react in an irritated way because he is reminded of a story of "losing things" as a sign of a possible disease that had already occurred within this family. An elderly woman may tell stories about her youth and everyone is delighted or—in another case—they ask her to please stop. Both reactions depend on the shared meaning of a behavior—that is, its potential consequences for the family as it is stored in family memory. This notion also comprises the idea of "private cultures" of single persons as depicted by Valsiner (2007), although these may clearly show an idiosyncratic character.

In summary, memory within culture may be reconstructed at the level of the individual and the surrounding microsystems up to the macrosocial level to use parts of the heuristic model of socioecological environment provided by Bronfenbrenner (1979). Memory in itself thus represents a co-construction of actors between the individual and those at different levels of the social context.

CONCLUSION

This chapter provided insight into the dynamics of memory development in a lifespan perspective. Emphasis was placed on the period of old age, which has become increasingly important in countries experiencing demographic changes due to lower fertility and longer life expectancies. The chapter showed that memory is a multifaceted phenomenon at both the individual level and the collective level. Moreover, and most essential, memory always involves the construction of meaning underlying people's personal experiences. It represents the interface between the internal and the external worlds and is used across all ages of the lifespan to both internalize and externalize experiences. In light of this, memory loss—as it is experienced by persons affected with a neurodegenerative disease— is a threat to meaning and thus the understanding of the self and the world, and it affects all persons involved in such a process. It is no wonder that there is a huge investment in assistive culture to prevent or compensate losses here. This chapter also discussed how semiotic resources are used to cope both at the individual level and at the collective level when irreversible changes have happened.

How the concerned person constructs meaning when memory starts decreasing and how he or she experiences this changed reality represent questions that need further study.

ACKNOWLEDGMENTS

I am deeply grateful to Brady Wagoner, Lisa Trierweiler, and Isabelle Tournier for their comments on this chapter.

NOTES

1. See "Population Structure and Ageing" at http://epp.eurostat.ec.europa.eu/statistics_explained/index.php/Population_structure_and_ageing#Further_Eurostat_information (June 2014).
2. Retrieved from the German Alzheimer Association's website at http://www.deutsche-alzheimer.de/unser-service/archiv-alzheimer-info/auguste-d.html#c767 (May 2014).
3. For a popular science book on these issues, see Diamond (2012).
4. This statement can be found in Wagner's comment on Robert's (2004) book, *Embryology, Epigenesis, and Evolution: Taking Development Seriously.*
5. All these efforts require a certain level of awareness and cognitive functioning, and one may mention here that the conditions for applying these models to a person affected by a neurodegenerative disease may no longer be given in the course of this disease, thus challenging at the individual level the conceptual significance of the term adaptation (Ferring, 2015).
6. Aristotle. (340 BC). *On memory and reminiscence* (J. I. Beare, Trans.). Adelaide, Australia: University of Adelaide. Retrieved from https://ebooks.adelaide.edu.au/a/aristotle/memory.
7. For an overview, see http://journal.gerontechnology.org/archives.aspx.
8. See http://www.aal-europe.eu/about.
9. As they aim at elaborating and strengthening ICT economy.
10. Robert Plunkett (1997, November 16). Love in the times of AIDS. *The New York Times.* Retrieved October 2015 from https://www.nytimes.com/books/97/11/16/reviews/971116.16plunket.html.

REFERENCES

Anderson, L. A., Day, K. L., Beard, R. L., Reed, P. S., & Wu, B. (2009). The public's perceptions about cognitive health and Alzheimer's disease among the U.S. population: A national review. *The Gerontologist, 49,* S3–S11.

Andrews, B. R. (1903). Habit. *American Journal of Psychology, 14,* 121–149.

Ballard, C., Gauthier, S., Corbett, A., Brayne, C., Aarsland, A., & Jones, E. (2011). Alzheimer's disease. *The Lancet, 377,* 1019–1031.

Baltes, P. B. (1997). On the incomplete architecture of human ontogeny: Selection, optimization, and compensation as foundation of developmental theory. *American Psychologist, 52,* 366–380.

Baltes, P. B., & Smith, J. (2003). New frontiers in the future of aging: From successful aging of the young old to the dilemmas of the fourth age. *Gerontology, 49,* 123–135.

Baltes, P. B., & Staudinger, U. M. (2000). Wisdom: A metaheuristic (pragmatic) to orchestrate mind and virtue toward excellence. *American Psychologist, 55*(1), 122–136.

Bouma, H., Fozard, J. L., Bouwhuis, D. G., & Taipale, V. (2007). Gerontechnology in perspective. *Gerontechnology, 6,* 190–216.

Brandtstädter, J., & Greve, W. (1994). The aging self: Stabilizing and protective processes. *Developmental Review, 14,* 52–80.

Bronfenbrenner, U. (1979). *The ecology of human development.* Cambridge, MA: Harvard University Press.

Buchhave, P., Minthon, L., Zetterberg, H., Wallin, A. K., Blennow, K., & Hansson, O. (2012). Cerebrospinal fluid levels of β-amyloid 1–42, but not of tau, are fully changed already 5 to 10 years before the onset of Alzheimer dementia. *Archives of General Psychiatry, 69,* 98–106. doi:10.1001/archgenpsychiatry.2011.155

Chalke, H. D. (1962). The impact of tuberculosis on history, literature, and art. *Medical History, 6,* 301–318.

Coppieters, N., & Dragunow, M. (2011). Epigenetics in Alzheimer's disease: A focus on DNA modifications. *Current Pharmaceutical Design, 17,* 3398–3412.

Cowgill, D. O., & Holmes, L. D. (Eds.) (1972). *Aging and modernization.* New York: Appleton-Century-Crofts.

Diamond, J. (2012). *The world until yesterday: What can we learn from traditional societies?* New York, NY: Penguin.

Diehl, M., & Wahl, H. W. (2010). Awareness of age-related change: Examination of a (mostly) unexplored concept. *Journals of Gerontology B: Psychological Sciences and Social Sciences, 65B,* 340–350.

Ferring, D. (2010). Intergenerational relations in aging societies: Emerging topics in Europe. *Journal of Intergenerational Relationships, 8*(1), 101–104.

Ferring, D. (2015). Alzheimer's disease: Behavioral and social aspects. In J. D. Wright (Ed.), *International encyclopedia of the social & behavioral sciences* (2nd ed., pp. 584–590). Oxford, UK: Elsevier.

Ferring, D., & Filipp, S.-H. (2000). Coping as a "reality construction": On the role of attentive, comparative, and interpretative processes in coping with cancer. In J. Harvey & E. Miller (Eds.), *Loss and trauma: General and close relationship perspectives* (pp. 146–165). Philadelphia, PA: Brunner-Routledge.

Gokhale, J., & Kotlikoff, L. J. (2001). *Is war between generations inevitable?* NCPA Policy Report No. 246. Dallas, TX: National Center for Policy Analysis. Retrieved from http://www.ncpa.org/pdfs/st246.pdf

Heckhausen, J., Wrosch, C., & Schulz, R. (2010). A motivational theory of life-span development. *Psychological Review, 117,* 32–60.

Henri, V., & Henri, C. (1898). Earliest recollections. *Popular Science Monthly, 53,* 108–115.

Hull, C. (1943). *Principles of behavior.* New York: Appleton-Century.

Hummert, M. L. (1994). Stereotypes of the elderly and patronizing speech. In M. L. Hummert, J. M. Wiemann, & J. F. Nussbaum (Eds.), *Interpersonal communication in older adulthood: Interdisciplinary theory and research* (pp. 162–184). Newbury Park, CA: Sage.

Hummert, M. L. (1999). A social cognitive perspective on age stereotypes. In T. Hess & F. Blanchard-Fields (Eds.), *Social cognition and aging* (pp. 175–196). San Diego, CA: Academic Press.

Jack, F., Simcock, G., & Hayne, H. (2012). Magic memories: Young children's verbal recall after a 6-year delay. *Child Development, 83*, 159–172.

Koivisto, A. M., Hallikainen, I., Välimäki, T., Hongisto, K., Hiltunen, A., Karppi, P., . . . Martikainen, J. (2016). Early psychosocial intervention does not delay institutionalization in persons with mild Alzheimer disease and has impact on neither disease progression nor caregivers' well-being: ALSOVA 3-year follow-up. *International Journal of Geriatric Psychiatry, 31*(3), 273–283.

Leist, A., & Ferring, D. (2011). Technology and aging: Inhibiting and facilitating factors in ICT use. In R. Wichert, K. van Laerhoven, & J. Gelissen (Eds.), *Constructing ambient intelligence: AM1 workshops. Revised selected papers* (pp. 163–165). Berlin, Germany: Springer.

Levenson, J. M., & Sweatt, J. D. (2005). Epigenetic mechanisms in memory formation. *Nature Reviews Neuroscience, 6*, 108–118.

Levy, B. R. (2003). Mind matters: Cognitive and physical effects of aging self-stereotypes. *Journals of Gerontology B: Psychological and Social Sciences, 58*, 203–211.

Markus, H. R., & Kitayama, S. (2010). Cultures and selves: A cycle of mutual constitution. *Perspectives on Psychological Science, 5*, 420–430.

Orwell, G. (1949). *1984*. London, UK: Secker & Warburg.

Peel, E. (2014). "The living death of Alzheimer's" versus "Take a walk to keep dementia at bay": Representations of dementia in print media and carer discourse. *Sociology of Health & Illness, 36*, 885–901.

Pillemer, K. (2015). *30 Lessons for loving: Advice from the wisest Americans on love, relationships, and marriage*. New York, NY: Hudson Street Press.

Ramakers, I. H. G. B., & Verhey, F. R. J. (2011). Development of memory clinics in the Netherlands: 1998 to 2009. *Aging & Mental Health, 15*, 34–39.

Robert, J. S. (2004). *Embryology, epigenesis, and evolution: Taking development seriously*. Cambridge, UK: Cambridge University Press.

Rowe, J. W., & Kahn, R. L. (1998). *Successful aging*. New York, NY: Pantheon.

Salthouse, T. (1996). The processing-speed theory of adult age differences in cognition. *Psychological Review, 103*, 403–428.

Snowdon, D. A., Kemper, S. J., Mortimer, J. A., Greiner, L. H., Wekstein, D. R., & Markesbery, W. R. (1996). Linguistic ability in early life and cognitive function and Alzheimer's disease in late life: Findings from the Nun Study. *Journal of the American Medical Association, 275*, 528–532.

Squire, L. R. (2004). Memory systems of the brain: A brief history and current perspective. *Neurobiology of Learning and Memory, 82*, 171–177.

Thomae, H. (1963). Ageing and problems of adjustment. *International Social Science Journal, 15*(3), 366–376.

Tulving, E. (1985). How many memory systems are there? *American Psychologist, 40*, 385–398.

United Nations, Department of Economic and Social Affairs, Population Division. (2013). *World population ageing*. New York, NY: Author. Retrieved from http://www.un.org/en/development/desa/population/theme/ageing/WPA2015.shtml

Valsiner, J. (2007). *Culture in minds and society: Foundations of cultural psychology*. London, UK: Sage.

Verghese, J., Lipton, R. B., Katz, M. J., Hall, C. B., Derby, C. A., Kuslansky, G., . . . Buschke, H. (2003). Leisure activities and the risk of dementia in the elderly. *New England Journal of Medicine, 348*, 2508–2516.

Wagner, G. P. (2004). The embryo of a dialogue. *Science, 305*, 1405–1406.

Wagoner, B. (2013). Bartlett's concept of schema in reconstruction. *Theory & Psychology, 23*, 553–575.

Wang, S., Baillargeon, R., & Brueckner, L. (2004). Young infants' reasoning about hidden objects: Evidence from violation-of-expectation tasks with test trials only. *Cognition, 93*, 167–198.

Weiner, B. (1995). *Judgments of responsibility: A foundation for a theory of social conduct*. New York, NY: Guilford.

Wortman, M., Andrieu, S., Mackell, J., & Knox, S. (2010). Evolving attitudes to Alzheimer's disease among the general public and caregivers in Europe: Findings from the IMPACT survey. *Journal of Nutrition, Health & Aging, 14*, 531–536.

Wright, N., & Lindesay, J. (1995). A survey of memory clinics in the British Isles. *International Journal of Geriatric Psychiatry, 10*, 379–385.

Zittoun, T., Valsiner, J., Vedeler, D., Salgado, J., Gonçalves, M. M., & Ferring, D. (2013). *Human development in the life course: Melodies of living*. Cambridge, UK: Cambridge University Press.

PART IV

Memory, History, and Identity

National Memory and Where
to Find It

JAMES V. WERTSCH ■

In today's interconnected, "flat" world, nationalism was supposed to be a thing of the past. Instead, it has remained very much a part of the global scene, although perhaps in a different form than in previous centuries (Brubaker, 1996). For example, Moscow sought to justify its attempts to dismember Ukraine in 2014 by appealing to common Russian national identity; in Vladimir Putin's view, Ukrainians and Russians are "not simply close neighbors" but, rather, "one people." In Asia, the appeal to national identity has also been part of recent political discourse, especially in China, where the Communist Party has increasingly turned to nationalist ideas to replace Marxist ideology for legitimacy (Lieberthal, 1995).

A key ingredient in all these identity projects is national memory. In Russia, this is reflected in Putin's calculated use of *Novorossiya* ("New Russia"), a term derived from the 18th century when Catherine the Great expanded the Russian Empire into the Black Sea region. Well aware of the patriotic response it would elicit among Russians, Putin suggested that annexing Crimea was part of a natural process of reconstituting the new Russia in the 21st century. In China, a cornerstone of the new nationalism is the campaign dubbed "Never forget national humiliation" (Wang, 2012). This well-known expression is a stark reminder of how much the Chinese Communist Party is counting on memories of colonial domination by European powers and Japan to mobilize the Chinese population today.

But what *is* national memory? For starters, we can say that it is part of a broader discussion of cultural psychology (Cole, 1996), memory studies (Wertsch & Roediger, 2008), and, specifically, collective memory. Given the massive resources and power that modern states devote to promulgating official accounts of their past, national memory presents a special case in this regard. These efforts at promulgation represent the largest and most sustained collective memory project in history. The national "mnemonic communities" (Zerubavel, 2003) that have grown up around them have proven capable of pursuing grand and worthy causes, but often they have also succumbed to what Amartya Sen (2006) calls "illusions of destiny" that foster brutal conflict.

National memory has been studied by a wide array of scholars and disciplines, and this is both a strength and a weakness. The strength derives from the richness of scholarship in history, political theory, sociology, and anthropology; the weakness derives from the fact that each of these disciplines has outlined ideas that often take little notice of what others have said. Hence, there is a need to search for points of integration. In what follows, I seek to do this by asking two basic questions: What is national memory? and Where can we find it? As it turns out, it probably makes more sense to ask these questions in reverse order because depending on where and how we search for national memory, we end up with different answers about what it is.

The question of where to search for national memory is seldom raised explicitly, but it is reflected in choices that investigators make about the methods they employ. Should we use content analysis to examine history textbooks? Ethnographic methods to interpret visitors' reactions to national holidays and monuments? Surveys to assess people's knowledge about historical events and figures? Historical analysis of how national memory has emerged and changed? These methods, along with others, have been employed when studying national memory, and they have yielded important insights. Each method provides only a partial picture, however, and some, including methods I have employed elsewhere (Wertsch, 2002), can take national memory out of living context in a way that misses some of its most vibrant aspects. For example, analyses of history textbooks can provide insight into what students know in a fairly neutral cognitive sense, but they tell us little about what will be effective in mobilizing members of a community around a national cause.

In an attempt to address these issues, I propose to outline two metaphorical "locations" where we can employ multiple analytic perspectives to examine national memory in its living context. The point about context provides a reminder of the importance of examining active, situated processes of *remembering* (Bartlett, 1932; Wertsch, 2002), as opposed to the more static orientation suggested by *memory* in English. One of the best places to examine active national remembering is the discursive space created when members of different mnemonic communities confront one another over the past. We often do not recognize or acknowledge the full outlines of our ideas until we find ourselves in confrontations over "what really happened" with members of other mnemonic communities, and the result is that we may end up making statements such as "I didn't realize how deeply I am committed to our version of the past until I started arguing with him." This discursive space can come into particular focus when national leaders invoke memory to mobilize the citizens of their country and to confront other mnemonic communities. These can be ideal locations for flushing into the open some of the deepest feelings and commitments that members of a community share about the past.

The second location I propose for the study of national remembering involves a different spatial metaphor, one of depth. In this case, the locations involve overt behaviors, on the one hand, and the underlying codes and habits we need to posit in order to understand the structure and motivation of these behaviors, on the other hand. Analyzing the surface form of what is said and written about the past can provide an incomplete, even misleading, picture if we do not complement this with the study of these underlying habits. In order to understand what surface utterances mean and why they can produce unbridgeable gulfs between national communities, we need to search for underlying codes that tie mnemonic communities together and separate them from each other. I argue that these are built around "narrative templates" that we must posit as investigators if we are to understand some of the more fascinating as well as dangerous aspects of national memory in the modern world.

NARRATIVE TOOLS AS SYMBOLIC MEDIATION

The line of reasoning I develop to address these issues has its foundations in notions of symbolic mediation in general and mediation by narrative tools in particular. In developing these ideas, I draw on the writings of Lev S. Vygotsky (1978, 1981, 1987) and other figures in Russia and Europe in the early decades of the 20th century. Their general argument was that humans are tool-using animals and that in order to understand human discourse and thought, it is essential to take the contribution of "cultural tools" (Wertsch, 2002) into account. For Vygotsky and others, such as Alexander R. Luria (1981), this meant turning first and foremost to natural language. Following in the footsteps of Wilhelm von Humboldt, Ernst Cassirer, and others in philology and semiotics, Vygotsky and Luria expanded the line of reasoning by examining psychological methods in a way that allows us today to incorporate insights from psychology, semiotics, sociology, and cognitive science into the broader picture of national memory. The crucial centerpiece that allows all these strands to be integrated is symbolic mediation.

Vygotsky was quite explicit about the centrality of mediation (*oposredstvovanie*) in his thinking, and in my view, it is the key to understanding the unique power of his ideas (Wertsch, 1985, 1991). Near the end of his life, Vygotsky (1982) asserted, "A central fact of our psychology is the fact of mediation" (p. 166). This had actually been a core part of his thinking for years, and a focus on mediation, especially as it concerns "signs" or "psychological tools," can be found throughout his writings. For example, in a 1930 account of "The Instrumental Method in Psychology" Vygotsky (1930/1981) included the following under the general heading of signs: "language; various systems for counting; mnemonic techniques; algebraic symbol systems; works of art; writing; schemes, diagrams, maps, and mechanical drawings; all sorts of conventional signs" (p. 137).

Such cultural tools are "by their nature . . . social, not organic or individual" (Vygotsky, 1930/1981, p. 137), which means that by mastering them, our speaking and thinking are socialized into a particular cultural and historical order. Vygotsky emphasized that this mastery involved transforming rather than simply facilitating existing social and mental functioning:

> By being included in the process of behavior, the psychological tool alters the entire flow and structure of mental functions. It does this by determining the structure of a new instrumental act just as a technical tool alters the process of a natural adaptation by determining the form of labor operations. (p. 137)

In making this argument, Vygotsky was part of a larger intellectual discussion of the time—a discussion that included figures such as Gustav Gustavovich Shpet (1927), a Russian student of Husserl and one of Vygotsky's teachers in Moscow, and the German philosopher Ernst Cassirer (1946, 1953, 1962, 1968). Although Cassirer was often dismissed by official Marxist–Leninist philosophers of the Soviet era for not being sufficiently materialist in his orientation, his insights had an important impact on Vygotsky, Bakhtin (1981), and many others who lived and wrote in the Soviet context.

Cassirer (1968) eschewed "the naive *copy theory* of knowledge" (p. 75) and noted that in science, for example, "the instruments with which it propounds its questions and formulates its solutions, are regarded no longer as passive images of something given but as *symbols* created by the intellect itself" (p. 75). From this perspective, human cognition and action are deeply shaped by "symbolic forms," which include, but are not limited to, language. Cassirer (1953) stressed that this is a double-edged sword, however, because "all symbolism harbors the curse of mediacy" in that "it is bound to obscure what it seeks to reveal" (p. 7). Taken together with Vygotsky's analyses of language as mediation in social and mental life, this means that to be human is to use cultural tools that are destined both to empower and to limit our understanding, including our understanding of the past. The aphorism by W. J. T. Mitchell (1990) that there is "no representation without taxation" comes to mind, and it applies nowhere more forcefully than in national narratives and memory.

Cassirer developed his insights by outlining how particular symbolic forms, such as myth, art, and science, hold the key to understanding the historical emergence and current state of human social and mental life. One of his most important interpreters, Susanne Langer (1949), summarized several of his points by noting that for Cassirer,

> the history of thought consists chiefly in the gradual achievement of factual, literal, and logical conception and expression. Obviously the only means to this end is language. But this instrument, it must be remembered, has a double nature. Its syntactical tendencies bestow the laws of logic on us; yet the primacy of names in its make-up holds it to the hypostatic way of thinking which belongs to its twin-phenomenon, myth. Consequently it led us

beyond the sphere of mythic and emotive thoughts, yet always pulls us back into it again; it is both the diffuse and tempered light that shows us the external world of "fact," and the array of spiritual lamps, light-centers of intensive meaning, that throw the gleams and shadows of the dream world wherein our earliest experiences lay. (pp. 391–392)

This line of reasoning finds parallels in the ideas that guided Vygotsky and his student and colleague Luria (1976) as they conducted their empirical studies in Central Asia in the 1920s. Employing oppositions that echoed those between the syntactical and hypostatic tendencies of language, they wrote of how "theoretic" forms of thinking differ from "practical" ones and how "higher" forms of mental functioning emerge out of "elementary" processes. However, in contrast to Vygotsky, who tended to set off the achievements of higher mental functioning from elementary forms, Cassirer made a point of emphasizing how even the most advanced forms of abstract thinking retain elements of what Langer called "the sphere of mythic and emotive thoughts."

Taken together, the ideas of Vygotsky and Cassirer suggest a world in which speaking and thinking are fundamentally shaped by the symbolic mediation, or cultural tools provided by historical, institutional, and cultural contexts. It is a world in which human mental and social life is socioculturally situated because of its reliance on these tools, including narratives, and these tools shape our thinking and speaking in multiple complex ways. Also in this context, the "double nature" of language as an instrument plays a complicating role in shaping narratives and memory.

In this approach, narrative tools do not mechanistically determine human discourse and thinking. Instead, the very notion of a tool implies an active user and suggests an element of variability and freedom stemming from the unique contexts of performance. Bakhtin (1986) made this point in his account of the speech utterance or "text." For him, any text involves a tension between two poles: a preexisting "language system" that provides the "repeatable" moment of an utterance, on the one hand, and a particular instance of speaking in a unique setting, which provides the "nonrepeatable" moment, on the other hand. All utterances reflect the influence of these two poles, but their relative weighting can vary widely. For example, a military command relies heavily on a language system and leaves little room for spontaneity, whereas informal discourse in everyday life relies more heavily on the unrepeatable, spontaneous pole.

Building on these ideas means that speaking and thinking about the past involve harnessing forms of symbolic mediation that are made available by the institutional and historical context in which an individual lives. When considering issues of national memory, the focus is on the narrative tools provided to members of a mnemonic community. What makes national collective memory collective in this view is that it is mediated by a shared "stock of stories" (MacIntyre, 1984), and the mediation involved brings with it the double nature of symbolic forms.

PROPOSITIONAL AND NARRATIVE TRUTH

The double nature of language outlined by Langer (1949) means that a national narrative has "syntactical tendencies" that "bestow the laws of logical on us" and "shows us the external world of 'fact'" (pp. 391–392). In what follows, these claims are associated with "propositional truth," which concerns the use of propositions to refer to and predicate about events, including events in a nation's past. On the other hand, the power of the "primacy of names" encourages "the hypostatic way of thinking" and "pulls us back into [myth and emotive thoughts] again" (p. 392). This is a tendency that I discuss under the heading of "narrative truth." Despite simplifying, discipline-based assumptions to the contrary—namely assumptions that it is possible to focus on one or the other of these tendencies in isolation— Cassirer and Langer assumed that they must be considered in tandem, and I attempt to do this in what follows.

Propositional truth has been a topic of discussion in analytic philosophy for more than a century. Debates about propositions and their use in making truthful assertions concerned figures such as P. F. Strawson (1950), and relatively recently John Searle (1979) continued this discussion in his reflections on how language can be used to make assertions with a "word-to-world" direction of fit. Assessing the truth of assertions about topics as complex as national history may require procedures for weighing evidence about this fit, and they can yield objective analysis and eventual social consensus. There is little doubt, for example, about the truth of the following statement: The American Civil War began in 1861. If someone were to claim that it began in 1761 or 1961, we would say this is not true, and if challenged, we could employ established, socially agreed upon procedures for consulting archives, memoirs, and other forms of evidence to resolve the matter and satisfy ourselves that our words fit the world in a true way.

Most hotly contested issues of national memory, however, do not arise over the truth of isolated propositions. Rather than being about particular dates or other facts as reported in propositions (or, more accurately, the use of propositions to make assertions), "mnemonic standoffs" (Wertsch, 2008) typically involve something deeper and more complex. They concern, for example, the emphasis that a mnemonic community gives to certain events and does not give to others or to its failure to recognize the "real" reasons and motives behind an action—in short, the sort of issues at the heart of narrative tools we use to represent the past. In such cases, we may respond, sometimes emotionally, that others' accounts are "just not true," but the dispute is over something other than propositional truth and no amount of information from archives, memoirs, or other forms of objective evidence may be capable of producing consensus.

These issues can even lurk in the background of seemingly simple assertions, such as the one presented previously about the beginning of the American Civil War. Although there is little disagreement about the date of 1861, stark differences regarding what events should be included in the story and the motives behind them come into focus when we consider referring expressions that stand in contrast with "the American Civil War"—expressions such as the "War Between the States" and the "War of Northern Aggression." Such referring expressions point to, or index, compressed narratives that are built into the very names (with their "hypostatic" tendencies) used in a seemingly straightforward proposition. Disputes over such episodes of naming are not about unadorned facts or their encoding in propositions. Instead, they are about the selection of some events and motives and the neglect of others—processes routinely accomplished by emplotting events in accordance with a particular storyline.

Kenneth Burke (1998) provided insight into this matter by observing that we use "literature as equipment for living" to name, and hence to "size up," a situation. For him, "*Madame Bovary* (or its more homely translation, *Babbitt*) is the strategic naming of a situation (p. 596)," and by naming it we know how to understand it. Burke made these points with regard to recurrent, everyday situations, but the same line of reasoning can be used to understand how we "size up" national events in the present or past. When we use a name such as "the War Against Northern Aggression," we are not simply picking out the same event as a referent that others call "the American Civil War." We are also sizing up an event from the past in accordance with one narrative tool that stands in stark contrast to another. This name "shows us the external world of 'fact,'" as Langer (1949, p. 392) stated, but it also "pulls us back into [myth and emotive thoughts] again" (p. 392).

What is crucial in all this is that narrative form contributes a unique kind of organization to our way of representing reality that goes beyond what propositions considered in isolation do. Also, along with an additional level of symbolic mediation comes an additional kind of truth claim. In a discussion of how this form of truth differs from that found in other, non-narrative forms of speech, or what he termed "direct discourse," the philosopher Louis Mink (1978) wrote,

> One can regard any text in direct discourse as a logical conjunction of assertions. The truth-value of the text is then simply a logical function of the truth-value of the individual assertions taken separately: The conjunction is true if and only if each of the propositions is true. . . . [In contrast] a historical narrative claims [narrative] truth not merely for each of its individual statements taken distributively, but for the complex form of the narrative itself. Only by virtue of such form can there be a story of failure or success, of plans miscarried or policies overtaken by events, of survivals and transformations which interweave with each other in the circumstances of individual lives and the development of institutions. (pp. 197–198)

We often appreciate the notion of narrative truth in some vague way, but it remains elusive and the source of confusion and frustration when we find ourselves in a mnemonic standoff. Speaking as members of mnemonic communities, we tend to assume that our utterances involve a word-to-world match of the sort that propositions have in the case of saying that the American Civil War started in 1861. We assume that we are stating the truth about what happened and that there are relatively straightforward procedures based on publicly available evidence to back up our claims. But as Mink and others have noted, there is an irreducible element of human choice and judgment involved in emplotting a set of events into a narrative, and for this reason there is no straightforward way to determine the "true" plot of an event on the basis of objective evidence.

William Cronon (1992) struggled with these issues in his analysis of the "place for stories" in historical writing. In reviewing two accounts by historians of the Dust Bowl in the American Southwest in the 1930s—one a "progressive" story of human determination and victory over adversity and the other a "tragic" form about human arrogance and hubris in the modern age that reflects "romantic and antimodernist reactions against progress" (p. 1352)—he notes that the accounts are so distinct that they "make us wonder how two competent authors looking at identical materials drawn from the same past can reach such divergent conclusions" (p. 1348). Cronon goes on to observe, "Although both narrate the same broad series of events with an essentially similar cast of characters, they tell two completely different *stories*" (p. 1348), and this leads him to observe that "the historical analysis derives much of its force from the upward or downward sweep of the plot" (p. 1348).

Both Mink and Cronon were concerned with the discipline of history, where scholars are called upon to observe the highest standards of documentation and rational argumentation. However, even in this context—with its explicit procedures for authenticating facts and strong sanctions for getting them wrong, with its insistence on not leaving out possible countervailing evidence, and with its methods for avoiding bias—there is no clear route to finding the right or true narrative to emplot a set of events. Historians are still left with the question, "Where did these stories come from?" (Cronon, 1992, p. 1348), and the point for Mink (1978) is that they do not—indeed cannot—come from a simple aggregation of the propositional truths. Instead of relying only on the techniques for evaluating the truth of propositions, a separate element of "judgment" (Mink, 1978) or "grasping together" (Ricoeur, 1984) must be involved. These are issues that come through with even greater force when we turn to how national memory, as opposed to history, produces accounts of the past.

AN ILLUSTRATION: USING WORLD WAR II TO REMEMBER THE 2008 WAR BETWEEN RUSSIA AND GEORGIA

As an example of how narrative truth plays out in the discursive space of confrontation between two mnemonic communities, consider Russian and Western accounts of the August 2008 war with Georgia. The "Russo-Georgian War" or "Five Day War" was a short but vicious conflict conducted largely in South Ossetia and Abkhazia, two breakaway regions of Georgia. It began on the night of August 7/morning of August 8 with a Georgian bombardment of Tskhinvali, a city in South Ossetia. This was followed within hours by a large-scale incursion of the Russian army into South Ossetia and Abkhazia and the rapid defeat of Georgian forces in these two regions and elsewhere in the territory of Georgia. The Russian invasion and aerial bombardment of these two areas, and of other regions within Georgian territory, continued for several days until a ceasefire was called at the urging of the international community.

Precisely what happened in this conflict remains contested. The most comprehensive and objective official account to date grew out of an independent fact-finding mission headed by the Swiss diplomat Heidi Tagliavini (2009) of the Council of the European Union. Her analysis concluded that Georgian forces opened fire first on the night of August 7/morning of August 8 but that Russia had made provocative moves beforehand and then proceeded to respond to the Georgian bombardment in a massively disproportionate way. Although the report's conclusions are widely accepted in the international community, they continue to be disputed by officials and the public both in Russia and in Georgia.

Russian leaders uniformly frame the 2008 war in a way that rejects any hint that aggression, let alone expansionism, on their part was involved. Instead, they present a picture in which the real agenda of Georgia was to create a launching point for NATO aggression against Russia. From this perspective, the Russian incursion into the breakaway Georgian enclave of South Ossetia was in response to outside aggression and an act of legitimate pre-emption—as well as liberation of the Ossetian population, many of whom indeed did side with Russia.

This perspective comes through very clearly in statements made by Russian leaders and media during and immediately after the August 2008 war—statements that were motivated in part by attempts to "spin" the conflict in a way that would shape the memory of it (Wertsch & Karumidze, 2009). For example, while the conflict was occurring, Vitali Churkin, the Russian ambassador to the United Nations, asserted in a US television news interview on August 12, 2008, "of course Russia was the victim."[1] This came as something of a surprise to Georgian and Western observers, given the massive invasion of Georgian territory by Russian armed forces. Churkin, however, viewed the bombardment in South Ossetia by the Georgian army on the opening night of the conflict as another instance in which a Russia that had been living peacefully and with no intention of interfering in the affairs of others was attacked without provocation.

A more detailed version of this interpretation can be found in comments made by Putin a few weeks after the war. Speaking to an international group of journalists and scholars of Russia[2] on September 11, 2008, he said,

> One of the most difficult problems today is the current situation in the Caucasus: South Ossetia, Abkhazia and everything related to the recent tragic events caused by the aggression of the Georgian leadership against these two states. I call them "states,"[3] because, as you know, Russia has made a decision to recognise their sovereignty.

In his statement, Putin presents "the aggression of the Georgian leadership" as objective fact or simple truth about what happened, and he spoke as if this is something that any reasonable person would recognize. In fact, however, it was a claim that was being actively challenged at the time. As such, Putin's statement could be interpreted as his attempt at spinning the event in an ongoing struggle against others, again pointing to the fraught discursive space of national remembering at the borders of confrontation between mnemonic communities. From all indications, however, Putin did not see it as involving spin at all. Instead, he seemed to be asserting what he took to be obvious truth, suggesting the conviction of deeply held belief.

During this news conference, British journalist Jonathan Steele made a point of noting that the opening salvo of the war was fired by Georgian forces and involved "atrocities" against South Ossetians. Steele went on to say, however, that the "moral high ground" had then shifted to Georgia as Russian forces pursued their attack beyond South Ossetia. Putin's response was one of incredulity, indicating that in his view this was not a matter of values or opinion at all but, rather, of truth, namely a sort of truth that anyone would agree with if they just had access to the facts. According to him, propaganda efforts by Western leaders and media had obscured this truth:

> You know, your question doesn't surprise me. What really surprises me is how powerful the propaganda machine of the so-called "West" is. This is just amazing. This is unbelievable. This is totally incredible. And yet, it's happening. Of course, this is because, first, people are very susceptible to suggestion. Second, ordinary people usually don't follow world events that closely. So, it is very easy to misrepresent the actual course of events and to impose somebody else's point of view. I don't believe there is one person among us here who is not familiar with the facts. At least in this room, everybody knows perfectly well how the events unfolded in reality. I have given the true account on several occasions, including my recent interviews with CNN and ARD.

It may be difficult for Western readers to understand why the army of Russia's small neighbor to its south should be such a threat to a large powerful country like itself, but Putin went on to make clear what he and others in Russia viewed as the real force of aggression:

> Our American partners kept training the Georgian military. They invested a lot of money there. They sent a large number of instructors there, who helped mobilize the Georgian army. Instead of looking for a solution to the difficult problem of ethnic strife and ethnic conflicts, they just prompted the Georgian side to launch a military operation. This is what actually happened.

Putin was, to be sure, an outspoken proponent of the claim that Georgia and NATO, rather than Russia, were the aggressors in this conflict, but his perspective reflected the general views of his mnemonic community. A survey conducted a few weeks after his comments in 2008 by the Levada-Centre, an independent Russian polling group, asked Russian citizens about the main reason for the conflict in South Ossetia, and nearly half of respondents (49%) answered that the conflict was caused by the United States attempting to exert greater influence in the Caucasus and incite tension between Russia and Georgia. Only 5% said that the conflict stemmed from a "divide and rule" strategy by Russian leadership, the only answer that attributed responsibility for the conflict to Russian aggression in any way.[4] The interference of the United States clearly provided strong explanatory power for Russian citizens, particularly the portrayal of the United States as contributing to the tensions between Russia and Georgia. A year after the war, another poll of Russian public revealed that opinion remained largely unchanged.

THE ROLE OF NARRATIVE TEMPLATES IN SYMBOLIC MEDIATION

The gulf that divides the Russian account of what happened during the 2008 war from the way it is remembered in Europe or the United States provides a case study of a discursive space in which opposing national memories surface in stark form. But getting to the bottom of this mnemonic standoff requires exploring another sort of metaphorical space, namely one between surface forms of discourse and the underlying codes we need to posit in order to make sense of them.

In Putin's 2008 press conference, for example, an underlying code is the key to understanding what led him to invoke World War II as a way of bolstering his claims about the "true account" of what happened in Georgia. In responding to questions about the Russian incursion into Georgia in 2008, he said,

> Now let's remember how WW2 started. On September 1 [1939], Nazi Germany attacked Poland. Then they attacked the Soviet Union [in 1941]. What do you think the Russian Army should have done? Do you think it should have reached the [German] border and stopped there?

Putin posed this rhetorical question in a way that appears to assume no one could possibly fail to see the logic of the analogy he was using and the power of his argument, but in fact it reflects a very Russian perspective. From that viewpoint, the parallel between World War II and the 2008 war is obvious and telling, and the reason was that both reflect the same underlying storyline. In contrast, to members of other mnemonic communities, linking these two conflicts appears strange, if not based on a superficial and insincere attempt at rhetorical manipulation. However, such gaps in understanding are precisely what are to be expected when the narrative truth claims of two mnemonic communities clash.

In drawing his analogy between what the Red Army did in Germany in 1945 and what the Russian army did in Georgia in 2008, Putin was assuming that the two events have the same plot line and that this provides insight into what happened in 2008. To him, it was the same story with different characters. This is an assumption that stems from the fact that the two events instantiate the same general underlying code and associated habits around which his mnemonic community is organized. This underlying code is a generic narrative used to make sense of repeated invasions by foreign enemies. This schematic story begins with alien enemies inflicting great suffering and humiliation on Russia, followed by their eventual defeat through the valiant efforts of the Russian people bound together by a distinctive spiritual heritage. It is a story that has been played out with different characters for centuries, including the Mongols (13th century), the "Germans" (Teutonic knights) from the same period, the Poles (16th century), the Swedes (18th century), the French (19th century), and the Germans again (20th century).

In each case, the invasion is recounted by using a "specific narrative" (Wertsch, 2002) that includes concrete information about setting, dates, and characters. The following is an illustration of a specific narrative:

On June 22, 1941, the German forces invaded the USSR brutally and without warning. After huge losses in the summer and fall of 1941, the Soviet Army stopped the Germans in Moscow, and they went on to defeat the Hitlerite invaders in Stalingrad, Kursk, and other major battles leading up to the March to Berlin and total defeat of Germany in 1945.

This qualifies as a specific narrative because it includes concrete information about actors, times, and places, and for this reason, it differs from other specific narratives such as the one about Napoleon's invasion in the 19th century. At the same time, however, this specific narrative about World War II employs the same basic plot line as the account of Napoleon and other invaders, suggesting the existence of a narrative template (Wertsch, 2002).

An initial inclination on the part of many is to assume that these multiple specific narratives of victory over invaders follow the same basic plot because the events in fact unfolded in a similar way. To be sure, Russia has suffered repeated invasions, and the point is not to deny this or to suggest that events in history are a mere figment of the Russian imagination. However, the pattern of interpreting these events has become so deeply embedded over centuries that members of the Russian mnemonic community sometimes have difficulty seeing events in any other way—even when others vehemently object to their interpretation.

For example, the 2008 conflict with Georgia was readily emplotted in Russia as another act of aggression by an alien enemy, but this contrasts sharply with the interpretation of people in countries such as Ukraine, Estonia, and Poland, let alone Georgia, who tend to view it as another episode of Russian expansionism. The Russian community's powerful habits for emplotting events produce several other surprises for members of other mnemonic communities as well. For example, major figures in post-Soviet Russia have discussed communism as an invasion by Western ideologies aimed at destroying their nation—a view that is surprising to many non-Russian audiences.

The general pattern of interpretation at issue reflects the socialization experience of repeated exposure to specific narratives with similar plot lines and leads members of the Russian mnemonic community to interpret events in a similar way—namely as threats from outside enemies. Based on an array of evidence (Wertsch, 2002) about this interpretive pattern, I have outlined the "expulsion-of-alien-enemies" narrative template as follows:

1. There is an "initial situation" in which Russia is peaceful and not interfering with others.
2. Then there is "trouble," in which a foreign enemy viciously attacks Russia without provocation.
3. Russia comes under existential threat and nearly loses everything in total defeat as it suffers from the enemy's attempts to destroy it as a civilization.
4. Through heroism and exceptionalism, against all odds, and acting alone, Russia triumphs and succeeds in expelling the foreign enemy.

As a narrative template, this is a theoretical entity posited to make sense of various texts and behaviors. As such, it is not something that appears in the form of surface utterances as specific narratives do, and this raises the question of what evidence supports claims about its existence. For starters, I note that members of the Russian mnemonic community, as well as others who are familiar with Russia's actions, readily agree that the expulsion-of-alien-enemies narrative template rings true. But beyond such subjective impressions, it is noteworthy that when asked about their history, Russians often run off a list of invasions (the Mongols, the Germans, the Poles, the French, the Germans again, and so forth), placing them side by side as similar. In some cases, the very names for past events reflect assumptions that the same story with different characters is at issue: Napoleon's invasion in the early 19th century, for example, is known in Russia as the Patriotic War (*Otechestvennaya voina*), and Hitler's invasion in the 20th century is known as the Great Patriotic War (*Velikaya otechestvennaya voina*). Expanding on a quip attributed to Mark Twain, we might say that history does not repeat itself (in specific narratives), but it does rhyme (with the help of narrative templates).

A crucial function of narrative templates is that they provide the foundation for assessing claims about narrative truth. In contrast to the kinds of evidence that we use to assess propositional truth, our judgments of narrative truth rely on these underlying codes and shared habits of mnemonic communities. Beyond being just a theoretical observation, this is critical for understanding—and perhaps even transcending—mnemonic standoffs. For example, it is useful for understanding Putin's frustration over how anyone in his audience could not know the "facts" of the 2008 war, how they could not know "perfectly well how the events unfolded in reality," and how they could deny that he had "given the true account on several occasions"—when in fact many in the audience did not view the situation this way at all. Recognizing the role of narrative templates in such encounters provides a means for standing back, gaining conceptual perspective, and dealing rationally with contradictory narrative truths.

NARRATIVE HABITS AS SYMBOLIC MEDIATION

In psychological terms, the quick, unreflective tendency to make judgments about narrative truth suggests the role of habit, a notion that has long played a role in discussions of memory, especially with regard to differentiating levels or kinds of memory. The psychological literature on this dates back at least to Henri Bergson's 1896 volume *Matter and Memory* (*Matière et mémoire*). Bergson (1896/ 2010) distinguished between two ways in which "the past survives" in humans: in "*motor mechanisms*" and second in "*independent recollections*" (p. 40, emphasis in original).

Bergson (1896/2010) proposed this distinction as part of an argument about the foundational role of memory in human mental functioning, including perception. In this formulation, "instantaneous intuition, on which our perception of the external world is developed, is a small matter compared with all that memory adds to it" (p. 34). Bergson had in mind the role of memory in, for example, the perception of visual images, but his general claim about how "instantaneous intuition" shapes "our perception of the external world" can be taken in a broader sense and applied to complex events in social and political history.

Nearly a century after Bergson was writing, Paul Connerton (1989) harnessed his observations on memory as bodily habit in his analysis of "how societies remember." Connerton begins by outlining two sorts of memory that both differ from habit memory and would qualify as forms of Bergson's independent recollection. The first is "personal memory," which corresponds roughly with what Endel Tulving (1972) called "episodic memory" or perhaps with what others have termed "autobiographical memory," and it is concerned with "those acts of remembering that take as their object one's life history" (Connerton, 1989, p. 22). The second is "cognitive memory," which corresponds roughly with Tulving's category of "semantic memory"—that is, memory that is not tied to any particular experience or episode in one's own experience. For Connerton, this sort of memory is about "the meaning of words, or lines of verse, or jokes, or stories, or the lay-out of a city, or mathematical equations" (p. 22).

Connerton (1989) notes that personal memory and cognitive memory have been studied extensively, especially in psychology, whereas "habit-memory, has for important reasons been largely ignored" (p. 25). In contrast to the "two heavily colonised territories" of personal memory and cognitive memory, "habit-memory . . . appears to be an unoccupied or non-existent space" (p. 28), and Connerton takes it to be the key to understanding much of the power of collective memory.

In developing these claims, Connerton (1989) draws on the ideas of Michael Oakeshott (1962/1991) about moral activity. For Oakeshott, a large part of moral life is a matter of "a habit of *affection* and *conduct* [in which] the current situations of a normal life are met, not by consciously applying to ourselves a rule of behaviour . . . but by acting in accordance with a certain habit of behaviour" (p. 467). He stresses that moral life "does not spring from the consciousness of possible alternative ways of behaving and a choice, determined by an opinion, a rule or an ideal, from among these alternatives; conduct is as nearly as possible without reflection" (p. 468).

Turning to the source of moral life, Oakeshott (1962/1991) asserts,

> We acquire habits of conduct, not by constructing a way of living upon rules or percepts learned by heart and subsequently practised, but by living with people who habitually behave in a certain manner: We acquire habits of conduct in the same way as we acquire our native language. (p. 468)

Oakeshott also notes that this form of morality does not lend itself to sudden, revolutionary changes. Instead, it "gives remarkable stability to the moral life from the point of view either of an individual or of a society; it is not in its nature to countenance large or sudden changes in the kinds of behavior it desiderates" (470).

A final point of elaboration on these ideas concerns the confidence with which we act on the basis of habit. In his account of "fast thinking," Daniel Kahneman (2011) outlines a form of automatic, nonconscious decision-making that shares many properties with habit and often leads to overconfidence in our conclusions. A hallmark of this "System 1" thinking in Kahneman's account is that it often focuses exclusively on information that is activated in attentional space at the time a decision is made, which is studied under the heading of "priming" in studies of cognition and memory (Roediger, 1990). The upshot is that fast thinking "excels at constructing the best possible story that incorporates ideas currently activated [i.e., primed], but it does not (cannot) allow for information it does not have" (Kahneman, 2011, p. 85). Fast thinking "operates as a machine for jumping to conclusions" (p. 85) that is unconstrained by slower, more reflective, "System 2" thinking, in part because of System 2's inherent "laziness" to step in and do the more arduous work of thoroughly assessing the validity of conclusions.

The overconfidence associated with System 1 thinking is due in part to its narrowed attentional focus that allows for speed. In contrast to System 2 thinking, which requires conscious attention and takes into consideration various forms of evidence, when following the dictates of fast thinking, "We often fail to allow for the possibility that evidence that should be critical to our judgment is missing— what we see is all there is" (Kahneman, 2011, p. 85), and the confidence we have in such judgments is often much greater than is merited.

Taken together, Bergson, Connerton, Oakeshott, and Kahneman present a picture in which much of remembering can be viewed as a matter of habit, with the implication that it is shaped by "instant intuition" (Bergson, 1896/2010) and "does not spring from the consciousness of possible alternative ways of behaving and a choice" (Oakeshott, 1962/1991, p. 468). Furthermore, these habits are acquired by daily experience such as that of living with members of a language community (Oakeshott, 1962/1991), and they allow for fast thinking that is often overconfident in what it decides. In the case of narrative templates, the habits are built around plot lines, and they provide the basis for assessing narrative truth, with the implication being that different national mnemonic communities with their different narrative habits can easily derive accounts of the past that stand in fundamental contradiction.

As Mink and Cronon emphasize, narratives involve an irreducible element of subjective judgment, a point that applies to specific narratives as well as narrative templates, and this means that narrative-based habits inevitably involve an element of subjectivity and bias. This is precisely what gives rise to frustration in mnemonic standoffs such as the one Putin seemed to be having with Western views on the 2008 War. An additional source of this frustration is that we often believe our arguments are over propositional truth, whereas they really are primarily about narrative truth, and we jump to conclusions about narrative truth because largely invisible narrative templates narrow our view in ways we do not recognize.

MANAGING MNEMONIC STANDOFFS

In the previous sections, I outlined an account of national memory that encourages a view that differences between mnemonic communities are stark, confrontational, and intractable. Fortunately, there are means at our disposal for ameliorating such pessimism. The ones I have in mind rely on bringing to light and, it is hoped, ameliorating the power of the narrative tools that shape our membership in mnemonic communities. They are consistent with Bartlett's comments on "turning around upon schemata" (Wagoner, 2013) and with attempts by figures such as Rauf Garagozov (2013) to encourage "narrative reconciliation." The two strategies I present are (1) using analytic history to check national memory and (2) encouraging irony and humility about the narrative truths we hold as members of national mnemonic communities.

Using Analytic History to Check National Memory

Using history to check national memory presupposes a distinction between history and memory in the first place, but this is a distinction that is questioned by some analysts. Indeed, it is not unusual to encounter claims that there is no solid line that can be drawn between these two ways of relating to the past, but I argue that it is not only possible but also ethically necessary to distinguish them (for a more thorough review of the issue, see Carretero and van Alphen, Chapter 12, this volume). This is a distinction that has been at the heart of countless discussions in modern historiography. For example, in his classic 1882 article "What Is a Nation?" Ernst Renan argued that national memory and history are not simply different but exist in tension, and relatively recently, Pierre Nora (1989) has made stronger claims of this sort in arguing that "memory and history, far from being synonymous, appear now to be in fundamental opposition. . . . History is perpetually suspicious of memory, and its true mission is to suppress and destroy it" (pp. 8–9).

For his part, Maurice Halbwachs (1980), the founder of modern collective memory studies, noted that "formal history" (p. 78) strives to create a "universal memory of the human species" (p. 84), a goal that he viewed as standing in opposition to collective memories that belong to, and in part define, groups. Jan Assmann (1997) has placed memory and history in a system that relates them in a broader picture that is more nuanced and principled. Assmann begins *Moses the Egyptian* with an example that lays this out:

> Unlike Moses, Akhenaten, Pharaoh Amenophis IV, was a figure exclusively of history and not of memory. Shortly after his death, his name was erased from the king-lists, his monuments were dismantled, his inscriptions and representations were destroyed, and almost every trace of his existence was obliterated. For centuries, no one knew of his extraordinary revolution. Until his rediscovery in the nineteenth century, there was virtually no memory of Akhenaten. Moses represents the reverse case. No traces have ever been found of his historical existence. He grew and developed only as a figure of memory, absorbing and embodying all traditions that pertained to legislation, liberation, and monotheism. (p. 23)

Assmann goes on to note that the distinction between history and memory is often more complex than suggested by this example and warns against assuming an "all-too antiseptic conception of history as 'pure facts' as opposed to the egocentrism of myth-making memory" (p. 23). Instead, he proposes that they are related because "history turns into myth as soon as it is remembered, narrated, and used, that is, woven into the fabric of the present" (p. x).

Weaving history into the fabric of the present is usually done in the service of self-interested identity projects, making the past into *our* past and one that appears to be less distant and separated from our present. Peter Novick (1999) noted collective memory's tendency to deny the "pastness" of events in general and "insist on their continuing presence" (p. 4). From this perspective, memory turns out to be "in crucial senses ahistorical, even antihistorical" (p. 3).

In creating a continuing presence of the past, a mnemonic community tends to streamline accounts of events in self-interested ways. Rather than being a conscious, reflective strategy, however, this is often built into the narrative tools and habits of a mnemonic community, with all the overconfidence associated with them. In particular, narrative templates with their proclivity for mythic and hypostatic thinking make it possible to ride roughshod over inconvenient facts, and the upshot for collective memory is that it "sees events from a single, committed perspective; is impatient with ambiguities of any kind; reduces events to mythic archetypes" (Novick, 1999, pp. 3–4). In contrast, analytic history is more inclined to acknowledge the complexity of the past and must have "sufficient detachment to see it from multiple perspectives, to accept the ambiguities, including moral ambiguities, for protagonists' motives and behavior" (p. 4). In a certain sense, there is a rough parallel between memory and history, on the one hand, and Kahneman's fast thinking and slow thinking, on the other hand.

How does the distinction between history and memory help us with regard to bridging the gulf between mnemonic communities? Specifically, how might analytic history be harnessed as a means for fostering productive discussion in overcoming mnemonic standoffs? As Cronon (1992) and Mink (1978) observed, we can never deduce narrative truth from the procedures used to assess propositional truth, so it might appear to be misguided to engage in argument at all. In fact, however, we do this all the time, striving to create accounts of the past that are more comprehensive and hence more accurate in the sense that they recognize ambiguity of motive, complexity of events, and multiplicity of perspectives. For example, the official historical account provided by Tagliavini (2009) outlined previously is more adequate and comprehensive than either the Georgian or the Russian account in this way and as a result is not completely satisfactory to either of these national mnemonic communities—a sign that it does not coincide with either community's memory project. It stands in opposition to both because Tagliavini's account is not framed as a simple, neat narrative of good versus evil, which is a strength because it acknowledges complexity but is a weakness because it is less likely to be easily remembered and used in public discussion.

Despite continuing criticisms of the shortcomings of analytic history, we generally recognize the importance of gaining Novick's (1999) "sufficient detachment" to review all the evidence about an event and produce a balanced and publicly defended account of what happened. In contrast to collective memory, such accounts are always open to further revision in an ongoing dialogue of critique and rebuttal, and there is nothing sacrosanct about the narrative used to emplot events. Given the power of narrative templates in mnemonic communities, we are asking experts to carry out a nearly impossible task, but the alternative is blind adherence to a single, simple narrative truth backed by relentless propaganda or just brute force.

Encouraging Irony and Humility About Our Narrative Truths

Along with the rational procedures of analytic history, there is another element to how we relate to the past that can bode well for transcending mnemonic standoffs: allowing for humility and irony. Our first thought when trying to overcome confrontations with other mnemonic communities is to learn more about them. Discussions about improving international understanding are filled with calls for increased appreciation of other groups' perspectives as a path toward mutual understanding. However, this often overlooks the need to reflect on our own views as well.

Such self-reflection requires a level of effort, coupled with equanimity and humility, that most of us find difficult to maintain. It is difficult to enlist any mnemonic community in a project of critical self-reflection and humility without seeming to suggest that it should give up its deeply held commitments to national narratives and memories. Given how central national narratives are to identity projects, this is an unrealistic expectation, however, and the challenge is instead to allow for the maintenance of national memories while simultaneously subjecting them to critical reflection that requires humility and allows for irony. We may find it easy to identify flaws in *other* communities' accounts of the past that we believe should lead to doubt, but it is much more difficult to acknowledge similar challenges to our own.

Some useful guidelines for how this can be done are provided in *The Irony of American History* by Reinhold Niebuhr (1952/2008). In this slim volume, which Andrew Bacevich (2008) has called "the most important book ever written on US foreign policy" (p. ix), Niebuhr struggled to understand how America found itself in the post-World War II years in a position it had never anticipated. Having spent much of its history focused on carrying out its experiment in democracy within its own borders, it was suddenly faced with tasks in the international arena that went against its isolationist proclivities. Niebuhr outlined his views in the early 1950s, but his reflections continue to resonate.

For Niebuhr (1952/2008), the basic problem is that "modern man lacks the humility to accept the fact that the whole drama of history is enacted in a frame of meaning too large for human comprehension or management" (p. 88). As a Christian theologian, he formulated human shortcomings in terms of the "original sin" of "egoism" that afflicts all humans, regardless of the period in history or type of society in which they live. For him, this is a tendency that has especially dire consequences in international relations because "nations are more consistently egoistic than individuals" (Niebuhr, 1944/2011, p. 182).

Niebuhr (1952/2008) outlined these views in the early years of the Cold War when

> we find it almost as difficult as the communists to believe that anyone could think ill of us, since we are persuaded as they that our society is so essential virtuous that only malice could prompt criticism of any of our actions. (pp. 24–25)

In the terms outlined previously, this amounts to a warning against the pitfalls of fast thinking based on habits framed by national narrative templates, which all too readily support the conclusion that "nations (and for that matter, all communities as distinguished from individuals) do not easily achieve any degree of self-transcendence" (p. 169). Fortunately, Niebuhr also believed that "even the collective behaviour of men stands under some inner moral checks" (p. 169), and this provides grounds for optimism.

In America's case, Niebuhr (1952/2008) noted, "we came into existence with the sense of being a 'separated' nation, which God was using to make a new beginning for mankind." However, in order to help his readers recognize the limitations of this national story, which had been overtaken by the rapid growth in American power, he urged them to recognize the deep irony involved—an irony that in his view should encourage humility about the American belief in its mission as a beacon of liberty. Specifically, irony requires

> an observer who is not so hostile to the victim of irony as to deny the element of virtue which must constitute a part of the ironic situation; nor yet so sympathetic as to discount the weakness, the vanity and pretension which constitute another element." (p. 153)

For those who are deeply certain that America is a beacon of liberty, it is all too easy to see the "element of virtue" they bring to the table and to overlook "the vanity and pretension"; however, for observers from other national perspectives, just the opposite may prevail. Niebuhr's (1952/2008) point is that *both* must be held in mind at the same time to appreciate the ironic situation and the challenges it brings to efforts to overcome misunderstanding and recrimination. Similar points, of course, apply to the narratives and memories of other national communities.

CONCLUSION

By searching for national memory in the space created when one mnemonic community confronts another and by recognizing the power of narrative templates to produce the confident judgments and impatience for moral ambiguity, it is easy to become pessimistic about the possibility of transcending the limitations of transcending mnemonic standoffs. This is especially so given that disputes about what happened in the past are formulated in terms of truth rather than opinion or ideology. Coupled with a focus on symbolic mediation, especially in the form of narrative tools, examining the two metaphorical spaces I have outlined in this chapter allows us to gain some analytic distance from the passions that often inflame international conflict. I have explored claims about narrative templates, habits, and fast thinking to help unpack the nonconscious processes that bias us in ways we are unlikely to recognize. It is often not difficult to see such bias in other national mnemonic communities, but self-reflection on our own perspective is more challenging.

   Fortunately, we have at least two means at our disposal for reining in the dangerous proclivities of national memory. Analytic history provides a way of relating to the past that differs from the tendencies of national memory. While recognizing the irreducible element of judgment involved in all narrative account, analytic history has institutionalized a set of practices that serve as checks and balances on the fast, unexamined conclusions about the past we draw as members of a mnemonic community. Also, by having the humility to accept that human events are "enacted in a frame of meaning too large for human comprehension or management" (Niebuhr, 1952/2008, p. 88), we can find some means for taming some of the most dangerous implications of national memory projects.

NOTES

1. See http://www.pbs.org/newshour/bb/europe/july-dec08/georgiadeal_08-12.html.
2. Russia has no imperial ambitions—Putin. (2008, September). *Russia Today*. Retrieved from http://www.russiatoday.com/news/news/30316.
3. Before the 2008 conflict, South Ossetia was part of Georgian territory, and it has not been recognized as independent by the nations that are members of the UN General Assembly except for Russia, Nicaragua, Venezuela, Nauru, and Tuvalu.
4. K godovschine voennogo konflikta na Kavkaze. (2009, July 17). *Levada-Centre*. Retrieved from http://www.levada.ru/press/2009080401.html.

REFERENCES

Assmann, J. (1997). *Moses the Egyptian: The memory of Egypt in Western monotheism*. Cambridge, MA: Harvard University Press.

Bacevich, A. J. (2008). Introduction. In R. Niebuhr, *The irony of American history* (pp. ix–xxi). Chicago, IL: University of Chicago Press.

Bakhtin, M. M. (1981). *The dialogic imagination: Four essays* (M. Holquist, Ed.). Austin, TX: University of Texas Press.

Bakhtin, M. M. (1986). *Speech genres and other late essays* (M. Holquist, V. McGee, & C. Emerson, Eds.). Austin, TX: University of Texas Press.

Bartlett, F. C. (1932). *Remembering: A study in experimental and social psychology*. Cambridge, UK: Cambridge University Press.

Bergson, H. (2010). *Matter and memory* (N. M. Paul & W. S. Palmer, Trans.). Overland Park, KS: Digireads. (Original work publishes 1896)

Brubaker, R. (1996). *Nationalism reframed: Nationhood and the national question in the New Europe*. Cambridge, UK: Cambridge University Press.

Burke, K. (1998). Literature as equipment for living. In D. H. Richter (Ed.), *The Critical Tradition: Classic Texts and Contemporary Trends*. Boston: Bedford Books (pp. 593–598). (First published in 1938)

Cassirer, E. (1946). *The myth of the state*. New Haven, CT: Yale University Press.

Cassirer, E. (1953). *Language and myth*. New York, NY: Dover.

Cassirer, E. (1962). *An essay on man*. New Haven, CT: Yale University Press.

Cassirer, E. (1968). *The philosophy of symbolic forms*. New Haven, CT: Yale University Press.

Cole, M. (1996). *Cultural psychology: A once and future discipline*. Cambridge, MA: Harvard University Press.

Connerton, P. (1989). *How societies remember*. Cambridge, UK: Cambridge University Press.

Cronon, W. (1992). A place for stories: Nature, history, and narrative. *Journal of American History*, 78(4), 1347–1376.

Ernest Renan, "Qu'est-ce qu'une nation?", conference faite en Sorbonne, le 11 Mars 1882, Accessed January 13, 2011.

Garagozov, R. (2013). Implicit measures of attitude change via narrative intervention in the Karabakh conflict. *Dynamics of Asymmetric Conflict: Pathways Toward Terrorism and Genocide*, 6(1–3), 98–109. doi:10.1080/17467586.2013.861919

Halbwachs, M. (1980). *The collective memory*. New York, NY: Harper & Row.

Kahneman, D. (2011). *Thinking, fast and slow*. New York, NY: Farrar, Straus, & Giroux.

Langer, S. K. (1949). On Cassirer's theory of language and myth. In P. A. Schilpp (Ed.), *The philosophy of Ernest Cassirer* (pp. 381–400). La Salle, IL: Open Court.

Lieberthal, K. (1995, November). A new China strategy: The challenge. *Foreign Affairs*, 2–15.

Luria, A. R. (1976). *Cognitive development: It cultural and social foundations*. Cambridge, MA: Harvard University Press.

Luria, A. R. (1981). *Language and cognition* (J. V. Wertsch, Ed.). New York, NY: Wiley Intersciences.

MacIntyre, A. C. (1984). *After virtue: A study in moral theory*. Notre Dame, IN: University of Notre Dame Press.

Mink, L. (1978). Narrative form as cognitive instrument. In R. H. Canary & H. Kozicki (Eds.), *The writing of history: Literary forms and historical understanding* (pp. 129–149). Madison, WI: University of Wisconsin Press.

Mitchell, W. J. T. (1990). Representation. In F. Lentricchia & T. McLaughlin (Eds.), *Critical terms for literary study* (pp. 11–22). Chicago, IL: University of Chicago Press.

Niebuhr, R. (2008). *The irony of American history*. Chicago, IL: University of Chicago Press. (Original work published 1952)

Niebuhr, R. (2011). *The children of light and the children of darkness: The vindication of democracy and a critique of its traditional defense*. Chicago, IL: University of Chicago Press. (Original work published 1944)

Nora, P. (1989). Between memory and history: Les lieu de mémoire. *Representations, 26*, 7–24.

Novick, P. (1999). *The Holocaust in American life*. Boston, MA: Houghton Mifflin.

Oakeshott, M. (1991). On being conservative. In *Rationalism in politics and other essays* (pp. 407–437). Indianapolis, IN: Liberty Fund. (Original work published 1962)

Ricoeur, P. (1984). *Time and narrative*. Chicago, IL: University of Chicago Press.

Roediger, H. L. (1990). Implicit memory: Retention without remembering. *American Psychologist, 45*(9), 1043–1056.

Searle, J. R. (1979). A taxonomy of illocutionary acts. In J. R. Searle (Ed.), *Expression and meaning: Studies in the theory of speech acts* (pp. 1–19). Cambridge, UK: Cambridge University Press.

Sen, A. (2006). *Identity and violence: The illusion of destiny*. New York, NY: Norton.

Shpet, G. G. (1927). *Vnutrenniaia forma slova. Etiudy i variatsii na temy Gumbol'dta* [*The inner form of the word: Lessons and variations on Humboldt's theme*]. Moscow, Russia: Gos. Akademiia Khudozhestvennykh Nauk.

Strawson, P. F. (1950). On referring. *Mind, New Series, 59*(235), 320–344.

Tagliavini, H. (2009). *Independent international fact-finding mission on the conflict in Georgia*. Report of the Council of the European Union, Brussels, Belgium.

Tulving, E. (1972). Episodic and semantic memory. In E. Tulving & W. Donaldson (Eds.), *Organization of memory* (pp. 381–403). New York, NY: Academic Press.

Vygotsky, L. S. (1978). *Mind in society: The development of higher psychological processes* (M. Cole, V. John-Steiner, S. Scribner, & E. Souberman, Eds.). Cambridge, MA: Harvard University Press.

Vygotsky, L. S. (1981). The instrumental method in psychology. In J. V. Wertsch (Ed.), *The concept of activity in Soviet psychology* (pp. 134–147). Armonk, NY: Sharpe. (Original work published 1930)

Vygotsky, L. S. (1987). *The collected works of L. S. Vygotsky: Volume 1. Problems of general psychology. Including the volume thinking and speech* (N. Minick, Ed. & Trans.). New York, NY: Plenum.

Wagoner, B. (2013). Bartlett's concept of schema in reconstruction. *Theory & Psychology, 23*(5), pp. 553–575.

Wang, Z. (2012). *Never forget national humiliation: History and memory in Chinese politics and foreign relations*. New York, NY: Columbia University Press.

Wertsch, J. (ed.) (1985). *Culture, communication, and cognition: Vygotskian perspectives.* Cambridge: Cambridge University Press.

Wertsch, J. V. (1991). *Voices of the mind: A sociocultural approach to mediated action.* Cambridge, MA: Harvard University Press.

Wertsch, J. V. (2002). *Voices of collective remembering.* New York, NY: Cambridge University Press.

Wertsch, J.V. (2008). A clash of deep memories. *Profession,* 46–53.

Wertsch, J. V., & Karumidze, Z. (2009). Spinning the past: Russian and Georgian accounts of the war of August 2008. *Memory Studies, 2*(3), 377–392.

Wertsch, J. V., & Roediger, H. L. (2008). Collective memory: Conceptual foundations and theoretical approaches. *Memory, 16*(3), 318–326.

Zerubavel, E. (2003). *Time maps: Collective memory and the social shape of the past.* Chicago, IL: University of Chicago.

History, Collective Memories, or National Memories?

How the Representation of the Past Is Framed by Master Narratives

MARIO CARRETERO AND FLOOR VAN ALPHEN ■

In this chapter, we argue that the nation, as both a conceptual and a narrative unit, greatly formats collective memories and history learning. By conceptual unit, we mean an abstract entity that integrates different social and political elements (e.g., population and territory) and generates a particular view of the past, not necessarily related to historical processes as such. By narrative unit, we mean the nation as the center and subject of historical narration. In both the collective production of accounts of the past and their individual consumption, national historical master narratives are pervasive. We consider master narratives as general patterns of imagining the nation, as seen, for example, in the myths of the origin of nations or narratives of national struggle or progress. According to Heller (2006), they serve as a general unit of analysis not only in psychology but also in the social sciences in general. National master narratives act as both official and general interpretations of the past but also legitimize the present and set an agenda for the future.

To clarify our argument, we first reflect on the relation between memory and history. These fundamentally different ways of representing the past become entangled in national history. After a contemporary example of how collective memory is framed by national experiences, we turn to the role of history education in this process. We discuss our empirical work that indicates the predominance of national master narratives over representation. Finally, it is suggested that disentangling history from memory, to critically interrogate the national narratives, might help expand collective memory beyond national memory.

MEMORY AND HISTORY AS REPRESENTATIONS OF THE PAST

The relation between memory and history is complex. Ricoeur (2004) argues that memory is "the womb of history" (p. 87)—that is, history as a discipline heavily relies on testimonies. Although the archives are a collective resource allowing the systematic investigation we call history, the testimonies that make up the archives rely on individual memories. Nevertheless, history is more than a kind of memory; it is "organized memory" (Le Goff, 1992). A notion such as "historical consciousness" (Rüsen, 2004) integrates history and memory as sources for identity and is very useful for thinking about how we commonly understand the past. However, we adhere to what might be called a "hyperdialectic" (Polkinghorne, 2005), an ongoing dialectic without synthesis, in which individual memory, collective memory, and history are different parts of a process of representing the past.

Memory, individually speaking, is the capacity to remember (Rosa, 2006) or "existential work" (Le Goff, 1992). In terms of autobiographical memory, it is important for our personal identities. Individual memory has been primarily studied as a cognitive function in a wide range of subcategories, from autobiographical and semantic to procedural memory (Tulving & Craik, 2000). Therefore, it is related mainly to individual perception and experience. Remembering also happens at a collective level, as a scaffold to collective identities and for many other (political) purposes. However, beyond metaphorical confusion, the collective does not experience or perceive the same way as does an individual. Nor does collective memory always refer to a collective experience. Often, events are collectively remembered that the individual member of the collective or the present collective itself has never witnessed. Wertsch (2002) illustrates the difference between individual and collective memory based on studies of state-dependent retrieval, showing that memory is more accurate when the individual state of mind at the time of retrieval is similar to the state of mind at the time of encoding. In this sense, talking about a collective state of mind and collective encoding is nonsensical, particularly because the collective is not a clearly defined organism situated in time and space. Collective memory is not a cognitive capacity but, rather, a practice that exists in objects collected in museums, monuments erected, and collective narratives told. This means that it transcends time and space. Here, cultural tools play a clear role, and they may also help to make a case for how both collective and individual memory are connected (Wertsch, 2002; see also Wertsch, Chapter 11, this volume).

According to Ricoeur (2004), the individual capacity to remember is connected to practices of collective remembering through a complex process of selecting and sharing testimonies. For Halbwachs (1992), this relation is inverse: Individual thought is capable of recollection because it is embedded in social frameworks for memory and participates in collective memory. As cultural psychologists, we can affirm that memory becomes interiorized through cultural means. In contrast, Ricoeur might argue that these collective means come from individual testimonies. Indeed, one could wonder whether witnessing is culturally mediated or a matter of perceptive mechanisms or both. Nevertheless, Ricoeur's statement that "history will offer schemata for mediating between the opposite poles of individual memory and collective memory" (p. 131) coincides with the position of cultural psychology (Wertsch, 1998, 2002). We agree that individual and collective memories are in a continuous and complex interaction. This is also indicated by Brockmeier (2010) in his exhaustive review of cognitive research on memory. He strongly criticizes the idea of "archive" as the key metaphor of memory, based on various trends of the present field. We think that both memory and collective memory are mediated mainly by narrative, in which the relation between past, present, and future plays an important role (Carretero & Solcoff, 2012). However, we should not let a "narrative imperialism" (Bamberg, 2011) make us believe that either kind of memory is reducible to the other. Nor is history just narrative or reducible to collective memory.

Remembering, individually or collectively, is at the same time forgetting (Ricoeur, 2004; Rosa, 2006). To constitute an individual or group as being the same through time, thus establishing its identity, is to tell a narrative (Ricoeur, 1992). A classic narrative has one protagonist. It describes certain selected events relevant for the protagonist while leaving others out. Forgetting, however, is something that the disciplinary investigation of the past tries to avoid (Rosa, 2006). Of course, historians make mistakes and can be manipulated or themselves be manipulative, but in their work both scientific and moral standards apply as truth values (Le Goff, 1992). Ideally, history does not forget and systematically investigates what memory leaves out, accidentally or on purpose. This can be done by not just looking at one testimony but also comparing many of them. Weighing sources against each other, and letting present questions interact with different remnants from the past, is part of the "historian's craft" (Bloch, 1953). Bloch and colleagues at the Annales School of history were key figures in what can be called "new history" (Burke, 2001). Instead of simply declaring the end of all great stories and throwing the history baby out with the modern bathwater, new history allows the introduction of different perspectives and the continuation of critical historical investigation. As Burke suggests, the ideal narrative for new history would be the multiple perspective account that we find in contemporary literature (e.g., Lawrence Durrell's *The Alexandria Quartet* (1962) or Milorad Pavić's *Dictionary of the Khazars* (1988) and film (e.g., Kurosawa's *Rashomon* (1950) or Fernando Meirelles' *Cidade de Deus* (2002)). In this way, forgetful memory, or strategic history manipulation, can be confronted with different accounts. Collective memory can be a source of such an account, for example, when narratives of political militancy in Latin America counter the official version of national history propagated by the dominant oligarchy or military dictatorships (Jelin, 2003; van Alphen & Asensio, 2012). As could also be seen in the fall of the Soviet Union, "popular archives" can correct "official archives" (Le Goff, 1992). In short, memory offers accounts and testimonies; history systematically compares and investigates them. As discussed in this chapter, Marxist ideas and experiences have been collectively remembered as liberating by certain Latin American groups, whereas these ideas have been represented as oppressing by Russian and Eastern European groups.

Note that national history is also a kind of collective memory when it propagates a particular national group's—or its political elite's—story or point of view. If we examine the discipline of history before new and multiple ways of doing history were introduced, we see that it was basically aimed at constructing national identities (Berger, 2012). In early history writing memory, identity and history were very much nationally entangled. History was national history, a very peculiar kind of collective memory, as the nation was basically invented (Anderson, 1983; Hobsbawm & Ranger, 1983). Other collective identities already existed, but national identity was new in the 19th century. National history was written to construct and legitimize this new identity, often rewriting significant parts of the past in national terms. Moreover, this history was developed in order to be taught, such that it could be used to make people into national citizens. With the rise of new history in the 20th century, and also all the different perspectives offered by collective memory, one might think that this is no longer the case. Yet, national identity has become so banal and naturalized (Billig, 1995) that it has invisible power over how people in societies remember. For example, how many times does the daily use of "we," "us," or "here" refer to the nation? In the construction of historical accounts, these tiny elements often indicate a restriction to national history or identity. In this chapter, we argue that history, memory, and identity are still very much framed in national terms. The national perspectives overpowering collective memory might even partly explain why history and memory are still being confounded, instead of acknowledging that there are in fact different kinds of histories and memories. Whereas contemporary historiography gives very critical accounts of nation (Alvarez Junco, 2011; Hobsbawm & Ranger, 1983; Rios Saloma, 2005), the common representation of the past is dominated by master narratives. This is a kind of narrative that celebrates the nation, its origins and its achievements, and generally functions to interpret the past in terms of a (national) group and its present goals. Examining the educational process where historical accounts and collective and individual memories meet is particularly illuminating for our argument. In the following, we first reflect on how collective memory is framed with a contemporary example and then explore the role of education in constructing frames for understanding the past.

WHAT FRAMES DIFFERENT COLLECTIVE MEMORIES OF THE SAME PAST?

Figure 12.1 shows a picture of students meeting in their school of education in Guerrero, Mexico, on November 23, 2014.[1] They are discussing protest actions in response to the disappearance of 43 fellow students on September 26, 2014.[2] These most likely violently abducted students were protesting against discrimination and other forms of political violence that defenders of human rights endorse. The incredible incident has produced the most important political scandal in Mexico

Figure 12.1 Mexican students of education in a meeting about civil rights. The mural quotes Karl Marx: "Until now philosophers have only interpreted the world. What is necessary is to transform it." © SAÚL RUIZ / EDICIONES EL PAÍS, SL 2014.

in recent years. As can be seen from the figure, images of Marx, Engels, and Lenin are part of the permanent political symbols at this school. The well-known phrase of Marx's thesis on Feuerbach is included in the image. It is an image very similar to those found in many places throughout Latin America. Plausibly, the presence of these images indicates that for this particular political movement, and probably many others in Latin America, Marxist and revolutionary characters are very influential in their interpretation of the past. For a majority of the Latin American youth, Marxist symbols and characters are no doubt representative or models in resisting political oppression, economic exploitation, and violation of human rights. In this vein, it is important to consider that the Marxist *weltanschauung* has traditionally maintained history as a social scientific support of its grand narrative of progress and emancipation, ultimately carried out by the Russian Revolution. It is very likely that this grand narrative is being represented on the Mexican mural in Figure 12.1. It is present in almost the same way in the famous Diego Rivera 1925 murals on the walls of the ancient Mexican Secretary of Education in Mexico City.

However, if we compare the image in Figure 12.1 with the numerous images showing the destruction of Marxist monuments throughout the former Soviet Union immediately after the collapse of communism (Figure 12.2), questions immediately arise. For example, how is it possible that Mexican students consider Lenin and Marx as cultural and political models of liberation and at the same time in other areas of the world these characters represent oppression? (For an analysis of the changes in history education in the former German Democratic Republic after the fall of the Berlin Wall, see Ahonen, 1997; and for a discussion about how former Soviet citizens did not consider the Russian Revolution a grand narrative at all, see Wertsch & Rozin, 2000.)

Figure 12.2 Sunday, December 8, 2013. Anti-government protesters dragged down and decapitated the landmark statue Sunday evening after hundreds of thousands of others took to the streets to denounce the government's move away from Europe and toward Moscow. © 2013 The Associated Press/Efrem Lukatsky.

Both representations are based more on collective memories than on historiographical research. As previously stated, collective memories involve selective forgetting. This can also occur in a historiographical endeavor, but the latter at least aims at systematically avoiding forgetfulness. For example, recent contributions such as that by Snyder (2012) have shown how Soviet regimes were characterized by an enormous repression of political adversaries and citizens in general, had an alliance with the Nazi regime, and produced more than 11 million victims. This is clearly "forgotten" by the Mexican students. At the same time, however, it can be argued that the massive destruction of Marxist monuments "forgets" the systematic repression of Marxist political leaders and citizens in general by military regimes in Latin America, often supported by the US government (for a discussion of the collective memory of political violence during the 1970s in South America, see Jelin, 2003). In short, it is clear that collective memories are basically contextual and to some extent reactive. In other words, they appear in the context of a particular inherited social and political past. In this vein, Mexican students vindicate the revolutionary role of Marxist figures because these represent their attempt to gain emancipation and civil rights. They probably do not consider Marxist figures as symbols of oppression because this has not been the case in their local and national experience. On their part, citizens from former communist countries see in monuments inspired by Marxism the oppression they experienced for decades in their specific societies. Historiographical research tries to maintain a broader view on social and political problems, and it takes into account more than one perspective on the past. Collective memories, however, are contextual and local, and the most relevant social, cultural, and political context for citizens is their own current national society.

Interestingly, these two divergent scenarios—Latin American countries and former communist societies—have something in common: the trend to base their history education and curriculum mostly on nationalist contents. In both cases, a nationalist view of the past is taken to be perfectly compatible with a particular position regarding the Marxist–Leninist grand narrative. This nationalist trend in history education has been analyzed in much detail (Ahonen, 1997; Carretero, 2011). For example, when the Mexican government tried to change school history content through an educational reform in 1992 and 2000, both students and teachers demonstrated and teachers went on strike (Carretero, 2011, Chapter 2). These historical contents were mainly related to national figures, such as the Child Heroes who fought against the North American army. These children are popular heroes in Mexico, even though their actual role in the military conflict has not been well documented until now. The Mexican government tried to implement a new history curriculum, in which these and similar figures were no longer present. The attempt to change the history curriculum, and to make it less nationalist, was perceived by a part of the citizenry as an assault on their collective memory. In another context, both Estonia and the former Democratic Republic transformed their history curricula radically after the collapse of communism in order to base it on nationalist narratives and concepts (Ahonen, 1997). This trend has become even stronger, taking into account the very nationalist and patriotic orientation adopted by Russia in recent years under President Vladimir Putin (Levintova, 2010). In comparing these examples of how collective memories are framed by certain contexts, the contribution of contemporary disciplinary history to constructing multiperspective accounts of the past can be clearly seen. On the other hand, particularly during the fall of the Soviet Union (Brossat, Combe, Potel, & Szurek, 1992), the contribution of collective memory to history writing is very clear. As Le Goff (1992) formulates, "*Popular archives* can correct *official archives*, even though the latter can hide and therefore reveal some truths that have been kept a secret" (p. 16; our translation from the Spanish version). Thus, collective memory and historiography combined can counteract the attempts of political, ideological, or economic powers to use, subdue, or manipulate history in their own interest (Le Goff, 1992).

THE ROLE OF HISTORY EDUCATION IN FRAMING THE PAST

Previously in this chapter, collective memories and historiography were compared as producers of representations of the past. However, formal and informal history education experiences, at the crossroads of collective memory and historiography, are essential to take into account in the construction of these representations. By formal history education, we refer mainly to school history contents and activities. By informal history education, we mean representations of the past that appear in patriotic rituals, museums, and heritage. As analyzed elsewhere (Carretero, 2011, Chapter 1), school history does not just consist of disciplinary historical knowledge. It is highly influenced by collective memories, attitudes, and other ideological aspects, as is historical research, although ideally it compares perspectives instead of choosing one and forgetting another. Therefore, historiography, collective memory, and history education have a complex relation in which mutual interactions are frequent. Specifically considering history education as a source of representation, and more generally considering cultural tools, a distinction has been made between production and consumption (Wertsch, 1998, 2002). The former refers to the produced cultural tools or elements of history education, such as textbooks and media. The latter concerns the representation and use of cultural tools by students and citizens, or history learning. As discussed later, a specific interaction between these two processes takes place.

Regarding the production of representations about the past, different researchers have considered the existence of competing objectives of history education (Barton & Levstik, 2004; Wineburg, 2001). Carretero (2011) has redefined these objectives as "romantic" and "enlightened" because their features and functions stem from their intellectual roots in Romanticism and the Enlightenment, respectively. In that sense, history has been taught in all national school systems so as to make students "love their country" (Nussbaum & Cohen, 2002) and to make them "understand their past" (Seixas, 2004). In a romantic vein, history education is a fundamental strategy used to achieve (1) a positive assessment of the past, present, and future of one's own social group, both local and national, and (2) an identification with the country's political history. In an enlightened vein, history education has aimed at fostering critical citizens' capability of informed and effective participation in the historical changes happening nationally and globally. This can involve a critical attitude toward their own local or national community, or even larger political units. Recently, this has been translated in several countries into the following disciplinary and cognitive objectives: (1) to understand the past in a complex manner, which usually implies mastering the discipline's conceptual categories (Carretero & Lee, 2014); (2) to distinguish different historical periods through the appropriate adequate comprehension of historical time (Barton, 2008); (3) to understand historical multicausality and to relate the past with the present and the future (Barton & Levstik, 2004); and (4) to approach the methodology used by historians, such as comparing sources (Monte-Sano, 2010).

The romantic and enlightened goals of history education have coexisted from the very beginning of school history teaching and have developed over time. The romantic goals were most influential from the 19th century until approximately the 1960s and 1970s. A testimony from Alvarez-Junco (2011), an academic historian, about how school history was taught in the mid-20th century is telling:

As for myself, I still remember the moment when I first heard about the heroic end of the Numantines [the inhabitants of Numancia, a town in what currently is northern Spain, who resisted a Roman siege], at the hands of the evil foreigners who had besieged them. . . . I imagined the scene of a great bonfire in the middle of the town square, into which two warriors were throwing the jewels, the furniture, and the bodies of the children and women that had been put to the sword. They finally killed each other, so that the triumphant enemy would capture neither slaves nor booty. This is how we Spaniards are, the teacher explained: We prefer to die rather than be slaves. We all felt horror, but also pride, and unconsciously resolved to do the same someday should the occasion arise. . . . It might be thought that a precocious interest in history is revealed by these stories, but that is not the case. Neither the former nor the latter were history; both were "school narratives." (p. xvii)

As can be seen, the teaching of history was not so much inspired by academic research. However, it was very powerful and effective, probably because it was directed at the construction of collective identities and emotional attachment to these identities. It is not surprising that Ferro (1984/2002), another academic historian, declared at the beginning of his classic book thatour images of other people, or of ourselves for that matter, reflect the history we are taught as children. The history marks us for life. Its representation . . . of the past of societies, embraced all of our passing or permanent opinions, so that the traces of our first questioning, our emotions, remain indelible. (p. vii)

Even nowadays, history education in a number of countries is exclusively romantic and nationalist. Therefore, national histories "were born to be taught." They are contained in a variety of records, such as museums (Knell et al., 2011) and monuments and patriotic celebrations important in many countries (Carretero, 2011, Chapter 4; Westheimer, 2007). Following the 1960s and 1970s, the disciplinary goals of history education became increasingly influential (Carretero & Bermúdez, 2012). Social sciences (economics, sociology, and anthropology) in general started to influence curricula in different countries. Included in history curricula were disciplinary objectives considered perfectly compatible with the romantic objectives. However, several studies (Carretero & Kriger, 2011; López, Carretero, & Rodriguez Moneo, 2015) have indicated the tension this might generate in students' representations. This is particularly clear in colonial and postcolonial history teaching. Spanish school textbooks have traditionally omitted essential features of the American colonization, such as the subjugation of indigenous people or slavery as a generalized social and economic practice (Ferro, 1984/2002; Todorov, 1997). Therefore, it could be said that aiming at "loving" the Spanish country has had serious consequences for understanding its colonial past. In contrast, these colonial issues are highlighted in Mexican or Brazilian textbooks (Carretero, Jacott, & López-Manjón, 2002). Similar findings are reported when former colonizers and the colonized are compared in France/Algeria, Great Britain/India, China/Japan (Ferro, 1984/2002) and Japan/Korea (The Academy of Korean Studies, 2005).

These tensions are not just a matter of controversial issues in recent history. Remote history is at the bottom. That is, the historical issues at the roots of national identity construction are a fundamental part of the problem. For this reason, it can be said that even nowadays, historical master narratives are playing an important role in the imagination of the nation. They serve the romantic goals of history education particularly well. Also, their influence is becoming more widespread and more intense with the emergence of new nationalism in Europe and other areas of the world. As Alridge (2006) and Straub (2005) have indicated, these "master narratives" of nation pervade underneath a variety of specific contents and through time. Whereas specific narratives may change frequently, these underlying master narratives rarely change, and they manifest once and again in subsequent revisions of history contents. Also outside of school—in monuments, rituals, museums, films, and other media—a narrative of nation is perpetuated.

So far, we have attended to the production or teaching of national history or, rather, national memories. However, do the conflicting views found in academic and public debates, and in school textbooks, influence how students and citizens ultimately understand the past? How do features of the social production of historical narratives translate into the processes of individual consumption of historical narratives? To these issues we now turn.

MASTER NARRATIVES AND THE REPRESENTATION OF THE PAST

Although there is an emphasis on national history in history education and its investigation, this does not necessarily determine how people represent history. The narrative of the nation is a dominant account of history, in and out of school, but people can also turn to historiography or alternative accounts of collective memory. In the theory of mediated action, there is an irreducible tension between the cultural tool, in this case the master narrative, and the agent who appropriates this narrative—the students and citizens who "consume" accounts of history (Wertsch, 1998, 2002). On the part of the appropriating agent, there can be opposition to, or rejection of, accounts of history. We find a very clear example of this in the historians who reject the master narrative as a myth (Megill, 2007). Also, collective memory, as in the experiences of a particular group of people, can resist and contribute alternative versions to "official" history. For example, Sandinista militants from peasant families in Nicaragua tell a very different story about the revolution in 1979 than the version propagated by the media and institutional powers (van Alphen & Asensio, 2012). Both on the basis of historical research and on the basis of alternative collective memories, people can resist and reject the national master narrative. Precisely these processes of resistance are important to study because they indicate the dynamic aspects of collective memories. In other words, they show how representations of the past change and generate new and different ways of remembering in both human beings and societies.

Nevertheless, research demonstrates that more often than not, students' representation of history, and of what is deemed important in history, is framed by the nation (Barton, 2008). Furthermore, Wertsch (2002; see also Chapter 11, this volume) suggests that schematic narrative templates—general narrative patterns that are found across specific narratives of historical events forming interpretation schemas in people's minds—are active when representing national history. Recent work, inspired by cultural psychology and history learning studies, indicates that the narratives that students construct about their own nation greatly resemble the national master narrative rather than a historiographical account of the national past. This has been found among university students in Spain (López et al., 2015) and high school students in Argentina (Carretero & van Alphen, 2014). To study the representation of national history and the appropriation of master narratives in more detail, Carretero (2011, Chapter 4; see also Carretero & Bermúdez, 2012) has suggested a model of master narrative production and consumption that can be applied to different countries. This model distinguishes six different narrative characteristics or dimensions. In this vein, the investigation of students' representations has turned to analyzing whether these characteristics appear, constituting master narratives in students' minds. The master narrative dimensions are as follows:

1. *A homogeneous historical and social subject*—that is, the narrative has one single subject that is homogeneous both in opposition to the historical other and over time. There is no variety or diversity of historical actors, and the subject has an idealized and timeless character. The establishment of this national protagonist, the main voice of the narrative, involves a process of inclusion/exclusion. For example, the voice of indigenous people living in the same territory is excluded from the national narrative.

2. *Identification processes*, in terms of a "we" versus "them" structure. The narrators identify with the national historical subject, or their use of the pronouns "we" and "they" reflect a present national identity projected on the past or their identification is both historical (between then and now) and social (with other nationals). Past and present subjects are merged into one national identity, as are different social actors.

3. *Heroic and transcendent key historical figures*: These individuals appear in the narrative to represent national virtue and set the national example. They are valued positively and considered outside their social and historical context, as quasi-mythical characters.

4. *A monocausal or teleological account of the historical events*, in terms of one main goal, such as the search for freedom or defending the national interest.

5. *Moral value judgments*—positive about the national subject and historical events and negative about the historical/national other. This national moral value is self-justifying or tautological: What is national is good, and the good is national. In this sense, the sacrifices made, from

dying for one's country to eradicating other groups and traitors, are for
the greater good.

6. *An essentialist conceptualization of nation and national identity*: Both
   are naturalized and timeless entities. In this sense, territory is also
   essentialized as, or predestined to be, national.

How do these characteristics concretely manifest in students' representations?
A study by Carretero and van Alphen (2014) provides some examples. It investigated how Argentine urban middle-class high school students represented
the historical event that occurred in 1810, which nowadays marks the anniversary of the Argentine nation on May 25. This event is therefore not just a
part of Argentine national history but also represents the very beginning—a
so-called *myth of origin* (Jovchelovitch, 2012; Smith, 1991)—and constitutes
an important theme in the Argentine national narrative: independence. It can
be compared to the Boston Tea Party in the United States and other histories of independence on the American continent (Ortemberg, 2013). Keeping
the master narrative characteristics in mind, we examine two different student
accounts:

> The Argentine people were tired of being governed by Spain. At that time
> there was a viceroy and the people went to overthrow him. They went to tell
> him that we were a free people.
>
> MARIO, 14 years old

> In the town hall, on May 25th, part of the Buenos Aires society held a
> reunion, to discuss about the government that had been in charge that
> was no longer legitimate, because Ferdinand VII (king of Spain) had been
> taken as a prisoner by Napoleon in Spain . . . and upon imprisoning him
> the Viceroyalty of River Plate, a Spanish colony of which our territory was
> part, because you cannot speak of Argentina at that time . . . the viceroy
> Cisneros, who was at that time the authority, was left without legitimacy.
> Some members of society, of the social upper class, decided that a meeting
> needed to be held urgently to dismiss that (Cisneros's) government and to
> form another based on the actual situation at that time.
>
> ANALÍA, 16 years old

Both Mario and Analía were asked to tell the interviewer about the same historical event. However, their accounts contrast dramatically with one another.
Apart from transcendent heroes and explicit moral values, all master narrative
characteristics can be found in Mario's version. There is a homogeneous historical subject, the Argentine people, opposed to another, Spain. That Argentines
are supposed to have existed indicates the essentialized conceptualization of the
nation and its nationals. The event was motivated by a desire to be free, or at the

very least of being tired of foreign rule. Here we also see something of a value judgment. Through the use of "we," a social identification process seems to be at work that at the same time is a historical identification process.

The four narrative characteristics are very much intertwined. The historical subject is homogeneous both in opposition to Spain and because of being essentially Argentine. The historical event is caused both by this opposition between the people and Spain and by essentially being different from Spaniards. The national identity sits in the people's need to be free and is affirmed by this freedom. This narrative coherence is not just a spontaneous feat of individual narrative thought nor is there a lack of learning. Mario has actually interiorized a collective memory: the master narrative of the origin of the Argentine nation. His account was learned, as was Analía's, because he cannot arrive at such an account on the basis of his individual experience: Something mediates his access to the distant past.

This is different for Analía. In her account, Argentina does not exist in 1810. The people are not unified by a national identity in opposition to another, as Spanish colonists constituted Buenos Aires society and differences existed in their sociopolitical status. Only some participated in a town council meeting that was held as a result of an international chain of events. There was a need for legitimate government, preferably representing those very protagonists calling for a town council. One could say that Analía's account reflects the other objective of history education: to understand the past. Her version unmistakably has a narrative structure, although it is much closer to historiographical accounts (Chiaramonte, 1991). Actually, she studied May 25, 1810, as part of her high school history curriculum a year earlier. The Argentine history textbooks used are quite precise in historical detail, even though they emphasize national history like many other curricula and textbooks throughout the world.

The general results of the study, however, do not suggest that the representation of the national past differs between 8th and 11th graders as a function of history education. Whereas a development toward history understanding in the 11th grade was found, some 8th graders did not manifest a master narrative representation but more than half of 11th graders did so. Their representations were mediated by the master narrative or by more historical accounts in different degrees. Therefore, there is no single way of individually constructing the collective narrative. However, the master narrative predominated overall, suggesting that some aspects of collective memory are difficult to change (Carretero & van Alphen, 2014). For example,

It is a step we took to fight against the Spaniards so that they respect our rights, because that place was in itself our territory. All those years of subordination to the Spanish Crown, with the viceroy and the king of Spain . . . we didn't need a government telling us what to do, if we want to be independent, we want to govern, we the Argentines.

CLARA, 16 years old

In this fragment, it can be seen how the establishment of an essentially national historical subject automatically, as a function of narrative coherence, involves and connects the other master narrative characteristics. There is identification with the national subject, its actions and supposed intentions. The territory essentially belongs to that subject and legitimizes a fight. The historical event, the fight, is inherently good because it was for independence, rights, and political autonomy of the national historical subject. Some heroism is involved, even though no specific heroes are mentioned. Later in the interview, Clara does give credit to the Argentine national hero of independence, responding to the question, "Was it Argentina that became independent?": "Yes, because of San Martín."

The overall results suggest that the students' narrative representation is more or less coherent. When, in the case of Analía, the historical subject is specified as urban political upper class, then the historical events are more contextualized. There is a narrative of nation, but the latter is understood in a long and complex historical process instead of a preexisting collective essence. Tensions arise when the students hold on to the master narrative, on the one hand, and enter into more historical detail, on the other hand. For example,

> Actually, we can say that in the beginning the population was a mix of Spaniards and aboriginals and I believe that the majority of the population was Spanish. When the country developed and they saw that they could have . . . they had the possibility to have their own country and a president or whatever. I believe they saw a possibility to become independent and create . . . a revolutionary movement . . . but putting it like this you realize that the major part of the population was Spanish and because of that, they maybe wanted to become independent from Spain themselves.
>
> Luisa, 16 years old

Here we see that as soon as a somewhat more contextualized historical subject appears, the events ("revolution" and "independence") that logically followed from the opposition with Spain are not so logical anymore. The historical protagonists are themselves Spanish colonists and not nationally opposed to Spain. Luisa has some difficulty with connecting the dots as the master narrative representation is disturbed by another possible historical subject. This tension might very well be a consequence of the two objectives in history learning mentioned previously. Other research in Argentina (Carretero & Kriger, 2011) suggests that for the students, there are tensions between master narrative and historical representations of nation—the same way that there are tensions between the two objectives of history education when it concerns the nation. Given the predominance of the master narrative, and its presence in the students' representations even after learning about the history of May 25, we could say that the objective of constructing national identities is more successfully accomplished. Aiming at history understanding, an educator would want students' representations to change, but they remain much restrained by the master narrative. In its wake, historical details are forgotten, such as the fact that women, slaves, indigenous groups, and creoles without political status in 1810 were not allowed into the town council. Can we therefore really talk about "the people" becoming "free"? Thirteen-year-old Manu is very skeptical: The idea of feeling Argentine to me seems something theoretical. The country is formed, not natural, in any moment it can change names: We're "Argentines" and all of a sudden we can be "troglodytes" (laughs). . . . I think it is kind of an egoist idea, in order for certain people to have power over society, and the rest of us we go along with those people so that they have the power and have more money, more dough. I think that for this reason the system of countries and of society in general is designed.

Interestingly, it was recently found that Spanish students, when telling about the origin of a nation that is not their own, do not construct a master narrative the same way they do about the Spanish nation (López, Carretero, & Rodriguez-Moneo, 2014). Particularly, they do not demonstrate the moral judgments and territorial claims that arise when the own nation is concerned. They do manifest the first narrative characteristic: A national historical subject is established. In the case of this recent investigation, the historical subject was Greek. Although the historical subject was not Spanish like these students, it was considered to be essentially and homogeneously Greek. This also suggests that the core dimension of the master narrative is its national historical subject, whether students identify with this subject or not.

MASTER NARRATIVES IN (RE-EN)ACTION

We argue that both kinds of representations—master narrative or more historical accounts—are learned and developed. Thus, in part, national identity is interiorized through master narratives, corresponding to the finding that these narratives were implemented in history education at the beginning of the 20th century to construct national identities in the populace (Bertoni, 2001). This interiorization does not happen in a purely cognitive way. In practices of remembering in Argentina, the so-called patriotic rituals that were also implemented at the beginning of the 20th century (Bertoni, 2001), the nation or the national historical protagonist is embodied. Patriotic rituals play an important role in many countries. In Argentina, Brazil, Chile, and Uruguay, at least four historical and patriotic commemorations take place in school every year. They are dramatizations of and discussions about the events, battles, and national heroes related to the processes of independence of each country. In the United States, these kinds of activities are performed at many historical and monumental sites (McCalman & Pickering, 2010), apart from those performed in schools.

Patriotic re-enactments, usually heroic and celebratory, unite stories in a long narrative chain that links them by virtue of the role they play in the construction of the nation. These narratives adopt a teleological form, also in relation to each other; destiny is already contained in the origins, and knowledge of the "roots" of a nation is indispensable for knowing how to act in the future. The patriotic scenarios convey an important amount of historical contents that influence student's understanding of the history contained in the formal curriculum and textbooks (Carretero, 2011, Chapter 4). Students consume and use national historical narratives that they learn from these kinds of events, in and out of school. Given the results and fragments discussed previously, it could even be said that patriotic ritual is more influential than history textbooks because no contemporary Argentine high school history textbook states that on May 25, 1810, the Argentines became independent from Spain. Independence was declared on July 9, 1816. Patriotic rituals in Argentina contain the central historical events of national history, expressing as well as enacting the master narrative. Being in the metaphorical shoes of national historical protagonists—"the people becoming independent"— is a very active way of remembering and identifying. Not only children but also their parents participate in these collective memories, such that the master narrative is converted into family memory (see Shore & Kauko, Chapter 4, this volume). These rituals make a timeless connection between the supposed historical protagonists and the primary schoolchildren interpreting them. Repetition is part of the strength of ritual in collective remembering (Connerton, 1989; see also Murakami, Chapter 5, this volume). Here, it strengthens the master narrative, such that it becomes increasingly more dominant in the child's representation of history. Patriotic rituals may play the same role in the common representation of history as the archives do in the historians' view on the past. That is, patriotic rituals likely provide a truth-value to a romantic representation of the past for the following reasons:

1. The child is involved in these rituals at an age (4–6 years) that does not yet allow critical thinking.
2. The national master narrative is repeated every year in a very similar manner.
3. No possible counter narrative or alternative account is offered.
4. Patriotic rituals in many countries are milestones of the school year, in terms of how the time is organized.
5. They are supported not only by the school but also by society in general.

In terms of the differences between collective memory and history discussed previously, one wonders whether patriotic rituals are implemented by national school systems as educational contents related to history or, rather, to collective memory. They are considered to be historical because they are about the past, but they are probably more collective memory than history. In this respect, the words of Le Goff (1992) should be considered: Memory is a conquest, it must seek and preserve that what allows it to construct itself from a perspective of truth. It must dispel false legends, black or golden, about such episodes of the past, collect the maximum amount of documents and confront contradictory memories, open up the archives and impede their destruction, know to look for the memory expelled to the taboos of history during certain periods in certain systems in literature or in art, and recognize the plurality of legitimate memories. (p. 15)

CONCLUSION

The implementation of the master narrative in early history education and in ongoing celebrations can help explain why an invented nation, according to contemporary historiography (Anderson, 1983; Hobsbawm & Ranger, 1983), or a national identity that is itself historical (Berger, 2012; Chiaramonte, 1989; Smith, 1991) can become so psychologically real. We have emphasized that it should not be taken for granted that people organize their past in a national key. Apart from explaining these national memories from a traditional social psychological viewpoint in terms of in-group–out-group processes, their proper history needs to be taken into account. That is, national identity is of course a matter of social psychology, but it is also historical. We have aimed to build an interdisciplinary bridge between history and psychology, taking the historicity of the master narrative as a cultural tool into account. Examining national history, it can be seen that the discipline is in fact quite young and that the concept of nation and the category of national identity started influencing the way the past was written in the 19th century. Since then, the master narrative has influenced education and started to frame how the past is represented. This means that there are other possible ways of representing the past, related to other collective memories or to different written histories. In the same way that there is no single collective memory, such as a national memory in narrative form, there is no single history. To some theoreticians, history is narrative and is the same as collective memory. However, this is a somewhat shallow interpretation, given the wide spectrum of histories written from new perspectives (Burke, 2001) and the attempt to compare perspectives instead of vindicating just one of them.

In this chapter, we have tried to distance ourselves from collective memory to see how it is centered in a generally nationalist perspective. We have seen that even in history education, history is understood nationally and that what is ultimately fostered might be more national memory than anything else. Students and citizens are capable of critically reflecting on single versions of the past when other versions are introduced. Contextualizing the essentially national historical protagonist of the master narrative seems a crucial step toward diversifying collective memory. In this way, we believe, historiography has something important to contribute to collective memory: It can help introduce new perspective. To open up collective memory for alternative not nationally formatted accounts particular historiographical techniques, such as taking a distance from history and critically interrogating the concepts and narratives we take for granted, are elementary. Paradoxically, therefore, we need to question collective memory in order to expand it beyond dominant national viewpoints.

ACKNOWLEDGMENTS

This chapter was written with the support of Project PICT 2012-1594 (ANPCYT; National Research Agency, Argentina) and Project EDU-2015-65088P (DGICYT;

Dirección General de Investigacion Cientifica y Tecnica, Spain), both of which have been coordinated by Mario Carretero. We express our gratitude for that support. Also, Mario Carretero expresses his gratitude for the Fellowship of the Ministry of Education (Spain) to stay as Visiting Professor at the European University Institute in Florence, Italy. During this semester Professor L. Passerini made insightful comments on this chapter.

NOTES

1. Retrieved December 18, 2014, from http://internacional.elpais.com/internacional/ 2014/10/17/actualidad/1413568451_060339.html.
2. See http://elpais.com/elpais/2014/11/10/inenglish/1415647071_871493.html; accessed December 18, 2014.

REFERENCES

The Academy of Korean Studies. (2005). *Nationalism and history textbooks in Asia and Europe*. Seoul, South Korea: Author.

Ahonen, A. (1997). A transformation of history: The official representations of history in East Germany and Estonia, 1986–1991. *Culture and Psychology, 3*, 41–62.

Alridge, D. P. (2006). The limits of master narratives in history textbooks: An analysis of representations of Martin Luther King, Jr. *Teachers College Record, 108*(4), 662–686.

Alvarez Junco, J. (2011). *Spanish identity in the age of nations*. Manchester, UK: Manchester University Press.

Anderson, B. (1983). *Imagined communities: Reflections on the origin and spread of nationalism*. London, UK: Verso.

Bamberg, M. (2011). Narrative discourse. In C. A. Chapelle (General Ed.), *The encyclopedia of applied linguistics*. Oxford, UK: Wiley-Blackwell.

Barton, K. C. (2008). Research on students' ideas about history. In L. Levstik & C. A. Thyson (Eds.), *Handbook of research on social studies education* (pp. 239–258). New York, NY: Routledge.

Barton, K. C., & Levstik, L. (Eds.). (2004). *Teaching history for the common good*. Mahwah, NJ: Erlbaum.

Berger, S. (2012). De-nationalizing history teaching and nationalizing it differently! Some reflections on how to defuse the negative potential of national(ist) history teaching. In M. Carretero, M. Asensio, & M. Rodriguez-Moneo (Eds.), *History education and the construction of national identities* (pp. 33–47). Charlotte, NC: Information Age Publishing.

Bertoni, L. A. (2001). *Patriotas, cosmopolitas y nacionalistas: La construcción de la nacionalidad argentina a fines del siglo XIX*. [*Patriots, cosmopolitans and nationalists: The construction of the Argentine nationality at the end of the 19th century*]. Buenos Aires, Argentina: Fondo de Cultura Economica.

Billig, M. (1995). *Banal nationalism*. London, UK: Sage.

Bloch, M. (1953). *The historians craft*. New York, NY: Vintage Books–Random House.

Brockmeier, J. (2010). After the archive: Remapping memory. *Culture and Psychology, 16,* 5–35.

Brossat, A., Combe, S., Potel, J., & Szurek, J. (Eds.). (1992). *En el este, la memoria recuperada.* València: Edicions Alfons el Magnànim. [First published in 1990 as *A l'Est, la memoire retrouvée.* Paris: Éditions La Découverte]

Burke, P. (Ed.). (2001). *New perspectives on historical writing.* London, UK: Polity.

Carretero, M. (2011). *Constructing patriotism: Teaching history and memories in global worlds.* Charlotte, NC: Information Age Publishing.

Carretero, M., & Bermúdez, A. (2012). Constructing histories. In J. Valsiner (Ed.), *Oxford handbook of culture and psychology* (pp. 625–646). Oxford, UK: Oxford University Press.

Carretero, M., Jacott, L., & López-Manjón, A. (2002). Learning history through textbooks: Are Mexican and Spanish students taught the same story? *Learning and Instruction, 12,* 651–665.

Carretero, M., & Kriger, M. (2011). Historical representations and conflicts about indigenous people as national identities. *Culture and Psychology, 17*(2), 177–195.

Carretero, M., & Lee, P. (2014). Learning historical concepts. In K. Sawyer (Ed.), *Handbook of learning sciences* (2nd ed.). (pp. 587–604). Cambridge, UK: Cambridge University Press.

Carretero, M., & Solcoff, K. (2012). The relation between past, present and future as a metaphor of memory. *Culture and Psychology, 18,* 14–22. doi:10.1177/1354067X11427463

Carretero, M., & van Alphen, F. (2014). Do master narratives change among high school students? A characterization of how national history is represented. *Cognition and Instruction, 32*(3), 290–312. doi:10.1080/07370008.2014.919298

Chiaramonte, J. (1989). Formas de identidad en el Rio de la Plata luego de 1810 [Forms of identity in the River Plate after 1810]. *Boletín del Instituto de Historia Argentina y Americana "Dr. E. Ravignani", 3*(1), 71–92.

Chiaramonte, J. (1991). El mito de los orígenes en la historiografía latinoamericana [The myth of the origins in Latin-American historiography]. *Cuadernos del Instituto Ravignani, 2,* 5–39.

Connerton, P. (1989). *How societies remember.* Cambridge, UK: Cambridge University Press.

Ferro, M. (1984). *The use and abuse of history, or, how the past is taught to children.* London, UK: Routledge. [2002: revised French edition, Paris, PUF]

Halbwachs, M. (1992). *On collective memory.* Chicago, IL: University of Chicago Press.

Heller, A. (2006). European master narratives about freedom. In G. Delanty (Ed.), *Handbook of Contemporary European Social Theory* (pp. 257–265). New York, NY: Routledge.

Hobsbawm, E., & Ranger, T. (1983). *The invention of tradition.* Cambridge, UK: Cambridge University Press.

Jelin, E. (2003). *State repression and the labors of memory.* Minneapolis, MN: University of Minnesota Press.

Jovchelovitch, S. (2012). Narrative, memory and social representations: A conversation between history and social psychology. *Integrative Psychological and Behavioral Science, 46,* 440–456. doi:10.1007/s12124-012-9217-8

Knell, S. J., Aronson, P., Amundsen, A. B., Barnes, A. J., Burch, S., Carter, J., . . . Kirwan, A. (Eds.). (2011). *National museums: New studies from around the world.* London, UK: Routledge.

Le Goff, J. (1992). Prefacio. In A. Brossat, S. Combe, J. Potel, & J. Szurek (Eds.), *En el este, la memoria recuperada* (pp. 11–17). València: Edicions Alfons el Magnànim. [First published in 1990 as *A l'Est, la memoire retrouvée*. Paris, France: Éditions La Découverte]

Levintova, E. (2010). Past imperfect: The construction of history in the school curriculum and mass media in post-communist Russia and Ukraine. *Communist and Post-Communist Studies, 43*, 125–127. doi:10.1016/j.postcomstud.2010.03.005

López, C., Carretero, M., & Rodriguez-Moneo, M. (2014). Telling a national narrative that is not your own: Does it enable critical historical consumption? *Culture & Psychology, 20*(4), 547–571. doi:10.1177/1354067X14554156

López, C., Carretero, M., & Rodriguez-Moneo, M. (2015). Conquest or reconquest? Students' conceptions of nation embedded in a historical narrative. *Journal of the Learning Sciences, 24*(2), 252–285.

McCalman, I., & Pickering, P. A. (2010). *Historical reenactment: From realism to the affective turn*. Basingstoke, UK: Palgrave Macmillan.

Megill, A. (2007). *Historical knowledge, historical error: A contemporary guide to practice*. Chicago, IL: University of Chicago Press.

Monte-Sano, C. (2010). Disciplinary literacy in history: An exploration of the historical nature of adolescents' writing. *Journal of the Learning Sciences, 19*(4), 539–568.

Nussbaum, M., & Cohen, J. (2002). *For love of country? A new democracy forum on the limits of patriotism*. Boston, MA: Beacon.

Ortemberg, P. (2013). *El origen de las fiestas patrias: Hispanoamérica en la era de las independencias* [*The origin of patriotic rituals: Latin America in the age of the independences*]. Rosario, Argentina: Prohistoria Ediciones.

Polkinghorne, D. E. (2005). Narrative psychology and historical consciousness: Relationships and perspectives. In J. Straub (Ed.). *Narration, identity and historical consciousness* (pp. 3–22). New York, NY: Berghahn.

Ricoeur, P. (1992). *Oneself as another*. Chicago, IL: University of Chicago Press.

Ricoeur, P. (2004). *Memory, history, forgetting*. Chicago, IL: University of Chicago Press.

Rios Saloma, M. F. (2005). From the Restoration to the Reconquest: The construction of a national myth. *En la España Medieval, 28*, 379–414.

Rosa, A. (2006). Recordar, describir y explicar el pasado, ¿Qué, cómo, y para el futuro de quién? [Remembering, describing and explaining the past: What, how and for the future of whom?]. In M. Carretero, A. Rosa, & M. F. González (Eds.), *Enseñanza de la historia y memoria colectiva* [*History teaching and collective memory*] (pp. 41–51). Buenos Aires, Argentina: Paidós.

Rüsen, J. (2004). Historical consciousness: Narrative structure, moral function, and ontogenetic development. In P. Seixas (Ed.), *Theorizing historical consciousness* (pp. 63–85). Toronto, Ontario, Canada: University of Toronto Press.

Seixas, P. (Ed.). (2004). *Theorizing historical consciousness*. Toronto, Ontario, Canada: University of Toronto Press.

Smith, A. D. (1991). *National identity*. London, UK: Penguin.

Snyder, T. (2012). *Bloodlands: Europe between Hitler and Stalin*. New York, NY: Basic Books.

Straub, J. (Ed.). (2005). *Narration, identity and historical consciousness*. New York, NY: Berghahn.

Todorov, T. (1997). *The conquest of America*. New York, NY: HarperCollins.

Tulving, E., & Craik, F. I. M. (Eds.). (2000). *The Oxford handbook of memory.* Oxford, UK: Oxford University Press.

van Alphen, F., & Asensio, M. (2012). The complex construction of identity representations and the future of history education. In M. Carretero, M. Asensio, & M. Rodriguez-Moneo (Eds.), *History education and the construction of national identities* (pp. 311–326). Charlotte, NC: Information Age Publishing.

Wertsch, J. (1998). *Mind as action.* Oxford, UK: Oxford University Press.

Wertsch, J. (2002). *Voices of collective remembering.* Cambridge, UK: Cambridge University Press.

Wertsch, J., & Rozin, M. (2000). The Russian Revolution: Official and unofficial accounts. In J. F. Voss & M. Carretero (Eds.), *Learning and reasoning in history* (pp. 39–60). New York, NY: Routledge.

Westheimer, J. (2007). *Pledging allegiance: The politics of patriotism in America's schools.* New York, NY: Teachers College Press.

Wineburg, S. (2001). *Historical thinking and other unnatural acts.* Philadelphia, PA: Temple University Press.

Media and the Dynamics of Memory

From Cultural Paradigms to Transcultural Premediation

ASTRID ERLL ∎

FROM "CULTURAL PARADIGMS" TO
THE TRANSCULTURAL MEDIA DYNAMICS OF MEMORY

At a conference in Germany in the late 1970s, literary historian Paul Fussell drew on his now-classic study *The Great War and Modern Memory* (1975) in order to elaborate his notion of "cultural paradigms" (Fussell, 1977):[1]

> In war memoirs the desire to communicate emotionally forces the writer back on the images and allusions most familiar and accessible in his culture. War memoirs are thus by their rhetorical nature quintessentially national. The idea of a war memoir written from an international point of view would be unthinkable. (p. 1f)

Following E. H. Gombrich's (1961) dictum that "the innocent eye is a myth," Fussell goes on to elaborate that "every beholder [of the Great War] carried with him a freight of largely unconscious paradigms or patterns of perception and interpretation which invited him to see and recall only what cultural conditioning had made him capable of seeing and recalling" (Fussell, 1977, p. 2). He explains that in their memoirs, British soldier–poets (Robert Graves, Siegfried Sassoon, Edmund Blunden, and others) tended to turn war into comedy (a legacy of Shakespeare) or portrayed the Western front in pastoral paradigms (a rich English tradition); they remembered it with irony or phlegm. On the other hand, according to Fussell, German soldier–writers such as Erich Maria Remarque and Ernst Jünger could mine the Gothic imagination (from "Grunewald to Struwelpeter" up to "the

paintings of Otto Dix") "as a standard natural resource," and they produced narratives that featured "overheated figures of nightmare" with all "the machinery of
Gothic romance" (Fussell, 1977, p. 5).

If Pierre Nora's work from the late 1970s onwards marks the re-emergence of
thinking about collective, social, or cultural memory in the discipline of history,
and Ulric Neisser's (1982) polemic "if X is an interesting or socially significant
aspect of memory, then psychologists have hardly ever studied X" (p. 4) indicates
a similar move in the field of psychology, then Paul Fussell's work heralds a new
beginning for memory research with a focus on literature and media. Criticism of
his approach aside,[2] Fussell has made an important point for memory studies: We
experience and remember with the help of paradigms that are part of our culture
and that come to us via the reading of texts and the use of other media. Such paradigms seem to be represented in our minds as a largely unconscious reservoir of
schemata. They may materialize as components of our rhetoric, helping us fulfill
the "desire to communicate" (often "emotionally") that arguably marks the origin
of all collective memory.

What Fussell described in the late 1970s still remains one of the most fascinating questions of media memory studies: the idea that certain paradigms travel
from medium to mind and to another medium—from works of the literary canon
to the minds of soldiers in World War I and to their memoirs, for example. Such
"travel" constitutes the fundamental dynamics of memory (all memory is "traveling memory", Erll, 2011a), and as Fussell's examples show, it is bound up in a
complex manner with individual and collective memory, with cultural traditions
and everyday experience, as well as with different media technologies and social
settings.

What needs to be considered in a slightly different way today, however, are
two assumptions that pervade Paul Fussell's writings as much as the prevalent
discourses on culture, media, and memory. The first is that culture is equal to
national culture and that memories operating beyond this frame would indeed
be "unthinkable." The second is that we can discuss mediation without looking at
concrete media. What I develop in this chapter, therefore, is a transcultural and
media-sensitive approach to "memory in culture."[3]

That cultural paradigms, social frameworks, symbols, or schemata are of
essential significance for memory—in the mind as well as in its sociocultural
manifestations—is an insight that dates back to the founding fathers of the
memory studies field in the early 20th century. However, it is usually paired
with a conspicuous lack of consciousness about both specific media and the
specifics of media. The sociologist Maurice Halbwachs (1925/1994), who
introduced the idea of *mémoire collective*, was interested in *cadres sociaux de
la mémoire*—that is, "social frameworks of memory." Only in passing does he
mention media such as maps, books, or buildings. And although these emerge
in Halbwachs' writings as links between the individual and his or her *cadres sociaux*, he never explicitly reflects upon the structural role of media as
strengthening and consolidating, expanding or connecting social frameworks
(Erll, 2011b, p. 129f).

A certain blindness to media also characterizes Frederic Bartlett's (1932/1954) *Remembering*. Although Bartlett already formulated the key question of what I describe as research on "transcultural remediation" ("what actually happens when a popular story travels about from one social group to another"; p. 64), he does not seem to take into account in which "vessel" the travel takes place. In his chapters on repeated reproduction, for instance, Bartlett does not differentiate between a story that a subject "dictated" to him (p. 70) and written reproductions (p. 77). [4] The first, however, implies orality and the second handwriting. Both media have their specific properties, for example, in terms of speed and style (Ong, 1982). Among the pioneers of interdisciplinary memory studies, it is only the art historian Aby Warburg who can be credited with providing some key insights into the transcultural dynamics of media memory, especially in his *Mnemosyne*-project (Warburg, 1924/2000), which views the travel of symbols in painting, from antiquity to modernity, as acts of memory (see also Erll, 2011b, pp. 19–21).

The idea of memory as an effect of "symbolic mediation" (Vygotsky, 1930–1934/ 1978; see also Wertsch, Chapter 11, this volume) and as often "mediated by narrative" (Carretero & van Alphen, Chapter 12, this volume) has been corroborated by wide sections of cultural and narrative psychology (Brockmeier & Carbaugh, 2001; Bruner, 1991; Echterhoff & Straub, 2003). It is an idea that was readily taken up in literary and media studies (Erll, 2009b; for cognitive narratology, which focuses on narrative schemata, see Fludernik, 1996; Herman, 2013). But in which medium does the narrative in question materialize or manifest itself? Is it a printed book, a VHS-taped film, an oral speech? These are important questions, as we are not dealing with "transparent media," with windows revealing the contents of memory, as it were. Instead, media are very specific assemblages of semiotic, technological, and social aspects,[5] which will mold available forms according to their specific affordances and restrictions; shape their messages while encoding them; and "never come alone" but, rather, are situated in complex constellations of pluri- and intermedial connection and filiation.

In tandem with the aim to provide insight into the medial specifics and dynamics of memory, this chapter is also concerned with how we can approach "memory in culture" through a transcultural and transnational lens. Both questions are related: In our globalizing age, many media products cross borders from the very outset (e.g., multinational modes of film production), and the travel and translation of key texts and images across national, regional, linguistic, ethnic, and religious boundaries have become the norm rather than the exception. In a historical perspective, it is also obvious that stories and images "on the move," such as Homer's epics or the Pietà, have always worked against an idea of memory paradigms as nationally or culturally "contained" schemata.

With his idea that war memoirs "from an international viewpoint would be unthinkable" (Fussell, 1977, p. 1f), Fussell appears to subscribe to what Ulrich Beck (2006) has called "methodological nationalism," an approach that characterized memory research especially during the 1980s and 1990s, with Pierre Nora's French national *lieux de mémoire* being the prime example (Nora, 1984,

1986, 1994). Although the significance of the nation as a framework or "scale" (de Cesari & Rigney, 2014) of collective remembrance should not be underestimated, there is no reason to believe that it is the natural container of memory. Admittedly, education and broadcasting systems have a strong national core, and the nationalist "invention of tradition" is still at work (as Wertsch shows in Chapter 11, this volume). However, the focus on *one* important framework of memory should not blind us to the existence and power of "traveling memories" that create fuzzy edges or may transversally run through the seemingly clear-cut containers of collective memory, such as "the national." Diasporic memories, subcultural memories, and religious memories, for example, challenge the concept of national memory in different ways.

The first widely recognized study to address traveling memories was Daniel Levy and Natan Sznaider's (2006/2001) *The Holocaust in the Global Age*. These authors show that as a "transnational symbol," the Holocaust has elicited and enabled the articulation of memories about genocide and the humiliation of human rights in widely different corners of the world, from Rwanda to Argentina to Palestine. The Holocaust has become a traveling schema, or, to adapt Fussell's term, a "transcultural paradigm." It is a paradigm that produces memories, which may be nationally inflected (Holocaust remembrance in Germany of course works differently than in the United States or Israel) and will always be locally specific. The paradigm itself, however, has become "de-territorialized" (Levy & Sznaider, 2001/2006, p. 153). In its basic shape, it transcends such national and local frames—arguably, though, only once it can manifest itself in media. Memories of Holocaust thus exemplify the very transcultural media dynamics that are the focus of this chapter.

Directing academic curiosity toward such transversal processes is the common goal of the new "transcultural memory studies," which emerged during the early 2000s and propelled the interdisciplinary field of memory studies into a further phase of vibrant research (Bond & Rapson, 2014; Crownshaw, 2011; de Cesari & Rigney, 2014). Under the umbrella term of transculturality memory studies addresses mnemonic movement not only across national frameworks, but also across ethnic, religious, gendered, generational, urban, rural or regional ones, the hybridization and transformation of cultural practices of remembering (see also Brunow, 2015). Although scholars of sociology, anthropology, history, literary studies, media studies, and philosophy are engaged in this "transcultural turn," voices from the field of psychology are not quite discernable yet. They would make an important contribution, however, because transcultural memory is only conceivable as both a sociomedial and a mental phenomenon.

MEDIA MEMORY: REMEMBERING ACROSS TIME, SPACE, AND CULTURES

Whenever we approach memory in culture—that is, when we are interested in processes of remembering and forgetting that take place within sociocultural contexts—we are dealing with mediation. This fundamental idea was already put forth by Lev S. Vygotsky (Wertsch, 2002; see also Wertsch, Chapter 11, this volume). In the following, my focus is on the "hardware" of symbolic mediation—on different media, their technologies, and the distinct "memory logic" they display.

The idea of "mediated memories" has gained renewed momentum in the digital age. In her study on digital photography and memory, José van Dijck (2007, p. 21) introduced her concept of mediated memories, emphasizing the co-construction or "mutual shaping of memory and media." However, it is not only in the age of the smartphone, Facebook, and Picasa that memories appear to be highly mediated. At a more fundamental level, mediation facilitates the externalization of memories we produce in our minds, their expression by means of gestures, linguistic utterances, handwriting, or typing e-mails. Conversely, through the internalization of mediated memories (from neighbors' gossip to the news at night), we participate in collective memory.

How the history of memory has evolved as a history of its ever-changing media was studied by Jacques Le Goff (1977), Aleida and Jan Assmann (J. Assmann, 1992/2011), and many other memory scholars. From orality to writing, from the handwritten manuscript to the printing press, from photography to film and the "new" digital media, media have generated key metaphors of memory, from Plato's "wax tablet" to Sigmund Freud's "Wunderblock" (Draaisma, 2000). They have furthermore determined the specific shape of our memories—visual memory, for example, appears to take on the rectangular shape of oil paintings, photographs, and the cinema screen[6]—as well our possibilities of storage and retrieval (compare the classical paper-based archive with the digital archive; see also Ernst, 2004).

In order to grasp the cultural dynamics of media, it makes sense to draw on a basic distinction made by media theorist Harold Innis (1951): "time-bound" and "space-bound" media. The typical storage media of memory, such as stone carvings or written manuscripts, are time-bound. Circulation media of memory, such as letters and television, are space-bound. Of course, one medium may operate according to both logics (e.g., on the time-bound book as a "portable monument," see Rigney, 2004). Digital archives, especially, tend to do both: Through digitalization, they save content that may be thousands of years old; at the same time, this content may be accessible in faraway places, indeed "traveling" the globe with a speed and spread formerly unimaginable. Although media may have certain affordances and limitations that make them prone to one or the other memory function, it will eventually be the cultural uses and scholarly perspectives that determine whether media either circulate or store memory.

New research on media memory has tackled older, static notions of media as mere "storehouses" of supposedly identical content or as representations that "mirror" the past. It has developed more complex and dynamic notions: Media construct and create, shape, and distort memories at the same time they purportedly "just encode" or represent them. They select and emphasize or they skip information about the past even if they ostensibly "just archive" it. Also, they fulfill an array of vital functions in memory culture. According to Ann Rigney (2008), for example, literature and other media can act in the collective construction of the past as "relay stations," "stabilizers," "catalysts," "objects of recollection," and "calibrators."[7]

Without the active participation of social actors, however, media cannot represent, store, or circulate any memories. Rather than subscribing to an exclusively media-centered perspective, memory research needs to take into account the "social arena" in which media appear and are used (Erll & Rigney, 2009)—the "social life" that memory media lead. According to the sociologist and media theorist Andrew Hoskins (2011), we are in fact dealing with complex media and memory "ecologies." A constitutive component of such ecologies, and the basis of all "social life" of media, are the individual minds that engage in the production and reception of mediated memories. It is here that media theory and cultural psychology meet within the field of memory studies.[8]

To illustrate how media memory studies have tackled the question of "remembering across time and space," the following introduces some influential research in this field. Special attention is paid to questions of the transcultural—that is, to the possibilities and problems of studying media as a means of "remembering across cultures."

The constitution of culture through the mediation of memory *across time* was the fundamental question that concerned Aleida and Jan Assmann when they started their memory research in the 1980s. What they call the normative and formative "cultural memory" (J. Assmann, 1992/2011) is established by "reusable" media, which, like the Bible, the Kaaba, or national monuments, stand the test of time; are curated by shamans, priests, historians, and other experts; and are continually reinvested with meaning. Social processes such as canonization and the appropriation of memory media by each new generation are the focus of the Assmanns' research. In *Cultural Memory and Western Civilization*, Aleida Assmann (1999/2011) distinguishes within the broad cultural archive of all existent media between a *functional memory*—those media that are in use, define cultural identity and value systems, and legitimize social and political order—and a *storage memory*—those media that are unused, inert, forgotten, but may (re-) emerge one time to become "functional" (again) to the mnemonic community.

A rather different but no less influential approach to mediated memory across time is Marianne Hirsch's "postmemory." In its earlier instances (*Family Frames*; Hirsch, 1997), it is a theory about the role of photography in remembering across generations. Family photography, Hirsch emphasizes, takes on meaning as a medium of memory only in conjunction with narrative: We need to be told the stories about the people we see in a photograph. (This is a reminder of the significance of intermedial interplay for the effectiveness of memory media.) The idea of postmemory is literary studies' contribution to the research on transgenerational trauma, which emerged in psychology during the 1960s, along with a second generation of Holocaust survivors. According to Hirsch, postmemories are those memories that members of a "second generation" retain (or better, construct) about their mothers' and fathers' traumatic experiences with the help of media. In her later work (*The Generation of Postmemory*, 2012), Hirsch extends the range of media she studies to other art forms (e.g., novels and paintings) and the idea of postmemory to "affiliative" memories that—in contrast to mere "familial" ones—can also operate across space and cultures (one of her examples is W. G. Sebald's (2001) novel *Austerlitz*).

Ultimately, it seems that the mediation of memories across time always carries the transcultural as a potential. Memories inscribed in time-bound media can be actualized and appropriated by groups that are distant to the contexts of original encoding and earlier use—not only in time but also in space and in their socio-cultural composition.

Studying the circulation of memories *across space* means taking on a synchronic perspective on the diffusion of memory. Levy and Sznaider (2001/2006) have addressed this question from a sociological perspective and introduced the notion of "cosmopolitan memory." Alison Landsberg's (2004) *Prosthetic Memory* provides a media studies view on the circulation of memory in the age of globalization. Landsberg studies representations of slavery and the Holocaust in literature, cinema, and museum exhibits. She is interested in mass media's capacity to make us "take on" other people's and groups' memories "like an artificial limb" (p. 20). With this reference to Marshall McLuhan's (1964) notion of media as the "extensions of man," Landsberg updates classic media theory within the horizon of memory studies. Using the metaphor of "prosthesis," of memory-as-a-limb, she emphasizes the bodily, experiential, sensuous, and affective dimensions of media memories in individual minds and indicates the interchangeability of commodified memories in the age of mass media. Although Landsberg is mainly interested in the sharing of memories between ethnic communities in the United States, her approach clearly lends itself to the exploration of wider transcultural and transnational dynamics.

Movement across space usually also means movement "across cultures." It can lead to the emergence of new transcultural mnemonic spaces. To understand the logic of mnemonic hybridization, we need to pay close attention to how media of memory are actually appropriated, made sense of, and localized in specific contexts of remembrance—for example, how Hollywood war movies are seen in a Vietnamese village or how museum exhibits are interpreted by visitors from different mnemonic constituencies.

Coming from literary history and Holocaust studies, Michael Rothberg has introduced with *Multidirectional Memory* (2009) a spatial metaphor to describe not only the movement of memories but also their entanglements and cross-referencing. Rothberg's concept of "multidirectional memory" is directed against the idea (still prevalent in much nationalized remembrance practice) that memory is a "zero sum game" and operates according to the "scarcity principle" (p. 3). Using the example of Holocaust memories, on the one hand, and memories of colonialism and slavery, on the other hand, Rothberg argues that recalling *one* victim group does not necessarily reduce the possibility of remembering *another* victim group. On the contrary, he shows that *one* discourse of memory can *enable other* discourses of memory (p. 6). Rather than understanding memory as competitive, he conceives of it as "multidirectional, as subject to ongoing negotiation, cross-referencing, and borrowing" (p. 15). Using a range of media, from literary works to philosophical tracts, movies, and paintings, he shows how during the 1960s in fact "Holocaust memory emerged in dialogue with the . . . struggles that define the era of decolonization" (p. 7). The idea of multidirectionality, however, despite its spatial imagery, refers not necessarily to the actual circulation of media across space but, rather, to the capacity of certain media products to express reflections about the affiliation of different histories and thus to perform—and elicit in their users—acts of transcultural memory.

The concepts of affiliative, cosmopolitan, prosthetic, and multidirectional memory are all characterized by their ethical concerns and a utopian moment. The authors are interested in how media memory may help create new forms of solidarity and new visions of justice. Although such normative approaches have gained great currency within memory studies—and for good reasons—I turn next to a concept that is located more on the descriptive end of the spectrum of possible forms of engagement with media and memory.

"REMEDIATION": FROM NEW MEDIA THEORY TO MEMORY STUDIES

The idea of "remediation" not only helps conceptualize memory across space and time but also introduces a further notion of movement—that of "remembering across media." It draws attention to the ongoing transcriptions of "memory matter" from one medium to another. Arguably, remediation is the very dynamics that keeps memories in culture alive.

"Remediation" emerged in the late 1990s as one of the most influential concepts within the field of new media studies. The term is derived from Jay Bolter and Richard Grusin's (1999) eponymous book *Remediation: Understanding New Media* (1999), whose title refers to McLuhan's (1964) classic *Understanding Media*, and which thus places itself within the genealogy of "media determinist" approaches—that is, those that examine how media technologies condition the shape of the mediated content as well as its reception and may thus influence society. Bolter and Grusin contend that "all mediation is remediation"—that "each act of mediation depends on other acts of mediation. Media are continually commenting on, reproducing, and replacing each other, and this process is integral to media" (p. 55). In this vein, video games remediate the "older" medium film as they create the look of "interactive movies"; digital photography remediates analog photography; and the Web absorbs and transforms almost all earlier visual and textual media (TV, film, radio, print, etc.). According to Bolter and Grusin, remediation is characterized by its "double logic"—its oscillation between "immediacy" and "hypermediacy," transparency and opacity, between creating "the experience of the real" and "the experience of the medium" (p. 71).

The idea of "remediation" was adapted and transformed for the uses of memory studies in Astrid Erll and Ann Rigney's (2009) *Mediation, Remediation and the Dynamics of Cultural Memory* (see also Hoskins, 2001; Kilbourn & Ty, 2013). Within memory research, remediation primarily describes the continuous transcription of memory content into different media. Memory content—stories and images about the past—is a transmedial phenomenon (Ryan, 2004). It is not tied to any one specific medium and can therefore be represented across the spectrum of available media: in handwritten manuscripts and printed newspaper articles; in historiographical books and novels; in drawings, paintings, and photographs; in movies; and on websites. If we look at "Odysseus," "the dark Middle Ages," "Napoleon," or "the Holocaust," we realize quickly that the key stories, concepts and images we retain in collective memory emerge and persist through their ongoing remediation. What is remembered about an ancient myth, a revolution, or a hero (or any other story or image) thus usually refers not so much to what one might cautiously call "the original" or "the actual events" but, instead, to a palimpsestic structure of existent media representations—to the narratives and images circulating in a media culture. Repeated representation over decades and centuries in different media is what creates a powerful site of memory.

The still most conspicuous instance of this nexus between remediation and a (virtually global) dynamics of memory is "9/11." It is also a good example of the power of *visuality* and *intermediality* in the making of collective memory, aspects often underrated in memory studies governed by the narrative paradigm. In fact, iconization is, along with narrativization, a key process of forming memory in culture. Both narrativization and iconization are set in motion through remediation.

During and after September 11, 2001, the burning twin towers quickly crystallized into the *one* iconic image of the event, and this icon has been remediated ever since: in television news, movies, comic strips, on websites, and so on. However, such iconization-through-remediation is not restricted to visual media. Another example connected with "9/11" is the icon of the "falling man," which stands for those people who were trapped by the fire on the upper floors of the World Trade Center and decided to jump rather than die in the flames. The first representation of the "falling man" was a photograph taken by Richard Drew. It shows a man falling to certain death, his body upside down and in eerie symmetry with the façade of the World Trade Center's North Tower. The image appeared in newspapers, on TV, and on the Internet, but it was also remediated in narrative form: among others, in a magazine story, a TV documentary, in Don DeLillo's (2007) novel *Falling Man*, and in Jonathan Safran Foer's (2005) intermedial novel *Extremely Loud and Incredibly Close*—which was made into a movie in 2011 (directed by Stephen Daldry). These remediations feature different semiotic systems and media technologies; they cover a spectrum of representational modes, including factual discourse as well as fiction; and they tell different stories and even convey contradictory meanings. At the same time, however, they all contribute to the stabilization and circulation of the "falling man" as a key icon of "9/11."

Memory studies have reinterpreted and in many respects transformed what was originally a new media studies concept. The particular uses, challenges, and possibilities of "remediation" for the study of memory can be summarized as follows:

1. Bolter and Grusin's (1999) term has been turned by memory studies into a broad (to some, perhaps overexpansive) concept, which understands

"remediation" in a more basic sense as "renewed" or "repeated" mediation.

2. Memory studies have so far placed emphasis on the mediation and remediation of certain *contents* of collective memory (mainly stories and visual icons), a process that Bolter and Grusin (1999, p. 45) would call "repurposing." However, remediation on the level of *technology* is another important aspect of memory in culture—for example, the digitalization of analog, black-and-white photography on Internet sites devoted to history. New approaches to "media archeology" (Parikka, 2012) may further open up this road of inquiry.

3. Bolter and Grusin's (1999) "double logic of remediation" is retained in memory studies as an interesting idea, although not in a strict determinist sense. The interplay of immediacy and hypermediacy will often, but need not always, characterize the logic of memory media. In memory culture, hypermediacy as a proliferation of different media (e.g., on history TV channels or in multimedia exhibitions) tends to create effects that are usually associated with immediacy: those of authenticity and experientiality.

4. Although not subscribing to strict media determinism, "remediation" in memory studies retains the original focus on the materiality and the technology of media. This is what distinguishes the term from other concepts of discursive and media filiations, such as intertextuality (Kristeva, 1969) or adaptation (Hutcheon, 2006). And although not arguing in an overly determinist way that "the medium *is* the memory," media memory research does continue to engage with the interesting question of how the "trace" of the medium may shape the memory it produces.

5. In memory studies, the emphasis on actors and social contexts is stronger than in Bolter and Grusin's (1999) theory. Because all preoccupation with "memory"—even in its media theory variety—is ultimately directed toward an understanding of social and mental processes, the study of remediation here tends to be coupled with research on social actors. These can be the producers, who create remediations in specific social contexts, possibly under certain constraints or with a political agenda, as well as the users of memory media, given that remediations will only have an effect when they are heard, read, seen, and committed to individual memory. In fact, a strong desideratum of media memory studies is an intensified dialogue with research on reception and media effects.[9]

6. Remediation itself implies reception: Before creating "renewed mediations," the producers of media products must have received and remembered "older" mediations. In this sense, the study of media filiations is a methodology that examines practices of reception and remembering (indirectly, through the analysis of media production). This approach to "reception" is very different from the synchronic, social

science-based reception studies that use qualitative methods. However, it can provide insights into histories of reception and into the changing cultural preferences in remembering stories or images. The more than 2,500-year-long media history of the *Odyssey* is one example of such diverse materializations of reception (e.g., remediations by Dante, Joyce, or the Coen brothers) across times and cultures.

7. "Remediation" is increasingly used to investigate transcultural and transnational processes of memory (Brunow, 2015; Rigney, 2012). These questions were originally not the focus of new media studies. Transcultural memory, however, is more often than not an effect of "transcultural remediation"—the transcription of "memory matter" into ever-new media and the capacity of these media to travel across time, space, and cultures.[10] With this capacity in mind, remediation lends itself to taking a fresh look at Bartlett's (1932/1954) question about stories that travel from one social group to another.

"PREMEDIATION": THE POWER OF MEDIA SCHEMATA

Remediation leads to premediation. The ongoing transcription of stories and images about the past across the spectrum of available media tends to produce, with time, a core of certain schemata of representation. Such media schemata will have narrative and visual properties, but they may also feature semiotic and tech-nological specifics or may be connected with distinct forms of social practice. At this point, we can often witness a reversal to premediation, revealing the power of such schemata to shape and preform new and other experiences, memories, and their mediation.

I have studied this double process using memories of the Indian uprising of 1857–1858 against British colonial rule as an example (Erll, 2007, 2009a). A sur-vey of the long series of Indian and British representations of the revolt—which materialized in a great variety of media and was never interrupted over a period of 150 years—shows how certain stories and images ("the Siege of Lucknow" and "the Well of Cawnpore") were remediated time and again, coalesced, and were eventually condensed into narrative and visual schemata. Apparently, such sche-mata of representation can be shared by antagonistic mnemonic groups, but their logic tends to be inverted when they find expression in different cultural loca-tions. While British media recalled time and again that Indians had raped English women during the uprising, Indian writers emphasized that the British imperial-ists had "raped" the Motherland India, Bharat Mata (thus inverting and allego-rizing the "slots" of the British schema). Eventually, such strongly schema-based media memory turned into a detrimental premediating force for the British, when "1857" shaped their understanding of (and military action during) the massacre of Amritsar in 1919.

Remediation and premediation go hand in hand. While remediation describes the ongoing transcription of mnemonic content from medium to medium, premediation draws our attention to the results of such pluri-mediated memories: the emergence of certain media schemata, which preform the ways in which future events will be anticipated, experienced, represented, and then possibly remembered. Returning to the example of "9/11," the American understanding and representation of "9/11" was clearly premediated by disaster movies such as Roland Emmerich's *Independence Day* (1996), the crusader story, and Biblical parables. I view premediation as cultural practices of looking, naming, and narrating—and eventually also of acting and legitimizing. Premediation means that the media circulating in a given context provide schemata for future experience. It is the effect of *and* the starting point for mediated memories. With this broad conceptualization, my idea of premediation diverges from the one developed by Richard Grusin (2010) in *Premediation*. For Grusin, premediation is a rather specific practice that emerged in the American media after "9/11." It describes the anticipation of further threats by means of incessant mediations of possible future wars and disasters.

Moving back a century in time, and also returning to Paul Fussell, we realize that "premediation" is one way to describe the emergence and workings of "cultural paradigms." Much of the "irony" that Paul Fussell (1975) finds in the experience of the Great War was a result of the fact that premediation did not work as a useful "cultural tool" (to adapt Vygotsky's term) to address reality. The narrative schemata, paradigms, or mental models were derived from earlier wars, such as Britain's small colonial wars in the 19th century—all rather short, led by cavalry, and thoroughly heroicized afterwards in media ranging from history painting to widely read juvenile literature. These models proved utterly outdated in the face of a modern, entrenched, and protracted machine war.

In today's world, the cinema has emerged as a major premediating force of war experience. Movies, especially popular Hollywood films, provide globally circulating narrative schemata and scripts for life experience: for friendship, courtship, weddings—but also for going to war. In *An Intimate History of Killing*, Joana Bourke (1999) shows how filmic representation of World War II premediated the way that soldiers entered into battle in Vietnam (for similar results, see also Welzer, 2002; Sturken, 1997). The following observations made by Bourke convey a sense of the media specifics of premediation—the visual, auditory, and visceral qualities of experience preformed and shaped by Hollywood cinema:

> Combatants interpreted their battle experiences through the lens of an imaginary camera. Often, the real thing did not live up to its representation in the cinema. A twenty-year-old Australian officer, Gary McKay, was slightly disappointed by the way his victims acted when hit by his bullets: It "wasn't like one normally expected after watching television and war movies. There was no great scream from the wounded but simply a grunt and then an uncontrolled collapse to the ground," he observed morosely. (p. 26)

Apart from the occasional conscious reference to a (here cinematic) premediation of experience, premediation remains largely unconscious. In cultural psychology and communication studies, the concept of "media priming" appears to deal with similar processes (Roskos-Ewoldsen, Roskos-Ewoldsen, & Carpentier, 2009). However, "media priming" describes the short-term effects of media contents (e.g., violence and politics in mass media) on users' knowledge, whereas "premediation" addresses the long-term effects of the exposure to plural mediations, deals with influence on more abstract levels such as narrative and visual schemata, and focuses on the power of such schemata to mold new memories and new mediations.[11]

Based on an extensive review of multidisciplinary schema-research in the past century, neuroscientists Ghosh and Gilboa (2013) define the following four "necessary schema features": "(1) an associative network structure, (2) basis on multiple episodes, (3) lack of unit detail, and (4) adaptability." From a media memory studies perspective it is clear that many of the "multiple episodes" whose commonalities will be extracted into a schema are not necessarily first-hand experiences, but may be mediated events—the raw material for premediation.

What role does premediation play in transcultural media dynamics? Media schemata help us make sense in situations of transcultural communication (from watching foreign films to international political communication). At the same time, they are themselves often transcultural phenomena, "traveling schemata" (Erll, 2014) as it were, which are used across ethnic, national, or religious formations to give shape to experience, memories, and media representations. Schemata "travel" as soon as cultures interact. In the ancient world, the Homeric narrative schema of "Odysseus' travels" and his search for home (*nostos*) materialized in various literatures across the Mediterranean. Today, mass migration and globalizing media cultures, with their wide circulation of printed, filmed, and digital contents, are setting stories and images on the move (Shohat & Stam, 1994).

The effects of Hollywood's pervasive worldwide dissemination of visual narratives are also palpable in experimental research conducted by cultural psychologists: In their extension of Bartlett's (1932/1954) method on repeated reproduction, Wagoner and Gillespie (2014, p. 635) found "narrative templates from Hollywood" among the "sociocultural mediators of remembering" that students at Cambridge University drew on to conventionalize the "War of the Ghosts," a story adapted from a North American folk tale. In their efforts to retell this "foreign" story, participants fell back on the plot structures of popular Hollywood ghost films (e.g., *The Sixth Sense* (1999) and *The Others* (2001)) and imagined something that had not come to the minds of Bartlett's participants in the early 20th century: A surprise ending revealed the protagonist himself to be a ghost. This is a clear indication of the premediating power of Hollywood story schemata, especially when it comes to understanding stories that have their origins in different cultural formations.

Memory studies have addressed the phenomenon of transcultural premediation mostly in research on the Holocaust as a "global symbol" that preformed the representation of other genocides and violations of human rights. A less conspicuous example is "District Six," an important memory site of post-apartheid South Africa. As a traveling schema, it has moved far beyond its original location in Cape Town, and it has been propelled into transnational spheres of representation through an array of media. It may now premediate the way people understand forced removals elsewhere (Erll, 2014).

The urgency to understand the transcultural dynamics at work in premediation is brought out in Dirk Moses's (2011) work on the "calamitization of history" in the Israeli/Palestinian conflict. Moses shows the tenacity of mental schemata derived from what he argues are "collective traumas," generated by memories of ongoing humiliation and suffering, which clearly have their own long history of mediation and remediation, and then turn (and are turned) again and again into powerful premediators of political action in the Near East. For Moses, this is an instance not of "liberal" but, rather, of bitterly conflictual transcultural memory: "Group humiliation is always a transcultural phenomenon, because it entails a lowering of status in relation to an other" (p. 94). Schemata that premediate action in the Near East are fundamentally related to the feared other—fueled by his actions but also by incessant mediations. It is in intricate constellations such as this that the necessity of knowledge exchange between transcultural media studies and psychological research becomes most evident.

CONCLUSION

Of course, ideas very similar to that of "premediation" have already been developed in psychology, the philosophy of history, art history, and literary studies. The advantage of the term *premediation* is that it opens up the possibility of bringing together existing research while focusing on the specific logic (*Eigenlogik*) of media (including their technologies, semiotic systems, aesthetic forms, contents, and social uses) as well as on the pervasiveness of media throughout the world— thus enabling development of a media-sensitive and transcultural approach to memory.

Aby Warburg's (1924/2000) "pathos formula," Ernst Robert Curtius' (1948/ 1953) "historical topics," the parables in Mark Turner's (1996) "literary mind," Lakoff and Johnson's (1980) "metaphors we live by," Hayden White's (1973) "tropes" and "plot structures," Paul Ricouer's (1983/1984) "prefiguration," Pierre Nora's (1984, 1986, 1994) "lieux de mémoire," Jan Assmann's (1992/2011) "memory figures," James Wertsch's (2002) "cultural tools," and Daniel Levy and Natan Sznaider's (2001/2006) "transnational symbols" are all condensed forms of remembering that must be mediated. They need "hardware," which, however, may work very differently, semiotically, technologically, and socially, in different times and places. The idea of premediation suggests that the schemata that lead our representations and memories along certain paths are more often than not derived from media culture—which is not a sphere separate from social interaction but, rather, irresolvably connected with it—and that these schemata will manifest themselves again and again in medial products.

Much of the research on cognitive schemata fuels the idea of premediation (Minsky, 1975; Rumelhart, 1975; Schank & Abelson, 1977). However, in the wake of cognitive science during the 1970s and 1980s, the idea of "schema" as "an embodied, dynamic, temporal, holistic, and social" concept seems to have lost its potential, as Brady Wagoner (2013, 2017) has argued in his re-reading of Bartlett's (1932/1954) work. I add that current notions of schemata also lack media sensitivity. Arguably, the reason for this negligence is that schemata tend to be related to the content level of media only, which in turn tends to be seen as unmediated or as contained by transparent hardware. If we understand schemata as *also* emerging from (and carrying the trace of) specific semiotic, technological, and social dimensions, then a more "holistic" idea of schemata and their mediation is possible.[12]

In *Remembering*, Bartlett (1932/1954) remains critical of the idea of shared "group schemata": "Whether there are literally group images, group memories, and group ideas must remain a matter of interesting but uncertain speculation" (p. 299). What we *can* study, however, are the recurrent forms, technological specifics, and social settings, which become manifest in and shape new medial representations. If we accept that the "media out there" are (albeit never in an easy or straightforward way) connected and co-constructed with "the minds in here," then the phenomenon of premediation points to the existence of certain (trans)cultural schemata—even as they may be denied by the individual, derided, or critically reflected upon.

Paul Fussell articulated his ideas about "cultural paradigms" in an environment of media and memory that was vastly different from the present situation. Today, World War I no longer comes to us primarily through memoirs or poems. The way we remember it is increasingly shaped by digital technologies. Enormous digitalization projects, making photographic and filmic documents of World War I, both official and private, available online, digitalizing objects and making extensive use of crowdsourcing,[13] characterize the media environment during the centenary of World War I. As a consequence, our memories may be increasingly shaped by eerily moving black-and-white images of the trenches, an effect of the increased remediation of "old" footage in the "new" digital media. The ubiquitous accessibility of such documents, their framing and hyperlinking on websites, and the way they can be explored (bodily) via mouse clicks or movements on the touchpad may all have a premediating influence on the ways in which younger generations will represent and remember World War I in the future. Clearly, the digitalization of memory materials related to the Great War facilitates their remediation across local, national, and cultural borders, thus potentially creating transcultural memories. However, users throughout the world will (and can only) draw on those archives that have chosen (or have the juridical and financial possibilities) to go online. It remains to be seen how these materials "travel"—how they are taken up and used to produce new media memories in different cultural contexts.

NOTES

1. The following excerpts are taken from the unpublished manuscript of a lecture on "Cultural Paradigms and Traumatic Testimony" that Paul Fussell gave at a conference at Siegen University in the summer of 1977. The text was translated into German (as "Der Einfluß kultureller Paradigmen auf die literarische Wiedergabe traumatischer Erfahrung") and published by Klaus Vondung in a collection called *Kriegserlebnis* [*War Experience*] (see Fussell, 1980). I am grateful to Prof. Klaus Vondung (Siegen) for retrieving and sending me the original English manuscript— an act of cultural remembrance in its own right.

2. Jay Winter (1995) and others rightly observe that Fussell focuses on memoirs of elite officer writers and therefore cannot draw conclusions about the memories and signifying practices of the common soldier.

3. "Memory in culture" is my term of choice to describe, very broadly, the different processes (mental, medial, and social) that are involved in the interplay of past, present, and future within sociocultural contexts (see Erll, 2011b, p. 7).

4. Later in *Remembering*, Bartlett (1932) does acknowledge that the "social stimulus" of oral settings is a "determinant of form" (p. 174), and he thus makes an important point about the social dimension within which media and acts of mediation are embedded.

5. I use the term "medium" here as a broad term covering aspects such as semiotic systems, technologies, contents, and forms as well as social settings of production and reception.

6. Interestingly, in their study on third-person images in autobiographical memories, Rice and Rubin (2011, p. 575) identify patterns of perspective location that correspond closely to the conventions of the camera angle in cinema. Similarly, the changes between observer and field perspectives in autobiographical memory as studied by Berntsen and Rubin (2006, p. 1193) bear comparison with a switching between establishing shots and point-of-view shots. It seems likely that conventions of the film medium and forms of autobiographical visual memory influence each other.

7. For research on media memory, see Morris-Suzuki (2005); Garde-Hansen (2011); and Neiger, Meyers, and Zandberg (2011).

8. For intersections of media theory and cultural psychology, see Slunecko and Hengl (2006).

9. On media effects, see Bryant and Olivier (2009); for an overview of reception studies in various disciplines, see Staiger (2005).

10. See also Hepp (2015) on transcultural communication.

11. Erving Gofman's (1974) "frame analysis", the study of social schemata of interpretation, offers a sociological perspective on the question of premediation.

12. Andrew Hoskins (2009) articulates a similar idea when he discusses the workings of "media templates" and describes the "new social network memory" as "fluid, deterritorialised, diffused and highly revocable, but also immediate, accessible and contingent on the more *dynamic schemata forged through emergent sociotechnical practices*" (p. 36f, emphasis added).

13. For example, the European Union-sponsored Europeana 1914–1918 (www. europeana1914-1918.eu), the Imperial War Museum's Lives of the First World

War (https://www.livesofthefirstworldwar.org), or the "centenary projects" of the Australian War Memorial (https://www.awm.gov.au/1914-1918).

REFERENCES

Assmann, A. (2011). *Cultural memory and Western civilization: Functions, media, archives*. New York, NY: Cambridge University Press. (Original work published 1999)

Assmann, J. (2011). *Cultural memory and early civilization: Writing, remembrance, and political imagination*. Cambridge, UK: Cambridge University Press. (Original work published 1992)

Bartlett, F. C. (1954). *Remembering: A study in experimental and social psychology.* Cambridge University Press. (Original work published 1932)

Beck, U. (2006). *The cosmopolitan vision*. Cambridge, UK: Polity.

Berntsen, D., & Rubin, D. (2006). Emotion and vantage point in autobiographical. *Cognition & Emotion*, *20*(8), 1193–1215.

Bolter, J. D., & Grusin, R. (Eds.). (1999). *Remediation: Understanding new media.* Cambridge, MA: MIT Press.

Bond, L., & Rapson, J. (Eds.). (2014). *The transcultural turn: Interrogating memory between and beyond borders*. Berlin, Germany: de Gruyter.

Bourke, J. (1999). *An intimate history of killing: Face-to-face killing in twentieth-century warfare*. London, UK: Granta Books.

Brockmeier, J., & Carbaugh, D. (Eds.). (2001). *Narrative and Identity: Studies in autobiography, self and culture*. Amsterdam, the Netherlands: John Benjamins.

Bruner, J. (1991). The narrative construction of reality. *Critical Inquiry*, *18*(1), 1–21. doi:10.1086/448619

Brunow, D. (2015). *Remediating transcultural memory: Documentary filmmaking as archival intervention*. Berlin, Germany: de Gruyter.

Bryant, J., & Olivier, M. B. (Eds.). (2009). *Media effects: Advances in theory and research* (3rd ed.). New York, NY: Routledge.

Crownshaw, R. (Ed.). (2011). *Transcultural memory. Parallax*, *17*(4). (Special issue)

Curtius, E. R. (1953). *European literature and the Latin Middle Ages* (W. R. Trask Trans.). New York, NY: Pantheon. (Original work published 1948)

de Cesari, C., & Rigney, A. (Eds.). (2014). *Transnational memory: Circulation, articulation, scales*. Berlin, Germany: de Gruyter.

DeLillo, D. (2007). *Falling man*. New York, NY: Scribner.

Draaisma, D. (2000). *Metaphors of memory: A history of ideas about the mind*. Cambridge, UK: Cambridge University Press.

Echterhoff, G., & Straub, J. (2003). Narrative psychologie: Facetten eines Forschungsprogramms. [Narrative psychology: Facets of a research program]. *Handlung, Kultur, Interpretation. Zeitschrift für Sozial- und Kulturwissenschaften*, *12*(2), 317–342.

Erll, A. (2007). *Prämediation—Remediation: Repräsentationen des indischen Aufstands in imperialen und post-kolonialen Medienkulturen (von 1857 bis zur Gegenwart)* [*Premediation—Remediation, representations of the "Indian mutiny" in imperial and postcolonial media cultures (from 1857 till present)*]. Trier, Germany: WVT.

Erll, A. (2009a). Remembering across time, space and cultures: Premediation, remediation and the "Indian mutiny." In A. Erll & A. Rigney (Eds.), *Mediation, remediation, and the dynamics of cultural memory* (pp. 109–138). Berlin, Germany: de Gruyter.

Erll, A. (2009b). Narratology and cultural memory studies. In S. Heinen & R. Sommer (Eds.), *Narratology in the age of cross-disciplinary narrative research* (pp. 212–227). Berlin, Germany: de Gruyter.

Erll, A. (2011a). Travelling memory. *Parallax, 17*(4), 4–18. doi:10.1080/13534645.2011.605570

Erll, A. (2011b). *Memory in culture.* Basingstoke, UK: Palgrave Macmillan.

Erll, A. (2014). From "District Six" to *District 9* and back: The plurimedial production of transnational schemata. In C. de Cesari & A. Rigney (Eds.), *Transnational memory: Circulation, articulation, scales* (pp. 29–50). Berlin, Germany: de Gruyter.

Erll, A., & Rigney, A. (Eds.). (2009). *Mediation, remediation, and the dynamics of cultural memory.* Berlin, Germany: de Gruyter.

Ernst, W. (2004). The archive as metaphor. *Open, 7,* 46–43. Retrieved from http://www.skor.nl/_files/Files/OPEN7_P46-53%281%29.pdf

Fludernik, M. (1996). *Towards a "natural" narratology.* London, UK: Routledge.

Foer, J. S. (2005). *Extremely loud and incredibly close.* New York, NY: Houghton Mifflin.

Fussell, P. (1975). *The Great War and modern memory.* London, UK: Oxford University Press.

Fussell, P. (1977). *Cultural paradigms and traumatic testimony.* Unpublished manuscript.

Fussell, P. (1980). Der Einfluß kultureller Paradigmen auf die literarische Wiedergabe traumatischer Erfahrung [The influence of cultural paradigms on the literary reproduction of traumatic experience]. In K. Vondung (Ed.), *Kriegserlebnis: Der Erste Weltkrieg in der literarischen Gestaltung und symbolischen Deutung der Nationen* (pp. 175–187). Göttingen, Germany: Vandenhoeck & Ruprecht.

Garde-Hansen, J. (2011). *Media and memory.* Edinburgh, UK: Edinburgh University Press.

Ghosh, V. E., & Gilboa, A. (2014). What is a memory schema? A historical perspective on current neuroscience literature. *Neuropsychologia, 53,* 1, 104–114.

Goffman, E. (1974). *Frame analysis: An essay on the organization of experience.* New York: Harper & Row.

Gombrich, E. H. (1961). *Art and illusion: A study in the psychology of pictorial representation.* New York, NY: Pantheon.

Grusin, R. A. (2010). *Premediation: Affect and mediality after 9/11.* Basingstoke, UK: Palgrave Macmillan.

Halbwachs, M. (1994). *Les cadres sociaux de la mémoire* [The social frameworks of memory] (G. Namer, Ed.). Paris, France: Albin Michel. (Original work published 1925)

Hepp, A. (2015). *Transcultural communication.* Hoboken, NJ: Wiley-Blackwell.

Herman, D. (2013). *Storytelling and the sciences of mind.* Cambridge, MA: MIT Press.

Hirsch, M. (1997). *Family frames: Photography, narrative, and postmemory.* Cambridge, MA: Harvard University Press.

Hirsch, M. (2012). *The generation of postmemory: Writing and visual culture after the Holocaust.* New York, NY: Columbia University Press.

Hoskins, A. (2001). New memory: Mediating history. *Historical Journal of Film, Radio and Television, 21*(4), 333–346.

Hoskins, A. (2009). The mediatisation of memory. In J. Garde-Hansen & A. Reading (Eds.), *Save as . . . digital memories* (pp. 27–43). Basingstoke, UK: Palgrave Macmillan.

Hoskins, A. (2011). Media, memory, metaphor: Remembering and the connective turn. *Parallax, 17*(4), 19–31. doi:10.1080/13534645.2011.605573

Hutcheon, L. (2006). *A theory of adaptation.* New York, NY: Routledge.

Innis, H. A. (1951). *The bias of communication.* Toronto, Ontario, Canada: University of Toronto Press.

Kilbourn, R. J. A., & Ty, E. (2013). *The memory effect: The remediation of memory in literature and film.* Waterloo, Ontario, Canada: Wilfrid Laurier University Press.

Kristeva, J. (1969). *Semeiotikè: Recherches pour une sémanalyse [Desire in language: A semiotic approach to literature and art].* Paris, France: Éditions du Seuil.

Lakoff, G., & Johnson, M. (1980). *Metaphors we live by.* Chicago, IL: University of Chicago Press.

Landsberg, A. (2004). *Prosthetic memory: The transformation of American remembrance in the age of mass culture.* New York, NY: Columbia University Press.

Le Goff, J. (1977). *Storia e memoria [History and memory].* Turin, Italy: Giulio Einaudi.

Levy, D., & Sznaider, N. (2006). *The Holocaust and memory in the Global Age* (A. Oksiloff, Trans.). Philadelphia, PA: Temple University Press. (Original work published 2001)

McLuhan, M. (1964). *Understanding media: The extensions of man.* London, UK: Routledge & Kegan Paul.

Minsky, M. (1975). A framework for representing knowledge. In P. H. Winston (Ed.), *The psychology of computer vision* (pp. 211–277). New York, NY: McGraw-Hill.

Morris-Suzuki, T. (2005). *The past within us: Media, memory, history.* London, UK: Verso.

Moses, D. A. (2011). Genocide and the terror of history. *Parallax, 17*(4), 90–108. doi:10.1080/13534645.2011.605583

Neiger, M., Meyers, O., & Zandberg, E. (2011). *On media memory: Collective memory in a new media age.* Houndmills, UK: Palgrave Macmillan.

Neisser, Ulric (Ed.). (1982). *Memory observed: Remembering in natural contexts.* New York, NY: Freeman.

Nora, P. (Ed.). (1984). *Les lieux de mémoire I: La République [Sites of memory I: The republic].* Paris, France: Gallimard.

Nora, P. (Ed.). (1986). *Les lieux de mémoire II: La Nation [Sites of memory II: The nation].* Paris, France: Gallimard.

Nora, P. (Ed.). (1992). *Les lieux de mémoire III: Les France. [Sites of memory III: France].* Paris, France: Gallimard.

Ong, W. J. (1982). *Orality and literacy: The technologizing of the word.* London, UK: Methuen.

Parikka, J. (2012). *What is media archaeology?* Cambridge, UK: Polity.

Rice, H. J., & Rubin, D. C. (2011). Remembering from any angle: The flexibility of visual perspective during retrieval. *Consciousness and Cognition, 20*(3), 568–577.

Ricouer, P. (1984). *Time and narrative* (Vol. 1). Chicago, IL: University of Chicago Press. (Original work published 1983)

Rigney, A. (2004). Portable monuments: Literature, cultural memory, and the case of Jeanie Deans. *Poetics Today, 25*(2), 361–396. doi:10.1215/03335372-25-2-361

Rigney, A. (2008). The dynamics of remembrance: Texts between monumentality and morphing. In A. Erll & A. Nünning (Eds.), *Cultural memory studies: An international and interdisciplinary handbook* (S. B. Young, Trans.; pp. 345–353). Berlin, Germany: de Gruyter.

Rigney, A. (2012). *Portable monuments: The afterlives of Walter Scott's novels.* Oxford, UK: Oxford University Press.

Roskos-Ewoldsen, D. R., Roskos-Ewoldsen, D., & Carpentier, F. R. D. (2009). Media priming: A synthesis. In J. Bryant & M. B. Olivier (Eds.), *Media effects: Advances in theory and research* (3rd ed., pp. 97–120). New York, NY: Routledge.

Rothberg, M. (2009). *Multidirectional memory: Remembering the Holocaust in the age of decolonization.* Stanford, CA: Stanford University Press.

Rumelhart, D. E. (1975). Notes on a schema for stories. In D. G. Bobrow & A. M. Collins (Eds.), *Representation and understanding: Studies in cognitive science* (pp. 211–236). New York, NY: Academic Press.

Ryan, M. (Ed.). (2004). *Narrative across media: The languages of storytelling.* Lincoln, NE: University of Nebraska Press.

Schank, R. C., & Abelson, R. (1977). *Scripts, plans, goals and understanding.* Hillsdale, NJ: Erlbaum.

Shohat, E., & Stam, R. (1994). *Unthinking Eurocentrism: Multiculturalism and the media.* London, UK: Routledge.

Slunecko, T., & Hengl, S. (2006). Culture and media: A dynamic constitution. *Culture & Psychology, 12*(1), 69–85.

Staiger, J. (2005). *Media reception studies.* New York, NY: New York University Press.

Sturken, M. (1997). *Tangled memories: The Vietnam War, the AIDS epidemic and the politics of remembering.* Berkeley, CA: University of California Press.

Turner, M. (1996). *The literary mind.* New York, NY: Oxford University Press.

van Dijck, J. (2007). *Mediated memories in the digital age.* Stanford, CA: Stanford University Press.

Vygotsky, L. S. (1978). *Mind in society* (M. Cole, V. John-Steiner, S. Scribner, & E. Soubermann, Eds.). Cambridge, MA: Harvard University Press. (Original manuscripts written 1930–1934)

Wagoner, B. (2013). Bartlett's concept of schema in reconstruction. *Theory and Psychology, 23*(5), 553–575. doi:10.1177/0959354313500166

Wagoner, B. (2017). *The constructive mind: Bartlett's psychology in reconstruction.* Cambridge, UK: Cambridge University Press.

Wagoner, B., & Gillespie, A. (2014). Sociocultural mediators of remembering: An extension of Bartlett's method of repeated reproduction. *British Journal of Social Psychology, 53,* 4, 622–639.

Warburg, A. (2000). *Der Bilderatlas Mnemosyne* [*The mnemosyne atlas*] (M. Warncke Ed.,; C. Brink, Trans.). Berlin, Germany: Akademie-Verlag. (Original work published 1924)

Welzer, H. (2002). *Das kommunikative Gedächtnis: Eine Theorie der Erinnerung.* Munich, Germany: Beck.

Wertsch, J. V. (2002). *Voices of collective remembering.* Cambridge, UK: Cambridge University Press.

White, H. (1973). *Metahistory: The historical imagination in nineteenth-century Europe.* Baltimore, MD: Johns Hopkins University Press.

Winter, J. (1995). *Sites of memory: Sites of mourning: The Great War in European cultural history.* Cambridge, MA: Cambridge University Press.